Two Roads to Dodge City

Nigel and Adam Nicolson

Two Roads to Dodge City

Weidenfeld & Nicolson

London

To Juliet

from her father and brother

with thanks and love

Maps and Diagrams

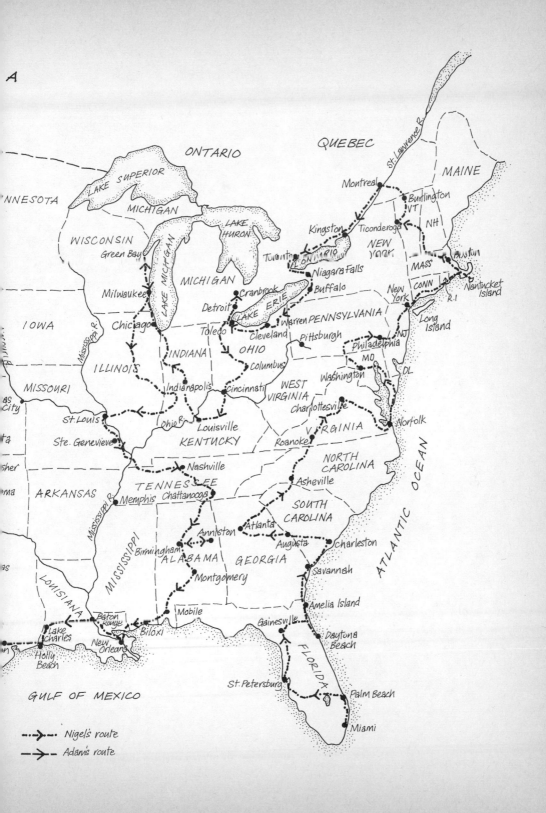

A

ONTARIO
QUEBEC
MAINE
LAKE SUPERIOR
St. Lawrence R.
MICHIGAN
Montreal
MINNESOTA
Burlington
VT
WISCONSIN
Kingston
Ticonderoga
NH
Green Bay
Toronto
ONTARIO
NEW
YORK
Boston
LAKE HURON
Niagara Falls
MASS
Milwaukee
Cranbrook
Buffalo
New
York
Nantucket
Island
MICHIGAN
LAKE MICHIGAN
Detroit
CONN
LAKE ERIE
R.I
Chicago
Cleveland
PENNSYLVANIA
Long
Island
IOWA
Toledo
Warren
NJ
Mississippi R.
ILLINOIS
INDIANA
OHIO
Pittsburgh
Philadelphia
Columbus
MD
Washington
DL
MISSOURI
Indianapolis
Cincinnati
WEST
VIRGINIA
Charlottesville
St. Louis
Ohio R.
Louisville
Norfolk
City
Ste. Genevieve
KENTUCKY
VIRGINIA
Roanoke
NORTH
CAROLINA
Nashville
ta
Asheville
sher
ARKANSAS
TENNESSEE
Mississippi R.
Memphis
Chattanooga
SOUTH
CAROLINA
ma
Anniston
Atlanta
Birmingham
Augusta
Charleston
MISSISSIPPI
ALABAMA
GEORGIA
Savannah
Montgomery
ATLANTIC OCEAN
LOUISIANA
Amelia Island
as
Baton
Rouge
Mobile
Gainesville
Daytona
Beach
Lake
Charles
Biloxi
n
New
Orleans
Holly
Beach
FLORIDA
St. Petersburg
Palm Beach
GULF OF MEXICO
Miami

- - ▶ - - ▶ Nigel's route
———▶——— Adam's route

Foreword

This book originated in a discussion between us late in 1985. Could we collaborate on a travel book? We would not travel together, for that would only result in two accounts of the same experience, but separately in the same continent, writing to each other every day, and converging on some mid-point.

We toyed momentarily with making Europe our continent, but soon agreed that it must be North America, the United States with excursions into Canada, and that our meeting would be in Dodge City, Kansas, because it lies centrally between the two coasts and has associations with one of the most heroic phases of American history. The title was suggested by Harry Eyres.

It took little argument to decide that Adam should tour the western half, the young man's country, and his father the eastern. We began our journeys on the same day, 15 March 1986, he in Los Angeles, Nigel in Miami, and we met as planned in Dodge City on 13 June, having covered between us 30,000 miles and forty of the fifty States, plus three provinces of Canada.

We drove all the way, Adam in a shaky Pontiac Catalina which he bought in California and sold in Dodge City, Nigel in a hired Toyota which he changed in Atlanta for a superb Ford Thunderbird. We completed the journey without illness and only one minor car-bump, Nigel's. We paid our own way throughout, so the compliments we address to our cars, accommodation and airlines are quite unsolicited.

Although we wrote to each other almost every day, we posted our letters by Express Mail only once a week to prearranged addresses, which accounts for the delay in replying to the other's observations and questions.

We normally used British terms when the two languages differed, but as we became gradually assimilated to American ways, their terms (gas, freeways, sidewalks, etc.) began to predominate. We have left them unchanged.

Our purpose was to sample American and Canadian life at many points, and to discuss our impressions with each other. Many of Nigel's engagements were planned ahead, but Adam's came about through chance acquaintances and opportunities, and the difference in our approaches is very evident. From our correspondence developed a secondary and unpremeditated theme, the contrasting attitudes of our two generations and our relationship to each other.

Both of us owe a debt to the many people, some of them total strangers, who gave us their hospitality. The least we can do to show our gratitude is to send them a copy of this book and ask their forgiveness for any inaccuracies, misreporting or leg-pulling.

We were fortunate to have in Juliet Macmillan-Scott, Nigel's daughter and Adam's sister, who lives and works in New York, a communications-centre through whom we passed messages to each other and from and to other people. We cannot express too warmly our thanks for her efficiency and solicitous care for both of us. She joined each of us for a few days during the three months, Nigel in Maryland, Adam in Las Vegas. It is to her that we affectionately dedicate this book.

Nigel Nicolson
Adam Nicolson

Saturday 15 March 1986

NIGEL *to Adam*   This address is a bit of a cheat, for I'm starting my
first letter at Sissinghurst two days before I leave it
for America. I will continue it on my knee in London Airport and finish it
on the plane to Miami.

Sissinghurst is a suitable place to begin, at my familiar desk in the place
where I first came to live in 1930. I regret that it is called Sissinghurst Castle.
That implies something more than it is, and more than I am. You know the
name was acquired only in the eighteenth century when French prisoners of
war who were incarcerated here called it 'le château', but few other people
know that, and they imagine it to be austere, stone and intact, when it's
domesticated, brick and a partial relic. Only one-third of a once splendid
mansion survives, and I live only in one-third of that third, where I hope that
you and Olivia will also live after I die, and Tom after you, and Tom's Tom
after that, to successive generations, for I am philoprogenitive about this sort
of thing, an attitude which I believe you secretly deplore.

What I mind most about this 'castle' image is that it stamps me as the sort
of person who owns a castle (I wish people realised that I don't own it – I
gave it to the National Trust in 1967, and I'm only their tenant here), and
must consequently have a castellated, antiquated, superior outlook on life,
which, I hope you'll agree, is a false impression.

When I was in America last November, I was asked to give an interview to
Mary Battiata of the *Washington Post*. She is a clever girl. We got on well.
But she fell for 'Castle'. When I read her article, accompanied by a photograph
of me which was fortunately unrecognisable, I found that she considered me,

> 6ft 2in. of elderly English ectomorph. Writer, biographer, publisher,
> former Member of Parliament, master of Sissinghurst Castle, true U with
> his dry, sly Oxbridge delivery, marbled skin and a voice that rises and falls
> the way an old hinge opens slowly, dramatically, with feeling.

She also wrote that I had 'slate-green peepers' and 'long fingers thick as
penny-rolls'.

Now that's good journalism. I have to admit that in the main it's accurate.
'Elderly' I must concede. More later about my elderliness. Height and
potted biography are true enough, except for the 'master' bit, and so is the
characterisation apart from 'sly' – can I really give that impression? But I
suppose that to Americans, who have preconceived notions of the British as
we have of them, I must fit a stereotype, which means almost always an over-
simplification.

Let me give you my own self-portrait in contrast to Mary Battiata's, for it's only in such a correspondence as this that fathers can recreate themselves for their sons. I am 69. It seems a dreadful age. When I read in a newspaper that a man is attempting something new, and in brackets after his name I see (69), my immediate reaction is that he's beyond it, forgetting that I'm of the same age, and, in my opinion at least, wholly competent. I certainly suffer a few disabilities – loss of hair, teeth, partial hearing, facial attractiveness, memory and quick response. But on the whole, I flatter myself that I am capable of almost the same degree of mental and physical energy that I enjoyed when I was your age (28). 'Almost' is a very necessary qualification, for I still remember the shame with which I turned back from one of your great walks in the Pyrenees. But my greatest gift is that my health has endured, by and large, up till this time, and I do not expect it to collapse in America.

Looking back on my life, I cannot trace in it any consistent theme. My public work has been adventurous enough, even on occasions reckless, but it does not seem to add up to a career. Another American journalist said to me that she was used to interviewing people who had done one thing successfully, but I seem to have attempted many things, unsuccessfully. That was pretty rough, but there's something in it. I've tried many alternatives (soldier, publisher, politician, editor, writer), written about many subjects (war, politics, travel, architecture, women), but where's the reputation? It's the reputation of a grasshopper. There's no self-pity in this, but there is self-reproach. I can say without sentimentality that you, Juliet and Rebecca* are the most enduring and lovable products of a very diverse life.

We have never been very close, have we? We have always had an affectionate relationship, but there's been mutual reserve, my fear of intruding on your life and setting rules of conduct which I'm not really qualified to give, and your reluctance to question what you regard as my privacy. When you were a child, I took you walking through the Sissinghurst woods and along the Roman Wall. We travelled through Norway together, we canoed the Kentish rivers. But I do not think that I ever exerted what is called parental influence, for good or bad. When you were at Summer Fields, at Eton and Cambridge, we often wrote to each other, but when we met, it was with a certain caution. Then you left Cambridge. You married Olivia. Tom was born. Olivia is now expecting another child, possibly William. You wrote your own books in a highly idiosyncratic style, displaying an enviable gift for observation, dialogue and narrative. Inevitably these achievements and divergencies created an extra distance between us, and I'm not so sure that we should attempt to bridge it now. But let our Dodge letters be not merely a record of our converging journeys, but an exchange between an ambitious, active son and his still-

---

* For Nicolson family relationships, see p. 281.

active considerate father. I have a feeling that you will be the more reticent of us two. I shall reveal confidences, but not induce them. When we meet in Dodge City at 3 p.m. on 13 June, we will exchange greetings, 'Hullo, Adam', 'Hullo, Dadda', and for a moment my hand may rest lightly on your shoulder, but not yours on mine. The Americans will think us very British.

That was written in a Sissinghurst mood. Now I'm in London Airport, not writing on my knee as I promised, for I have no knee to write on. All benches being occupied, I'm standing up, scribbling against a pillar. A tired Arab is lying across three whole seats, but I have not the heart or courage to disturb him.

We are both somewhere in this huge concourse, you waiting for the 10.30 plane to Los Angeles, I for the 11.30 to Miami, but by arrangement we do not meet. We said everything we had to say yesterday, and I do not want to throw a paternal blessing over your farewells to Olivia, which I imagine might be tearful on her side. I watch your departure vicariously on the huge indicator-board, and think of you in flight, soon to follow your jet stream on the 4,425 miles from London to Miami, while you continue a further 3,000 across the continent.

Pan Am Flight 99 is now airborne. We are Jumbo-full. I am seated right at the rear of this elongated auditorium. I look at the backs of four hundred non-corporeal heads. I have a lady beside me, my first American, of whom I shall tell you more later.

But first let me confess a slightly discreditable story about a previous encounter with an American on a plane, chiefly as a warning to myself about my conduct towards this lady in the next seat. It was a couple of years ago, and I was flying from New York to Dallas. There was an empty seat between me and her. I was deep in *War and Peace*, and she, who was about 30 and blondely attractive, was looking up from a script from time to time, muttering to herself, and memorising, I soon decided, the lines of a play. She must be an actress. For three hours we did not speak. Then I dropped my Bryant & May. She picked it up. 'Only the British', she said, 'would keep the same label on their matchboxes for 120 years.' So we talked. There was an hour to go before we reached Dallas. It was one of the most enjoyable conversations I've ever had. She was utterly delightful. She told me that her name was Fink. She thought it an unsuitable name for someone in her profession, and asked me if I could suggest another. Laughter rang through our end-corner of the plane. When we landed at Dallas, we exchanged a Fink-wink over the shoulders of the people who had come separately to meet us.

Now that's not the discreditable part of the story. It's its sequel. She had given me her New York address. So when I returned to Sissinghurst, I sent her six coloured postcards of the garden, writing on the back of each a description of the picture side, ending with an unfinished sentence like, 'I wonder if you . . .', which was continued on the next. I posted the cards one a day for the next six days so that they would arrive in New York like a serial story. I never had any response. Fink must have thought me disappointingly vulgar.

My present neighbour and I have now been flying for $4\frac{1}{2}$ hours, speechless. I am strongly tempted to speak. She's not so young or elegant as Fink, which makes it easier for me. She is reading one of Christopher Lloyd's books on gardening. She has a notebook in which she writes the names of plants, and from another source, *Country Life*, the names of birds, all in Latin. On a separate page of the notebook she wrote, in a curly script rather like yours, 'Things to buy in Miami'. Various items have been added under this heading, but they're written too small for me to read. She's a great smoker (Rothmans, tipped) and has had three miniature bottles of white wine, so far. Now this is just the sort of American woman I like most. Unruffled, occupied, no puritan evidently (smoke, drink), full of talk if only I dared release it, and presumably (from the literature she carries) Anglophile. I do not expect her to be typical Miami, but then Miami is not typical American.

I have been to the United States many times, you virtually never, for I don't count your skiing trip to Utah when you were 18, since you saw little more than a single mountain and then flew straight home. Yet never in history have the inhabitants of one country known so well the appearance and people of another which they have never visited. We've met many Americans in England, read their novels and their history, seen their movies, and become familiar with every aspect of their home and public lives on television, and I don't think that much of what you will find there will come as a surprise.

The pleasure which the continent gives me takes three forms. The first is purely selfish, the hospitality I've enjoyed there, and this will surely be a recurrent theme in our letters. Secondly, I love the country, from city to wilderness, from old New England houses to the glass pinnacle-buildings of Chicago, its superb roads, its forests and its rivers. Thirdly, its history. (She's just written down *Auricula mollis*.) I must guard myself against writing too much about that, but you can imagine with what eagerness I look forward to standing on the site of Jamestown or New Harmony, canoeing down the Ohio just to get the feel of it, and seeing Monticello and the Indian mounds near St Louis.

I have now spoken to the lady next to me. It was not a Fink situation, positively or negatively. She is not even American, except by birth. Married to an English stockbroker, and living in an old rectory in Northamptonshire, she is turning its garden into a scene of bucolic delight. She has a mother in Buffalo, a 'fun-person' who would be pleased to see me, but, if I was her mother, I would regard the appearance of an English stranger with much misgiving. We talked horticulture. She had visited Sissinghurst. She is a Vita-fan.

So we landed in Miami. If the infusion of the passengers at Heathrow was awful, our extrusion at Miami was purgatory. In the concourse there were posters everywhere welcoming us to the United States, but the message does not seem to have penetrated to the officials employed to implement it. The airport buildings may have been very lovely. I did not notice them. All I noticed were thousands of tired people like me humping and pushing their luggage (no porters, no trolleys, no space) towards a narrow funnel where sat a man who clearly did not like the human race, and would have been astonished by the very suggestion that some day, some place, someone would devise a better way of organising these things.

If you wished to test to the limits your capacity for goodwill, try arriving at Miami International Airport at 5 p.m. on a Saturday. Nearly everyone behaved with extraordinary calm, except one woman who rounded on me with the false accusation that I was breaking out of line. 'You look as if you might once have been a gentleman,' she said. I replied, 'Well, I don't feel like one now.' When I eventually reached the Avis counter after two hours of being processed and compressed, I found that I'd been allotted a Toyota, my least favourite car. Too crushed to request a change into something more American, I edged out into the Miami traffic, the darkness and the pelting rain, not feeling at all welcome to the United States. But I suppose one has to pass through hell to enter heaven.

Venice, Los Angeles, California

Saturday 15 March 1986

ADAM *to Nigel*   It's raining, great warm Pacific gobs of it, and flood-ing in the streets. The only noise is the sluicing of the cars tyres through the puddles and the breaking of the surf. The palm trees are bent over in the wind off the ocean and their fronds are blown sideways like hair. Some people on the TV in Westwood have had their garage roof blown off. They're Catholics and the priest is round there commiserating.

But I must tell you about the flight. There was the sad goodbye to Olivia and Thomas – not too long and not too tearful – and then eleven hours in the Pan Am clipper. After twenty minutes in the air my neighbour, a large man with a thin moustache and half-moon glasses, began clipping his nails with a gilt nail-clipper that he took out of a suede *pochette* from Aspreys. Things looked worse when he found a pair of tweezers slotted into the same case. He began to use them to trim his nasal hair. 'No, no, not here dear, not *now*,' his wife whispered at him and he complied. There were still $104\frac{1}{2}$ hours to go.

Nothing else happened except for the sudden, beautiful appearance of Greenland out of the window, half-way through the dreadful movie. The pilot announced it and there it was, the west coast of Greenland, part of the curved earth, salmon pink where the sun caught the mountains, green in the long shadows across the glaciers. It looked just like it should, a piece of wedding cake left out in the rain, with long glacier cuts and smooth plateaux. Over on the left, Louie complained about the amount of ice in her fruit juice cocktail.

So I'm here, feeling rather battened down by the rain, odd with the time difference, with my hired Toyota Corolla parked outside this hotel and my mind laden like any immigrant with all the baggage of my prejudices about America. The television's doing the best it can to confirm them. Someone called E. Joseph Cossman, who has an auburn toupee and speaks as if he's holding a live toad in his mouth and is frightened of crushing it, is telling me that 'artistic talents are highly problematical. Nothing, and I mean *nothing*, is more difficult to sell than *art*.' The heavy emphasis comes regularly every seven words. 'Nevertheless, with Patience, Postage and Perseverance' – these words come up on the screen – 'and with the E. Joseph Cossman/American Institute of Success 18-Part Course in *Selling Yourself and Your Work*, you' – he points at the screen – 'can do it. All you have to say is: "That is action and I want a bit of it." I'll say it again: All you need to get what you want out of life is a strong desire, not a wish, not a whim, a *strong desire* to make money and the E. Joseph Cossman/American Institute of Success 18-Part Course in *Selling Yourself and Your Work*.'

On another channel a basketball player is explaining to a beautiful woman in a yashmak why Islam seemed the right road for him. She nods and seems to be smiling. Like every other presenter she announces 'messages' all the time, but these aren't commercials – they're quotations from the Koran read by an English actor with a plummy voice. I suppose the implication is that Allah, far from being a terrifying, radical Khomeini lookalike, is actually a graduate of some nice establishment or even an English school. Reagan's now calling the Sandinistas a cancer. I must go to bed.

GEORGIA

FLORIDA

ATLANTIC OCEAN

o Cumberland Island
Amelia Island
Kingsley
Jacksonville •

St. Augustine

Hastings
Gainesville

Daytona Beach

Orlando •
Cape Kennedy

Weeki Wachee •

Tampa •

St. Petersburg •

Holmes Beach •
Arcadia
Okeechobee
Hobe Sound
Jupiter Is.

Brighton •
Palm Beach

Lake Okeechobee

GULF OF MEXICO

Naples •
Ft. Lauderdale
Miami Beach

MIAMI •

The Everglades

Florida

• • > • • Nigel's route   15–25 March

0   50   Scale
MILES

Miami, Florida

Sunday 16 March

NIGEL *to Adam*   One of the unexpected pleasures of Miami is that it's
                         half Spanish. We've all known about the Cuban
exiles who took refuge here in the 1960s, and in successive waves later, and
I'd imagined them poor, distressed, transient and unstable. On the contrary,
the refugees have turned, for the most part, into hard-working entrepreneurs,
who have improved a whole quarter of Miami, now known as Little Havana,
and many of them have established themselves here as middle-class Americans
with a Spanish accent.

The result is startling. When I arrived tired and cross last night, and tried
to find my way to the Howard Johnson, I stopped at a garage, a liquor-store
and a café to ask for help. The garage-hand, who was old, looked at me
uncomprehendingly. The liquor man, who was also Cuban, helped a lot. In
the café I began slowly, 'Do you speak English?', to which the reply was 'A
leetle'. In the city centre I came across a young man and woman in evening
clothes. They also were Hispanic, and today I saw them multiplied to five or
six hundred at a concert given, it appeared, exclusively to sustain their culture.
Mingling with the audience, I did not hear a single word of English spoken.
Miami has adapted well to this cosmopolitanism. Even in the smartest hotels,
most notices are bilingual as in Wales. I read under the printed greeting 'Have
a good day' an alternative, '*Que tenga usted un buen dia*', as if someone might
need a translation.

However, Miami doesn't *look* Spanish, even in Little Havana. It is super-
American, as if the map of the United States had been tipped sideways and
all the money had emptied into Florida. There's a lot of industry here, I'm
told, but I didn't see any, and although Miami is one of the country's greatest
ports, almost the only evidence I saw of it were five huge cruise liners moored
end to end along an outlying quay, as if commerce itself, the source of all this
money, had to be given a façade of leisure and luxury. I'm not complaining.
It is one of the most amazing cities in the world. Europe can show nothing
like it, not the French Riviera, certainly not the Costa Brava, for the sheer
audacity of the whole enterprise and the architectural variety that expresses
one aspect of the American dream.

The climate, and the beaches, explain the multi-billion dollar success of
this coast. Today it was 75°. The temperature seldom drops below 70°, and
when it rises above 90°, some hotels give you a day free to compensate for
the discomfort. The vegetation is tropical – palms, hibiscus, cane, a grapefruit
tree dangling yellow globes immediately fit for the breakfast-table. And those
beaches! It's a bit disconcerting, but for Miami scarcely surprising, to hear

that they are artificial, siphoned from the sea-bed to replace eroded sand. Broadening to 200 yards or more, they stretch for miles. I walked to the ocean's playful fringe, feeling foolish in my tea-planter serge and knotted tie as I stepped carefully between recumbent bodies, near-nude (but never Mediterranean nude), and wondered, not for the first time, what pleasure there was in such a day-long basting, sleep without comfort, wakefulness without activity of any kind. I longed to plunge into the ocean, but I had no swimming-trunks, and if I had, where on this vast open populated runway of a beach could I change? In any case, as I learnt later, this was the gay section of the beach.

You'll have gathered that by this time I was on Miami Beach, which is separated from Miami proper not only by a salt-water lagoon but by a whole difference in life-style. And I was no longer alone, no longer a tourist, but a guest.

My hosts were Mr and Mrs Fred J. Lighte. I had not known them before. Two months ago I met their son Peter at a London party, and he suggested his parents as my first American rendezvous. We corresponded, and we converged. Mr Lighte is a retired busness-consultant, I'd guess about 70, a man of outstanding gentleness and courtesy, with a profound interest in the arts. Mrs Lighte is different, but in a highly acceptable way. She's more extrovert than her husband. I imagine that she could be formidable if crossed, and it came as no surprise to hear that she once ran for public office. They both wore beachlike clothes, Mr L. a marbled silk shirt which I envied.

They took me to their house, a low white jewel of a house on the shore of an artificial island in the lagoon. I noticed two warnings displayed outside the door. One was to beware of the dogs (but they turned out to be as courteous as my hosts), and the second a picture of a crossed-out cigarette woven into the doormat. I hid my packet quickly. Inside there is a large drawing-room filled with a creditable diversity of art-objects – a Dali, a seventeenth-century Bavarian cupboard, nineteenth-century landscapes in watercolour, a twisted modern statue in bronze, a chain of bell-like objects which I took to be Indonesian, for they are great travellers – and books everywhere, mainly on art, and all, to my joy, still wrapped in their untorn paper covers. House-pride has never gone further than this. I was given a muffin to eat with my coffee, but it looked and tasted like no muffin that you or I have ever eaten, being dark and crumbly, quite delicious. It was in their garden, beside the pool, that I saw the grapefruit tree. Mrs L. gave me one of its fruit. I do not quite know what to do with it. I hold it like the Queen an orb.

We toured Miami Beach, the Art Deco of the older buildings (but old here means thirty years) lying behind the vast palaces of the newer hotels. I was anxious to see the greatest, grandest, most famous, most expensive hotel in

America, the Fontainebleau Hilton, and they took me there for lunch. One wonders how people could ever be worthy of such magnificence. It would-surely be like populating the Baths of Caracalla with pygmies. Not at all. There was an ease about the place, a succession of comforts and intimacies which reduced the great lobbies to a human scale, and a rise and fall of levels, as in Canterbury Cathedral, which break the monotony of hugeness. You can eat outdoors by a cascade, or inside in a sort of garden-room. We ate inside. I still have to learn the euphemisms of American menus. Fish is not fish but seafood. Salad is not what you and I mean by salad, but a pot-pourri of garnished viandes. My Florentian Salad was a pottage of tuna resting on half a pineapple. I did not dare glance at the bill which the Lightes were paying. But the Fontainebleau is not all that expensive. You can spend two Deluxe nights of your honeymoon here, with presents added by the management, for $311 per couple. I owe them that advertisement.

Miami Beach, and much of the waterfront of Miami itself, is studded with condominiums between the hotels. They are huge buildings like grounded liners, divided into as many as four hundred separate apartments of which you buy the freehold. Architecturally few of them can be called distinguished. Their external patterning is always the same, tiers of balconies, one for each apartment, on which nobody ever sits, but they add square-footage to the advertised floor-space, and hence to its price. Many of these condos are occupied by widows in retirement. I noticed them everywhere in the streets and foyers, holding the hand of a reluctant granddaughter, asking total strangers where they're from, or delaying their party by insisting on talking to 'my friend', the friend being a harassed assistant in a boutique. Their final years seem rather pathetic. They give to Miami a strange diversity, the wrinkled, often crippled, old, side by side with the hale, fun-seeking young. It's a combination of a discreet old people's haven with the ultimate in holidaying. But then so, on a very different scale, is Bournemouth.

Mr Lighte took me afterwards to see what he clearly regards, and rightly, as Miami's greatest showpiece for the architectural connoisseur. It's called Brickell Avenue. Until quite lately it was an indiscriminate collection of up-market houses on each side of a broad tree-lined street. They kept the trees, some of them to grow through the lower storeys of the new buildngs (an odd effect, like columns in the palace of Darius), but pulled down the houses, and in their place they have erected, and are still erecting, office blocks and hotels in glass, steel and marble. I am not a good judge of modern architecture. When Mr L. pointed out to me the tallest building in Miami and regretted its design (little glass cubes, each one-room large, mounted in a vast mosaic), I thought it lovely but didn't like to say so. I shared his enthusiasm for a building with a huge square hole cut through the middle, one corner of it

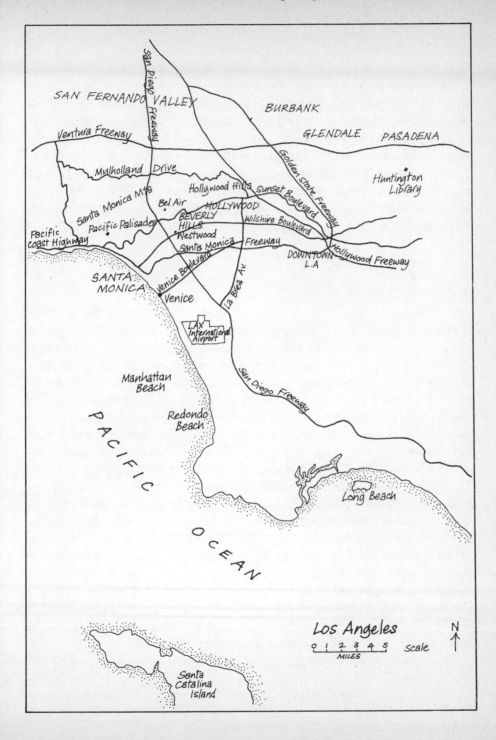

occupied by a spiral staircase painted in brilliant red, like an intestine; and for the Intercontinental Hotel, just completed, faced outside and inside with roseate Italian marble. There's a large Henry Moore in the same material standing central in the foyer. Best of all is the CenTrust Tower, so new that its terminal crane still perches, like a crane, on its topped-out roof. It is all of glass, mounting in three half-moon tiers, and striped like the sort of silk pyjamas I've always wanted to possess. The green bands light up at night. This is indeed Brave New World.

It's hard to leave such a place after only two nights (one harassed) and a single day. I would never have seen or learnt so much without the Lightes. Mrs L. called me at the hotel after dark to give me the addresses of friends along my road. How can one repay the kindness of these people? I'll send her a bouquet.

Venice, Los Angeles, California

Sunday 16 March

ADAM *to Nigel* The rain's gone and it's beautiful. I've spent all day walking around Venice. ('This is the Venice of America', a man in a fast food store told me, 'and thank God those crazies in the planning department just haven't got hold of it yet.') I love it. Just from walking around I get a little quickening in the pulse. It is obvious that once there was some great development scheme to make Venice look like Venice. It was a 1905 amusement park, with gondolas and gondoliers. There are a few canals here and there, and fragments of half-boarded up loggias and arcades, with a couple of semi-Venetian windows above them, but that style has disintegrated under the pressure of people doing their own thing. There is not a square yard of what feels like public space here, only endless privacies strung together with telephone wires. It's all private domains, high hedges, landscaped lots, nurtured privacies. Not a single house joins up with any other, but they all creep to within a few inches of the edge of the lot, so that between them all is this little canyon, a tiny cordon sanitaire, guaranteeing somehow a sense of isolation. I've just seen an ad. in the property section of the *L.A. Times*. 'For those who set themselves apart ...' it begins, and that says it all, doesn't it? Even if the prairie is squeezed down to only 18 inches wide, there is something important about it still being there.

Inside these moats anything can happen. Spanish baroque, Massachusetts weather-boarding, Tudor (one house in Venice, not satisfied with a slightly wobbly effect in its stuck-on beams, has an S-shaped door and leaded windows in which the lines of lead wander backwards and forwards across the glass),

Chinese, something apparently called Moderne and even Egyptian. 'It's wild, isn't it,' a woman said to me as I was standing outside a particularly flamboyant example of half-timbered Los Angelethan, whose roof was speckled in miniature gilded dormers, like a slice out of Chambord. Then the punch line: 'And it's *mine!*' That's the climax, the ultimate remark. Ira Funk (I am not joking) gave me a cup of coffee in this incredible pad and showed me round. 'We had the entry hall walls upholstered in Florentine silk,' she said and stroked them. 'And then, if you move through, you can see that we progress to the warmer and softer felt for the dining room walls, enhanced with a brass trim.' It was obvious she had done this before. The felt was scarlet. 'We decided to have direct-access to the center-island kitchen, for ease and convenience.' We swept on, through the suede-lined family-room, the cork-lined laundry room, more silk for the bedrooms, Sicilian if she was to be believed, culminating in raw Yosemite granite surrounding the hot-tub. 'Those Tudors just could never have dreamed up even one small bit of this,' Ira said.

The best part of it was that she knew how funny it all was, how fantastic it was to bring in 4 tons of granite to line a bathroom that was meant in some odd way to be part of a Norman-manoir-cum-Ightham Mote in a place called Venice on the edge of the Pacific. It wasn't exactly eclectic, nothing had been assimilated, but it was – the whole of Venice *is* – wonderfully acquisitive, wanting to get its hands on anything that's going. There's no reserve, it's all fluorescence and excrescence. Or at least that's how I see it at the moment, skidding across the first surface of enthusiasm and real delight in being here.

It seems that I've been coasting around inside the myths. I've spent all afternoon at a lecture. I stumbled into it by mistake. A large, rather dull building in the middle of Venice called 'Beyond Baroque' – the name apparently of a late '60s poetry movement which the city of Venice had adopted as its own – advertised a lecture called 'Los Angeles: Behind the Myths – the Underside of Tinsel Town'. There was a van parked outside, with a super-tanned young man sitting smoking at the wheel. The van said, 'C'est Si Bon Mobile Dog Grooming Parlor' in a sort of curly gothic script, with the question 'Have you hugged your dog today?' underneath. 'How are you doing?' the man said. 'Just fine,' I said. 'What about the lecture?' 'That can suck,' he said, so I went in.

There were about forty people inside, all of them looking blindingly self-aware and in touch with themselves, as I've learnt to say, in the most relaxed and laid back way that California can provide. I felt unreformed, grubby and worried next to these supple calfskin people, with their laminated tans, their tans on tans like the forty-five coats of paint that go to make up the gloss on a Rolls Royce, and their discreetly optimistic clothes, the pure pastel shades and the slight looseness, everything cotton. As I say, I felt northern and unreformed. I still had no idea what this lecture was going to be about. In the pre-talk hubbub, it was all art/aestho-chat. 'Ya, Davina, she has this emotional intensity, one-liners from *really* deep down in there, but she's no strategist. She's getting too old now just to be flying ... what am I saying? I'm saying those pants she's flying by are getting pretty thin.'

To my amazement the lecture wasn't like this at all. It was a very long, very serious analysis, in two parts, of the role of Mexicans or *chicanos* as they're called, on the one hand and of women on the other in the history of Trade Unionism in Los Angeles. It was worthy and interesting up to a point – the great villain was the Huntington whose house became the library in San Marino. Before the war, apparently, he ran his railway businesses on the most exploitative and racist of lines, discriminating against white American labour in favour of Mexican because he knew they would take lower wages and that the white labour unions were indifferent to the fate of an inferior racial group. It *is* interesting, but it's pretty dry and what amazed me was the turn-out. Forty people on a sunny Sunday afternoon for two hours of this! And they weren't hardline activists, but rather beautiful, glamorous, well-off people, who asked complicated and informed questions at the end. I thought to begin with that it was just a group of middle-class Americans taking vicarious pleasure in the history of labour problems, some of them letting out rather silly giggles at the stories of minor triumphs won by the workers over the bosses, impotent, uninvolved, voyeuristic giggles about something no one would have giggled about at the time. Was this, I wondered, just another Sunday afternoon luxury for a pampered class? Do some people go surfing and drink margaritas, while others go and hear about the strikes of Mexican railway workers in the 1920s? Would both sets slide back into their Yosemite bath-tubs when it was over? I really don't know. I suggested this in a roundabout way to one of them after the talk was finished, and he of course, as he would, said that I had got it all wrong and that a lot of people here spent a lot of their time and money trying to do something to compensate for the imbalance in the system. 'It's different in this country,' he said. 'Even mildly liberal people are made to feel pushed out on to the margin. And when you have a President who lies so often and so blatantly lies about what's happening in Central America – you know that man wants to invade Nicaragua, don't you? and he's chucking in anything he can lay his hands on – Khadafi, Khomeini, drug pedlars – to try and convince the dumbos out there that's what has to happen. I tell you, son, we live in a bad time and we've got to hang together. That's what we're here for now, if you're honest about it.'

I've no idea what to think. There's a demonstration on Tuesday against aid to the Contras. Perhaps something'll come a bit clearer there.

Miami–Palm Beach, Florida

Monday 17 March

NIGEL *to Adam*   I got a rather different angle on Miami from Barry Caswell-Brooks with whom I lunched in the Convention Center before I left. As a resident, but claiming no expert knowledge, he cannot help noticing the contrast between the declining tourist traffic and the building explosion. I told him about the five cruise liners I'd seen. Surely they must bring trade to the city? 'But they're just there to load people from the airport. The passengers never go near Miami Beach.' All the apparatus is here to give anyone a good time, but not enough people want this particular sort of good time. He pointed to the swank new high-risers I'd so much admired. 'It's all very fine, but who's paying for it? Who will occupy all those tourist beds, all those spacious offices?' Barry is not a grouchy old pessimist. Still in his thirties, he fled Beverly Hills, where he had been brought up, to run from Miami semi-academic courses for Americans in Oxford and Cambridge colleges during vacation time. It's been going three or four years, and unlike Miami it's booming. He's bringing one of his twenty-five-strong courses to Sissinghurst in August.

I must say that Interstate 95 is about the most depressing and frightening highway I've ever travelled. Running through dead-flat country, with unpleasant factories and supermarkets on each side for miles, it carries north from Miami a cataract of competing cars and trucks which switch from lane to lane with demonic skill. Nursing my Toyota, with whose habits and potential I'm still unfamiliar, I took the safest, slowest line, like an unpractised skier on a championship slope, and after $1\frac{1}{2}$ hours escaped ruffled but intact by the slip-road to Palm Beach.

I'd been told to expect a manicured and sanitised version of Miami Beach. But it's wholly different. In the centre there's a cluster of superb hotels and shops, and such shops! Imagine Cranbrook's High Street newly carpentered and painted, all outdoor advertisement, all ugly street furniture removed, and for those familiar names, White's, Jones (fish), Miles Travel, International Stores, substitute Cartier, Hermes, Laura Ashley, Gucci, Sotheby's. From this centre spring north and south the domestic roads with cross-streets at intervals, forming a grid-pattern the length of the island. Some houses towards the north end, where I stayed, are relatively modest. The others are on a palatial scale of luxury, in every style from the South African stoep to the Palladian villa to the Greek revival, some built of mottle-grey coral, others stuccoed white, lilac, peach (pastel colours to match the women's clothes), and all are in unbelievably perfect condition – every lawn mown it seems with nail-scissors, every hedge barbered to the smoothness of a wall, not a tile missing, not a blemish on acres of fresh paint, the sanded drive-in ways innocent of the faintest tyre-mark. For someone like me who delights in visual perfection and prefers regularity to irregularity (that's what makes me an eighteenth-century man), it was very heaven. Yet the strange thing is that I saw nobody creating or maintaining this beautiful effect. There must be an army of workmen who emerge only after dark, for one of the principles of the Palm Beach style of gracious living is that everything must be achieved without apparent effort. Another is exclusivity. One expects to see a notice 'Tourists will be Prosecuted', but there are no tourists, as if by general consent a communal privacy has been created from a multiplicity of individual privacies. It's the most highly policed section of the United States. People feel safe here.

Following Barry Donahue's instructions I found his rented house without difficulty, 'white with blue shutters' he had said, and there it was, 200 Ocean Terrace, white with blue shutters. His wife Linda (black tousled hair, fine eyes) was walking up from the beach as I arrived. Would I like to swim? Would I just. The best bathe I've ever had was in about 1960, alone among the Atlantic rollers off the coast of Liberia. This was undoubtedly the second best. One walks barefoot up a short stretch of road to a white door, usually kept locked to guard the private beach, and beyond the door is the ocean. A narrow strip of sand, both firm and yielding like a carpet, shelves into the water. The waves buffet you with a giant's tenderness. The calm water beyond the surf is warm, silky and supportive. But I needn't go on. You will soon, I hope, experience the same delight in the Pacific.

There was quite a party at the Donahue house, half a dozen grown-ups and three sweet miniature children. With one of the other guests, Anne Schirrmeister, who is assistant curator of costume at the Metropolitan, New York, I went bicycling. One of the only concessions which Palm Beach people make to public enjoyment of their affluence is a bicycle-track, an aristocratic right-of-way, which extends for 3 miles between their gardens and the lagoon. On one side you have the water with elaborate piers for mooring yachts, and on the other a view, denied us from the streetfront, into the lit intimacies of these stupendous villas. A party was going on in one of them, and in another garden, three men were talking, with drinks. Otherwise we saw nothing but an occasional light in an upstairs bedroom, and many houses were completely darkened, for wealth on this scale allows you to leave your Palm Beach house unoccupied for ten months in the year while you visit your others. The track was asphalt-smooth with only the sightest rise and fall, but so narrow that we were obliged to ride in Indian file. We turned on reaching the centre of the town. The sun was setting as we looked across the water to West Palm Beach on the mainland. In daylight the far shore is unattractive, but as the lights came on in the tall buildings and, at the tip of a slender radio-mast, a warning beacon glowed redder than neighbouring Mars, all against a peach-coloured sky, the effect was magical. We biked back in near-darkness to find that you had telephoned from Los Angeles, where it was cold and raining.

At dinner that evening I talked to Barry's sister, Mary-Ellen McCarthy, who had spent five years in Palm Beach earlier in her life. She told me that contrary to the impression we had formed during our bike-ride, parties are incessant. Once she had attended sixty-eight parties on sixty-eight successive days. Was this not a bit overdoing it? No, she had enjoyed it, for, while the parties were undeniably competitive and status was measured more by money than by achievement, they were excellent parties, hostesses vying with each other to introduce some novelty, an unexpected star-guest, entertainment or delicacy. It was regarded as an insult to refuse an invitation, and the thank-you bouquet you sent round next day must come from the most fashionable of Palm Beach florists, otherwise it didn't count. She did not give such parties herself. Small dinners were more her line. Clearly she was torn, as a woman of intelligence and taste, between her enjoyment of this high living and her doubts about its conspicuous consumption. I did not press her further.

Someone said that the chief benefit which Palm Beach confers is that you can relax there. 'Relaxation' is a favourite American word and aim, but I have never quite understood what is meant by it. Does it mean doing nothing, or doing something different? Once after a lecture to a women's club in Philadelphia I was made to stand for a hour greeting members of my audience, and a lady said to me, 'It must be so nice for you to be able to relax', little realising that at that moment I was under maximum tension. Surely the social life of Palm Beach must lead to equivalent strains, the fear of not being invited, the performance expected of you if you were, let alone the gossip of which you might be centrally or marginally a victim? It would not be the life for me. What then, they asked, did I regard as the most pleasurable experience? 'This,' I replied. They wouldn't accept that. So I invented another. Lying on a summer's day beside a sweet river reading Jane Austen's *Emma*, while beside me, fast asleep, lies a much loved companion. Bruce Schnitzer, another guest, agreed, 'but I would prefer her to be awake'.

Santa Monica, Los Angeles, California

Monday 17 March

ADAM *to Nigel*   I've moved up the coast a bit, out of Venice and all
its eccentricities. Santa Monica is more conformist,
richer, less violent at nights, so they tell me. There's a huge monument to
money with Merrilp Lynch stamped on it in 6-foot letters across the street
from my motel. I've just been for a drive around Beverly Hills to have a look
at the money. It coats the place like a sort of poison ivy. The only people you
see are the Mexican gardeners picking up the specks from the Surrey-style
driveways. (I now realise what it is that Chertsey and environs is modelled
on: Surrey is an imitation Beverly Hills.) I have never seen a place where
money has so efficiently organised a landscape. Without any dollar signs,
everything can be read as evidence of those dollars somewhere in the background. The Renaissance gatehouse: $250,000. The four-car garage (with
contents): $520,000. The wife (with emeralds) standing under Tuscan portico
in sable: $1.2 million (including wife).

Bulldozers belonging to a company called Landscapes of the Heart were
removing the seventeenth-century Dutch garden (pleached lime alleys) from
in front of a Spanish Baroque mansion, as I passed. This was on Dawn Ridge
Drive. I stopped and asked one of the Mexicans what was happening. 'They
want a Japanese stone garden,' he said. A skip full of boulders stood on the
roadside, waiting for the limes to go. The new garden had been ordered the
day before; it would be installed by the end of the week, when the owners
would be back from Brazil. The inspiration for Landscapes of the Heart
pulled up for a second. She was about 35 and had diamonds in the frames of
her glasses. 'How are you doing?' she shouted at the Mexican. He pulled off
his baseball cap and said it was all going very well. 'Don't let these tourists
get at you,' she said and smiled at me like a toothpaste advertisement. Her
car, which is *the* car of the moment, was a black Porsche Carrera, widely
called, and without affection, an ego blanket. The Mexican couldn't tell me
whose house it was.

I must tell you about one other marvellous woman I met called Betty Merjil
('That's a Latin name,' she said). Betty sells a map on the roadside just off
Sunset Blvd of the streets of Beverly Hills and Bel Air, showing 'the mansions
and each and every one of the stars'. 'You know the producer of Dynasty
lives just over there,' she said, pointing at an ivy-swathed gateway with a
picture of a snarling Alsatian fixed to it. I didn't. And didn't the stars mind
fans being shown straight to their front doors? Betty had to admit there had
been one or two mildly unfortunate incidents when young girls – quite a
group of them in fact – had gone up to Paul Newman's front door and a

couple of them had fainted away there before anything could be done about it. And then there had been an incident with Robert Wagner in the Polo Lounge of the Beverly Hills Hotel, but she didn't think she could go into that. And who was her favourite star? This was one of the great sorrows of her life. Her favourite, I mean the man she felt really quite *weak* about, was Julio Iglesias, and although he wasn't a film star, it was one of the great sadnesses of her life that Julio did not feature on her map. She had no idea at the moment where he lived, but like everyone else in California, she lived in hope.

Palm Beach–Jupiter Island–Okeechobee,
Florida   *Tuesday 18 March*
NIGEL *to Adam*   At 6.30 I went to the deserted beach, walked a mile
                      barefoot throught the spreading surf, plunged in, returned to the Donahue house to write to you about yesterday, and was given breakfast of squeezed orange juice, coffee and pomegranates.

How's that for the beginning of a letter, and of a day?

Barry drove me and Linda round the whole of Palm Beach, pointing out, with an amused display of his detailed local knowledge, the properties of famous names (Estée Lauder, Yoko Ono, Henry Flagler, the man who started it all at the beginning of the century), the marinas, the single school (looking like Palladio's Villa Maser), and the famous shops. Then it was time for me reluctantly to go.

Let me get out of my system a grievance I have against American roads. Not the roads themselves, but their signposting, at least in Florida. No highways have ever been more liberally placarded with notices, but they are never the right ones. You come to a V-junction. One branch will have an enormous sign saying that 150 yards ahead you can have your shoes expertly repaired while you wait. The other warns you that in half a mile you will come to road construction. But not a word to indicate which branch you should take for Hobe Sound. Americans have explained to me that you must follow the route-numbers. That's not much help, unless you have an elephantine memory for numerals, or a companion beside you who can read a map, not a gift that is widely in evidence in this country. Another excuse is, 'But everyone knows where Hobe Sound is. There's no point in advertising it. It's a secretive sort of place.'

So I arrived at Hobe Sound an hour late for lunch, having discovered *en route* that Hobe Sound itself is a tatty little village with a gas-station and half a dozen shanties which has inexplicably given its name to my true destination, Jupiter Island, miles away from it.

My hostess was in New York, and it was not to her that I made my apologies, but to Kitty and Frank Giles, her guests. They were enjoying ten days of the most exquisite hospitality the world can offer. I misled you in suggesting yesterday that Palm Beach represents the ultimate in gracious living. Jupiter Island does. Its dominant quality is discretion. You conceal your beautiful property behind shrubberies through which winds a gravel drive, unlike Palm Beach, where a flamboyant façade is a public advertisement of your success. There is only one road down the centre of the island, with a bridge at each end, the houses being ranged down each side, facing alternately the ocean or the Sound, but scarcely one is visible from another. The life-style of this paradise is equally discreet. You will not be re-invited there if you publicise it. As I want to be re-invited, I won't.

All I need to say is that I ate under a huge ficus tree the best luncheon I can remember, that we discussed with the candour born of long friendship (indeed cousinhood) what book Frank should write next – I was for Lafayette, he for Lord Bute – and that butterflies played between the orange trees as we lunched. We walked through the garden to the water's edge, and then Frank returned to his painting, Kitty to whatever Kitty does return to, and I to my Toyota which was looking, in these surroundings, ostentatiously cheap.

I crossed a third of the peninsula along straight roads through unenterprising country (where are all those orange-groves I'd been promised?) to Okeechobee, a sprawling little town famous only for the lake of the same name and the battle fought here in 1837 between Colonel Zachary Taylor and the Indian braves under their chiefs Wildcat, Alligator and Sam Jones. I don't know who won. (Later, Alligator did.)

I went to look at the lake, or rather a corner of its 750 square miles. Rather disappointing. Sad boat-people, sadder anglers, and a marshy verge. More endearing is a photograph in the *Okeechobee News* of Dixie Wherrell, the 1985 Miss Speckled Perch, who was about to crown her successor. Then I took a room in a cheapish motel ($30), thinking it high time that I reasserted my true nature and deserts after three days of luxury living.

Okeechobee–Holmes Beach, Florida

Wednesday 19 March

NIGEL *to Adam*   Still in search of the American way of life, I visited this morning an Indian Reservation and an orange farm. The 'Brighton' Reservation is one of those allotted to the Seminole Indians, whose persecution by the Spanish, then the Americans, is one of the grimmest episodes in the Indian wars. I shall not give you the story in detail because I want to examine the whole drama of the subjugation of the tribes when I reach Kentucky and Indiana. It's one that fascinates me, particularly because present-day Americans do not seem to feel the same degree of shame for what happened as they do about Negro slavery.

The Florida Seminoles can claim, 'We are the unconquered; we never surrendered; we signed no peace treaty,' but the effect was just the same as with the Sioux, the Apaches, the Nez Percé, the Creeks and the Kiowas, who did. They are now few in number and confined to the poorest land. They have not lost their identity and culture, but it can scarcely be denied that they have lost their pride and energy.

So I entered the Brighton Reservation with a certain diffidence, as if trespassing in a synagogue. I felt that I had no right to be there. I drove slowly down the road which bisects the Reservation (it's 40,000 acres), looking for evidence that this was Indian territory. There is little. The occasional thatched house looks odd in Florida, but in recent years they have built for themselves bungalows in the American manner, and the clothes of the few people I saw were indistinguishable from those of poor whites. I went into both the stores which advertised cool drinks, and was met with sullen courtesy. In the second, the woman was clearly unwilling to talk. I bought a pair of moccasins for Kit Walton, and looked around at the other clothes. They were well made but over-gaudy. The most pathetic evidence of their depressed state were the tomahawks and hunting knives. They were made of wood throughout.

The orange farm was the sort of thing which the Seminoles might have undertaken if they had not lost the enterprise of their warrior days. It lies only a few miles beyond the Reservation, near Lake Placid, and it belongs to R. R. Grigsby. I never learnt his first name. Our meeting came about like this. Driving steadily along the dead-straight highway, I was delighted to see that the endless scruffy plains, grazed sometimes by cattle but more often left derelict, suddenly sprouted a large grove of orange trees planted with the precision of twenty battalions on parade. A little further on was a cluster of buildings, and a notice, 'Sunray Orange Farm'. I knocked at the office door.

A girl of startling beauty, with blonde hair that lifted at the ends like Js, looked up interrogatively. I said my piece. 'I'm from England. I am writing a book about America. I have never seen an orange farm before. Can I look round?' She would ask her boss. A few minutes later Mr Grigsby appeared. He did not at first seem very pleased by my intrusion. He said 'Huh?', an international expression which conveys not just enquiry, but suspicion and a certain irritation at being interrupted in the middle of a busy day, particularly by a 'journalist'. I explained I wasn't.

This first impression was soon dispelled. He was a delightful and helpful man, about 65, not unlike old Mr Ewing in *Dallas* who came to such an unfortunate end, gruff, competent, solicitous, and with a laugh, wholly unforced, which expressed a character, experience and goodwill that I found immensely attractive. He drove me round the farm, or about 1,000 of its 3,600 acres, all planted with orange or grapefruit trees at various stages of growth, some little sticks a few months old, others which had been there twenty, even fifty, years. To my eye all were in perfect condition, fed by an ingenious irrigation system which his son had computerised, to make sure that every tree received exactly the same amount of moisture. It's a most rewarding crop. Apart from spraying, watering and weed-suppression, it requires little attention. When I was there, the trees were in flower (those little white blossoms with glossy leaves that brides used to carry), and the only fruit visible were the few that had been missed at the last harvest. He let me pick some of them, and I shall arrive at Gainesville like a greengrocer.

When we returned to the office, I asked him what he called his property. A farm, an estate, a ranch, a plantation? 'No,' he said simply, 'a grove.' *Et in Arcadia ego*, I thought (Arcadia was the name of the next town on my road), for this was a truly idyllic spot, a fecund nursery for the world's most acceptable fruit except bananas. He wanted above all to visit Israel, with an eye, I suspect, on Jaffa. I told him about our book, and promised to send him a copy. The girl with J hair offered us coffee, but couldn't find the pot.

I drove on until I hit the ocean, crossing a bridge to an island called Holmes Beach, where I hoped to find a room for the night. Not one to be had. The tourist season was still in full swing. In despair I opened the conversation with the manageress of the fifth motel by asking if I could swim in the ocean. 'Not in the ocean,' she replied, 'the Gulf.' 'But it's all the ... ' I began. 'It's not in the least the same.' This was a bad start. I pleaded with her. 'The coast of the Gulf of Mexico' (emphasised) 'is 3,000 miles long' (I made this up), 'and all I'm asking is to rent 10 feet of it for a single night.' This specious argument appeared to convince her, and she gave me her last room. I swam happily in the Gulf.

Santa Monica, Los Angeles, California

Wednesday 19 March

ADAM *to Nigel*   'This is the city that is relaxciting,' it said on my car radio yesterday. I spent almost the whole of it driving around, feeling marvellously relaxcited. It's the one adjective that bridges that place. I don't quite understand how somewhere can be so sedate and frenetic at the same time, but Los Angeles manages it. The traffic slides along at 35, the eye in the sky on the radio announces snarl-ups on the San Diego Freeway southbound between Rosecrans and Artesia or clogging on Ventura where three large bits of metal are blocking lanes 5 and 6. Everybody slides along undisturbed, enjoying the freedom of their cars. It's famous that Los Angeles is the city designed around the car, but no one says what fun that makes it. Everything fits when you're driving here, everything works. There's no sensation of the car being a large unwanted intruder. Traffic is the blood in the veins of this city, endlessly flowing, pumping between the parts. From the plane when I arrived the other day, Los Angeles looked like a hard white rash on the edge of America, with only the clean cut of the Pacific shore and the lines of the freeways, snaking between the hills, giving it any shape at all. This is why it's relaxciting here, because everything goes, everything is fluid and easy and you never bump up against a sharp corner. Traffic on rubber wheels – that's the ideal picture of life in southern California, all neuroses ironed out, all awkwardness removed, leaving you with nothing but a seamless fluency of movement, gliding round the clover leaves, an existence made up of one long liquid slide.

Of course that's not true. Or at least it's only partly true. Money is the lubricant of this extraordinary ease and in some parts of town it's obvious that the money has simply run out. Shops boarded up, no-hopers on the street, an air of withdrawal and decay. Parts of Venice are like this. Even parts of Pasadena less than a mile from the Huntington's spreading lawns are rotten with poverty. Money in Los Angeles is like hot fat on water, shrinking into tight little globules and leaving large parts of the place without. It's a city riddled with frontiers that you cross without any warning. A general rule is that money heads for the hills and if you're up a bit, with a view and a breeze in the air, then that's where the dollars are to be found. But it's not fail safe and without any good reason you can cross a boulevard and find yourself in another world. There's a sort of psychological capitalism behind it: good neighbourhoods become better because they're good to start with. Money goes where money is. It's because Los Angeles is an invented city, where the idea and the image is the only reality (these are Californian thoughts) and where everything is bendable to a sort of communal imagination which makes things how it wants them to be.

I went to a demonstration last night with Kanthi Barry (do you remember her?). She works for Tom Hayden who is a left-wing Democrat assemblyman for Santa Monica and Jane Fonda's husband. The demo was against aid to the Contras. There's a vote about it in the House on Thursday. The demonstration was in the evening, about 6, at the peak of the rush-hour, at the corners of Wilshire and Westwood Boulevards. We parked some way off and started walking towards the Federal Building, a beautiful skyscraper with great concrete fins sticking out from its huge façades, like the ruffled feathers on a goose. I said about the ruffled feathers to Kanthi but she told me I was not meant to be thinking about that sort of thing. People in Sandinista T-shirts pointed us in the right direction. Everywhere you looked, on all the placards, was the one word: 'Vietnam.' Kanthi said that she would never have thought, when she was here demonstrating on this very street in the '60s, running away from policemen with batons, that she would be back here in the '80s. A group of right wing nasties with a placard saying, 'Go Go Get Em, Ronald Rambo Reagan', came up to us and said 'You looking for Red Square? You looking for the Annual Gathering of the Los Angeles Communist Party? Well, it's right over there, comrade.' We ignored them, feeling martyrish and superior and joined the crowd. There must have been two or three thousand, lined up along the pavements, pushing the Save Nicaragua banners at the windows of the rush-hour cars. The businessmen stared ahead. An earnest young woman asked me if I had sent a mailgram to my Congressman yet. An old man asked me to come to a multi-media show called 'From Ellis Island to El Norte: An inter-weaving of Jewish and Central American Experiences'. I had to tell him I would be in Vancouver by then. 'NO, NO CONTRA AID', we all shouted at the traffic. Kanthi said that there wasn't the feeling here that she remembered in the '60s, none of the passion.

Somehow it was all more tired, more arranged, less heartfelt. The only real passion was coming out of the right wing group, who seemed to believe that a Marxist government in a country of three million people 1,000 miles away was a threat to the United States. One of them came up to within an inch of my face – he had a terrible skin condition – and shouted, 'You couldn't do this in Managua, you know.' I smiled a smile of sublime ignorance and gave him a copy of *The Militant* I had bought a few minutes before. 'Read that,' I said. 'I wouldn't even wipe my butt with that,' he said and threw it on the pavement. Kanthi said we should move on. More shouting of 'NO, NO CONTRA AID' and gesticulating at cars. It had been arranged for some people to be arrested in a polite sort of way and they were led off smiling by smiling police into a police car, and then someone said something about the next demonstration in a few weeks' time and then we all drifted off. Nothing had happened, and in Washington Reagan was calmly buying off a few more Democrat congressmen to get the majority he needed. That was my feeling anyway: impotence, irrelevance, rather a self-confirming party. But Kanthi thought it important and necessary. People wouldn't have done it in England, would they? In England there is not a single issue of foreign policy except for the missiles, which people care enough about to come on to the streets and demonstrate. A tired, old, hopeless country we come from.

Holmes Beach–Gainesville, Florida

Thursday 20 March

NIGEL *to Adam*   On the way to St Petersburg there is a turning to the beach where Hernando de Soto landed in 1539, one of the most historic sites in America. It has been tidied and annotated by the National Parks people in a way that I like but you wouldn't, but I don't think you could fail to look unmoved at that strip of sand where the Spaniards landed at the start of one of the most extraordinary journeys in history.

There were six hundred of them, quite an army, most mounted, and they entered America by this beach with infinitely less fuss and in higher spirits than I did through Miami Airport. Their troubles started when they began their trek inland to discover the gold-plated cities of their imagination. Arrows to left of them, swamps to the right of them, rode the six hundred. They pushed their way through, as the local guidebook puts it, 'as an enormous questing centipede', for three whole years. They found no gold, saw no cities, endured the mounting hostility of the jungle and the tribes. Their route, plotted on a modern map, shows by its inconsequential twists that they hadn't the faintest idea where they were going. Florida, Georgia, the Carolinas, Tennessee, Alabama they discovered and explored but did not name, and eventually they emerged at the greatest river any white man had ever set eyes upon, the Mississippi. There de Soto, worn out, died. His body was sunk by night deep into its waters, for fear that the Indians, who thought him a god, might find out that he wasn't after all immortal. Three hundred of the six hundred managed to reach Mexico by the river and the Gulf.

One of the clever things that the National Park has done is to run a path round the little peninsula on which the beach stands, the first few hundred yards of that awful 3,000-mile march, between exactly the same vegetation through which the Spaniards had to hack their way – figs, vines, mangrove, yucca, the prickly pear – some sporting aerial roots to trip a foot or hoof, others spiked with sharp-pointed needles that would pierce the heaviest leather jerkin. How did they ever get through? Lizards scuttled out of my way, and in the sand I saw the prints of a racoon, just like a baby's. How unhostile that once hostile world has now become! A beautiful bay with little sail-boats on it, a couple of people lazily swimming, a balmy sky, and in the distance a column of smoke, not an Indian signal now, but someone's camp-fire.

The road north leads over an astonishing feat of engineering, the Sunshine Skyway Bridge. Goodness knows how long and high it is, but exceedingly both. There are in fact three bridges side by side, one which you use, a second under major repair after a tanker smashed into it, and a third under construction. The unfinished bits rise yearning towards each other from opposite shores (*ripae ulterioris amore*), and terminate with terrifying abruptness like the take-off point of a ski-jump. Dwarf engineers could be seen among the girders, spidermen weaving a steel web.

I skipped St Petersburg, Tampa and the Interstate, and took what I assumed would be a prettier coast-road, US 19, hoping for fishing villages. I must suppress my indignation at what Americans have done to the main approaches to their cities, but will allow it for the moment a little play. It's the hideousness of the roadside advertising that appals me. For 30 miles the road is lined with huge billboards of competing ostentation. What they must cost! A 50 × 30 ft. board saying 'Come to the country where the Marlboro's come from' is mounted on a pillar substantial enough to support Blenheim Palace itself. These ads have two functions – (a) to inform at a distance of a quarter of a mile, and (b) to proclaim the superiority of their goods and services over all rivals. The yellow camel-humps of McDonalds top the lot. It's terrible. If only, I thought, the advertisers would stage a major convention and agree to reduce their typography by a couple of points, no commercial advantage would be lost and some serenity regained, but bigger, higher, better, brighter is the unrelenting aim. Then I reflected that I was being stuffy. This is only the Americans letting off commercial steam. It's confined to this one road. In the neighbouring streets and in the open country no such pollution is allowed. Besides, it's fun. Modesty would be ineffective and inappropriate here. Perdita's little hamburger stall has as much right to shout her wares as McDonald's, whom one day she may rival. It's all part of the dream.

There's a wonderful place on the road called Weeki Wachee which advertises itself as 'Live Mermaid City' (oh America!), and I stopped to see what it meant. I didn't enter the garden of delight where the mermaids perform, but from the postcards I gathered that fish-tailed girls cavort underwater and recline in becoming attitudes between the waterfalls and the rocks. I longed to see how they managed to enter and leave the stage with dignity, but thought

$7 too much even for this experience. There was a splendid Holiday Inn opposite which tempted me. But I'm economising. When I'm not lunching under a fig tree on Jupiter Island, I lunch off Hershey Kisses in the car.

I reached Gainesville at 5.30, and was immediately arrested. Being half an hour early, I parked on the road to read. That was a mistake. A lady in a neighbouring house telephoned the police that a man of sinister appearance was loitering outside it. Within minutes the city police drew up alongside me. What did I think I was doing? I explained my nationality and innocent purpose. I produced my documents, including a British Rail certificate that I was a Senior Citizen, hoping that this would mollify them. All menaces changed into smiles. That's quite OK. I was breaking no law. It's simply that this is a Crime Watch Neighbourhood, and they had to watch for crime.

My hostess for the next two nights is Kit Walton. When she was Kit Macdonald nineteen years ago, she came with me and Ian Graham on the long car journey through Europe which resulted in *Great Houses of the Western World*. She typed my descriptions of the houses as fast as I wrote them, kept the accounts, researched for pictures and fixed the accommodation and the drinks. She was an admirable companion. (You met her in Norway at the very end of the trip, when you were aged 9, and she was much impressed, she told me, that you knew the word 'pylon'.) When she returned to Gainesville, she married, bore three children, divorced, and in her mid-thirties, with creditable gumption, she began to study law, successfully sat the Bar exam, and is now a fledged attorney. We had not met for fifteen years. There she was at her door to greet me. She still had those smiling eyes, that seal-flip of the hand by which she dismisses improbabilities, and phrases like 'Wasn't that terrible?' 'Isn't that awful?', which I remember so well from our thousands of miles on the European roads.

Westwood, Los Angeles, California

Thursday 20 March

ADAM *to Nigel* I've moved. The hotel in Santa Monica, with its lovely view of the Pacific and its Art Deco bedrooms, was costing too much. So I've moved in for a few days with a journalist from the *New York Times* called Aljean Harmetz and her husband Richard. They give me delicious stir-fried vegetables for dinner and let me do anything I want to in the day. It couldn't be nicer or they more friendly to an utter stranger. Haven't the English got something to learn from that?

I swing around this city, buoyed up on the friends of acquaintances and the acquaintances of friends. Mary-Agnes Donahue, a friend of *your* Florida Donahues, gave me dinner in a Japanese restaurant. She is a screen-writer and, having just finished a script and sent it off to a few directors, was wildly distracted. All she could think of was those powerful men flicking through her worked-on, cared-for dialogue with the sort of blasé knowingness that comes with power. I can't think of a fate worse than being a Hollywood writer. No, of course I can, but the image of these little ants nibbling at the huge supine bodies of the studios, hoping for a little chunk of something and meeting year after year the vast immobile bulk of indifference – that is not a good picture. Mary-Agnes sold a script ten years ago and nothing since. But she was hopeful for this one. It was about a love affair between a very young man, about 20, I suppose, and his godmother, his mother's best friend. The title is *Rules of Engagement*, which is brilliant except that it's too like *Terms of Endearment*. Never mind. If she sells it, she expects to get $250,000 or more. That's why one sale every ten years is perfectly viable and why this whole city is teetering on the edge of a tantalising future. Nothing is fixed or permanent. A writer scraping along at one moment is flush with dollars the next, choosing the stars for the parts, deciding whether Streep would be right or not, suddenly driving when all she'd been doing before was watching the traffic. Kanthi Barry said to me that this was the root of the Los Angeles 'I-can-do-your-job, you-can-do-mine' syndrome. That waitress in the run-down diner will, after her screen test on Monday, be installed in a Malibu penthouse and on the cover of *Vanity Fair* within a fortnight. I've never been to a place where the future is so dominant, where it is always the possibility and the potential that matters more than the present and the actual. Los Angeles is founded on the idea that hope is the only human happiness. It makes me feel giddy. At the end of dinner we had those fortune cookies. Do you know them, biscuits with a message inside? Mary-Agnes's said: 'You have a potential urge and the ability for accomplishment.' She loved it. Mine said: 'You will be travelling and coming into a fortune.' That was fine.

I went to see Stewart Granger, the film star, this afternoon. One of Olivia's enormous number of cousins, Kitty Black, had helped him write his autobiography a few years ago. He lives in a small apartment just off Sunset Boulevard in Pacific Palisades. (Aren't these names wonderful?) It is jammed full with the carcasses of animals. He'd shot them all. Two pairs of elephant tusks scraped the ceiling. A table was covered in an Indian leopard, the floor carpeted in lion and zebra skins, the walls encrusted with the horns of various creatures. This was quite alarming, but worse were the guns – not in a nice glass case but leaning up against the furniture as if we were in the Alamo. A huge revolver lay on the table between us as we talked. 'This is a nice one,'

I said, stroking the head of a leopard. 'I shot that one from the back of an elephant. Had trouble seeing it at first but then *boom*,' he made a little pistol with his fingers and thumb, '60, 70 yards. The elephant was shaking like a jelly.'

Mr Granger was sitting on a sort of high stool near the window overlooking the Pacific, but there was nothing else to sit on within about 10 yards. I wasn't quite sure what to do. Should I sit down 30 feet away and shout questions across the room or should I come nearer and be forced to stand? I decided to stand, about 4 feet in front of Mr Granger, with my hands in my pockets to show I was relaxed and quite used to talking to sitting-down film stars while standing in front of them. Mr Granger felt ghastly but looked marvellous, ruddy with swept back silver hair. 'You look marvellous,' I said. 'Yes, I know, with this colour, but I'm ashen underneath.' It was a tricky start, but as he talked about his extraordinary life (Had I seen *King Solomon's Mines*? No. Had I seen *Scaramouche*? No Had I seen the *Prisoner of Zenda*? Yes. Relief. 'You were marvellous in that Mr Granger'), as he talked about all of this, his chaotic life, I warmed to him. He's only got one lung – the other was taken out by mistake when they thought he had cancer. He lost all his money in the property crash in the early seventies and he dreams rather sadly of becoming a big star again. He even had to say to me, 'I was a very big star, once, you know.' There's a chance that he might play Sylvester Stallone's father-in-law in some big Rambo-style film that's coming up. But it's not the same. He feels sad that the glamorous romantic days, the swashbuckling and the really beautiful women, – all that has gone. Woody Allen is not Errol Flynn. This was the other end of the I-can-do-your-job, you-can-do-mine pendulum. Here was the past, once a beneficiary and now a victim of fashion.

Gainesville, Florida

Friday 21 March

NIGEL *to Adam*   I got your first batch of letters (15–17 March) here. I'm glad that Olivia behaved with dignity when you left her at Heathrow, that your flight was not entirely spoiled by the nail-clipping man, and that Venice, on the second day, partly lived up to its plagiaristic name. But what is this 'baggage of prejudice' with which you say you arrived in America? I want to know more about its sources, its gradual confirmation or removal, hoping you won't look for evidence of your pre-conceptions, because you'll be sure to find it if you do. I liked the sound of Ira and Betty of the Beverly star-map, and so I think did you. You even enjoyed the Trade Union lecture which I would have found intolerable.

Clearly you're getting into the swing of California, its eccentricity, display and occasional unexpected earnestness. On my coast things are a little more sedate.

Kit took me to meet the Director of the Center for Gerontological (old age) Studies in the University of Florida, Professor Otto von Mering. That may sound rather a grim thing to do immediately after breakfast. It was the very opposite. The professor told me he was 63, and looks just what I would like to look at 69 – a full mop of grey hair, a ruddy prairie face, eyes as bright as stream-washed pebbles. We talked for an hour, but I'll give you only a sample of his wisdom:

> Old people must be protected from younger people who want to help them. If they are cossetted too much, they will come to feel sorry for themselves. They only feel old because it is expected of them.

> They should stop agonising about the past, about what went wrong with their careers, and plan for the future, for every age has a future.

> Younger people are much nicer to you when you retire, because you no longer pose a threat to them.

> The sandwich-generation, young marrieds, with children and elderly parents (that's you, Adam), would think it disgraceful to neglect the latter in favour of the former. That's the ethos here.

Then we talked about the American way of death. You must learn to die gracefully. There's a complete thanatological profession which studies and teaches the method. I didn't like to ask what the method was, but we did touch on the delicate subject of whether you should pull the plug on life-support systems when life has ceased to have much meaning, a half-way stage to euthanasia. Some people write this merciful provision into their Wills. That's a good idea – I think I'll write it into mine, but not quite yet. Anyhow, Professor von Mering clearly suffers from none of the disabilities which he studies. He didn't exactly say 'Life begins at 60', being too articulate a man to descend to such banalities, but I think he meant it, and was an example of it.

In the afternoon we went to the Courthouse, and I sat in on the trial of two teenage girls who had run away from home, stolen a car, and were arrested at 3 a.m. this morning. They were dressed in penitential clothes, white blouses, blue jeans, looking sweetly innocent, but weren't. One girl, weeping, asked to be allowed to go home, and although her mother said she wasn't to be trusted, which I thought a bit harsh, the judge released them with a caution.

I talked to him afterwards, and to two other judges, of whom one, Stephan Mickle, is the only black judge in the Gainesville circuit. I asked him about Civil Rights. He said that since the assassination of Martin Luther King, and under the influence of Reagan conservatism, there has been a slight retrogression. Some of the momentum of the '60s has been lost. Anti-discrimination laws (housing, education, jobs) are not strictly enforced. But there is no doubt that more opportunities now exist for blacks than when he was young. His 16-year-old daughter was astonished by the notion that racial prejudice existed. 'That's all history,' she'd said. Yet he knew well that it still takes subtle forms, like depriving black students of their proper share of grants, filling schools in black areas with more than their designated quota of blacks, and schools in white areas with too many whites, in spite of bussing them to and fro, a 'creeping re-segregation' which he deplored. However, attitudes were slowly changing. People had been moved by TV dramas like *Roots*, the dreadful example of South Africa, and his own elevation to a judgeship in a predominantly white community.

I asked him, as were getting on so well, whether he felt himself to be wholly integrated. He was honest about this. Professionally he had had to study the 'majority culture' of the whites having been raised in the 'minority culture' of the blacks, but he still did not think of himself as belonging to both jointly. He said a remarkable thing: 'If I go to a meeting or a party where there are twenty whites and five blacks present, I instinctively gravitate towards the five.' That this decent, clever, highly respected man could feel and act like this shows how far there still is to go. I thought of our racial problems at home. We have experienced, stage by stage, in the last twenty years what America has struggled with for a century.

In the evening a party was given for me in a neighbour's forest-house. This description is apt, because although the suburban houses sit on quarter-acre plots, the trees, flowering dogwood, azaleas and wisteria, conceal and cushion them, giving the whole place a Red Ridinghood feel.

I wish – but what's the use? – that I was a better guest at parties like this. Enormous pains had been taken by Lucille Maloney to gather eighty of Gainesville's citizens and give us the pleasure of good drink, decorative food and each other's company. My feeling of inadequacy arises from two causes. First, I cannot hear properly in a hubbub. The decibels augment in proportion to the mounting number of guests, until one finds oneself yelling inane remarks like, 'BOYS ALWAYS BENEFIT FROM CLOSE ASSOCIATION WITH GIRLS!', in an attempt to sustain a serious conversation on co-education with a man who is obliged to assent or dissent at equal pitch. It cannot be done. Secondly, the 'guest-of-honour' is inevitably torn away from guest 32 to be introduced to arriving guest 56, just as he has begun to like 32 very much, and never meets her again. 56 may start off, 'My wife and I visit Zimbabwe on average once every five years,' or, 'My niece had a lovely holiday in Devon in 1972 – or was it 1973?' – conversational openings with which I'm absurdly incapable to deal. One person began, 'I have seven wives, and this is one of them,' which I thought quite funny, though perhaps it was his party-piece. His wife didn't look too pleased. I met the Mayor of Gainesville (a fine Ferraro woman), a member of the Board of the American National Trust who was interesting about preserving small towns (one is Arcadia), a Welshman who teaches Virginia Woolf at the University, and a lady who owns a castle near Oban. As the company thinned and the noise and pressures abated, the last hour of the party was as enjoyable as the first. It was the middle that found me wanting. The departing guests kissed each other lip to lip, but not me.

Westwood, Los Angeles, California

Friday 21 March

ADAM *to Nigel*   Aljean took me to the Publicists' Guild of America Annual Lunch and Award ceremony today in the Beverly Hilton. I had to borrow a tie off Richard. Aljean looked mildly disapproving at my wrinkled English trousers but said nothing. The other guests – there must have been a thousand – were smart, blousy and breezy. The vast ballroom of the hotel – chandeliers, soggy lettuce – was filled with the invisible puffs of these professional enthusiasts. We sat at the Universal Studios table, right next to the dais where Robert Wagner and James Stewart and other stars I hadn't heard of stared a little glassily across the room. The publicists are not an admired breed. They get paid a lot, they confuse their business with their friendships, they spend most of their time in the awful business of persuasion. Fanny May Candy shops had provided little bits of candy for every place setting. Everybody ignored theirs. Too cool. The woman next to me had masterminded the marketing of *Out of Africa*. She was happy with the way it had gone. A Universal executive across the table was one dissertation short of a PhD at Harvard but had been wooed away by film money. Sometimes – that was the crucial word – he didn't think the hassle was worth the money. Sometimes. A beautiful actress presented an award to someone who wasn't there. More lunch. 'There is simply no cuisine', I was told, 'between Santa Fe and New Orleans. That is one big cuisine desert out there.' Then the speeches. Reminiscence, fumbling with the microphone, endless gratitude to the people who *really mattered*, who were either still picking at their soggy lettuce or were dead. Robert Wagner had first met Glen A. Larson when he (Larson) was hitching a lift in the rain. Someone in a shop in Rodeo Drive in Beverly Hills had asked Sheilah Graham, an antique English gossip columnist who had an affair with Scott Fitzgerald, if she was 'the late Sheilah Graham'. This extraordinary mixture of boredom and sentiment, of soft-palped cherishing and ruthless dropping of the no longer adequate – I feel I'm on the fringes of a world of unintelligible complexity, which somehow, *somehow* produces wonderful films. Have you seen *Out of Africa*? But publicists are hardly at the centre of any world. The film-makers are not to be judged by the people who promote them. One of the speech-makers, a lobbyist called Jack Valenti, said: 'I say to you with all the passion and fervour I can summon: I feel comfortable with you.' That does not inspire trust, does it?

Two fat women came up to Robert Wagner in the lobby after the lunch was over. He looked beautiful in a grey Parisian suit and a mild tan. They looked awful in turquoise and peach. 'I'm trying to take some of it off,' turquoise said up at the beautiful profile. 'Oh? Where?' 'Here in Los Angeles.' 'No, I mean where.' 'Oh, right here,' she said squeezing a bit of turquoise hip, like a piece of raw tuna in silk. 'Have you tried drugs?' Wagner asked. The fruit cocktail giggled. Then Wagner swung off down the lobby while we all watched. He had an odd way of arranging his hair on his forehead, with a practised, feminine gesture that left it looking as if he had just come in off the track at Le Mans. I like looking at stars. There is a satisfied air about them, like a properly inflated tyre.

I rang up Pamela Granbery, the daughter of your friends from New England, and she took me to some dives on Friday night. Some hip joints, she said. First was the Atomic Café in Downtown Los Angeles. Polynesian waitresses in figure-hugging black leotards served up cheesecake with custard all over it. Leotard-clad Natalie from Hawaii had made it. This was hip. We had tea and **Sid Vicious** did it his way on the juke box. A man in an orange shirt and a thin grey moustache who had appeared perfectly normal for the first ten minutes seemed to go mad. He stood up from the stool at the bar and pulled a gun out of his pocket. (This was a mime.) He then held it up to the head of Hawaiian Natalie and shot her. Natalie continued to adjust her bra straps. Johnny Rotten sang 'God Save the Queen' on the juke box and there was a slight confusion in the red plastic booth next to ours: were they talking about the Kennedys (the famous New England political family) or the Dead Kennedys (the almost equally famous new wave band)? Not that it mattered.

Then on. More driving on the freeways, with Brown Sugar on the stereo. I love the freeways at night more than anything else. So easy, fast and beautiful. A police helicopter hung over an empty lot illuminating it like one of those seventeenth century pictures of God discovering Guilt. This is how they catch murderers here. The evening tailed away at a vegetarian jazz club in Venice. 'A new age of humankind has evolved,' the menu said. 'At the

Comeback Inn we satisfy (and also stimulate) the body, the heart and mind. We are sincere in our quest for the Good Life.' I had a beer and a woman sang about the pain of existence. Pamela is so nice. She paints beautiful pictures of Icarus in Beverly Hills. You know the kind of thing. In one of them an angel arrives to save someone in a brown Ford van. In another the Hollywood Hills are blood orange red. I told her that her clouds are like Constable's. 'I know,' she said.

Too much is happening. I feel kaleidoscoped by it. You must be able to tell from these letters. I can't maintain any sort of distance or cool. I feel like a bit of luggage on a fast complicated system of conveyor belts, hurrying me along here, whirling me past there, dropping me for a second in a backwater there. I know this word has been devalued but Los Angeles is *dynamic*. The population is growing by a *twelfth* every year. This must have been the feeling in the great industrial cities in Europe in the nineteenth century, the crowding in, the sucking in of people, feeding the great money/people hoover of this city. No wonder people have to be so laid back here. Elizabeth, the Harmetz's daughter, does nothing but tease me about my absurd English accent, my decrepit English teeth and my use of the phrase 'laid back' every other sentence. It is, apparently, part of the usual disease to which every Englishman who comes here succumbs: over-use of 'laid back'; wanting to buy a 1974 Pontiac Catalina convertible; eliding of the consonants in an attempt to fit in; buying a pair of sunglasses with silverised lenses; thinking that nobody does any work in LA. To virtually all of these temptations I have fallen prey, but I will tell you about them in my next letter.

Gainesville–Daytona Beach, Florida

Saturday 22 March

NIGEL *to Adam*   Kit and I drove to the Atlantic coast, my second crossing of Florida, through woods bursting into leaves as crisp as lettuce. The inland country at this latitude is richer than further south, and fewer acres of it are left barren. Hastings, a small town on our route, calls itself 'The Potato Capital of the World' (they're very keen on superlatives in Florida), and just beyond it, I think by coincidence, is a village called Spuds.

I wanted to go to Daytona for several reasons. Because the Macdonalds own a condominium there where we could stay; because it is one of the best places from which to view Halley's Comet in this particular week; because you can drive at 20 m.p.h. along the same beach where Malcolm Campbell drove Bluebird at 207, breaking the speed record in 1928; and because it is 'spring-break', the week when students from all the campuses in eastern America pour into Daytona and Fort Lauderdale to celebrate the coming of spring and their latest love-affairs.

Of all these enticements the most rewarding was the beach-drive. A strong wind was still blowing and the beach was narrowed by a high tide, but there was just room enough between the scudding surf and the dunes to give the Toyota a 12-mile canter. The sand is firm and almost white. The ocean advances towards it in curly parallel ridges some 10 feet apart, very regular for something so unstable as a breaker, and looking exactly like waves drawn by schoolchildren round their maps of New Zealand.

When we reached Daytona we ran into the students. It was difficult to miss them. They congested the streets and beaches in thousands. I felt that you should have been there rather than me. I prefer students, like architecture and woods, to be neat and orderly, strolling handsomely round a campus, not hanging out of car-doors high on beer or drugs, shouting obscenities or scrawling them with spray-guns on the metal sides of their cars. You may think this betrays my age. It doesn't. It betrays my character, for I was just like that when I was myself an undergraduate. I loathed rags and bump-suppers which involved a forced display of high spirits. Perhaps that was why I wasn't more popular. I noticed with sympathy a shy pale girl inside one of the cars (*Delta Sigma Phi* from somewhere like Duke University) who was obviously made the same way as me and was dreading the wet T-shirt contest advertised as the evening's main attraction. We made our way through this honky-tonk, Kit's preferred name for razzmatazz. She was uncertain whether to applaud or resent it, but on balance she took the more puritanical line, perhaps because I'd expressed it so firmly, or because of a Calvinist streak in her. She was born Canadian.

Earlier, she'd sprung her surprise. Her family's condo was occupied by tenants. We couldn't go there. Instead, her father had booked us two rooms in the Daytona Hilton, and prepaid for them. When I set out on this journey, I imagined myself, when I was not staying with friends, taking rooms in mean motels, saving my budgeted $60 a day for a Holiday Inn treat once a week. But the Hilton! It was everything that you can imagine, from ochre-coloured bath-towels to a roof-top candle-lit restaurant. I am glad that my travels are not pampered migrations from Hilton to Hilton, for how can anyone relish luxury, as I did, if it is the norm?

Halley, I'm afraid, was a flop. We each booked a 5.30 a.m. call to see the phenomenon in the south-eastern sky. Kit had a star diagram to guide us. But clouds and the glare of city lights obliterated it. Now I shall never see Halley. Instead I dressed as dawn swept in from the ocean, and wrote this.

Daytona—Amelia Island, Florida

Sunday 23 March

NIGEL *to Adam*   Kit and I said our goodbyes affectionately, and I drove north, waving a Kit-flip at Jacksonville as I passed through on the Interstate, and turned off it to cross a whale of a bridge which gently deposited me on a long, slim, flat island – Amelia Island.

It is one of those barrier islands which give this part of the US a double coastline. Reading outward—inwards, there's the ocean beach, on which I walked for an hour playing with the blowing balls of surf. Then comes the wooded centre of the island, with a west coast of marshy rushes laced by broad creeks. Next, a mile-wide strip of open water known as the Intercoastal Waterway, and on its far side the continental shore. I am staying in a house on the marsh side.

My host is Charlie Atkins, Juliet's new friend. I was startled to find him so young (31), but he appeared less startled to find me so old, having been warned, I expect. He's the sort of person who gives one immediate confidence that he could fix anything, from a new airline to a children's party, but he's also a man for the open air, politics and the arts – he could be put on exhibition, and nobody would dispute his right to typify the young American male. His wife is in Arkansas, expecting their second child. Their house overlooks the marsh, grey outside and white within, single-storeyed, with verandahs and a great shapely hat of a roof with broad brims, the sort of house that a former Governor-General of Nigeria might wish he'd had in Lagos, but didn't. It is extremely comfortable, and so clean that I scarcely dare put down a coffee cup. Everything electrical or mechanical of course works.

We dined in a country club where girls in pale blue lead you to a table in pink. I asked Charlie to explain why it was that no other country has managed to create a material civilisation at this level. His answer was interesting. He said it was due to three things. The competitive energy of the people, which he acknowledged might have something to do with their pioneering past. The absence of government restraint upon private enterprise. And the comparatively low level of taxation – currently 50 per cent of the highest incomes. I suggested a fourth, the early development of the credit system which allowed people of modest means to make a start. He agreed, and commented that the US tax system actually subsidised borrowers by permitting full deductibility of interest expense while fully taxing interest on savings. (In case you detect a change in tone, and a gain in authority, in that last sentence, I must explain that it was written in by Charlie when I gave him a draft of his speech to check.) He said that there was little jealousy of the wealthy. Even if there is a yawning gap between them and the poorest, the poorest never lose hope that they might one day become the wealthiest, and it happens all the time. He gave me as an example the New York taxi-driver who will quite naturally turn to his Wall Street passenger and question him about the latest movement in stocks and bonds. That would never happen in London or Paris. 'Take the four hundred richest men in the country,' he said. 'One hundred of them will have inherited great wealth. One hundred will have inherited a little, and made much more. But two hundred will have started without anything.' One has heard this before. All the same, it still seems to me remarkable that the United States, with no special advantages of geography, raw materials or population (Russia, China and most of Europe had the same) should have managed to raise 70 per cent of their people to levels of affluence almost unimaginable to the rest of us. I must talk about this to James.

We spoke of many other things, including women's lib. Charlie had not been greatly impressed by it, nor had his wife. It was a social phenomenon which is rapidly losing its momentum. It has had a few positive results. For example, a Board will now generally add a woman director to their number, and many of them are excellent (he instanced Marietta Tree), and lower down the scale female employees are more vocal in claiming equal salaries. But the truth is that the women crusaders were besieging castles whose gates were already half-open. The universities, the arts and most of the professions have welcomed women for decades, so there was not all that much for women to protest about. The 'movement', at its strongest in the 1960s and '70s, was essentially confined to the north-east and far west, liberal, Democrat, upper-middle class, and intellectuals. It never inspired working women to join in. Older women were actually hostile to it. 'Why? Because they saw in it a criticism of their lack of enterprise in the past?' 'Possibly.' Their daughters (like mine) have a different attitude, seeking jobs and widening their interests, but it's not the result of women's lib.

When I went to bed, I read for an hour one of the books Charlie had left in my room, *D. Brahm's Report on the General Survey in the Southern District of North America* (ed. Louis de Vorsey Jr.), about the survey of this coast in the 1760s. This is the kind of book I enjoy most. His mapping and soundings were astonishingly accurate, and he endured hurricanes, Indians and jealousy of his achievements with splendid equanimity.

Amelia Island, Florida

Monday 24 March

NIGEL *to Adam* This has been a lovely day, fine, warm and educative. Charlie Atkins took me in his boat along the Intercoastal. It is a small open boat called by its makers a Boston Whaler, but by Charlie, Frances IV. (If it were my boat, the white hull and fittings would by this time be off-white, and the engine wouldn't have started.) We clove the water at 35 m.p.h., the same as the speed limit for cars on the island and for birds on the waterway, except the pelicans who dawdled. We landed after half an hour at the Kingsley Plantation on Fort George Island. Although it now belongs to the State of Florida and is regularly open to the public, few people visit this lovely spot. Within a few yards of the beach where we grounded Frances IV, stands a grey and white house built in the 1800s. I am astonished that so delicate and original a building could have been designed by people who had no architectural training and no architect, sited on a remote island under Spanish rule, constantly threatened by buccaneers, the Indians and the British, and plagued by mosquitoes. One would have expected from these circumstances a rough-hewn, semi-fortified, insect-repellent, ranch-like bungalow. Instead, we have a two-storey clapboarded house, with porches back and front and a square pavilion at each corner. On the roof, which is tiled by wood shingles, is perched a gazebo or look-out over land and water, the only sign of troubled times. The house would have been an ornament in Williamsburg. From where came this instinct for perfect proportion, this concept of domestic felicity? Beyond, and linked to the house by a charming latticed walkway, is a building containing kitchen and storerooms. To one side stands a barn, its walls built of 'tabby', a type of concrete made partly of intact oyster shells which speckle the walls with tiny shadows. A quarter-mile away along an avenue lined with palms and moss-dripping live-oaks (Kew Garden conservatories in the open air) are the slave quarters, a curving line of huts built of the same tabby.

Of course, this idyllic scene must be harshened in imagination. Although the owner, Zephaniah Kingsley, is reputed to have treated his slaves leniently, he never questioned the justice of the system which enabled him to make a fortune from their unpaid labour in the rice and cotton fields, and even had a hand in importing fresh slaves from Africa. For them there was no appeal possible from a brutal overseer, and when their master died, they might be bequeathed to as many as six new masters, breaking up their families ruthlessly. The contrast between their miserable huts and Kingsley's elegant house illustrates a relationship which in the free world we would have regarded as intolerable. Or would we? I thought of Mr Bertram's estate in the West Indies, and how his family in *Mansfield Park* took for granted this cruel source of their income. I thought too of the servants' cold dormitories in houses like Knole and Hardwick, and wondered whether servitude under a kind master was altogether so terrible for men and women who had never known or imagined anything else, and were given lifelong security in return for their labour. After the Civil War, the slaves won their freedom but many lost their employment. Their former owners could not afford to pay them wages, and those who did not volunteer to remain as slaves in all but name were turned away to face destitution. I felt a little ashamed to be making these excuses.

We lunched in a fishing inn on the St John River, and afterwards motored (the boat is as easy to handle as a car) up the Intercoastal to another barrier island called Cumberland, where in the 1880s the Carnegies built a vast house like something in Surrey, but not your Beverly Hills version of Surrey. Its interior was burnt to a cinder in 1959, and the calcinated roofless walls are preserved as a memorial to America's tycoon period. Less melancholy, and far prettier, is the Victorian town of Fernandina on Amelia Island, where we dined tonight, and talked of the Revolutionary and Civil Wars. I will spare you our conclusions. There's too much history in this letter already. You'd have liked the Palace Saloon, the oldest in Florida. It has a 40-foot bar along which I could have slid a bottle of whisky end to end if only a cash register hadn't interrupted it in the middle.

Westwood, Los Angeles, California

Tuesday 25 March

ADAM *to Nigel*   Another of Olivia's extraordinary connections got me an invitation to the Playboy Mansion in Beverly Hills last night. (It is the first time in the history of Playboy that a wife 6,000 miles away has procured such an invitation for her husband. But then Olivia has a habit of doing rare and generous things.) Anyway, I wasn't going to pass up this opportunity. The first thing I did (this is a shameless LA habit) was to ring up and ask if I could bring someone along. 'We would feel very glad to welcome along any female guest you might consider able to bring,' the voice said on the phone, 'but if any male is to bring a male guest with him then that male guest must meet with the personal approval of Mr Hefner. And I regret that Mr Hefner is not available at this moment.' This was the longest version of 'No' I had ever heard, but, since the person I proposed to bring happened to be a man, it meant that I turned up alone.

I had asked on the phone what I should wear. 'The girls usually wear something nice,' the voice had said, 'but the men, they don't usually bother with anything more than chic casual.' So I put on a new pair of socks and drove off to the mansion. Its address is 10236 Charing Cross Road, which is in fact a sort of rambling Devon lane, snaking its way between the usual assortment of New England colonial, Mediterranean (which means *tuiles canales* and knobbly plaster) and the sort of sub-Bauhaus sheen known as 'moderne'. Not that any of these categories are fixed. One of the Harmetz's neighbours remoulded his Massachusetts weather-boarded mansion a year or two back, but wasn't keen on losing all those clear-cut, puritan associations. (This was the age of *Roots*.) The building – it's rather difficult to call it a house – now has a sort of weather-boarded Mussolini effect, a kind of homey brutality like Joe McCarthy kissing a little girl. Apparently the owner is quite pleased.

Anyway, I found my way to 10236 Charing Cross Road. Not a sign, not a bunny icon to be seen, just a pair of huge metal gates. I waited in the horrible Toyota Corolla while a Lincoln Continental the size of the Astrodome drew up behind me. What on earth was I meant to do. Perhaps there was a doorbell to ring? I started to get out of the car to look for it. 'Stay where you are, sir,' a boulder next to the gateway said. I recognised the Voice from the telephone. Was I chic casual enough? 'Are you Ivan Nicole, the English author,' the boulder asked. 'Yes, yes, that's me,' I shrilled back, unbuttoning my button-downs in case that was a little too chic and a little uncasual. I had now spotted the grille set flush into the boulder. 'Please drive up, sir,' it said in the most appropriate, lapidary tones.

It's axiomatic here that you are what you think you are. I imaged (LA for 'thought of') Paul Newman and oozed on to the gravel in front of the mansion. Black men in scarlet dinner-jackets drove my car away somewhere, recognising a film star when they saw one. Another butler opened the 4-inch thick English oak door with overdesigned handles and studs into a marble hall. Paul Newman had his photograph taken by a woman in a brown suit who then asked him what his name was. 'Ivan?' she queried professionally. 'No, *Adam*,' Paul said a little testily and swam off towards the champagne. (Wasn't I meant to be doing the *low* life in this book?)

It was the strangest party I have ever been to. Large numbers of extra-ordinarily attractive girls swanned around between a smaller number of extra-ordinarily unattractive men, of which I was the youngest by about twenty years. (None of the women was older than me.) Mr Hefner (who began the evening as Mr Hefner, progressed to Hefner and ended up plain Hef by midnight) eased between the rooms in purple silk pyjamas, a relaxed move-ment like a pop star's Oldsmobile on a freeway. It was Oscar night. There was at least one television in every room showing the ceremony Downtown.

For hours minor stars presented statuettes to cameramen and special effects teams. No one watched. An embarrassing song-and-dance show was put on by a collection of superannuated actresses. The refrain went, 'Once a star, Always a star, Wherever you are', something which needed to be said only because it was so blatantly untrue. The men jeered when the director who had made the best foreign film mispronounced the word 'proud'. 'I am such a prude, I am so prude to be here,' a man said in the sort of cap deep-sea fishermen and garage mechanics wear. And the girls displayed their bosoms, not overtly but not discreetly either. They all had the same face, the same awful pert preparedness which the Playboy culture has taught them, making them all readiness and passivity, like rows of apricots served up on platters. There was nothing lewd in the way they behaved – there wasn't enough life in them for that – nothing raunchy, just the leached, bleached version of sex that *Playboy* has been gratifying America with for thirty years. I have never seen a collection of people who look so exactly like their photographs. People complain that the trouble with the Playboy aesthetic is that it distorts and corrupts the image of women. But here it was happening back to front: these women (and even to call them that feels strange, so effectively had they been filleted) had *in themselves* become the deodorised, anaesthetised non-people at whose bodies men would look so lovingly in the magazine. The real shock is that *Playboy* photography is so unflinchingly realist in its approach. From the evidence at the Playboy mansion that night, the camera simply records what's there. It was a sort of Disneyland in which the cartoon characters didn't even have to wear masks for you to recognise them from the pictures.

And, of course, in a way, I loved it, talking about nothing to these semi-naked beauties. One of the strange features of the party was that the other men didn't seem to notice them. They talked across their cigars to each other about Libya. 'Now that's what I call an exercise,' one of them said about the Gulf of Sirte. 'That is America defending the freedom of the seas.' I talked to the girls about their careers. 'I'm Florence Pololena Rebolledo,' a dazzlingly beautiful woman said to me. 'I've just ditched my agent but I'm presently studying acting, I'm interested in Real Property Investing and also studying a bit on Health and Fitness.' She took me on a tour of the mansion and explained her Filipino–Spanish–Chinese background. 'My husband says I'm a mongrel,' she said. I denied it but understood the warning. The mansion itself is a sort of solid 1920s Jacobean, the stuffiest and most turgid version of Californian architecture. I suppose you could look on it as some sort of anchor for a puff-ball life. Pololena said she liked it because it was so English. The best part was the grotto. White peacocks stalked past the floodlights. A toucan in a cage bellowed for Peru. 'Hef is just in love with animals,' Rebolledo said sweetly. The grotto occupies a sort of peninsula that juts out into the swimming-pool. (I say swimming-pool, but really it's a magnificent artefact modelled partly on Lake Maggiore and partly on a remote section of the Colorado River.) Pololena led me into the grotto. Faint murmuring came from inside and a breeze of warm wet air. It was virtually dark, lit only with dim submarine lights. Half-seen bodies sipped half-seen vodkatinis and Rebolledo whispered that it was lovely wasn't it. The water in the grotto frothed with the jacuzzi jets. I couldn't make out what was going on at all. My only possible reference for this was Suetonius, but, as I said, the lights were low. I was glad about that. All those puritan anxieties which you might have thought this place would bury were for some reason summoned by it. I felt straitlaced, hostile and exposed. I suddenly hated the plastered together rock ceiling and the lush air. I don't know why. Pololena said she would stay, but I went back to the party.

A slightly drunk and sad man came up to me. 'Hi.' 'Hi.' 'I'm Adam Nicolson.' 'I'm John O'Donnell. Well, I say I'm John O'Donnell but I'm an actor and there already is a John O'Donnell and so I appear as Johnny O'Donnell. But I hate that. I hate that John*ny*. The stupid thing is that O'Donnell isn't even my real last name. My family name is Bender, but Bender doesn't sound too good does it?' 'Bender sounds fine to me.' 'You think so?' He tried it out a few times. 'Ya, "John Bender", I like it.' So in a minute and a half I changed a man's life – or his name anyway. He looked like Robert de Niro and like every one else was floating on his fragile, vulnerable hope balloon.

Moving on, I smiled past Hefner. 'Nice to have you here,' he said. 'Nice to be here,' I said back. *Out of Africa* was winning all the prizes and no one could understand why Jane Fonda looked so tense. 'Has she been drinking?' some one asked. 'No, she's standing next to Alan Alda.' The amazing parade of bosoms continued, the scoop, the droop, the keyhole, the soft over-chiffon, the one shoulder, the frankly-exposed-from-the-side, and the world seemed indifferent. I sat down on a vast leather sofa in a baronial hall. 'Well, what do we have here,' an enormous Texan woman asked me. I was sitting on the end of the sofa next to the arm but she managed to squeeze her body between me and the arm like an overcoat packed into a suitcase. 'MMMM,' she said and blinked five times while arranging her hair. 'You are *gorgeous*,' she went on. 'Thank you very much,' I said. Only then did I notice the fingernails – an inch and a half long and sky blue. 'I'm Carole. Here's my card.' It said Carole de la Hautois in a fluted palace script. 'And this here is Linda.' Linda was very young, about 17, and literally wringing her hands with embarrassment. 'Now you must be nice to Linda,' Carole said with a sort of Danish-pastry smile, 'because this is her first visit here.' Poor Linda, who was dressed up in some awful doll's uniform, smiled and blushed and wrung her hands. Carole mmmed again for about four seconds and then pushed those nails into my thigh. Linda couldn't bear to look and Carole let out another vast smile revealing a set of teeth like Mount Rushmore. 'No, you are *delicious*,' and then, seeing across the room a man she thought she knew, squealed 'Tony!' 'Tom,' he said. 'Tom, I mean,' she said and rushed over to hug him.

Poor Linda sat down on the sofa. 'You don't have a car here do you? I am desperate to go to sleep.' I said I'd give her a lift to her hotel. I ordered the car from the men in scarlet dinner-jackets, and waited with Linda on the porch. An enormous man I had never seen before came up to me and asked, 'Are you going to take this girl home?' I was. 'Now, please, I beg of you, please don't embarrass us all. She's a young kid.' I said I knew and I wouldn't. He came over sentimental. 'Now let me tell you something. When you're my age you'll probably find yourself acting the shepherd. You may find it difficult to believe now. I wouldn't have believed it at your age but I can tell you something.' He took a slug of whisky. 'It's much better in life to be the shepherd than the ram.'

It was a half hour drive through the empty streets of Los Angeles to her hotel. She had been offered $25,000 by Hefner to do what she called a fold out. The girls at the mansion had tried to persuade her that it was an art-form, but she knew that it wasn't. 'It's just stripping isn't it, however much they pay you for it.' She was tempted for the one reason that it might be a way into films. 'But I hate back doors, I hate them.' Outside the hotel I kissed her good night and wished her good luck.

Amelia Island, Florida–Savannah,
Georgia   *Tuesday 25 March*

NIGEL *to Adam*   At breakfast Charlie told me the news of the Libyan–
                              American clash in the Gulf of Sirte. No war, please
God, no war. Otherwise you'll be attending anti-Khadafy demos instead of pro-Sandinista. But is it really true, as you say (p. 25), that the British never feel strongly enough about a foreign issue to shout about it in the streets? There was Munich, there was Suez, there was the European Referendum, and the Falklands. I dispute, in the ambassadorial role I've assumed here, that we are 'tired, old and hopeless'. 'Tired' is incompatible with the energy we still display in science, invention, the arts, TV and radio, people's holidays, design, building, and in your own letters. 'Old' is something you can say of civilisations, but is not a term you can apply to nations any more than to rivers, for both are constantly being renewed. Are the Greeks old in your

sense, the Russians, the Jews? 'Hopeless' I simply don't follow, unless it is a synonym for apathy. I think that our stability is a sort of national bottom, a clearer guide to Thatcher of what we will tolerate and won't than American volatility can be to a president. We have steerage-way, even when the engines temporarily fail.

Charlie left for New York, and I stayed on in his house for a couple of hours. I had great fun answering his telephone calls, employing fancy phrases like, 'This is Mr Atkins's residence. It's his house-guest speaking. Can I be of assistance to you?' but none of the callers was taken in for a moment. I'll meet him again in two days' time at his other house near Charleston.

Soon after quitting Amelia Island, I crossed my first stateline into Georgia, leaving behind me the only State with an interesting silhouette on the map, and feeling that perhaps I hadn't done justice to Florida. I'd missed the Everglades, the Kennedy Space Center and Disney World near Orlando. But we are not seeking tourist sites. If someone tells me, as they do, that if I've not seen Disney World I don't know America, I reply, 'Well, that's just too bad.' I'm fast learning the lingo and that dismissive tone of voice.

Georgia leads off with signs pointing to a submarine base which Charlie told me is costing billions. But thereafter it appears extraordinarily empty, a vast forest crossed by a single magnificent road. Rivers as wide as the Thames in London flow under the road at intervals of 3 or 4 miles, reminding me that I no longer have a peninsula on my left, but a continent. I see how easy it was for the first explorers to discover it. You simply sailed from the sea up the middle of rivers, out of bowshot from either bank, until you came to the first rapids. Then you returned to the sea, and tried another estuary. What is surprising is that they and their successors, right up to the present day, never cleared more than a tiny part of the forest for settling, but pressed ever onwards into the West. I must go into this puzzle more thoroughly in Virginia. I suppose there are economists somewhere claiming that America is already over-populated and within fifty years will be strangled by its own web, but to me it still looks a land which could absorb the entire population of Israel overnight and hardly notice it.

I'll keep Savannah till tomorrow when I've really seen it. Driving this evening through the usual tangle of exclamatory placards and blockages by traffic-lights and snarls, I was exhilarated to swim clear into the old town and find it not only clutter-free and avenue-conducive, but beautifully laid out in grids and squares composed of large unshabby houses which show what the Victorians could do when they tried. Charm it has, and elegance, all in a lively spring dress of azaleas, magnolias and judas. Self-conscious, yes, but I have never seen that term, as applied to places, any more derogatory than when applied to a woman who takes trouble with her clothes. Even the Ramada Inn, where I'm staying two nights, has lacy ironwork balconies as its contribution to the general air of civility.

The man responsible for much of this, for he was President of the Historic Savannah Foundation, and now of the Savannah Landmark Rehabilitation Project (I have to put all this in because they deserve it), was my host at dinner, Leopold ('call me Lee') Adler II. We met in the Ramada lobby with a mutual display of smiles, and he drove me not direct to his house where his wife was waiting with guests and quails, but to the riverside, simply because he had spotted through the trees a moon more circular and bronze gong-like than any previous moon, and he wanted to see, and me to see, its reflection in the water. That was a good beginning. I could not take in at a gulp all the historical information he was pouring out, and begged temporarily for mercy, which he readily conceded, but I got the impression in the darkness of many statue-centred squares, houses actually joined to each other to form streets, and a succession of openings which reminded me, oddly enough, of Bloomsbury.

His house is stone and tall over a basement, the rooms bright and capacious. In the wide hall the walls are hung with maps and pictures of old Savannah in bird's-eye perspective, and a truly horrible parody of a Reynolds, about 1800 I'd say, of a mother with her simpering children. The nineteenth-century Americans, for all their cleverness in architecture, furniture, glass and silver, took extraordinarily long to pass the limner stage in portraiture.

The dinner was Southern. By that I don't mean only that rice was served with the quail and green salad as a separate course, but that there was a relaxed sobriety about the table in contrast to the animation of a dinner-party further north. Only one glass of wine was served to each of us, after a cocktail before dinner, and for this I was grateful, for I'm going through an abstemious phase; and a fellow-guest threw a rubber bone to a dog, not once, but again and again till the dog got bored. I asked them whether the distinction we're apt to make between South and North is any longer valid, or is it a fallacy derived from reading Mark Twain and Uncle Tom, and seeing, too many times, *The Wind*? They thought so. Once it had a meaning. The South was slower, softer, gentler, made much of courtesy and family life, rocking away a summer's afternoon on the porch. But now, with the mobility of the people, the spread of industry and commerce, a common parlance induced by TV, the wars, the universities – all that is fading fast. I asked Mrs Adler if she ever spoke of 'Yankees' contemptuously. Her mother did. She never. In a way, she missed the old tradition. She spoke sadly of the new violence, of the quick dispersion of families once the children are grown, of hurry and indifference that accompanies hurry. But a nice girl there, in a cherry dress, an Adler cousin from New York, said that she did find in Savannah a greater considerateness between strangers. The very name of the city implies a feminine grace, but how I wish they wouldn't over-egg it by calling it the Hostess City of the South.

We made plans for the morrow, and a lovely lady who is keen on Sussex gardens drove me with her husband to my elegant Inn. My bathroom has fourteen towels, one of which is just the size of my face, so convenient for after-shave.

I suppose that we are now at the most opposite psychological poles that we'll find in this country, you still in LA, I in Savannah. You are finding fun in absurdities and effervescence, I in the ocean, forests, quiet streets, good old buildings, and the norm. I've not so far met anyone as crazy as Sid Vicious, so importantly self-pitying as Stewart Granger or a waitress who yearns for a Bel Air penthouse. But just as the distinctions between North and South have been eroded, so too, I expect, have those between East and West. Let me make a list of my likes and dislikes so far, and compare it to yours:

Bad	*Indifferent*	*Good*
Radio and TV	Gardens (except the best)	Hospitality
Outdoor ads		Roads
No nationwide banks	Crowded parties	Cars
Waiting in line to be seated in an almost empty restaurant	Lunch	Breakfast
	Signposting in Florida	14 towels
	Police politeness	Helpfulness, except at Miami Airport
		Students in campuses
		Black bellmen

Savannah, Georgia

Wednesday 26 March

NIGEL *to Adam*   Today I toured Savannah, after Charleston the most attractive city in the south, and I toured it in company with the man to whom most of the credit is due for its restoration, Lee Adler.

I must give you a little background first. In 1733 James Oglethorpe, a Liberal MP, sailed 15 miles up the Savannah River with a group of poor emigrants to found the last of the thirteen English colonies, Georgia. He landed at a point where a low cliff or bluff drops into the river, forming a deep-water anchorage alongside it. He cleared a scoop of land from the forest, established friendly relations with the Indians, and laid out the future city in a traditional grid pattern of streets and avenues, with the significant difference that many of the intersections were widened into squares and oblongs, much like Georgian London. He showed astonishing foresight, because the settlement consisted at first of mean little huts with gardens, yet his town plan was perfectly suited to the large and often sumptuous buildings which replaced them long after he was dead. As you walk down these broad tree-lined streets or sit in one of the squares, you are conscious of this genius who staked out with little more than a theodolite a perfect pattern of urban felicity. With equal prevision he designated the plain beyond, which he devided into 45-acre farms for the settlers, as communal property, so that, when the village expanded into a town, and the town into a city, there were no private interests to consider. The Council, or whatever it was then called, simply added another set of Oglethorpe squares, until there were, and are, twenty-four of them. It sounds simple. It is simple.

Little of the eighteenth-century town survives except its shape. There were two disastrous fires in 1796 and 1820 which effectively destroyed it, but the strange thing is that the nineteenth-century town was visually lovelier than the one it replaced – strange, because we associate, at any rate in England, the 1830–60 period with over-ornamentation and a deplorable lapse of taste. Central Savannah was rebuilt in brick, sometimes stuccoed. There were short uniform streets for the relatively poor, not unlike our terraced houses, neat brick domestic boxes for the middle class, free-standing mansions for the wealthy (mainly Regency, neo-Georgian and Greek Revival), and some splendid public buildings, like the rebuilt 1819 Presbyterian church which has one of the loveliest interiors I've ever seen – a vast coffered oval ceiling, galleries supported by giant Corinthian columns, a pulpit in mahogany, and outside, a tower spire that rivals St Martin-in-the-Fields.

Bear with me a little longer, for I'm quite hooked on Savannah. The buildings I've mentioned exhibit a wonderful inventiveness. Many of them have external balconies in wrought iron, rather like the more famous but inferior balconies of New Orleans. Others are clapboarded over the brick, or were built wholly of timber when better fire-precautions made it once more possible to take the risk. One of their pleasantest features is that, in order to catch the breezes, many of the houses, not only the largest, are built high above basements and the main floors are approached externally by delicate staircases. Repeated identically along a row of contiguous houses, they form a shadowed frieze, varied in the neighbouring street by a quite different array.

Finally, you must add to this image a profusion of trees and flowering shrubs, pansies in tubs, wisteria clambering to the balconies. But it's not a Williamsburg. It's a vibrant working town, to which new buildings are constantly added in sympathy with the old, violated only recently by two outrageous hotels, a Hilton and a Hyatt.

Now comes the second part of the story. The man driving, walking and talking me around, Lee Adler, could be called Savannah's second Oglethorpe. In the late 1950s he and some others (I cannot go too deeply into the fascinating history) determined that the centre of the city, which was falling into decay as the richer inhabitants moved out to the suburbs and the poorer took over their houses, must and could be saved. Many of the century-old buildings were uninhabitable, others converted into tenements. Some were abandoned, lacking even their front doors, and porches and staircases were life hazards. Others were threatened with demolition for the sake of their bricks and their sites for use as parking-lots. A few survive in this condition as perfect before-and-after illustrations of what has been achieved.

Where was the money to come from to rescue the old town? Where were the new purchasers or tenants to be found bold enough to reoccupy a blighted district and repair the houses? Adler devised a most ingenious scheme. Modestly he says that he got the idea from what had already be done in Charleston, but it was his energy, his powers of persuasion, his refusal to take the first three Noes as answers, that created his famous Revolving Fund. He raised among his friends and sympathetic bankers enough money to buy a few of the crumbling buildings (one whole street cost only $24,000), and then sold them unrepaired to people who undertook to restore them. They were controlled as far as the external appearance went, but inside they could do what they liked. With the money from the sales, and occasionally a small profit from them, he (which now meant the Historic Savannah Foundation) bought and sold other houses on the same conditions. He taught himself the intricacies of the real-estate game. He became, at no profit to himself, a major entrepreneur. The project gathered momentum, enthusiasts multiplied, the City and then the Federal authorities, and the American National Trust, became interested, and in the astonishingly short time of less than thirty years, 1,500 houses were restored, 500 of them under Lee's personal management, and Savannah became not only the prettiest town in Georgia, but a tourist attraction that brings to the city $200 million a year. That convinced the sceptics who remained. Lee, with his growing influence, even managed to save the cobbles, brought in ballast from England, which pave the steep ramps leading down to the quays.

That's not all. This incredible man, who has a gentle smile and from whom I had to squeeze the story of his achievement, next undertook an even more intractable project. He restored the Negro quarter. This consisted in late Victorian houses on the southern outskirts, not architecturally so distinguished as in the centre, but large and decorative, in which black families lived in near-slum conditions. Few believed that Adler could repeat his miracle there. He did. He founded a new association called Savannah Landmark. He bought the houses one by one, but this time did not sell them to outsiders or the sitting tenants. Instead, he raised local and national funds to subsidise the restoration of the houses to almost the same standard of outward attractiveness as the grander houses of the old town, and let the Negro tenants remain. Of course, they were delighted. Cynics had said that they would never look after them properly. But as we drove round the quarter, I could see from the expressions on hundreds of black faces a joy (I'm not exaggerating) that with the restoration of their ramshackle dwellings they had recovered their dignity and pride. What had started off as a preservation project on a major scale has become a social, moral and even political gesture of enormous significance. The Savannah Landmark experiment has already inspired imitations in many cities throughout the United States.

I returned to Ramada dazed with admiration. But that was not the end of my day. Lee Adler took me as his guest to his exclusive Madeira Club. Fortunately I had a dinner-jacket. The club (a 'grape and gravy' club) has only fifteen members, all men, and meets half a dozen times a year, rather like my Dilettanti in London, to dine, sip Madeira (we had a bottle of 1898 said to be one of only two surviving), talk, and listen to a paper read by one of their number. This time it was about the Russian character, and how it has changed (it hasn't) in the last two centuries. We then discussed the paper, and broke up at 11 p.m. with many cordial promises to meet again.

Savannah–Mulberry Plantation,
South Carolina   *Thursday 27 March*

NIGEL *to Adam*   One thing I've noticed about Americans is their pre-
                               occupation with fame, their adulation of Number
Ones. It's the winner–loser tussle which motivates this country, and you're a loser even if you win the silver, let alone the bronze. I find this attitude a little ungenerous, but American's don't, because with their worship of success goes an unjealous acceptance of defeat. They want desperately to come out on top, but if they don't manage it themselves, they're glad to see someone else on the centre step of the podium. Its simple outline might be America's logo.

I was reminded of this when reading the local newspaper at breakfast. It reported that the TV audience for the Academy Award ceremony dropped 9 per cent last year because unknowns like F. Murray Abraham and Haig E. Niger won Oscars, and stars like Jack Nicholson, whom the fans really wanted to see win, didn't. This year the organisers and judges are determined to honour 'names'. But aren't Abraham and Niger names for having won in 1985? Not at all. Nobody had ever heard of them before. You are not a star until you become a triple-star. Nobody now remembers the man who knocked out John McEnroe in last year's Wimbledon. Americans are slow to bestow the supreme accolade, but once bestowed, it is seldom withdrawn. Your Stewart Granger and Hugh Hefner are examples. You might say that Savannah is another. People flock here because other people flock here.

My newspaper provided an illustration of another facet of the American character, their sentimentality. A man wrote to the editor as follows: 'My wife is fat. So am I. We love each other. When I look at her, I do not see a fat old lady. I see a nymph on the beach in moonlight.' I don't think that any British editor would dare to publish such gush, and most Americans would find it as embarrassing as we do. But that it could be written and actually printed suggests a tendency to cover up unpleasant facts (in this case obesity and old age) by fake gentility, which also shows in their coy euphemisms for sexual and other natural functions (but that's a coy euphemism in itself). It's very strange for so impulsive and vigorous a people.

I went to a small town on the coast called Beaufort, a mini-Savannah, where several houses are fronted by a double porch, one above the other, a delightful Southern conceit of which the only example I know in England is West Wycombe. I bought a painted bowl for Charlie Atkins.

I was on my way to stay two nights at his second country house, Mulberry Plantation. I can't tell you (but I'm doing just that) how lovely it is. It lies on a bluff above the Cooper River about 30 miles north-west of Charleston, in a park studded with live-oaks and pine. To one side is the broad shining river which in the early days was the only communication with Charleston, and on another, large flooded fields where they grew rice. But the point is the house. It was built in 1711 on what must then have been the very edge of the frontier. For that situation and date the design is extraordinarily graceful and original. I know of no prototype in England which could have suggested it. The main block, built of bricks the colour and texture of Sissinghurst's, with white shutters folded back against them, rises two floors to five tall dormers set in a mansard roof. At each corner is an attached gazebo, known as a flanker, capped by a high spiked roof like a cuirassier's helmet. Inside, the main rooms are large and airy, and the flankers provide delicious closets with windows on three sides. I am writing in one of them, overlooking the river. The only signs that this was hostile Indian territory are its old name, 'the Castle', and loopholes for muskets at basement level.

To live here then must have been rather like living grandly in Ireland during the '20s, a social agricultural community under constant threat. Add, of course, the slaves, who toiled all day under a cruel sun, tormented by mosquitoes. Their huts, of which an illustration survives but no actual example, were beehive African in shape, more decorative than hygienic. On the whole they were well treated here. Charlie lent me an excellent book about the Carolina slaves, *Down by the Riverside* by Charles Joyner, which I read in bed far into the night.

Westwood, Los Angeles, California

Thursday 27 March

ADAM *to Nigel*   I've spent two days trying to buy a car. The rental I picked up at the airport was a mean un-American thing. (Only an un-American can say that without it sounding racist.) So I decided to get rid of it and buy myself a car, a real American car. Almost certainly, this was nothing but another exercise in confirming prejudice. The plan was to expose myself to all the brutalities of the second-hand car market as an experience of the capitalist system in the raw.

That – thank God – didn't work out either. Of all the good chances in the world I fell into the hands of David and Kanthi Barry. Kanthi, you remember, took me to the anti-Contra demo the other day and David, among many other things, writes for a car magazine. He's a wonderful man, in his 40s but looking about 32, extraordinarily handsome in a big-boned New England way and with a wild passion, a real deep-seated addiction to American cars. He can talk for hours about the history and spirit of America through its cars, the way that the 62 Corvette moulted into the Sting Ray some time later in the '60s and then bulged into the Mako Shark, a grotesque bloating of the earlier cool, the automative equivalent, as he said, of Elvis at Vegas. (All this was late at night over dinner at their house in the Hollywood Hills, looking out over the lights in the San Fernando Valley, with the mountains behind and the constant hum of the freeway traffic, an ever-present noise in Los Angeles like the surf on a beach.)

So here was someone at least who would understand my delight and fascination for something as American as a real American car and my impatience with compact, economy and all the rest of it. 'What you need,' David said, 'is a Pontiac Catalina convertible.' Of course, I had no idea what he was talking about, but I would have taken anything from this man. And he found me one for $900. This was a coup. We went to see it yesterday. It's vast, about thirty feet long and ten feet wide, what David calls 'a real boat, a land yacht, a cream puff'. But it's not really a cream puff, it's more like a wide flat sliver cut from a side of salmon, all horizontal, not bright and perky like European cars, but slit-eyed, low and lazy. It's a crook's car and I love it. You don't need to do anything by hand: the gears of course are automatic, the windows electric, the lowering and raising of the roof at the push of a button. Even the adjusting of the position of the seats is done by electric motor. The aerial for the radio extends and contracts automatically when you turn it on and off. But better than all of this is the ride. The engine accelerates like a millionaire growing angry, the suspension slides it around bends as if there's a rudder at the back, the power-steering means that one finger can swing the whole cruiser on a corner, the sheer length of it rounds off bumps in the road into no more than a mild swell. Of course it's wildly out of date and guzzles gas but I don't care!

Do you know that song by Dionne Warwick 'LA is just one big freeway / Put a hundred down and buy a car . . .'? That was on the radio this morning, so I did. The man selling it was an architect called Dave Miller. He had wide ostrich feather sideboards and a wife who told Kanthi that her liberalism had died a bloody death many years ago. Kanthi didn't ask her what on earth she was talking about. Miller had a tired, affectionate voice which dropped away at the end of every sentence. I said to him after a short test spin around the block that it was like sitting on a sofa while trying to drive a tennis court. 'Oh no,' Miller said slowly. 'She's a beaut. Looks good, goes great. There's 4,000 lbs of car there.' That made it slightly under 25c a lb. 'You couldn't get anything at that price,' Miller said smiling, and that clinched it. I'm now in possession of my own bit of mobile real estate. I lie back on the seat like a redneck, thinking the world is automatic and watching it slide past the windscreen like a long-running TV show.

Of course, the buying was only a tenth of it. Endless bureaucracy was involved in the transfer of title. Queuing for hours in the Department of Motor Vehicles in Hollywood, taking the written Californian driving test. (Not difficult: the first question showed a one-way arrow and asked, 'Does this sign mean:

    1.   No trucks here
    2.   Vehicles must travel in this direction only
or   3.   Go into reverse'

I felt inordinately proud of scoring 100 per cent.) I fixed the insurance but could only get the minimum legal cover, so that if I run over a film producer I'm ruined for life. Kanthi took me to the AAA, of which I'm now a member.

Endless free maps from a man called Art and the promise of a pick-up truck wherever the Catalina finally decides to give up the ghost. For the moment it's wonderful, goes 80 m.p.h. on the flat and is slowly eating away at any modesty or reticence in me that has survived ten days in Los Angeles. By the time we get to Dodge, I'll be chewing a cigar with a black wet end, wearing a big domed cap with the word 'Pontiac' across the brow. Olivia, Thomas and William will all be transported across the Atlantic and we'll set up home on a ranch in Wyoming. All because of the Catalina. One bastion of Englishness remains: I have yet to buy a pair of dark glasses.

Mulberry Plantation, South Carolina

Friday 28 March

NIGEL *to Adam*   This has been a plantation and garden day. I feel a bit guilty, being so close to Charleston, that I never went there. But I knew that if I did, I would be bound to repeat my ecstatic Savannah letter, and you'll have had enough of architecture for the moment. Besides, I know Charleston from previous visits, and within 20 miles of Mulberry are three famous gardens I've never seen, and this is the best time of year to see them. They are Middleton Place, the Magnolia Garden and the Cypress Gardens. I'll leave the last till tomorrow, but I've been to the other two.

I prefer Middleton Place to the Magnolia Garden because it is more open. The garden is related to the house by lawns so trim and undulating that if I were a golfer, I would want to take a No. 3 iron to approach it. It is not unlike Stourhead, but instead of a lake you have the river, and instead of classical temples, little functional brick buildings once connected with the running of the estate. On each side, but not obstructing the view, are 'wildernesses' in the eighteenth-century English sense, woodlands slashed with azaleas, camellias and sweeping daffodils. More conventional Victorian gardens, patterned in box, lie nearer the house. I have never seen a more successful combination of formality with controlled abandon.

It is beautifully displayed. Small numbered sign-posts at foot-level relate to the same numbers in the guidebook. Shall we copy this idea? I think you might disapprove of garden gates labelled Push or Pull, and of sandy paths scored by this morning's raking. You would say with reason that a Secret Garden is no longer secret when a notice points the way to it. But you would enjoy the undoubted splendour and glamour of the place. 'Rich is the robe, and ample let it flow,' wrote Humphrey Repton of a somewhat similar landscape, Antony in Cornwall. It certainly flows here.

The Magnolia Garden is more harum-scarum. The 'wilderness' aspect is predominant. There is little landscaping, and few open spaces apart from the view over the river on the far side and a paddock filled with miniature horses to amuse the children. The paths wind between big clumps of azaleas, leading to swampy pools in which stand cypresses up to their ankles in water. There's a mini-route which you can take if short of time or breath, but I took the maxi. Being so closely wooded, it provides more surprises than Middleton. I found the tomb of the Drayton family, who created the garden, in a hidden corner, a marble mausoleum with putti sculpted on the side-panels, the cheeks of one baby's bottom pockmarked with bullet holes dating from the Civil War, for Sherman passed this way, as did Cornwallis eighty years earlier. Wisteria coils 40 feet up cypress trunks. It's all a bit tangled and left deliberately wild, a place to wander in, more secret and mysterious than any part of Middleton, and less showy, but definitely not my sort of garden, nor Vita's.

I lunched at the Medway Plantation, Mulberry's neighbour. It belongs to Gertrude Legendre, who explored Abyssinia and shot big game when she was young (stuffed heads, going a bit mouldy, line the walls of a log barn), and was the only American woman to be captured by the Germans in the Second World War. After six months in prison, astonishingly she escaped to Switzerland, and wrote a book about her experiences. Now she divides her time between travelling, energising the Republican Party, and entertaining her friends on this beautiful estate.

There was a large party, including two couples whom I particularly want to remember – Leslie and Rugers Barclay; and the Agnews, she from Philadelphia, he English, neighbours in London of George Weidenfeld, from whose celebrated drawing-room they are separated only by a wall. She had read your English *Walks* and loved it. Always your warmest advocate and publicist, I said that your French *Walks* and *Frontiers* were even better. I asked cautiously whether she had read your much-praised article about the Alps in the *New York Times*. She hadn't, and nor have I.

We lunched in the open air beside a lake in which alligators were breeding, so Mrs Legendre cheerfully informed me, and I was lent a straw hat against the sun. Afterwards, the entire party, as in a nineteenth-century novel, drove over to Mulberry, not in carriages but in Mercedes. My final wish is that just once in my remaining years I shall drive myself in a Mercedes 80 miles in 60 minutes, but I know it will never happen.

Charlie Atkins and I were alone for dinner, he cooking it. How much I have come to like this man! Very successful in business, his heart is really in this place and Amelia Island, and his interests in history and the arts. Together we pored over old maps of the Mulberry Plantation. He also has a modern one, a 1/24,000 published by the US Geological Survey, only obtainable from them. Why are these beautiful sheets not more readily available and more in demand?

Hollywood, Los Angeles, California

Friday 28 March

ADAM *to Nigel*   This is the morning I leave Los Angeles and I feel I'm shedding a skin. I've spent the night at the Barrys' house on Woodrow Wilson Drive, on the sofa, after a bottle of Bollinger yesterday evening. David said it was champagne because he wanted to launch me like the *Queen Mary* and Bollinger because I'm like a character out of Evelyn Waugh. (Elizabeth, the daughter of the Harmetzes and one of the most inventive manipulators of language I've ever met, asked me if it was really true that my father lived in a castle type place. 'Isn't that majorly freaky? I mean is it majorly big or what?' I told her that she must come and ask you one day.)

Mulberry Plantation—Aiken,
South Carolina

Saturday 29 March

NIGEL *to Adam*   Soon after Charlie left to join his doubly expectant wife at Little Rock, Arkansas, I went to the Cypress Gardens. There I was greeted by Kathy Townsend, a pleasant girl wearing a bright-green skirt and an even brighter smile (I'm catching your style), who had been warned by Charlie of my coming.

She took me first to the swamp, where I embarked alone in a wide canoe. It took me only a few minutes to relearn the technique of turning the paddle sideways at the end of the stroke to maintain direction. Less professional canoeists switch the paddle from side to side. I gave some black children a lesson in the art. It is not really a swamp. It is a huge expanse of clear, still water about 3 feet deep, bordered by artificial dykes to contain it, and filled with cypresses up to 100 feet tall. The trunks flare bulbously at the foot to give their roots purchase in the mud. There are thousands of them, growing in the water as close as 6 feet apart, and this canoeist showed great skill in gliding between them without hitting a single one. They are not handsome trees, being deciduous, unlike the Italian cypress, and they deserve their unflattering name Bald Cypress, but this solemn parade of Grenadier-straight columns, and their survival for four hundred years in water, create an impression of eerie solemnity. As I slid forward, the alignments slowly changed.

If that were all, it would be a worthwhile experience, but the Cypress Gardens owe their fame equally to the flowering shrubs which line the banks. You may be bored by azaleas, but I shall never be, nor by camellias, the most perfect of flowers when you find a perfect specimen. Here there are more than 57 varieties of them. Leaving my canoe, I walked a mile among them. The guidebook told me to watch for birds. I love guidebook language:

> Look for the handsome yellow-throated warbler and the tiny parula, or listen for the ringing whistle of the prothonotary warbler or the drumming of the pileated woodpecker. Listen also for the hunting call of the red-shouldered hawk or the raucous squawks of egrets and herons. The liquid call of the Carolina wren blends with the melody of the mockingbird, and, if you are lucky, you may see the brilliant painted bunting.

I looked, I listened. Not a warbler warbled. I did not see a single bird in flight. What I did see was a swallow-tail butterfly. How well I remember going with Rebecca to Wicken Fen near Cambridge, reputedly the only remaining habitat of our swallow-tail, and how we walked for miles in vain, only to be told by the lady selling postcards that she had not personally seen one for fifteen years. Here I saw a dozen. The guidebook, admittedly with reservations, also promised turtles, racoons, bobcats, white-tailed deer, opossums, otters, snakes, rabbits and squirrels. I saw a squirrel.

I struck west, away from the luxury plantations into the first genuine farming country I've yet seen. The coastal plain is very wide at this point, and I'm longing for the ground to heave and moan a bit. However, it was very pleasant scooting along minor roads between the crops. The small towns are disappointing. What this part of America lacks are villages, which is strange, as most of the early settlers came from villages. Instead, I passed through Denmark, Blackville, Williston, Windsor, each labelled with entrance plaques like, 'Williston is a great town'. Unhappily, Williston isn't. It's the usual trouble – too much space between buildings, no plan. If the space is grassily neat, I have no complaint. More often it is litter-strewn and scarred. There are no gardens. Mobile homes are beginning to give every small town the appearance of a campsite. It's not just their impermanence which offends me, but their long narrow shapes, travesties of a home. One was advertised as 'Methodist Church'.

Turning into a small state-owned forest, I found peace and loveliness. How well America does these things! There's just the right degree of orderliness and access. No litter, except nature's detritus. I walked a marked trail through virgin forest. So this is what the pioneers found! We've been misled by Western to imagine that the whole great adventure took place on open prairies. On the contrary, most hacked their small farms out of swampy jungles just like this one. I was quite alone. It was warm and intensely quiet.

I found a pleasant motel at Aiken, near Augusta, seeing no point in lodging in yet another vast city.

Carmel Valley, California

Saturday 29 March

ADAM *to Nigel*   I left Los Angeles on the Pacific Coast Highway, in love with America's sense of its own epic scale. There is a sign on the Santa Monica Freeway, a couple of miles inland from the beach, which says in cinema-screen letters 'Christopher Columbus Transcontinental Highway'. Like the PCH, as it's called, most people use the freeway for no more than their daily commute, but always there, in the vast sign, is the reminder of size and possibility. You hate the enormous billboards (p. 26). I love them, like I love the enormous and perfectly clean American trucks. It's where America is entirely itself, unaffected, unworried by any trimming or clipping or by the awful disease of tastefulness, which when Americans suffer from it pushes them towards the Disneyland disaster.

I've now driven up to this beautiful green valley, running in from the ocean through the Santa Lucia mountains. I wanted to come all the way up the coast but the highway (California 1) was blocked by a landslide and I had to come inland before cutting back down here. I'm staying with a charming lady called Nancy Morrow, who is Ambassador Dwight Morrow's daughter-in-law. These odd connections. Like the Harmetzes, she simply said 'Sleep there and do what you want.' Don't you find this immediate hospitality extraordinary and wonderful?

It was sad to miss the coast, but I'll be getting a good deal of that later. And sad to leave Los Angeles. I really knew I had left when I stopped for a sandwich – 'Give me a tuna melt,' I said – and there was a sign on the counter saying, 'All our waitresses have husbands, brothers or fathers. And they all have shotguns.' They told me in Los Angeles that I had yet to arrive in the United States – LA, like Texas, is different – and now I knew what they meant. On the radio a man from Malibu, who had championed public access to the beaches, was complaining that, of the ten signs pointing the way for non-property-owners to get down on to the beach, six had been cut down in

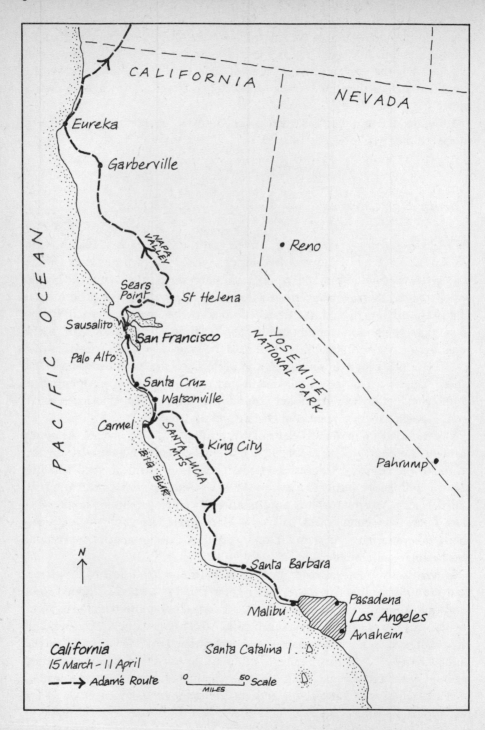

CALIFORNIA

NEVADA

PACIFIC OCEAN

Eureka

Garberville

NAPA VALLEY

• Reno

Sears Point

St Helena

YOSEMITE NATIONAL PARK

Sausalito

San Francisco

Palo Alto

Santa Cruz

Watsonville

Carmel

SANTA LUCIA MTS

King City

Big Sur

Pahrump •

N

Santa Barbara

Pasadena

Los Angeles

Malibu

Anaheim

Santa Catalina I.

California
15 March – 11 April
- - -➤ Adam's Route

0 ___ 50 Scale
MILES

the night with a chain saw. There is violence somewhere here. People wouldn't do that in England.

Aiken–Atlanta, Georgia

Sunday 30 March

NIGEL *to Adam*   I've another item to add to my list of good things in America – their motels. I wrote last night that Aiken Inn was pleasant. It's much more than that. It's quite cheap, $35, and for that you get breakfast too. It's attractive, it's very clean, it's quiet, and it provides every convenience a traveller could want, from bedside telephone, TV and radio, to ice-cubes on demand. No advance reservation is needed. You park your car right outside your door, so luggage-humping is no problem. You pay on arrival, and leave as early as you wish. The Aiken Inn is one of hundreds of thousands in the US like it. For a single-night, single man, like me, they're perfect. Why can't we do more of the same thing in England? We continue to make do with Trusthouse Forte and bed and breakfasts. A fortune is to be made, and a benefit conferred on mankind, by establishing a chain of Aiken Inns throughout Britain.

It is Easter Sunday. That has not made on me the impact which it should, and everything seems to work normally except that it is forbidden to serve wine with meals in Atlanta hotels. I drove through sunny Georgia, left arm brown, right arm white. The country is charming – lakes, woods, sown fields, the Oconee National Forest – and I was glad to find small towns like Monticello (not Jefferson's) held together by central squares. It's Jimmy Carter country, Baptist churches and peanut farms. I love the almost universal trimness of the farmhouses. Once, driving up the Hudson valley with Jane Lancellotti, I exclaimed with delight at a small white house standing alone on a sloping meadow. Jane, astonished, said, 'You're very easily pleased.' Yes, I am. I like the unselfconscious elegance of these homesteads, to which in the South a rural version of a columned porch is often attached. I like the hedgeless fields, woods trailing like flung garlands down a hillside (the country is just beginning to roll towards the Appalachians), and soothing water, running or still, is everywhere. The country roads are straight and smooth, bordered by wide grass verges which fade, without any barrier, into the forest. Georgia satisfies every instinct in me for the orderly and the romantic.

I did little today but drive, 200 miles to Atlanta. I have a problem. I cannot find on my car radio anything but pop and country music. It may be that Toyota thinks it stimulating, and talk soporific. When there is a verbal interruption to this endless soapy stream, it comes in very short bursts, as if the listener couldn't take in more, usually about the weather which I can enjoy without being constantly told to. I cannot believe that people on their long and unadventurous drives do not want something a little more informative or exciting. There is Public Radio, but it's beyond the reach of my little set. In Savannah I was told that it could be found 'on the extreme left', but on the extreme left of my narrow band I find 'A Hard Day's Night' and 'Never on Sundays'. Where is Kissinger on Nicaragua? Where, oh where, is Susan Stamberg? Nowhere, at least not on this Sunday. Then there's the short range of local radio. Just as I'm getting fairly used to Augusta's offering, it goes croaky and then watery, till finally it gives up altogether, passing the cultural torch to Atlanta, which seeps in watery, croaky, with the same offering, getting louder and clearer as I approach the Big A, as they call it.

I am staying at Holiday Inn, South, one of my weekly treats, pre-paid in London through Pan Am Fly/Drive. But here the cheerful receptionist had never previously heard of this convenient method. My voucher was examined with curiosity and disbelief, and eventually dishonoured. However, she made up for it when I gave her the last few of my typed pages to photocopy, and she asked me what it was all about. I told her. I said that I would put her into today's diary–letter. Well, I have, and she can photocopy it tomorrow.

Carmel Valley, California

Sunday 30 March

ADAM *to Nigel*   I've been in the wilderness all day and I can hardly stand up with exhaustion. It was the only wilderness I've ever come across that had a name: the Ventana Wilderness. Whenever I saw Nancy yesterday she said, 'Just you do what you want, my dear,' and so I decided to go for a walk – as some sort of antidote to LA, if nothing else. A friend of hers down the road called Corky Matthews, a mature woman with a thick mat of grey hair and an enthusiast's twinkle, told me where to go and lent me the maps. She had a poster saying 'Reagan for Führer' on her dining room wall. I had been told the night before that Carmel and Carmel Valley were the richest places, per capita, on the planet, making Beverly Hills look like a part of Brixton. But Corky was a member of the Sierra Club and it was Reagan's indifference to the environment that got her going. I told her that I couldn't understand how a Republican could be an environmentalist. 'Look at Teddy Roosevelt,' she said. 'But he shot anything that moved,' I said. 'That was in the old days. It takes time to understand these things.' We let it go. I had a suspicion it was my negative-attitude problem surfacing again. But Corky was passionate about the survival of the wilderness (or was it

Wilderness?) and the administration was indifferent. (I'm almost sure she meant the federal government, but Carmel is in the throes of a mayoral election, in which Clint Eastwood is standing as the business candidate, and everyone refers to the current Mayor of Carmel, a well-built woman with hair like a shower cap, as 'the Administration'. The main issue is whether ice-cream can be sold in Carmel or not. Eastwood says yes, the Administration says no. The election is next week, when I will be well away.)

So with Corky's maps in hand I set off early in the morning, hauling the Catalina miles up a dirt road into the mountains, hawks hanging on the wind beside me, the engine overheating until it got too hot and I decided to park it on the side of the track and walk. A beautiful, hard, hot day. The mountains about four thousand feet high and utterly desiccated. My favourite sort of place, nothing cushy, nothing into which you can sink. I read some Steinbeck stories yesterday about homesteaders, or at least the memories of homesteaders here, all in that rhythm which is no more than the Bible translated into American. But sweetness here and there too – high meadows with flowers called Baby Blue Eyes (they were exactly the colour of Carole's finger-nails) in sheets across them. Fifteen-foot high bushes of ceanothus in flower, black butterflies I had never seen before and smaller ones like Chalk Blues. The names of the places come straight out of a pioneer story – China Camp, Church Creek Divide, Divide Camp, Pine Valley, Tassajara Hot Springs (but I didn't get as far as them). I must have walked about 15 miles, up on to a ridge and then down into a valley, with always the idea that the Pacific, the end of the continent, was just over the last of many horizons. It was incredibly beautiful, the hill-ridges stepping back into the blue distance, the great elephant corpses of dead pines laid out across the path and made silver with the drought and the altitude. I was in seventh heaven and now I must sleep.

Atlanta–Asheville, North Carolina

Monday 31 March

NIGEL *to Adam*   A small disaster, which turned into a blessing. My car's ignition key snapped in the lock. I was left with a stub and an impotent tip. The Holiday Inn's manageress (no less) helped a lot. She called Avis, and Avis came with a brand-new car, a Ford Thunderbird, silvery and sleek, to replace my now dusty Toyota. I moved luggage from one to the other, feeling quite sorry for the Toyota, for although I have never grown to love it, and, like you, somehow feel it's wrong to drive a foreign car on American roads, it has served me well for my first 600 miles. The Thunderbird is so splendid that I've almost transferred my allegiance to it from Mercedes. It has powered steering, powered windows, and a device which turns off sidelights after four minutes when you've parked it without remembering to do so. It has so many gadgets that I had to master a small volume to understand them. It rides as lightly as an albatross. Finally, I got away at 1 p.m.

Atlanta is formidably beautiful. Owing to the car delay, I did not have time to visit the birthplace of Martin Luther King, as I'd hoped, but passed through on the Interstate looking right and left as much as I dared. The city centre bristles with high-risers – cylindrical, rectangular and trapezoid – and yellow cranes pierce the skyline to raise it still higher. I like these buildings. People call them cold and impersonal. So they should be. An office-block should not look like a house or warehouse. It should look efficient, to suggest efficiency within, it should proclaim from a great distance that you are approaching something important, and it should be beautifully made. All this is true of Atlanta's Downtown. The dome of the Capitol shimmers in gold. Huge brontosaurus machines, preparing new foundations, new flyovers, savage the ochre earth which Rhett and Scarlett crossed to escape the blazing town. I was sorry to streak between a million people none of whom I shall ever meet. The Interstate is so well curved, graded and signalled that you might be travelling on rails. Lane discipline is something you learn here on your mother's knee. I was shot out of Atlanta in a cataract of cars and juggernauts.

It is a long drive, over 250 miles, to Asheville. I noticed, as a sign that I was moving north, that the trees are not yet in leaf, but it is still hot, in the middle 80s. As I approached the town, the Smoky Mountains rose behind it, a welcome third dimension after all this flatness. Asheville lies in a saucer between hills, with a great deal of space between the buildings, very un-Atlantalike. My hotel, where I am the guest of the University of North Carolina, is polite and comfortable, but the management have made the error of dressing their waitresses in short shorts which are not becoming to big bottoms. People telephoned – my host, Arnold Wengrow, my doctorial sponsor, Merritt Moseley, and my professorial host at Charlottesville, three days ahead, Martin Battestin. How happy I shall be to re-enter the academic world, and talk to people after three days of virtual and virtuous silence.

Dream Inn, Santa Cruz, California

Monday 31 March

ADAM *to Nigel*   There was an earthquake last night. I slept straight through it, but Mrs Morrow thought there was a man at the end of her bed shaking it. It was only 5.3 on the Richter scale but I curse myself for not noticing it. What on earth am I here for if not to experience earthquakes when they happen? The movement, apparently, was not on the San Andreas fault but on another line parallel to it which seismologists had never recognised before as a 'suture' (the word they used in the *San Francisco Examiner*). This whole part of California is shot through with fractures along which the continental plates move past each other at an inch a year. In fifty million years' time Los Angeles will arrive opposite the Golden Gate like a vast, garish liner. No one was killed in this particular quake (more Examinerese) but a man had to go to hospital after hitting his nose trying to dive under a table and a parrot belonging to a woman in San Jose was killed when the shaking knocked its cage off a table. The woman appeared on *Good Morning America* half distraught and half delighted at her exposure. The television crew refrained from filming the dead parrot and the woman said it was a shock in more senses than one.

Mrs Morrow had known worse – a double jolt last January when the ground had jerked up a foot and then dropped back, only to do it again a minute later; and a terrifying rippling of the whole valley a few years ago, which she heard coming from miles away like a tidal surge, a deep booming roar. Her whole house and garden had floated up on the wave and then down again with no damage. The house is wooden and can bend with the movement of the earth. It's brick buildings that crumble, but most damage is done by the fracturing of gas pipes where they enter the foundations of the building and are held rigid in the concrete. (I got all this from Mrs Morrow's gardener, who, incidentally, said that my car looked fine but the trouble was you couldn't tell the difference between the fuel gauge and the speedometer. 'Turn that thing on and she drinks a gallon,' he said.)

Fractured gas pipes lead to fires. Everyone thinks of San Francisco in 1906. If a novelist had invented this threat of destruction hanging over such a rich, tanned and beautiful society, the editor would have cut it out as too crude a metaphor. Most people don't seem too bothered about it anway. An 8.3 could come tomorrow and there would be no warning. (5.3 sounds quite near 8.3, but the Richter scale is geometric and every rise of 0.1 represents a doubling of intensity, so that an 8.3 shock is more destructive than a 5.3 by a factor of 2 to the power of 30. Do you follow me? It means 5.3 is a baby and 8.3 a whopper. I find these things interesting.)

Southern California will eventually disappear under the Aleutian Islands, but by then other things will have changed too. I sometimes wish I was a geologist. I don't think a geologist would mind that his Pontiac Catalina was brown or that his nose had a great lump half-way down it. Or perhaps that's naive. The seismologists have discovered no way of predicting earthquakes with any reliability, but I was interested by another man who appeared on the television (this was the local news) who claimed that his cat was magnetic and that because some change occurs in earth magnetism immediately before a quake, his cat was a fail-safe indicator of impending disaster. Its fur sticks up all over its body (the cat was called Jason) for several hours before an earthquake happens. We were shown Jason, post-shock, with fur smooth and then a man from Berkeley being sceptical. Jason's owner said that the academic establishment had its head in the sand and its nose in the air. The man from Berkeley said they were pursuing every reasonable avenue of research. The reporter, in the extraordinary way that American TV reporters do, said, 'Meantime, the residents of King City, California, continue to find the predictive powers of Jason's fur', and then a long pause, as if something of extraordinary wit and perception was going to be said, '*very* interesting.' They say there might be some more earthquakes in the next few days. I hope I'm awake this time.

I'm in Santa Cruz now, staying in the hotel you stayed in. It's my first 14-towel experience in America. It's OK, a little boring and hugely expensive.

Now how do I know this is the hotel you stayed in? Madeline Moore told me. I drove up to the University on top of its beautiful hill and hidden by its redwoods to find her. To Kresge College, all post-modernist colours and walls with holes through which you can see the trees. Students kicking a football around the vaguely Japanese spaces pointed me towards the English faculty. I found Room 224, where a notice on the door said that Professor Moore would be counselling students at 3.15. I waited outside feeling 18. Madeline showed up at 3.25, looking extremely professorial, with her hair much shorter than I remembered it and a certain briskness in her greeting. She had no idea who I was and for a few seconds I let her think I was an exchange student queuing up for counsel and then said, 'Your hair is much shorter than I remember it.' This was something out of a bad film and she played her part, looking nonplussed. But then I explained, all professoriality went out of the window and I've just come back from having supper with her now. She asked how you were. I said you were enjoying a string of dinner parties on the East coast. I told her about the Father–Son Relationship Exploration Scheme (the FSRES) for the book and she held her head in her hands, more in the way that people watch climbers half-way up the Eiger Nordwand than hear the news of a plane crash.

She, like everyone I have met in the past two weeks, is bursting with energy and life and new enterprise. A novel is half-written, poetry is being published, her daughter Rebecca is going to a dance school in LA and leading backpacking expeditions in Death Valley. The English are tired, old and hopeless because they don't have these multiple lives. There's a heaviness, like an overweight jogger, in English culture, which makes life singular and slow. I'm impatient with the steerage way you claim we have (p. 44); stability is a boring virtue and consistency all too often the mask for a lack of invention. I'm for variety with the chance of failure or vulgarity, if that's what's required. The English suffer from taste and a lack of daring. You can tell that I'm an anti-ambassador here, doing more damage to the image of Britain than Johnny Rotten and Edward Heath put together. But you will not like these remarks, made so easily in the Californian sun.

I asked to sit in on Madeline's Woolf class, but she wouldn't let me. Instead we had dinner in a fish restaurant on the pier. Delicious it was. I quizzed her about the feminist attitude to *Playboy*. She saw it as a financial arrangement, a simple buying of bodies for dollars, actual and photographic prostitution. The result of that, explaining something I had not understood at the party, was a polarisation of the sexes. Women become cipher-women (the bosom), men become cipher-men (the dollar and the cigar) and any humanity, because humanity is necessarily androgynous, disappears. The reason, she said, that the men at the party did not notice the girls was because they already in some senses owned them. It would be like talking to your car. She saw this as a particularly American affliction because of the simple identifications made in one part of the American soul between money, pleasure and masculine prowess. Buying is fucking is being happy. (Those are not Madeline's words but it is the sort of bitter and violent language used by the most radical feminists. There is a group here in Santa Cruz who display a really flamboyant anger. Earlier this year a group of them staged the Myth America Pageant to coincide with the *Miss* Am. Pag. It consisted of various women walking up and down a catwalk clothed head to toe in slices of salami. The same group constructed a giant penis with a hydraulic system inside it. They filled it with liquid cake icing and then visited all the porn shops in Santa Cruz, pumping the stuff over the magazines. Twice yesterday I was told that America was a visual and not a verbal culture.)

Asheville, North Carolina

Tuesday 1 April

NIGEL *to Adam*   I did a shameful and uncharacteristic thing. I wanted to visit Biltmore, the vast house of the Vanderbilts, just on Asheville's outskirts. At the reception-centre I paid for entrance ($15!, which makes our £2.60 at Sissinghurst sound modest), and the lady gave me two small brochures about the property. In one of them was tucked a ticket. I did not notice it. It must have fallen under the feet of a hundred other tourists. At the next barrier, where you drive into the park, a man asked me for my entrance ticket. What ticket? I showed him the brochures. 'That's not a ticket!' 'No, but it's proof that I've paid. I was never given a ticket.' We argued, and my impatience took over. Suddenly I stepped on the accelerator and left him spluttering. That was a most unwise thing to do. I had not reckoned with Biltmore's high-tech communications. A patrol car caught me up after a mile, klaxon blaring. I must return at once. I persuaded the ranger to radio the reception-centre and ask whether they remembered a tall, elderly Englishman with an indignant face. God be praised, they did. I must be very obvious. With this verbal ticket, I was allowed to proceed, shamefaced and slowly cooling.

Biltmore is one of the largest houses I have ever seen, and without question the ugliest. It seems to me incredible that George Vanderbilt, a man of culture with a special interest in architecture, should have chosen the French Renaissance style for his great house in the mid-Carolinas, and that on its completion in 1892, stood back and said, as presumably he did, 'Yes, that's exactly what I wanted.'

It is built of a hideous yellow stone. It has an external staircase badly modelled on Blois. It has spiky turrets. But the true horror is reserved for inside. It is not a house. It's a railway station. Huge atria open one into the other, with palms and settees 16 feet long. There are quotations from Chambord, Azay-le-Rideau, Hatfield, Glamis and Sans Souci, all mixed up. The dining-room can seat sixty-four people, and at one end, above a baronial fireplace, is an enormous frieze depicting peasants at their labours, to remind the Vanderbilts of one source of their wealth. Upstairs (you could mount the staircase on horseback) is even more ghastly than downstairs. Vast bedrooms contain furniture of unexampled brutality and discomfort. Every chair is knobbled with encrustations to suggest antiquity. The beds are broader than the Great Bed of Ware. Only in one bedroom, I imagine for Guest No. 22 in the pecking order, is the furnishing reduced to human scale and the dressing-table looks like a table where you might conceivably dress. The brochure said, 'The House Tour takes two to three hours.' Mine took ten minutes. The park, I must acknowledge, is very beautiful, in the English style. As I drove out of it, I averted my eyes from my enemy at the gate.

My reasons for coming to Asheville were four. To stay in a hotel called Smoky Mountain Inn on the Plaza, a name I couldn't resist. To drive from here to Charlottesville along the famous Blue Ridge Parkway. To talk to some of the students in the University about Virginia Woolf. And to meet Arnold Wengrow, Professor of Drama, who has written an excellent study of Robert Sharpe, the theatre-designer. I gave my talk in an airy classroom to some twenty students, but they were too scared by the presence of a large faculty contingent to ask questions afterwards. The faculty did. Did I ever see Virginia mad? (No.) What did she think of Arnold Bennett? (Not much.) In the edited version of my father's diary, how much of the original did I leave out? (19/20th.) It will be that sort of thing again in the University of Virginia, and I feel a bit of a fraud in replaying a much-used record, especially as UNCA (work that out) gave me a wholly unexpected honorarium of $150.

I lunched with some of the faculty (Wengrow, Moseley, and a visiting lecturer from Oxford), and the talk was good. I said that Americans were the most patriotic people I've ever known. The Union flag, national anthems (plural) and hands-on-hearts are in evidence at the least excuse. From time to time they rise collectively to a high level of shared emotion, as during the Tehran hostage saga and the explosion of the shuttle last January. Moseley said that it was true about these emotional highs. As the country is so huge, there is almost a psychological need for such events to unify the people. Personally he didn't derive much jingoistic pleasure from American successes in sport, foreign wars, academic triumphs, etc. He couldn't imagine himself saying, 'By Golly, I'm glad it was an American!', when the latest Nobel Prize for Physics is announced, but he might think it momentarily, omitting the 'By Golly' bit. (I'm simply giving the sense of what he said.) The others agreed. One young teacher surprised me by saying that she was shocked by the revelations about President Kennedy's call-girls and love-affairs. I had imagined that people would accept them as proof that he was both normal and virile, highly desirable qualities in a president, and that they would enjoy, posthumously and vicariously, his small peccadilloes. But no, she was distressed by these revelations. A wholesome family life (not her words) at the White House is what the nation wants. I wonder.

This evening, the Chairman of the Literature Department, Dr Jeff Rackham, asked a few people to meet me at his house, with wine, shrimps and strawberries. It's a neat, very clean house in a quiet street, with verandahs on two sides, and I noticed similar houses climbing the hillside behind, in a pattern of villas strangely reminiscent of Fiesole above Florence. The party was exactly of the kind I enjoy most, some fifteen people in several uncrowded rooms. There were basket chairs on the verandah where one could sit in coolness.

Asheville–Roanoke, Virginia

Wednesday 2 April

NIGEL *to Adam*   The Blue Ridge Parkway is a marvel. No other nation could have built such a road purely for the motorist's enjoyment. Trucks and vans are barred from it, and it passes (but does not enter) only three large towns, Asheville, Roanoke and Charlottesville. There are no traffic-lights and very few intersections. It is nearly 500 miles long, of which I drove half. In appearance, it is a country road, one lane wide in each direction, and it twists and climbs up the mountain sides in easy curves and gradients. It is beautifully made and geographically sensational, for it runs almost all the way along the Eastern watershed. I passed many places where a bucket of water emptied on the road would be divided by the camber into two streams, one destined for the Atlantic 400 miles away, counting meanders, and the other for the Gulf, 1,500 miles via the Ohio and the Mississippi. Since it is the Divide, there are no rivers or cascades to excite you till you reach the lower ground in Virginia. You overlook on both sides a tossing mass of forest-covered hills, and every few miles a scoop or driveway leads you aside to a vantage-point where the designers hoped you would be amazed by the view. You are, for the first three or four times, but the views are inevitably very similar. When you are running along the top of a long, long ridge, on average 3,500 feet up, the surrounding country unfolds very slowly and no scenic surprise can be left. Local variety is provided by the road itself, twisting this way and that between woods.

The ride was lovely, all 250 miles of it to Roanoke, but lonely. I could have done with a companion. Everyone has warned me against hitch-hikers, and the hikers have almost given up hitching. I have spoken to nobody all day except for checking out and checking in. At the latter desk, they said that very few non-Americans come to Roanoke, and I'm not wholly surprised. It is a night-stop sort of place except for those condemned to stop a lifetime.

Santa Cruz, California

Wednesday 2 April

ADAM *to Nigel*   I couldn't afford more than one night in the Dream
                        Inn and so I'm staying with Colin and Karen Hend-
erson. I can't remember if you have ever met them. He's 26 and she's 34.
He's about to start training to be a doctor and she is nearly qualified as a
chiropractor, someone, as far as I could make out, who rearranges bones and
straightens nerves. He's also working as a carpenter, and is, as he says, very
up-front. He was worried that I was going to misrepresent Karen and him
and the whole set-up in Santa Cruz. If I was going to stay at all, I should
stay at least a week. (This sounds hostile, but it wasn't.) I said that, if he
preferred, I wouldn't stay at all. This was slightly awkward. He said he
thought it must be the archetypal reaction of anyone we come across – a
mixture of enthusiasm to communicate everything and a suspicion that it
wouldn't be taken in the right way. I reassured him as far as I could, and I'm
staying here for one night only.

Colin took me to a Phone-a-thon which began at 5.30, and was intended
to raise money for a charity show called *Peace Child*. About twenty young
men and women gathered in the marble banking hall around the magnetic
and excited figure of Madeline Keller, a woman of extraordinary mobility.
Everyone was issued with the sort of hooters that unroll and make a squawk
when you blow into them. 'All *right*!' Madeline said when everyone had their
hooter. 'Now I want this to be fun and I want you to remember you are here
to make money. Now how much are you going to make? I want to hear your
targets. Anders, how much are you going to make for *Peace Child* tonight?'
Anders fingered the feather on the end of his hooter and rather sheepishly
said '$500'. 'All *right*,' Madeline said again, with the emphasis on the second
word. (It is strange that a phrase which implies no more than mute acceptance
in England, in America becomes the most positive of approbations.) We went
round the circle. Everyone laid claim to a large slice of the wealth of Santa
Cruz and the target for the evening was $10,000. 'Now go to it,' Madeline
said. 'Step out of yourself. Make them *want* to give money.' My role was
distributing organic apple juice in plastic cups. A few rather grim figures from
the staff of the Bank sat at their desks analysing Individual Retirement
Account percentages while Madeline tried to turn it into the Democratic
Convention. 'All *right*,' she said whenever one of the phone-a-thoners got a
pledge. Then everyone blew their hooters. I was given a tambourine with
which to greet every new pledge. 'Twenty-five big buckaroos,' Anders shouted
and I shook the tambourine as required. The girls did infinitely better than
the men and the star was a sweet soft-seller called Chelsea who whispered

into the telephone and came up with $25 every time. 'I don't hear enough noise in here,' Madeline shouted. 'This is meant to be fun. Have a good time. Communicate your happiness!' Tentatively Colin, Mary, Robin, Terri and the others approached complete strangers for their money. 'Remember: don't argue and don't talk to ansaphones,' Madeline shouted. I distributed apple juice. '$45,' Chelsea announced demurely. A macho hulk in the corner had failed to raise a penny for an hour and Madeline took him off the phone. 'We need money off that line,' Madeline said and the hulk silently expanded his neck muscles. They managed to raise about $3,000 dollars in three hours. At the end of it Madeline was looking desperately bright and exhausted. 'Remember, this is for peace,' she said as I distributed Mexican tortilla chips, stone-ground. Someone had spilt the last of the apple juice over the bank deposit forms and the evening had been a success. 'Very best of luck,' I said to Madeline. 'You should try and lose some of that reserve,' she replied.

Roanoke–Charlottesville, Virginia

Thursday 3 April

NIGEL *to Adam*   Thomas Jefferson, I wrote twelve years ago after my first visit to Monticello, is the most Periclean figure in American history. Today I wouldn't use so fanciful a comparison, but what I meant by it I still feel, that he was the great all-rounder, his interests manifold, his style patrician, his humanity attractive, and his influence still felt to this day, all of which happens to be true of Pericles too. By his grace of manner, his wide knowledge and his intelligence, Jefferson (or TJ, as someone called him here so I'm adopting it) was the man who above all others convinced Europeans that Americans were not a bunch of cloutish rebels but civilised people, and his conduct at home set the pattern for the decent approachability of the presidential line. It wasn't always like this. In his lifetime he was thought a bit dandified, aloof and Francophil, and it was said that he always proclaimed the superiority of the Old World to the New, which was then nothing but the truth. Strangely enough, it was Franklin Roosevelt who restored Jefferson's reputation, by quoting him frequently and putting the silhouette of Monticello on the nickel piece (look at your loose change), and now he is regarded as the greatest of all American patriots, though in character he was much more like an English Whig peer of the best type.

Monticello, which I revisited this afternoon with Freddy Nichols, the great authority on Jeffersonian architecture, illustrates TJ's character far better than any other eminent man's house I know – for instance Chartwell, which is pretty in a way that Churchill wasn't and was the product of his wife's taste

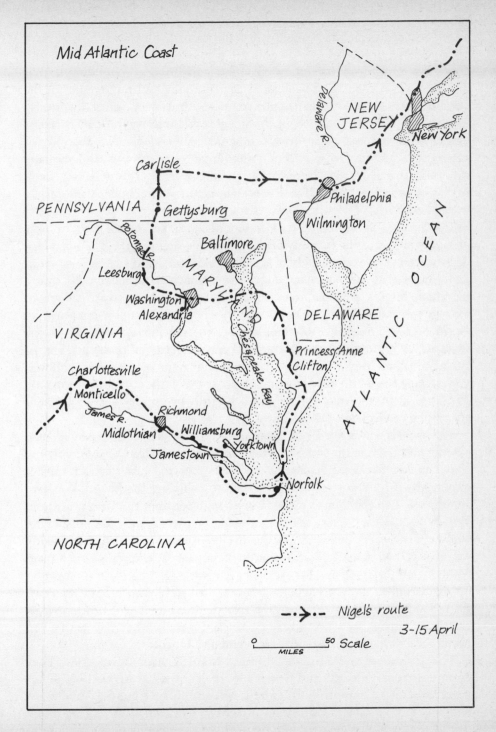

Mid Atlantic Coast

NEW JERSEY

Delaware R.

New York

Carlisle

PENNSYLVANIA

Gettysburg

Philadelphia

Wilmington

Potomac R.

Baltimore

ATLANTIC OCEAN

Leesburg

MARYLAND

Washington
Alexandria

DELAWARE

VIRGINIA

Chesapeake Bay

Princess Anne
Clifton

Charlottesville

Monticello

James R.

Richmond

Williamsburg

Midlothian

Yorktown

Jamestown

Norfolk

NORTH CAROLINA

--->-- Nigel's route

3-15 April

0   50 Scale
MILES

more than his own. Jefferson's wife died very young, and Monticello is entirely of his own design and decoration. It has the three qualities which Bacon said were essential to any domestic building – 'firmness, commoditie and delight'. Firmness comes from its setting on a flattened hilltop. Commodity in the arrangement of rooms as a succession of intimacies, and the removal of the slave quarters to galleries half-underground with wooden walks, like decks, laid on top of them. And delight in the agreeable interplay of half-octagons and classical porches, all in brick of a good colour with white boarding or plaster set against it. One talks about 'wandering round a house', and normally means by that its rooms. Here one means its exterior, with its lovely views over Virginia as far as the Blue Ridge Mountains where Indians still lurked as the first bricks of Monticello were laid.

Inside, on this second visit, I found his mistakes troublesome – ugly skylights let into ceilings, many of the rooms too high for their width, a lack of delicacy in the workmanship of cornices and doors, and staircases so mean and furtive that the big room under the dome was turned by TJ into a playroom for his grandchildren, almost the only people small enough to manage the stairs. There's no doubt that the conveniences of the interior were sacrificed to the elegance of the exterior; the placing of windows is one example. A professional architect would have solved the problems. But as Freddy Nichols reminded me, TJ was the amateur of amateurs, and was undertaking a revolutionary experiment. He says that the influence was mainly French, but to me Monticello appears English to its very core, a brilliant adaptation of Georgian Palladianism.

Mr Nichols looks like Fred Astaire, and knows it, because people keep coming up to him in the street to say so, and latterly he has taken to replying, 'But I'm not like Fred Astaire. I *am* Fred Astaire,' just to deter further impertinences. He put on a straw boater to complete the image. We were accompanied on the tour by some twenty students from the University, and Freddy kept putting questions to them like, 'Why is there grass outside the window instead of stone?' and, when the boy or girl looked blank, Freddy would say, 'Oh come on!' and then explain that TJ didn't want the sun bouncing off the stone into his eyes as he sat working. There was no mention in his discourse of Sally Hemings, the mulatto slave who bore TJ at least three children, but I have a suspicion that the bunk above his bed, a narrow closet approached by a tiny spiral stair, was for Sally when TJ was feeling tired. I didn't like to ask Freddy. He seemed so innocent.

The University of Virginia is different from all other universities. They don't call their Professors and Doctors by their titles, but Mr and Ms. They never refer to a Campus, but to The Lawn and The Grounds. They won't have anything so vulgar as 'precision-marching' by cheer-leaders. They didn't even admit girls till the 1960s, and then only because two girls, or their parents, sued the State of Virginia for sex-discrimination and won. It was the alumni who were anti-girls, as alumni are always anti any change. 'We got on without girls', they said (I bet they didn't), 'so why can't these kids too?' So there are girls now, lying about the Lawn like mermaids, and the boys are said to like them.

All the new buildings in the Grounds reflect TJ's passion for columns. It's a stone forest. But I mustn't exaggerate. These brick and plaster temples, Monticellos blown up to five times the size, dotted around little hills, look extraordinarily attractive in the mass, like a Poussin landscape. But the best is the Lawn, TJ's conception of an academic village, designed by him to the last architrave, and finished in the year he died, 1826. It has been declared the Most Distinguished Architectural Group of Buildings in the USA, or words to that effect. The Lawn is a long wide sweep falling prettily downwards in grassy cascades, terminated at one end by a later building which the architectural historians deplore, and at the upper by TJ's great Rotunda which he modelled on the Pantheon in Rome. Down each side are pavilions for the professors linked by low rooms for the students, all in a pure classical style, as if Palladio had come down to Charlottesville and pupped. It's very successful and very beautiful. I'm staying in one of the pavilions, the Colonnade Club, and it's only right that not everything works quite so well as it would in a motel – lamps not aways lighting, water not always hot, coat-hangers made of wire – but what do I care, when I am the guest of the University of Virginia, in TJ's own bed for all I know?

I lunched with Mrs Battestin, the wife of my host and sponsor, Martin Battestin, in her garden of weeping-cherry, forsythia and judas, and went back there to dine before my lecture. As I sat at the front of the auditorium waiting for Mr Battestin to introduce me, a stout lady came tripping down to say how simply *lovely* Sissinghurst was looking when she was last there. There's nothing I hate more than being talked to gushingly when I'm about to give a lecture. I gave it. Unlike the University of North Carolina, the University of Virginia did not give me an honorarium because Amy Henderson, who had fixed it from Washington, told them that, as a British aristocrat, I'm totally indifferent to money, and if offered a cheque would reject it with contempt. In every way they were most hospitable. There was a post-lecture reception, at which I went around making myself pleasant to my ex-audience. I enjoy scholarly chaff, but the *jealousy* of academics is amazing. 'Some creep in Minnesota published the letter from Henry James to Adams which *I* had found at the Berg, and he *knew* that my note was about to appear in the Bulletin of Current Literature.' That sort of thing. I'm glad that, like TJ, I can plead the privileges of the amateur. I crept back to his imagined bed at

11 p.m., and read your letter from California (25 March) laughing out loud over Hef and the poor scared 17-year-old kid whom you rescued from a centre-fold.

Galilee Harbor, Sausalito, California

Thursday 3 April

ADAM *to Nigel*   This is a beautiful place. I'm sitting on top of a houseboat, looking out across the bay, smoking. Two Filipino fishermen are catching shoe-shaped fish from the quay next to me. An old Irishman is fixing a telephone line on to his boat next door. A woman rows past in a slide-seat rigger and a bulk carrier the length of fifteen blocks takes Korean novelties to the dock in Oakland. I'm being lulled by California. Its absurdities are gradually sliding under the generalised wash of well-being.

I will tell you about Jeanne and Bob, whom I am staying with, later, but I mustn't let Colin and Karen Henderson go past. We had a long and very up-front talk at breakfast this morning. The issue was masculinity – or at least that was the core of it; we fringed into other areas: Lazaris, the absent consoler, a guru who has no physical existence but communicates his wisdom by using other people's voices and bodies or even by remaining completely silent and absent. His flyer (Amex, Visa and Mastercard all acceptable) said that people who met him would find questions answered which hadn't even been asked. The health obsession – my contribution was something I had heard on the radio: an estimated 500,000 lb had been lost by slimmers in the Los Angeles area in the first quarter of this year, a remarkable achievement of collective denial. The insanity of sensory deprivation pods, which are warm, dark, fibreglass eggs filled with water. The idea is to sit inside them and experience nothing because experience is stressful and stress is *bad* because stress is a negative sensation. (I say this as though it was God-given truth. Imagine my surprise when I found a book in a bookshop here this afternoon called *The Joy of Stress*. That has to be the cutting edge, the new frontier of Californian existence. I'm told sensory deprivation pod manufacturers are going out of business by the dozen. Everything is fluid in the brutal market.) Anyway, we talked about masculinity. California is four steps ahead of the world in this as in every other issue. No longer is masculinity a problem for men; it has now become the goal. Colin explained that the culture had taught him while he was growing up that men are unpleasant. Almost everything good in the world was female. Love, beauty and truth all belonged to women, while men were full of greed, aggression and brutality. Colin came to dislike his own maleness, even to hate other men and envy women for whom the path of life appeared so smooth. Meanwhile, the women he knew were adopting rather masculine attitudes and habits – control, strength, direction and so on. The whole of Colin's world was becoming an androgynous soup in which he felt himself to be drowning. But then the lifeboat: a workshop (California for seminar) on Men, Sex and Power. $400 for the weekend. The facilitator, a man called Justin, would make people angry by shouting at them an inch away from their face and then turn around to the rest of the workshop and say in the most relaxed of voices 'I'd like you to notice the dominant/submissive interplay here' before returning to his all-male shouting match. Colin found his maleness satisfactorily reinforced by the workshop and by the Men Support Team weekends he has been on ever since.

A small group of men go off alone together and really get into their masculinity mountaineering or white water rafting or what have you. This is not about homosexuality, it's about being a man and loving other men. I said I could relate to that. And the effect on Colin? It has turned him into the Boss, he said, and Karen into the Leader. These are technical terms which, he said, allowed him to shout at Karen but meant that Karen made all the decisions. I told them that's how my marriage worked too. They said that in Vermont people saved up for a new load of firewood, in Florida for a new car, but in California the dream experience was another workshop. There is a psychological condition here, during which it is unsafe to drive a car, known as 'The Workshop High'. They recommended it; I didn't have the money.

But now I'm on the Bay and I've exhausted all my superlatives. This must be the most beautiful situation for a city on earth. I'm in Sausalito, or at least floating on the edge of it, tied up to a rickety quay, on a northern arm of the bay, across the Golden Gate bridge from San Francisco itself. Sausalito calls itself a city but of course it is really a suburb of SF, like all the cities around the bay. I'm staying with Jeanne Petry and Bob Hypio ('Oh God,' he said this morning, 'we're not going to have last names in this, are we?') I met them when coming down from the Ventana Wilderness on Sunday. 'Come and see us in Sausalito,' they said and so here I am – up the freeway from Santa Cruz, the number of lanes growing with every mile until at the almost Mississippi width of fourteen the first sign to the Golden Gate bridge appeared. I made straight for it, the most golden of all destinations in America and no disappointment.

At dusk this evening Jeanne took me up on the hills in Marin County which separate the Pacific from the bay. She's a photographer and said that it was Utopic here. We could see everything – the ocean, the great flat wishbone of the bay itself, with its short stub at the Golden Gate, holding apart the Marin peninsula and its twin to the south, where the City peaks in the glass towers of the business district. Over on the far side, the industry and slums of Oakland, blending into Berkeley. Jeanne said that America, the real America, began on the far side of the Bay, over there, where it was grittier. On this side, connected only by the threads of the bridges, was a sort of off-lying pleasure-island, where different constraints operated. Money was no problem here. The lawyers and bankers who work in the City come back on the ferry across the Bay.

It must be the most beautiful commute in the world, seeing that bridge against a green sunset, matched only by the twinkling towers of the money-citadel they are leaving behind for the night. I said this to Jeanne. She said she had been on the ferry watching these things. The bankers and lawyers had been down in the hold somewhere swilling G & Ts. One gets indifferent to regular beauties. They come back loaded with money and money is no problem. Different anxieties take over. This is the land of hot-tub hedonism and instant gratification. (Have you had a jacuzzi yet? It's completely addictive and a far more dangerous drug than cocaine. I'm amazed Falwell hasn't called for the outlawing of the hot tub.) But as you know instant gratification is a contradiction in terms. I said this to someone in Carmel and he told me that was the sort of remark only someone from an emergent third-world nation like England could make. For once, I bristled in defence.

At least it's true to say that instant gratification has its problems and they're everywhere here. It's a society floating in cream. I've been reading Galbraith and the opening words of *The Affluent Society* are as follows: 'Wealth is not without its advantages and the case to the contrary, although it has often been made, has never proved widely persuasive.' He's a witty man. 'But, beyond doubt, wealth is the relentless enemy of understanding.' The rich man, and this is the description of Marin, 'can assume or imagine a much greater variety of ills and he will be correspondingly less certain of their remedy. Also, until he learns to live with his wealth, he will have a well-observed tendency to put it to the wrong purposes or otherwise to make himself foolish.' That should be inscribed over the Golden Gate bridge. It would immediately be defaced with graffiti about freedom. You ask for evidence. I will collect it tomorrow. And I haven't yet told you about my amazing hosts.

Charlottesville—Williamsburg, Virginia

Friday 4 April

NIGEL *to Adam*   What a lot we are packing into these days! I perhaps even more than you, because I'm now approaching the centre of the east coast where the action lies, and I arranged months ahead to see many people, while you, perhaps more wisely, have no appointments except those you make at an hour's notice.

Today was typical. A tour of Jefferson's famous Rotunda to start with, drive to Richmond, lunch on its outskirts, drive on to Williamsburg where I drop luggage, visit the site of Jamestown, visit the new Art Gallery, dinner-party, bed after midnight. No time to write a word to you, so this letter is started at 6 a.m., 5 April. I find it essential to record one enthusiasm before the next enthusiasm smothers it.

At Richmond I lunched with Gay Fraser, an English friend who married in America and has lived here for thirty-five years. (We knew each other in London when we were young – I young, she younger.) She still feels English enough to take a critical view of America, but there was little in her woodland home and her neighbourhood, Midlothian, that I could find fault with. I may have regretted the absence of villages in this country, but they have raised the despised name of suburb to unforeseen levels of sublimity. Just beyond where Gay lives is such a suburb or 'development' called Salisbury. 'When you move into Salisbury,' said Gay, 'you have *really* arrived.' I'm not so sure that she wants to. The houses are spanking-fresh, bright, colonial and very expensive. Each must be set on a minimum of an acre of gound, must cost no less than $ so-and-so, must expose no garage to the public view, must conform in size, style and graciousness to its neighbours and be maintained to a high standard of elegance. The curious thing is that Salisbury's inhabitants put up with rules laid down by the 'developer' that they would hotly resent from the State, which cannot prevent an American doing whatever he wishes with what he owns. Another developer has built a shopping complex near Salisbury called Sycamore Square. I thought it lovely. Our tastes differ widely on this sort of thing and I know you would hate its prettiness, calling it fake gentility. You want a supermarket to look like one, with all its entrails and ads exposed, but I want my Sainsburys to lie within an outer casing to which some thought has been given, which, in other words, does not pollute by its appearance. Sycamore Square has its super-market, its inn, its florist and its drugstore, but it looks like a section of Colonial Williamsburg mocked up for an international Expo. I'm laying this on a bit thick, just to shock you. I found it immensely attractive.

Gay is a schoolteacher. She teaches high-school juniors, 14 to 16. She stands no nonsense from them. She quotes herself, 'We're here to learn English grammar, not to fix up our faces', to a pert miss freshening her lipstick in class. She was interesting about the effect of Salisbury-type affluence on the young. It's not good. The satisfaction of every need leads to the assumption that it will always be satisfied, and so minds and wills grow mushy. Money, and more money, is the general expectation. Too much TV except in well-ordered families. Too-early dating. Parents scared of their children. Too little home support for school-learning. But these are the complaints of teachers world-wide, and Gay loves her job, has many bright children to teach, and is herself an example to them.

I am staying the night with Anne and Jack Willis in Williamsburg. He is Chairman of the English Department at the College of William and Mary. She had thought ahead of everything I might need or like, down to bananas by my bed. In what remained of daylight we drove to Jamestown, and by special arrangement had it entirely to ourselves after normal closing-hours.

In my first letter of this series I said that two of the places I most looked forward to seeing were Monticello and Jamestown. Monticello yesterday, Jamestown today, both in beautiful weather and under the most knowledgeable of guides. The spot is an island-meadow girt by marsh and forest-trees, lying on the James River 15 miles from its mouth. There in April 1607 a company of 150 men and boys landed to found the first permanent British colony in America. There was no Spanish fuss of religious dedication or territorial claims when they stepped ashore. They simply tied their three ships to the trees, and began constructing a fort. Here English America began. Only 12 miles away, at Yorktown, it ended.

The site has long since been deserted, and all that remain are foundations and memorials. There is John Smith in stone gazing over the river, Pocahontas, the Indian Princess, in bronze like Joan of Arc, a tall obelisk, the brick ruins of a later church, foundations which outline some of the earliest houses. At intervals excellent explanatory notices are set on sloping boards, and beside the foundations are drawings of what the buildings might have looked like – very English, wattle and daub, thatched, such as you might see today in any Sussex lane. What are missing are the shouts, the stench, the fear, the wild animals except deer, the Indians, the disease-laden swamps. They were like amphibians crawling ashore hoping to survive and somehow turn into land-animals. No colonists can have suffered greater hardship, but one feels little sympathy for them, for they were a cruel and feckless lot, many of them criminal types out for loot. There was no loot. After three years fighting off the Indians, malaria and starvation, the survivors gave up. They sailed away. By a strange chance they met at the mouth of Chesapeake Bay our ancestor (admittedly only by a knight's move) Lord De la Warr, bringing fresh supplies and colonists from England, and he persuaded them to return. The tablet to his memory in the ruined church reads, 'Saviour of the Colony in the starving time of 1610'. It's strange that the colony, a toe-nail-hold on Virginia, was not snuffed out by the Spaniards who by that time had colonised a large part of South and Central America. It slowly became economically self-supporting when one of their number, John Rolfe, imported from Trinidad a weed which seemed to grow well. It was called *Nicotiana tabacum*.

We returned to Colonial Williamsburg in the dusk. I shall not describe what is so well known, only recall what Thomas Jefferson astonishingly thought of it in its prime. He said of the smaller houses that 'it is impossible to devise things more ugly, uncomfortable and happily more perishable'. The Capitol he found the best of a very poor lot. The Governor's Palace 'is not handsome without', and the College and Hospital for Lunatics 'are rude mis-shapen piles which, but that they have roofs, would be mistaken for brick-kilns'. To us the reconstructed buildings are charming, decorative and finely balanced. The Hospital is the latest to be completed, with money from Wallace of the *Reader's Digest*, and contains a museum of English and American art of the eighteenth century, a Wallace Collection of shining objects of high quality. We were shown round by John Davis, the Associate Curator. I felt sad to rush so quickly through such a treasure-house.

Galilee Harbor, Sausalito, California

Saturday 5 April

ADAM *to Nigel*   There is no evidence. It's a feeling. I suddenly remember an incident from years, maybe fifteen years ago. We were looking at a magazine article together. The man said that he *felt* something or other was wrong. You said that whenever you saw the word *felt* or *feeling* in an article or a book you stopped reading. 'The man hasn't thought enough', you said, 'if he's still feeling things.' I thought that was a bad thing to think but it was a silent period in my life and of course I said nothing. And nothing either when Jo Trautmann was at Sissinghurst one year, editing the Woolf letters with you, and you said to her that psychology was a science without any basis in reality because no stranger could discover any more about a man than what he himself already knew. That struck me as nonsense then and nonsense now. It's the sort of thing I spend my time talking about here, a function of too much spare time – mine and theirs. I couldn't live here for that reason. It would be life in a theme-park in which the themes were money and absurd anxieties, muddled in with a desperate desire to get it right, to make the soul match up to the coloured, optimistic clothes they all wear.

Jeanne showed me a book by someone called Shakti Gawain, who lives in Mill Valley, a couple of miles from here. She is a Workshop Facilitator and the book is called *Creative Visualisation*. It makes my blood run cold. 'Everything you need or want is here for the asking,' Shakti says. 'You only need *believe* that it's so, to truly *desire* it, and to be willing to *accept* it, in order to have whatever you wish.' To think that anything is wrong with the world, Shakti says, is a false belief which 'limits us all from realising our natural state of prosperity'. All you've got to do is visualise creatively and the world will be nice. Shakti recommends 'Affirmations' you should make every day in order to turn the world into a nice place and *you* into a nice person. These include:

- Financial success is coming to me easily and effortlessly.
- Life is meant to be fun and I'm now willing to enjoy it!
- I'm rich in consciousness and manifestation. (Don't really understand that one.)
- I have more than enough money for my own personal use.
- I now have a satisfying income of $____ a month.
- I am rich, well and happy. (That is the great Marin tautology. It means 'I am rich, rich and rich'.)

This is a terminus for a civilisation, don't you think? A dissociation from reality leading to a self-castrating dream of private happiness. All you can do is make desperate jokes and attend to the body, making it neat and handsome like volunteer members of the Society for Disused Churches. Example of desperate joke: A wealthy, middle-aged woman is trying to manoeuvre her Cadillac into a parking slot in Mill Valley. A flash young man in an open top Porsche Carrera whips into the space and shouts, 'That's what you can do when you're young and agile.' The woman accelerates her Cadillac straight into the side of the Porsche. 'And that's what you can do when you're old and rich,' she says.

This is a world of which I have only glimpsed the fringes. Jeanne and Bob are not part of it. Galilee Harbor is a small pocket of another version of the Dream. It was once a proper boat-building yard. Liberty ships were built two by two on the slips here. The enormous salmon skeleton of a tea-clipper called the *Galilee* is laid up on one side, rotted and romantic, and the whole space of the harbour and the sides of the decrepit quay are taken up by about thirty half-crumbling, half-tended-to houseboats. It's a co-operative and everyone who lives here is an artist or artisan of some kind. (That alone is not distinctive in California. I went to see Clayton Carlson yesterday, who runs the Harper & Row office in San Francisco. He gets ten thousand unsolicited manuscripts sent to him every year. It's a good year if ten of them get into print.)

The people are eccentric here. One man has divided his boat down the middle and painted everything on the left red and everything on the right green. He runs a Volkswagen beetle, painted in the same way and organises his life on the principles of port and starboard. Another has filled every bit of space in his boat with toys. A third has constructed a miniature Mississippi paddle-steamer using parts from lorries to turn the big red wheels. They all had a big party in the Sausalito Cruising Club last night. Dancing and Drunkenness. An earnest woman, the wife of an architect, talked to me for hours about her fear of bulldozers and nasty developers, the military/industrial complex and the future of America. I drank a Bud or two. A glamorous boat-builder said the drug of the moment was called Ecstasy. It was the drug everyone should have been doing in the '60s and had only been made illegal three months ago. There's glamour for you.

Bob and Jeanne have only been here since last August and everybody loves them. He is from Michigan, she from Pennsylvania. They met at graduate school in South Carolina. When Jeanne first saw Bob in the corridors of the school, she went straight up to him, shook him by the hand and said 'I'm Jeanne. Who are you?' That's her style: fearless. Bob thought 'Oh, oh, here's trouble.' That's his style: careful, making jokes you could never tell he thought were funny. I've never met people who love each other so much – they're shiny with it. They rent their boat and it's the smallest here. The shell – the hull – is a lifeboat from one of the Liberty ships, which has been lined and roofed with redwood planks. The effect is an Austrian ski-hut which bobs about now and then in the wash from one of the ferries. Bob does carpentry for the rich in Mill Valley. At the moment he is building a cedarwood-clad garbage cabana, as he calls it, for a lawyer. It's about half the size of the boat they live on. Jeanne works in a print shop and rolls her head around inside a photocopy machine making Xerox self-portraits. I tell them it's the ideal life and Jeanne says it's wonderful to lie awake at night thinking of all the people in Galilee Harbor floating up on the flood tide and then back down again on the ebb. But already life in the pleasure zone is cloying.

Before coming here on the four-day drive across country in the Dodge Dart, with everything they had in the back seat (these American pictures!), they lived in a house in the woods in Michigan. There was no Californian lying-around there. All hard work, keeping things going. There are people here, even in Galilee Harbor, who live perfectly good lives simply on the stuff they find rifling through other people's rubbish. The 400-cubic-feet garbage cabana is Bob's central symbol for life in Mill Valley. It wouldn't happen in Michigan and part of Bob is pining for the woods. Jeanne talks about Bali now and then. This has yet to be resolved. I tell them I will find them here in ten years' time living in a houseboat modelled on the Taj Mahal. (There's already a reproduction Blue Mosque from Isfahan floating a couple of hundred yards away. They say it leaks. The remains of a Tudor cottage only appears at low tide.) But when I say that they both look aside.

Williamsburg–Clifton, Maryland

Saturday–Sunday 5–6 April

NIGEL *to Adam*   I'll run these two days into one letter, being so cushioned by hospitality and busy with planned activities.

I drove over the famous bridge-and-tunnel which crosses the mouth of the Chesapeake Bay from Norfolk, practising for our own Channel Tunnel, but the tunnel parts are short, the bridges long, and fog welled up each side of me, obliterating the view, or rather the non-view, for so long is the bridge that there comes a point where in fair weather the shore on either side is invisible. The toll is $9, worth the experience.

At the far end you are still in Virginia, but before this great tongue of land, the Eastern Shore, merges northwards into the continent, it becomes Maryland and then Delaware. I thought them lucky thus to be represented by six senators. On the contrary, some of them say that they feel neglected, cut off from the mainstream of American life. Others glory in their isolation. The farming and fishing people don't mind being thought inbred, clannish and old-fashioned. They tell you with pride that on Smith Island they still speak Elizabethan English. They do not accept as natives people who were not born here. When a woman of 99 died here the other day, having been brought to the Eastern Shore as a babe of three months, the headline in the local newspaper read, 'Baltimore woman dies'. There is a tradition of family life and hospitality warmer than in any other part of the US. They are hard-working, strong, humorous and brave.

I have certainly found evidence of this in my own entertainment. I am staying with Kathy Cousins and her husband Wid Washburn, at Clifton, their plantation house some 30 miles north of the Virginia–Maryland border. It's an ample brick house of about 1810, looking across its garden to a wide river-mouth. Juliet and James had driven from New York, and Amy Henderson of the National Portrait Gallery came from Washington. There was also a delightful lady from Georgetown, Catherine Morrison – a painter would find it almost impossible to catch the sparkle of humour in her eyes. Many other guests were added for meals. We sat down sixteen for lunch on Sunday. One of them was the most famous living American after the President, Frank Perdue. Never heard of him? Nor had I. That shows that we don't watch American television. In a recent poll he achieved '99 per cent recognition in Manhattan'. The remaining 1 per cent mistook him for Mayor Koch. He breeds chickens in millions, and appears on his own commercials making wry jokes about them. That's why he's famous.

Our party's motorcade travelled many miles over the flat country. We saw the little town of Princess Anne, boxed together in tight white houses, and were received cordially in one of the largest of them, a collector's dream-house belonging to William Fehsenfeld. In the open country we visited Liberty Hall, the property of Ted Dorman, seventeenth-century in origin, from the evidence of adzed beams in its cellar. Its garden is patrolled by peacocks. Earlier, by myself, I'd seen Eyre Hall (Furlong Baldwin). All these country houses sustain the legend that the Eastern Shore preserves something of an older way of life – little altered for two hundred years, isolated, within easy reach of creeks, hospitable and calm. It's not unlike parts of East Anglia.

The most original of our expeditions was to learn about crab-fishing. We were too early in the season actually to meet a crab, except frozen in plastic packets and later sautéed for lunch, but the process was explained to us by a wonderful Captain Courageous figure called Bob Kolscher. The crab has a dull life, which only at the very end turns adventurous and cannibalistic, when it crawls after bait into a large wire creel, and can't get out. Mr Kolscher was a cornucopia of information about its habits, and even more about the habits of the fishermen. When he said that one of them would never drink on Sundays 'because the Master would disapprove', Juliet asked innocently who the Master was. 'God,' he replied. That's one characteristic of the people, a deep Methodist faith. Another is their intense commercial rivalry. Even brothers (and the trade here seems to be dominated by a single family, the Bozmans) will not reveal to each other their deals and methods.

As we were leaving the crab-harbour, I asked Kathy if the motorcade could stop for a moment beside a small wood on our way to the next house. Kathy said, 'Oh they've got several restaurants there.' At least, that is what I thought she said, being almost as deaf and dumb as a crab. I replied, 'I don't think you quite understand my need.' 'Rest-rooms,' hissed Juliet, scarlet with shame at her father's obtuseness.

Most of the guests left on Sunday evening, and I was alone for dinner with Wid and Kathy, and Richard Conroy and his wife Sarah Booth, she a staff-writer on the *Washington Post*. They talked politics, Republican (our hosts) versus Democrat, and almost for the first time I saw where the divisions lay. Should black girls be discouraged from having bastard children by denying them child-aid? Should the unemployed lose their compensation if they consistently refuse jobs? Is Russia still committed to world domination? How can we de-escalate the arms race? I kept quiet while this articulate, animated debate continued round the table, and loved these people for their vigour and concern.

Galilee Harbor, Sausalito, California

Sunday 6 April

ADAM *to Nigel*   I went to a lesbian basketball match last night. A friend of Madeline Moore's had a ticket to spare and of course I went like a shot. The match was between San Francisco and Los Angeles and the idea was to raise money for the Gay Games to be held here in August. The lady I bought the ticket from explained that it should have been the Gay *Olympics*, but, even though there had been the 'Special Olympics' (US euphemism for disabled) and even the 'Nude Olympics', the Supreme Court had ruled that the gays weren't allowed to use the term. So Gay Games. I turned up at the stadium in the Haight district of the city. It was 8 at night and I put on my tweed jacket to look straight. Strictly the observer. Two thousand lesbians were queuing to get in. 'Everything is extremely negotiable,' I heard across the waiting crowd, but lost the rest of the message in the hubbub. 'He's a snotty little yuppy at the moment, but you wait, he's working up to be a pissy queen ...' 'They have some quite *terrible* diseases over there ...' 'Did you see that in the papers? Sixty-eight people in the city died of AIDS in March?' And the answer: 'Some people just don't know how to behave properly do they?' I checked this figure this morning: 68 deaths in March, 75 new cases. Almost ten thousand people have died of AIDS in the US, over a thousand of them in San Francisco. But that wasn't the tone here at all. No sense of the gay community battening down. This was explosive. 'What's the matter, Baby,' a nun with a beard and sparkle all over his eyelids said to me. 'Got no date?' 'I'm fine thanks,' I said like Lord Hailsham and he walked off, holding his habit out on either side like a spinnaker and saying, 'Oooooh, I see.' 'No, it's *not*. It's the *exchange* of bodily fluids ...' Only in San Francisco. I looked around me. There was something strange in a gathering of two thousand people simply on the basis of their sexual proclivities, but if I hadn't known that was the reason they were there, I couldn't have guessed it. A complete spectrum surrounded me, all the way from snotty yuppy to pissy queen, moving through austere, superior New York nose-lookers, chummy vegetarians, and muscle-bound sports fanatics, bypassing all too ordinary ordinaries like me on the way.

The heart of the evening was the basketball but that was by no means everything. Our hosts were Patrick Toner, Mr International Leather (distinguished by a sculpted black codpiece) and Sister Boom Boom, who, the rumour went, had recently got married. Toner was overshadowed by Boom Boom. She/he was carried in shoulder-high by four near-naked men. Surrounding her on the platform were several small palm trees to go with the leopardskin coif (is that the word?) 'I knew this was a big game', she said, 'and so I thought I'd wear my big-game outfit.' Cheers from the crowd. Then the Pre-Game Entertainment. The San Francisco Gay Freedom Day Marching Band – nice uniforms, pretty tunes. Then the crowning of the Homecoming Queen, Sister Chanel 2001, in scarlet silk with an oversize crucifix in her hair. Then thanks to the organisers, the Sisters of Perpetual Indulgence, particularly Sister Sadie Sadie the Rabbi Lady, Sister Loganberry Frost, Sister Hysterectoria, Sister Nocturnal Submission and Sister Krishna Kosher, who had done the lighting. Sister Amazing Grace Cathedral and Sister Salvation Armée then ran up and down the court with brooms, preparing it for the game. More applause and then the National Anthem by the San Francisco Gay Lesbian Chorus. They had already featured quite heavily in the crowning of Sister Chanel 2001. They too were in scarlet silk. (I'm not sure if I have adequately conveyed the fact that these people I am talking about are *men*. Most of them had beards, incredible figures and hair like Jackie Onassis. A gay lesbian, I think, is a man who dresses up as a woman but still is attracted only to women. I may be wrong about that.) The 'Star-Spangled Banner' began and to my amazement everybody stood up. *There* is the strength in this country. Even this incredibly marginal and wild crowd stands up and looks serious for the National Anthem, as if they were delegates to a bankers' convention in Kansas City. No wonder rebels feel frustrated here. Then we sat down and Sister Vicious Power Hungry Bitch announced the names of the players.

The game was a steal, as the saying goes. Los Angeles walked it 106–78. They had one genius and beautiful player. 'Hasn't that No. 4 got a cute body?' the woman sitting next to me asked. 'She plays basketball very well,' I said. 'I've always wanted a body like that,' she went on ambiguously, trailing off in a string of adjectives. I was the only person to cheer for Los Angeles, having developed an affection for that city. (Jeanne says I have a Los Angeles accent, but I know she's a clever flatterer.) Whenever San Francisco managed to pop one in, the band played a snatch of 'Ain't Misbehaving'. At half-time we had a thrilling display of karate by a woman who looked like a colonel in the Green Berets. Everyone sat in awed silence while she destroyed invisible enemies.

Clifton–Washington, DC

Monday 7 April

NIGEL *to Adam*   Here I am in the capital, after a three-hour drive through Maryland. Usually I love the way Washington draws the new arrival into the city by avenues and tree-lined creeks (of all the capitals I've known, it proclaims its importance most graciously), but on this occasion I foolishly lost my way and got snarled up and shouted at in the city centre. Nothing is more tedious than other people's traffic problems, nor more quickly forgotten when the sufferer eventually makes it, in my case to the house in Alexandria belonging to Roger and Frances Kennedy.

Their house lies with others on a hill. That might mean almost anything – a chute of bungalows on an ancient coal-tip – but here it means a multi-variety orchard rising and falling in quite strong undulations to conceal widely spaced multi-variety houses of the American upper-middle suburban type, what Hugh Brogan has called 'one of the great civilised achievements of all history'. It is *rus in urbe*, privacy within a community. There's a fence between the Kennedys' property and their neighbour, but although the posts stand sturdily in line, they are not filled in by horizontal slabs. This seems to me symbolic of the American character – you stake out your own territory and defend it stoutly, but you do not resent a passer-by looking in. If he looked into the Kennedy house, he would notice its creaminess, its faintly Japanese air, its open plan, its clean geometry, the incorporation of old coloured glass in the windows, and its efficiency – everything works. It's also a smoke-free zone, which does marvels for my health and self-control.

I walked through Alexandria. I suppose that with its companion, Georgetown, these are the two places where American Juliet/Jameses must aspire to live one day. Georgetown is for the more ambitious and the successfully retired, Alexandria for those who take life a little, but only a little, more easily. There is more privacy here, fewer competitive parties, less rush, a more generous mix of rich and less rich. It shows in the façades of the eighteenth/nineteenth-century streets. Some houses would qualify as mansions, others are apparently one room up, one down, and from outside they look like a row of playing cards dealt from a dozen different packs, all beautifully restored, Anglophile, door-knockers shining, street numbers written in italic script, toy lanterns, pansies in tubs, windows with shutters tied back. One might be in the smarter part of Norwich. The modern town has piped down to conform. McDonalds are denied their yellow hoops, which appear only in miniature as door-handles. The Holiday Inn looks like a caravanserai in Fez. Shopping areas are patioed. I went into the old church, all white and balconied inside, and was offered the choice between General Washington's pew and General Lee's. I took Washington's, and thought, as far as I could remember or imagine them, the thoughts he had on the morrow of his victory over us.

I reached Georgetown by the new subway and walked a few blocks to call on Susan Mary Alsop in 29th Street. Her downstairs rooms look more French than English, and her maid is French, for she spent part of her early life in Paris, but Susan Mary herself is unmistakably American, overflowing with energy and offers of help. No sooner had I unfolded my now grubby sketch-map of our two routes than out came her address book and she was fast scribbling names of friends in Chicago for me and of her daughter in Salt Lake City for you, and the telephone went to work to ensure that neither of us will feel lonely in the middle of the middle-land.

The Kennedys are an eager couple. John Julius Norwich, who introduced us, told me that seldom has he taken more instantly to a man, and I felt the same about both of them. He is not an academic by upbringing, but has made money in business, run for Congress, written several books on architecture, remodelled his house to *House and Garden* worthiness, and was appointed Director of the Museum of American History because it was thought, rightly, that he would bring to the job a fresh flair. His wife Frances has American-Indian blood in her (how much they are not quite sure), and it shows slightly in her physiognomy and slender figure, in the precision of her movements – or am I imagining this? – when cooking or tending seedlings, and in her concern for pure foods, some of which she grows herself in the garden. I enjoyed my dinner alone with them. He is a thoughtful man. There are pauses between his sentences while he ruminates for the exact phrase to follow.

Washington DC

Tuesday 8 April

NIGEL *to Adam*   I was driven to the Museum of American History by its Director. It is a huge building, and needs to be because it contains huge exhibits, like the oldest steam-engine to run on American rails, Washington's campaign-marquee, and the giant flag (fifteen stars, eight stripes) which was raised over a Baltimore fort in 1814 and inspired Francis Scott Key to write 'The Star-Spangled Banner'. It is so precious a relic that to protect it from glare it is concealed behind a painted screen which once every hour moves slowly and religiously to reveal the original for a few moments, while the famous tune is played to crowds of awestruck children. The Museum suffers a bit from having been a Museum of Technology as well as of History. While there is little about the colonial period and the discovery of the West, there are great halls filled with pieces of machinery. Roger Kennedy is changing much of this. He wants to focus attention on what the common man and woman achieved, and move away from the hero concept of history.

Washington was looking lovely in the spring. Everyone said how lucky I was to be here in a week when cherry-blossom and mild sunshine are coinciding. I walked a mile to the Library of Congress, where in a deep-piled and soothing office I met my sponsor, Robert Saudek, and my intermediary, Ms McCormick, who had arranged for me to see a senator, Charles Mathias of Maryland, a Republican on its more liberal wing. Everyone I'd met had spoken of him with affection.

His office is not in the Capitol but in a vast building to one side of it, and you approach him through security checks and then a succession of outer offices womanned by aides of mounting courtesy, until you reach the sanctum. There stood Senator Mathias to greet me, a man of about 60, imposing, open-faced, skilled at pleasing, frank, every inch a senator, as solid as the Constitution. His private office was not so smart as I'd expected. No bare leather-topped desk flanked by flags, but a workroom with books around it and a mass of urgent paper. We sat. We talked. His lawyer came in, remained silent.

I asked him about Civil Rights, nothing else. As a boy he had actually known old men who had been slaves when they were boys. He told me how black families moved north slowly, after emancipation, and later, during the 1930s Depression, very rapidly, 'the greatest mass-movement of people in the history of the world', he said with surprising hyperbole. They were country people who on arrival found it difficult to adapt to urban life, and there were difficulties. After the Second World War, under Truman, Eisenhower and Johnson (his presidential roll left a few significant gaps), Civil Rights slowly advanced. Names made famous by the long controversy – Brown, Little Rock, Meredith, King – slipped in and out of the conversation.

'What exactly did Martin Luther King achieve?' I asked.

'I have a strong feeling about that. We went through a dreadful civil war basically on this issue. We went through a hundred years at the end of that war of very uneasy race relationships. Although the Civil War ended slavery, it did not reconcile the American people, in the sense that black and white would live easily together. And I think that Martin Luther King primarily brought about that reconciliation.'

'You think that the two races are now reconciled? But any visitor to your country like myself cannot fail to see evidence that the blacks live in the poorest conditions, that there is a higher rate of unemployment among them, that they are less well educated.'

'I would agree absolutely with that, and I wouldn't argue that reconciliation is perfect. Economic equality will take time, but reconciliation means in my terms that for the first time in American history, a black American has an opportunity to climb out of the ghetto, to have an education, a better life. But there's a long way to go.'

'Do the poorest blacks feel they have the respect of the whites?'

'I genuinely think they do. I'm really amazed that in my lifetime there is a genuine feeling of acceptance and respect between black and white. It's a profound change. You see it in so many respects – business, judgeships, academic life. What we must do is to increase blacks' opportunities for education and training. Only if we do that will young blacks get the better jobs.'

'How about children? Do they sense a colour bar?'

'Well', replied the Senator, 'take my own children. They have no such feelings whatever. They're absolutely colour-blind.'

I was impressed by his optimism. How far a man like this has come from Jefferson's grim prophecy:

> Deep-rooted prejudices entertained by the whites, ten thousand recollections, by the blacks, of the injuries they have sustained, new provocations, the real distinctions that nature has made, and many other circumstances, will divide us into parties and produce convulsions which will probably never end but in the extermination of the one or the other race.

I did not quote this to Senator Mathias, though I had it in my notes. I thought it would be painful to this kind man. Having promised me thirty minutes of his time, he gave me forty, as the tape shows.

This evening the Kennedys took me to a dinner-party given by James and Sylvia Symington to celebrate the publication of Roger's latest book, *Architecture, Men, Women and Money in America 1600–1860*. That's quite a title, and it was quite a dinner. Twenty people sat down at three tables set up in contiguous rooms. I was given a little card which said Dr, not Doctor but Dining-room. For the social record, I must say that not a single person smoked a single cigarette throughout the evening, eighteen of us because we didn't want to, and two because we didn't dare. Speeches were made. Songs were sung, one of them Irish, 'for the benefit of our British guest'.

Frances Kennedy had given me a run-down of the guest-list beforehand, and I tried to relate her descriptions to their faces. I failed terribly. Who was the woman 'who represents all that is good in Washington' (Bitsey Folger)? Who the TV commentator whom Roger praised as the most agile in the country (Jim Lehrer)? They were present, but where? I spoke to John Reinhardt, former US Ambassador to Nigeria, a black man with so humorous a face that one could not help but beam when talking to him. And to Edmund Morris, whose book on Theodore Roosevelt was so sensationally successful that Reagan has now invited him to be his official biographer. He sees the President once a month. What a strange experience that must be! We talked briefly about discretion in biography. How much should a biographer tell? He looks a little like Lytton Strachey, but is obviously less vituperative. I sat between his wife Sylvia and our hostess. This is a world, I thought, whose only equivalent in London are George Weidenfeld's parties – politics, the arts, journalism, business – all combined in easy familiarity, relaxed, merry and sophisticated. People of power and influence, but not displaying it.

Galilee Harbor, Sausalito, California

Tuesday 8 April

ADAM *to Nigel*   We spoke on the phone last night and you asked why
                         I didn't respond more to what you say in your letters.
There are various reasons, some superficial, some more deep-seated. First, and easiest to explain, is that there is so little time and space to get everything in and everything done. We are both finding ourselves awash in the sea of information and ideas that America pours over us. Too much attention to what's happening in our letters means less attention to what is happening outside, and I feel more of a responsibility to get out and do that and think about that, than towards any immediate reaction to what you have to say. But that, I think, is either an excuse or a symptom of something that lies much deeper. I could say that our dialogue should consist merely in the laying down of attitudes and reactions side by side, with the differences displayed and the response no more than implied, but that too is a rationalisation. I feel – and this is hardly examined – a strong desire to communicate with you and an equally strong reluctance to do so. This is why the Oedipuses were such a tense and peculiar family. I have of course often tried to think why this should be so, but with little success. It is no good saying that it is the archetypal father–son relationship (which I nevertheless imagine it to be). The question is why this interbedded reluctance and desire should *be* the archetype.

The orthodox psychologist *would* say that the roots of it must lie in some early event or series of events in my life, which are, of course, irrecoverable, but I can at least remember as a teenager trying to talk to you and feeling hopelessly powerless in any conversation. I would make a sally and you – as I saw it then, or at least as I remember it now – would pick that small thing up, toss it around, dissect it and effectively destroy it. Any cruelty was of course unintentional and I understand now that you must have been at least as desperate as I was to make some sort of contact beyond the absurd formalities that we occasionally engaged in. The effect was to destroy any trust on my part. The point about any real communication is that each side must leave open, trailing, vulnerable edges, which the other person will either string on from or, if he is insensitive, will bruise or even crush. If that happens too much, as I felt it happened between me and you, then the child, who is obviously the weaker and the less competent of the two, will no longer leave those vulnerable edges exposed and will present closed-off nuggets of himself to his father, which are as hard and shiny as he can make them. They are no longer friendly things, but more like debating points or propaganda positions. And the father, who may not even be aware that this is happening, is left with his trailing edges untaken up, neglected and spurned.

This is my picture of what has happened between us over the last fifteen years or so. Those nuggets I have been bowling at you for all that time have had a great deal of love bound up inside them, but it has had no chance of penetrating beyond the armoured shell. The result (another picture, but I think in pictures) is like two electric poles (are they called diodes?) set a few inches apart but with a massive voltage across them. For most of the time they are silent as if there were no energy there at all, but occasionally, with a mild fluctuation in the air or the temperature or something, a huge blue electric flash will cross that gap. There is no room in this arrangement for a steady, equable flow of current between the two poles. It's either nothing or everything, the reluctance or the desire. There is another possibility, which this picture does not fit. The father and the child can simply play rather public roles to each other, affably communicating on a level that doesn't even recognise this problem of power and love, of inheritance and usurping. (*Lear* is the best thing that has ever been written about the way that fathers and children can and cannot communicate.) That affability, it seems to me, is the way in which you and your father managed so well and how you and Juliet have always communicated. My electric pole system is how you and I, you and Rebecca and, maybe, Ben and your parents have/have not managed. This is late at night. I'm not sure how much sense it is making. I've been on the campus at Berkeley all day, but I must tell you about that tomorrow.

Wednesday 9 April

NIGEL *to Adam*   I was sorry to miss seeing again the Treasure Houses
                       of Britain (silly title) exhibition at the National
Gallery. If I'd been more foreseeing, I'd have asked to meet Carter Brown,
its Director. I saw it on the day after its formal opening last November, and
was amazed by the triumph of persuasion, organisation, transport, insurance
and display it represented. It shows, of course, our best in the best possible
conditions, and it could be said that no English house looks like this because
everything here is perfect – no clutter, no flaked paint, scuffed carpet or
chipped enamel – but the purpose was to illustrate the finest things of which
our artists and craftsmen were capable during our centuries of glory, and it
does just that. There's a decline after about 1780. We lost our instinctive
taste more rapidly than the Americans (I'm still haunted by Savannah), and
the twentieth-century exhibits are tawdry in comparison with what preceded
them. The exhibition has been a wild success. Superlatives have multiplied
during these six months. Now it is ending, and the silver table will return to
Knole, the great sofa to Kedleston, the chinoiserie bed to Calke Abbey, the
girandoles to Plas Newydd, and we'll see them next in their familiar homes,
more in context there but looking a little less splendid.

I've driven only 50 miles today, to Burr Ridge, a house near Leesburg, north-
west of Washington, but 750 feet more elevated, which shows in the backward
growth of spring flowers and leaves. The house belongs to Powell and Agnes
Harrison. It is a white-columned house with a large drawing-room and a tiny
suite of bedroom, bath and study which they have allotted to me, in addition
to an upper-floor room where I can type. The view from the window is across
the Potomac to the Blue Ridge Mountains, perfect Virginia country, where
the Confederates manœuvred against the Union. I cannot get that war out
of my mind. More Americans were killed in it than in the First and Second
World Wars combined. It is like the battlefields of northern Europe, each
bloodstained patch marked by a metal plaque. To one of the Harrisons'
other guests I called it 'the unnecessary war'. She reproved me strongly.
She was not going to mention the unnecessary wars that we have fought.
1812?

I arrived to find the Harrisons distressed by an absurd incident which
occurred today. Agnes had publicly opposed some application by a political
eccentric called Lyndon LaRouche, who has stood three times for President,
and he had rounded on her and some others by calling them Soviet fellow-
travellers and connected with the international drug traffic. It was all in the

newspapers and on television. Why such a ridiculous charge has become national news I cannot explain, but Agnes took it all with creditable calm. She has sent packing a *New York Times* photographer who pleaded for a picture. And in the middle of all this she gave a dinner-party for eighteen people. Tomorrow is her birthday.

It was quite splendid. Silver, black servants, candles, peanut soup, Virginia ham, strawberry shortcake, husbands with wives, wives with husbands, and Powell made a speech. I replied shortly, but he urged me to tell them the story of our book and travels. So I did, the first time I've semi-publicly described it. I notice that it arouses wonder, curiosity and slight apprehension in that order. I assured them that I would not quote the lady on my right about American doctors, nor the eloquent lawyer opposite me on the menace of the libel laws. I'd like to, for both were formidably outspoken. Another lady told me that her daughter's life had been radically transformed by *Portrait of a Marriage*, and a man that Leesburg was the fastest growing town in Virginia, though it has lost its trains, the very tracks uprooted in surrender to the car. I met a fellow Napoleon-buff, who had actually read my book. Of such conversations are my days composed. I never cease to relish them. As my father once said to me, and you have since quoted, only one person in a thousand is a bore, and he is interesting because he is one person in a thousand. There were no bores at Burr Ridge.

Galilee Harbor, Sausalito, California

Wednesday 9 April

ADAM *to Nigel*   I got to Berkeley at half past six in the morning. The Bay was looking beautiful as I slid over the Golden Gate and then through the City, over the Bay Bridge, an incredible steel thing, no grace in it, but a double-decker from San Francisco to Oakland, hinged to an island which the two-level freeway, westbound on top, eastbound below, drives straight through in a tunnel. There's no room for these engineering heroics in England. So I was pleased with America when I arrived at the UC campus. This was a country where things were great, where people could measure up to the scale of their surroundings. None of the itsy-bitsy National Trust æsthetic here, but daring, confidence and achievement. (This is sounding more like you, the result of a great deal of work on my negative attitude problem.) And the look of the campus, even so early in the morning, shared that pushed-out-chest style of American confidence. The faculties ranged up the hillside like opera patrons in an auditorium, large semi-classical buildings with BIOLOGY or HISTORY incised on their friezes in 10-foot-high Garamond. But I wasn't here for architecture. I heard on the radio Monday night that the students were going to blockade California Hall (or Winnie Mandela Hall as they have renamed it), where the university administration has its headquarters. Last week there was a major riot, the biggest since the early '70s, in which about ninety people had been arrested. The local press had a field day over this because forty of the ninety were not students but 'outside agitators'. The riot had been sparked off when the police tried to remove a shanty town from outside California Hall built to symbolise the students' solidarity with the people of Crossroads. The blockade was a follow up to that. Nobody was there when I arrived except press and TV people (about sixty of them) and the police, standing around with truncheons in their belts and riot helmets swinging from their hips. 'The worst part of this is the waiting,' a policeman said to me. He had been at the riot last week. 'Now you will have read in the papers', he said to me through his dark glasses, silver rims, getting slightly less dark towards the bottom, 'that we hit people over the head. There is no truth in that. We do not hit people over the head. We use the shoulder as a disabling point,' and touched my shoulder to show what he meant. 'Most of these kids are here for an education,' he went on and then added a few remarks about the outside agitators, calling them 'bozos', which, so I'm told, is a patronising variant on 'jerk'. He chewed gum and was a little nervous. It was now 6.50. The blockade was due to start at 7. Disabling with a blow to the shoulder was a 'standard procedure' he repeated. I said I'd got the point.

The reporters talked to each other, looking over each other's shoulders with that quick, acquisitive look I realise I must share. Most of us were shabby. Only the local TV news reporter, a young woman in a hair-do and plum-coloured wool suit, looked as if she had any style. At 7 on the dot the students turned up, about two hundred of them, some with the word 'Banned' pinned to their hats or jackets. Others were labelled 'Outside Agitator'. Nothing is more easily manufactured than martyrs. The police chewed their gum a little faster and the protesters sat down in front of the four doors of the building. Everything quite relaxed. The staff were not due to arrive until 8. 'Hey, hey, ho ho, Apartheid has got to go,' the blockaders began but it tailed away. 'Too fucking early,' someone said. The University of California has $2.4 billion invested in companies that deal with South Africa. The protest wanted that money out. 'You see that guy over there?' a student said to me, pointing at a grizzled man in a blue anorak and dark glasses. 'That man is a policeman. He nearly killed a guy last week.' The man stood slightly apart with his hands in his pockets. 'We call him Choke Hold.' I looked at him more closely. He hadn't shaved properly in a patch just under his jaw on the left hand side. There was no telling if he was violent or not. He suddenly pulled at the top of his anorak and spoke down into it. There was a radio inside.

It was now coming up to 8 o'clock. The number of protesters had risen to about a thousand. There were still only twenty or thirty policemen. Nobody wanted another riot. 'They don't want to arrest more than they have to,' my informant said. 'They don't like the paperwork.' There were tom-tom drums going now. A woman in a turquoise T-shirt had brought in a collection of placards which she distributed. I said I was a member of the press. People not sitting down at the doors were marching round and round the building. 'No standing around allowed,' the organiser of the event shouted through a megaphone. To me, perhaps deliberately, he looked like Malcolm X, a tall thin man with a scratchy beard. There was some real energy and excitement here, a sense of something building to a crisis, but behind it all, not voiced but in everyone's mind, was the memory of the '60s, when it was not one issue at stake but a whole world, a whole life revolution. In a way it's like the memory of an affair that went wrong. It's too near in the common memory for a repeat version to have any conviction. 'If this had been 68', a man outside the east door said, 'that damn thing would have been down half an hour ago.' 'And if this had been 68,' the guy next to him said, 'Managua would have been bombed two years ago.' The memory cuts both ways.

Behind the door the policemen pushed their faces against the glass, whitening patches on their cheeks, to see what was happening in the now loud and chaotic mêlée outside. 'Get your asses out of classes, Come on out and join the masses.' A priest in a dog collar, corduroy cap and Nike sneakers said this was great. A woman repainted the smears on the CND mask her friend had drawn on her face while the crowd chanted 'Fired up, shut it down. Fired up, shut it down.' A young black girl was speaking into a TV camera while the plum suit stood by nodding. 'There was no holding back there *at all*,' the black girl said. 'One of those guys, he was from Alameda County PD, he said "Look, we're going to break your ass. We're going to twist your wrists, so shut the fuck up."' I didn't see that getting on to the early evening bulletin. A sudden kerfuffle outside the west door. A police cameraman was filming the faces of people blocking the door. Students were trying to put placards between the camera and the faces. 'What's the matter with you?' someone shouted at the cameraman. 'Can't you get another job? Can't you worm your way into some other little hole?' Then the man who was shouting these things was interrupted by a marshal, a student officer of some kind, who said that they had agreed not to harass the police. 'OK, but I'm an individual aren't I? If I feel like asking the guy a few questions, I can ask them can't I?' 'Yeah, but it's probably better not to.' 'Yeah, but I can if I want to, right?' And while they argued the cameraman sloped off with his escort to capture more faces elsewhere. It was now 8.15. One or two of the university administration employees were standing around at the edge of the crowd in beige dresses and make-up. 'I have sympathy with what these guys are doing,' one of them said to me. 'I've been working here twenty-five years and whenever something like this happens the administration usually does something about the issue.' Then she talked about the thousands arrested here in the old days – this ubiquitous nostalgia – and said 'But I don't like the violence. I don't like that at all.' 'Apartheid, apartheid, apartheid's on fire. We don't need the water, let the flames burn higher' suddenly emerged, spreading like its metaphor all the way around the building, a great roaring uncoordinated chant. This felt like the beginning of something really violent, and it was frightening and thrilling but, as it turned out, it was the climax. The rumour ran round that the employees had been told not to come to work until 1.30 in the afternoon. The Malcolm X figure announced this at the west door with tangible dis-appointment in his voice. 'So it looks as though there are going to be no arrests this morning. But' – and with this a rewinding of the enthusiasm spring – 'I think we should see that as a victory. We have closed down Calif . . . Winnie Mandela Hall for an entire morning!' Cheers of encouragement and self-encouragement from the blockaders. But the sting had been taken out of it.

I sat down on the grass next to a large man with a huge head of black hair. I went and had breakfast with him in a café. He was older than most of the students and before coming here had worked and lived in the slums of St Louis. He felt a sort of hopelessness or at least an irrelevance in everything that we had seen. He saw the people playing little more than a self-gratifying game. 'You only have to look at the faces of those people who are wearing their "banned" stickers to see what it's about. There's a sort of self-con-gratulation there, another item for their private résumé of Things I Have Done in My Life: Gone to Berkeley; Banned from Campus; Became a Tax Lawyer. There's nothing in it.' I liked him. His mother was the daughter of an admiral and had been something of a wild girl. His father was Japanese–American and had been interned in one of the camps during the war. With that background it must have taken some courage to marry him. What would he do with his life? He thought he might go into the State Department. I asked him if he was thinking about Burgess and Maclean. 'You could say that's one model,' he said and laughed. He was one of those people you couldn't tell whether he meant what he said or not. Then we talked about *Frontiers*.

Later on at midday there was a large open air meeting about the plan to remove ten thousand Indians (or native Americans as I should call them) from Big Mountain in Arizona in order to strip-mine the billions of tons of coal that lie beneath it. Only one man spoke with any great persuasion. He was Bill Wahpepah, a native American and lobbyist for the Indian cause. 'There is a silence about the American Indian peoples,' he said. 'The Americans are blind to the struggle in their own country. They talk about South Africa, about Belfast, about Central America, but there is a silence about the American Indians and their struggle with the profit-orientated mechanisms which are taking away and destroying their sacred lands here in the United States. I am happy to see you people here today, but don't let this be a trend, a fashion. Make this a commitment. Think of those blind robots, those power-seekers lined up under the garage over here. Don't let this be a small memory when you are in your lawyer's office or your accountant's office or your comfortable home. Fight for justice for the rest of your life, justice for the robots next door, dressed up to harm other human beings. Be brave, brothers and sisters, be brave.' We were all cheering at the end of that.

Today I went to visit the Green Gulch Farm Zen Center. I had met a French woman called Luce at a play on Sunday. She was wearing a black and yellow skin, a cyclist's uniform which had 'Peugeot' written down the length of her thigh. 'Do you like bicycling?' 'I've never done it in my life,' she said. But the image was good. Nothing goes down better than dynamic health. 'I like you because you are serious,' she said. ('Serious', like 'intelligent', is one of the major plus adjectives in California at the moment. No one who is really hip or great says hip or great any more. They (we) say 'Hey, that's *serious!*' or 'What an *intelligent* choice!') But then she went on, 'You know, I don't think your head is attached to your body,' and drew her finger across her throat like a razor. I said I still believed in rational thought. She said, 'It's one Universe, right?' and then claimed that Plato had destroyed western civilisation. I mentioned Descartes. She said, 'I know where you're coming from, but you've got a long way to go.' She told me to go to the Zen Center to try and catch up.

It's a beautiful place, a collection of neat tree-fringed buildings in a long green valley running down from the Marin County ridge to the ocean. I went for a long walk down the valley and back up with the director, a New Yorker called Norman Fischer. He used to work on the *Wall Street Journal* but is now a Buddhist priest and poet. People were working in the narrow fields, tending and watering the vegetables they grow for grocery stores and a restaurant in the city. I asked him – it was a stiff, prepared, first question – if the incredible wealth of Mill Valley and Sausalito stimulated or dulled the appetite for a spiritual side to life. He roared with laughter. 'I haven't the faintest idea!' he said and spat at a bush. This was a Zen answer. The great Zen masters in Japan have been known to slap people in the face when

confronted with this kind of question. I had got off lightly. Then we talked
about less pretentious things – the running of the farm, the economics of the
place (it is slightly less than self-sufficient), the connections of this centre with
the sources of the idea across the Pacific (not strong and not constant). Like
any missionary church, the Californian version of Zen is moving off along its
own tracks, influenced and moulded by the culture in which it is now to be
found. There was a real seriousness in this man which I admired. Traditional
Zen, he said, had placed insight or wisdom at the core. A subtle shift had
occurred here. Traditionally Japan was a communal society in which wisdom
had come to be seen as an isolated and private affair. In America, this had
turned upside down because of America's insistence on the individuality and
isolation of its people. Wisdom in this kind of society could be equated with
a sense of compassion, a recognition of the things that tie people to each other.
It was the wisest thing I had heard for months. He gave me a book of his
poems. It was called *Why People Lack Confidence in Chairs*. I had once read
something by Koestler who said that, when he learnt that most of the atoms
of which chairs were composed are no more than organised emptiness, he felt
a sudden vertigo and nausea. Was this in the back of Fischer's mind? No, it
was far more ordinary than that. Only that whenever people sat down in a
chair, unless they were extraordinarily circumspect, they weren't actually
looking at it. There was an ever-present anxiety, he said, that the chair might
not be there. I'm not sure yet if this idea can be generalised for America as a
whole.

Leesburg–Gettysburg–Carlisle, Pennsylvania

Thursday 10 April

NIGEL *to Adam*   Noticing signposts to Gettysburg, I could not resist
                    diverging to see the most famous of American battle-
fields. I was left in no doubt that it is the most famous, for never have I seen,
not at Waterloo, not at Borodino, so many memorials nor so brilliant an
exposition of what happens in a battle. There's a museum, a cyclorama, and
an immensely tall observation-tower. There are marked routes for touring the
battlefield by foot, bicycle or car. Don't let me give the impression that it is
overdone. All the new buildings are sited away from the main battlefield, which
is left clear except for small effigies and inscribed rocks. The diagrammatic map
is wonderful. It lies on the floor of a square auditorium, and as the voice-over
tells the story of the battle (in July 1863, in case you'd forgotten), little
coloured lights indicate the movement and clash of armies. The diorama is
less successful. You cannot imagine yourself in the middle of a painted battle

scene because the eye hasn't got a 360° span, and the end of the diorama has to fuse with the beginning.

I walked the central part of the battlefield against a wind that had suddenly turned icy. I wondered yet again how so many thousands of young men, all of the same nation, could have found the spirit to endure what they endured and slaughter each other for a cause which was in any case nebulous from the start, and must have faded as the war progressed. They probably hated their sergeant-major far more than the enemy. Wars, including my war, cannot be fought except with the consent of the private soldiers on each side, and they are the very people who stand most to lose (their lives) and least to gain by victory. Why do they do it? Because the momentum of an army is unstoppable? Because its cohesion in drill and on the march prevents a man from dropping out, and when battle is joined, the same applies – he cannot escape, so he goes on?

That's the only way I can explain the horror of Gettysburg. Fifty thousand men died, were wounded or missing on these fields and ridges. Photography came just in time to record the scene, corpses lying in rows like game after an Edwardian shoot. They were not beautiful. Uniforms were shoddy, young faces prematurely aged by beards, and death came in its most ungainly forms. The beauty lies only in the melancholy of the recollection, and in the manuscript of Lincoln's address, shown like the holy grail alone in a dimly lit cubicle. As I read the familiar words written by his own hand, I remembered how once Virginia Woolf opened a discussion on style by asking whether '. . . shall not perish from the earth' would not be better as 'this earth'. I still think it would.

Carlisle is only 30 miles north of the battlefield. I parked the car, shopped for 10 minutes, and returned to find it ticketed for misparking. When I paid my $2 fine at the police station, they said, 'Welcome to Carlisle', quite nicely. But my real welcome was delayed till I rang the bell at the house of the President of Dickinson College, Samuel Banks, and his wife, my former collaborator and closest American friend, Joanne Trautmann. She came to the door. We embraced. She showed me to a bedroom of presidential magnificence and sybaritic comfort, but they would not allow me to change out of my campaigning clothes for dinner. We three were alone. They considered that the ultimate proof of friendship was that no special effort should be made by me. It was by them. The dinner was delicious.

Afterwards Sam walked me round part of the College in the darkness. We went to the library which at 10 p.m. was still in full operation, and then to his own office, where the latest in high-tech helps him manage the affairs of this famous place. He spoke of Jo's contribution to his and its happiness.

First lady of the Campus, and still a teacher in her own right, an author too, she is perfect for the role, and finds the role perfect. Jointly they entertain the faculty, the students, the alumni and distinguished visitors in this lovely spacious house. Sam gave me a very funny description of how he raises money for his College, one of the President's main jobs, which I would hate. He gave up hating it thirty years ago. 'How much?' asks his pinioned victim. '20,000 dollars ...', says Sam (relieved consent shows on the donor's face), '... annually for the next five years.'

St Helena, Napa Valley, California

Thursday 10 April

ADAM *to Nigel*   A thrilling day. David Barry had fixed up for me to visit a motor racing school half an hour north of the city. (I've now left the Bay and I haven't even described to you a long walk I took through San Francisco the other day, my dominant impression one of undistributed wealth, that ever-present and disregarded conscience of this country. But of course it was exciting too. I went to visit the 800 feet high obelisk office block called the Transamerica Tower, which has become a symbol of San Francisco almost as potent as the Golden Gate Bridge. I met a lady called Beatrice in Corporate Communications. Was it true, I asked her, that the building reflected the corporate structure of Transamerica and that the President's office occupied the very topmost point of the building, with the vice-presidents and the various assistant vice-presidents descending in layers below him? No, Beatrice said, the President's office was on Level 24. The spike of the obelisk was a solid spire. But surely the architect wanted to embody the upward-thrusting myth of the dream? No, not true either. The intention was to create more light in the streets surrounding the building and to avoid the Wall Street canyon effect. Ha ha, I said. What a disappointment.)

So I left this morning on the freeway through green, flowery hills, with cows grazing on the view and the Catalina smoothing through America. The Sears Point International Raceway lay just off the highway. A large sign said 'Bob Bondurant School of High Performance Driving'. I remember when I was small reading about Bob Bondurant in my green monthly *Motor Sport* when he was a Grand Prix racer. He had been in Ferraris but when I knew him it was a BRM like Jack Brabham's. Never an undiluted hero, but he once came fourth at Monaco. Bob is a cheery, large-faced man with a wide body. For some reason I had always imagined that racing drivers were small. How on earth did he fit inside a racing car? I didn't ask. Various middle-aged executives sat around the foyer of the school in racing overalls that said

Goodyear, Ford and Bob Bondurant all over them. Bob was in casuals. 'I think the best thing to do is to have a look round the place,' Bob said. There were pictures of Bob and Paul Newman, Bob and Elke Sommers, Bob and James Caan all the way around the walls. This was the stratosphere, the dream come true, with the boiler-suited executives hoping to nibble at the edges. I signed away my life on a dense, unread form Bob called 'a release' and then put on a helmet. It was ten sizes too big. 'Don't worry,' Bob said, 'I'm not planning to use it.' We climbed into a car whose name I didn't catch and Bob strapped himself into a sort of parachute harness. I had an ordinary safety belt. Bob described his arrangement with Ford, the size of the engine, the particular qualities of the shock-absorbers and the anti-roll bars, the experimental suspension system. I was speechless with excitement, my lips withdrawing up my teeth in terror and anticipation. We started slowly, rolling past the lined-up Mustangs and Formula Fords on which the students learn. Yes, yes, I nodded, now hungry for speed. We circled a small oval loop a few times at about 20 m.p.h. while Bob explained his patented trailing brake technique and heel and toe downshifting. Paul Newman had been through all of this. 'Then we get them to go a little faster.' I was beyond moving a muscle at this stage, let alone speaking. Bob took the car out on to the raceway. I was already as far back into the seat as the upholstery would allow me to go, so that the only effect of the acceleration was an enormous, uncontrolled smile splitting the bottom of my face like a canyon. We were going 115 at a sharp right-hander within a few seconds. Bob continued to talk about his Executive Chauffeur Anti-Kidnap Course as though we were travelling along your Virginian Parkway at 42. 'We like to take them through 180 degree skid turns by the second day,' he smiled across at me as we took the corner sideways on, the car travelling down the track in a direction exactly perpendicular to the way in which the wheels were aligned. 'Ng,' I said with my mouth now wide open as I watched the landscape going the wrong way past the windscreen. This was meant to be an interview. I knew I was in the Shuttle. Bob was pointing at features out of the side window. 'It's a little like the Nürburgring,' he said, turning the steering wheel in ways that seemed completely unconnected to the direction we were going. 'Fun, huh?' he asked as another impossible corner slewed out of the rear window. 'Yep,' I managed to squeeze out, 'Great.' I was feeling like one of those films of astronauts undergoing g-force tests on a rocket track, with all the skin and flesh on my face pulled back away from the bones like hair. Bob looked normal enough, if a little flushed. I suddenly remembered: he had just returned from a business lunch. 'Only the CIA run an equivalent course,' he said as the car crested a rise, pirouetted on yet another mindless corner and sank into a hollow, leaving my stomach on the roof. 'I wanted to do a deal with them, see what we had going here.' Pure, glorious rip-up down a straight and that same first bend again. 'Do you know what they said? "We've already put a couple of people through your school, Bob, and you're doing a nice job there."' A curious sensation of ease now, recognising at last that this man knew what he was doing. 'And I'd checked out everyone who came on that course. There was no one who didn't come from a major corporation.' 'Is that right?' I said. 'You could say', Bob went on as at last we slowed down and off the track, 'that we are the premier road and race training establishment in the United States.' 'I can believe it,' I said.

Carlisle, Pennyslvania

Friday 11 April

NIGEL *to Adam*   Carlisle has two prestigious institutions – Dickinson College and the US Army War College. I'd asked Jo whether I could visit the latter too, wishing to squeeze in for both of us (for you're not likely to do so) at least one visit to the armed services. I said my subject was military history. She passed on my request. I'd expected to meet a fresh-faced young captain for half an hour's talk. That was all I needed and deserved. Instead, the whole USAWC was mobilised for my instruction and entertainment. I was given an operation order, detailing where I was to be for every minute of an entire morning, starting with the arrival of my 'escort', Colonel Orlov, at 7.45 a.m.

It was fun re-entering a military establishment after so many years. I was soon reminded (for this doesn't differ from one army to another) of the subtle relationship of rank to rank – the burly sergeant at the outer desk, the offices of the majors (no captains), the grander offices of the colonels, the superb office of the General, the only one to be allowed flags as supporters for his desk – and of their social manner to each other, combining manly ease with graded deference. In this college the tradition is broken to the extent that Christian names are normally used, except for the Commandant. It is a staff-college for 250 senior officers who stay here a year to be freshened for even higher command, and students and faculty are regarded as equals, all being lieutenant-colonels or colonels. There are all the appurtenances of a military station (they call it 'the Post', which seems a bit monolithic for so widespread and distinguished a campus), with banners on poles, statuettes on tables, and shields on walls commemorating past commanders and campaigns. All that's missing are soldiers. It's like a vast officers' mess, with corresponding comforts. Officially it's called the Carlisle Barracks. Anything less like a barrack I've never seen.

From war to peace. I attended a class at Dickinson College, taken by Professor Kim Rogers, an historian. The question for today was, 'You are divorced. You have two children of three and one. How do you cope?' This seemed an odd subject for a history class, but Kim explained that it was contemporary history. The young men and women (did you know that the term 'girls' except for small children and centre-folds is now regarded as offensive?) were amazingly responsive and articulate. There were two in particular whom everyone admired: a man, arrogant, bronzed, wearing a shirt hooped in many colours, his feet permanently on the next chair; and his opposite number – grey jersey, classic face, audacious, beautiful line between chin and throat. From time to time they caught each other's eye. Professor Rogers conducted the class like an orchestra, signalling in the horns, the violins, and making her own contribution with rotund and animated gestures. The subject was thoroughly explored. They seemed familiar with the problems of divorce, perhaps expectant of them. Who would look after the kids? Grandmother. How will you react emotionally? 'I will look for someone to share myself with.' 'I'd seek a counsellor.' The language is a mixture between academia and the couch, but campus-talk keeps breaking through. A lot of 'you knows' speckle and help forward the dialogue. 'I'd be staggered for a while, you know.' And once to my delight, 'I don't know, you know.' Kim herself has caught the habit, although I don't suppose she knows it, you know.

The Banks gave a dinner-party. Among the other guests were Stanley and Rodelle Weintraub. The industry of that man amazes me. Having just published a long book about 11 November 1918, he has completed nine hundred printed pages on Queen Victoria. Yet he has a full social life and helps other people write their books, like me. Jo is a skilled hostess, steering the conversational barque away from shoals like the Civil War, and directing it into the deeper channels of literary style and the nature of youth. I had half an hour with her alone to discuss her editing of the *Selected Letters of Virginia Woolf*.

Eureka, California

Friday 11 April

ADAM *to Nigel*   At last I'm on my way north. I've been treading water in the warm, smooth pool of California for almost a month now, while you've been climbing up the east coast, clocking off states and climates, and I've been doing no more than looking at the corners of one sunny and rather strange picture. There is one question I am always asked in California. 'Will you be going to the West?' At first I used to reply that I thought I was in the West, but the answer to that would always be: 'No. You're in California.' Jeanne was wrong when she said that Marin County was an offshore island; the whole state is. The American West is to the east of here, as if the country were an orange, and the flesh itself began only after you had penetrated this bright pleasure-rind. People promise me Montana as a goal.

I've been driving all day, up the Pacific rim. Eureka is a horrible place. No one would ever have put ! at the end of its name on arriving here. But the redwoods were beautiful and the sense of encroaching northernness some sort of relief. Little has happened all day. I gave a lift to a man outside Garberville. He was more rough and ready than anyone I had seen for weeks and was bemoaning the recent clamp-down on Marijuana farming which until recently was the main agricultural enterprise of the area. Until 1981 the annual financial statistics for Mendocino County listed the drug as the most valuable cash crop grown there. Now anyone found growing it will have his entire property confiscated. 'It's doing terrible things for the employment statistics,' the man said and then asked to be let out in the middle of nowhere.

The road was full of logging trucks and its surface scattered with lumps of the flaky red bark. I couldn't resist taking the Catalina through the Drive-Thru Tree. It squeezed through, an inch to spare on either side while a man in shorts took a photograph. What a thing to do to a tree! The hole has to be hacked out again a little wider every year because the tree itself, trying to forget the rape, squeezes in on either side. In a few hundred neglected years it might repair itself and close the gap. A poem was written up on a board next to it.

'Here, sown by the Creator's Hand,
In serried ranks the Redwoods stand.
This is their temple, vaulted high,
And here we pause with reverent eye,
With silent tongue and awe-struck soul,
For here we sense life's proper goal.'

The powers of self-deception are limitless.

Carlisle–Philadelphia, Pennsylvania

Saturday 12 April

NIGEL *to Adam*   If you look at my schedule, you will see '12 April. Philadelphia. No fixed address.' That was still true three days ago. Then I received an unrefusable invitation – to dine/sleep in the middle of Philadelphia at the house of Henry McIllhenny. I'd not met him before, but we knew of each other through his friendship with Ben, Eddie Sackville-West, Raymond Mortimer and James Pope-Hennessy. He is a man of 75, whose face 'wrinkles well' as a recent magazine article said of him, and he has devoted his life and inherited fortune to the collection of works of art, said to be the second finest private collection in America. Imagine my delight when he asked me to stay in his house on Rittenhouse Square in the very centre of Philadelphia, where all these treasures are kept! It is not in the least like a museum. It is a large private house sumptuously and beautifully furnished. Orchids are in all the main sitting-rooms, and a vase of Madonna lilies in my bedroom. Mine is one of the largest, but even the smallest contains objects which would make our Sissinghurst sitting-room look like Baba Metcalfe's in Eaton Place. Besides that, the house is staffed by butler, maids, chef, and is of an unbelievable luxury and comfort. My high road will never lead higher than this.

I've been re-reading your latest batch of letters, received at Jo's house. Your unsensed earthquake (p. 63). How you confronted Madeline Moore at Santa Cruz without warning. Why did she hold her head in her hands when you told her about the father–son element in our letters? Because she found such self-exposure improper, like another woman you met earlier who said sneeringly that it was typical of the Nicks? It may be, but I'm not embarrassed by it. I wouldn't have enjoyed the Colin Henderson party (pp. 69–70). I was never good at tambourine-shaking, money-begging or gurus, but strong on British reserve, as indeed you are, but you're capable of putting on a performance if required. I'm sorry, but I still believe what I once said to Jo, that psychoanalysis is an obsession here, since no trick-cyclist can possibly know more about you than you know yourself, and it's simply paying a man to listen to your self-dissatisfactions, 'absurd anxieties' as you express it (p. 80), which would bore anyone unpaid. That's a side of American culture I loathe, like your Lesbian basketball match (p. 84). I repeated your story to a man tonight, and he said that in New York there's a female voyeuses group who pay to watch near-naked men dancing, and stuff dollar-bills into their G-strings, without touching flesh. 'Disreputable women?' I asked. 'Not at all. They're often from the social élite, and not in the least ashamed of it.' I think this shows a lack of stability, a tendency to be attracted by the latest fad, a febrile search for novelty. But you deplore the absence of these very qualities in the British. We're dull. The Americans are excitable and exciting.

I feel (there's me feeling) that your west-coast adventures have been almost wholly eccentric, while my east-coast adventures have been, by American standards, conventional. Down-market, up-market? Different aspects of the same thing? I think not. You relish the ludicrous, I the upper culture, which is often flamboyant, but as in Henry McIllhenny's house a very real appreciation of the best things in life, and a wish to share them with strangers like me. America is a society which develops its energies from opposite poles. Below the outward gloss and fantasies is a deep seriousness, which makes them what they are, a seriousness of purpose, personal and national. You've found the personal, but not yet the national, nor the historical roots of both. Tell me what you think about the influence of the past upon the present in your strange half of the continent.

Tillamook, Oregon

                                                          Saturday 12 April

ADAM *to Nigel*   More miles and a new state. I crossed the state line
                       in a forest near the coast and then later this afternoon
the 45th parallel, half-way between the Equator and the North Pole. I leave California with regret. I had the time of my life there. Now there will be a slowing down. That may be the result of Californian propaganda, but I'm an easy victim to it.

Fog rolled in off the ocean for part of the day and for the rest of it rain dropped out of a low sky. Ferny wetness in the forests and non-talking people. More long patches of silence today. I went for a long walk on an empty beach, with the Pacific surf half a mile wide to the west of me and dunes to the east. I always have some days when I feel futile and this was one of them. But I hate self-pity. I had booked this horrible motel early in the afternoon, thinking that it might be difficult to find somewhere later on. (And I couldn't agree less with your great encomium to the motel (p. 59); they're monuments to a peculiarly nasty sort of individualist hygiene, as though sociability were a disease.)

But Tillamook has nothing and so I left in the car again and went north to Fort Clatsop in the far northern corner of Oregon. I can't remember if you have been there. It's a marvellous place, hidden in a wood near the slimy, reedy banks of the Lewis and Clark River. That's the clue. It is the site of Lewis and Clark's winter camp, where they spent three months from December 1805

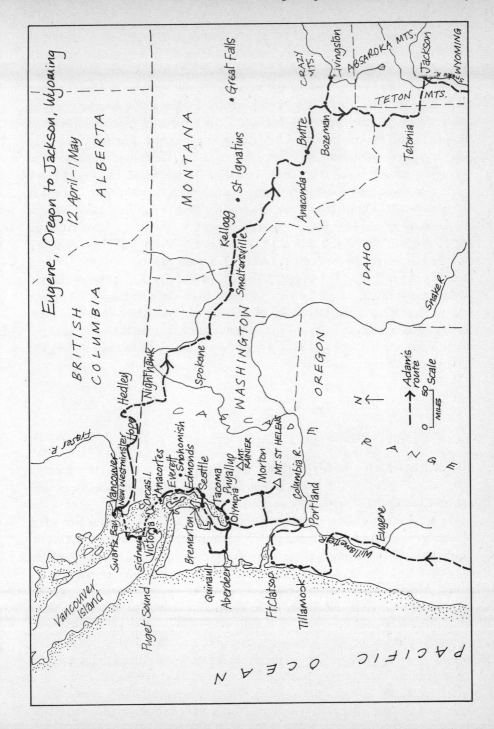

Eugene, Oregon to Jackson, Wyoming
12 April – 1 May

to March 1806 after crossing the continent from St Louis and before setting out home again. The National Park Service has built a replica of their fort and it's beautifully done – a tiny log stockade only 50 feet square and with only seven raw pine rooms inside. 'Great joy,' Lewis had written a week or two before, 'we are in view of the ocean ... which we have been so long anxious to see, and the roaring or noise made by the waves breaking on the rocky shores ... may be heard distinctly.' Imagine that after the silence of the plains and the mountains. They had a terrible time. For only 12 of the 106 days they spent here was there no rain. Fleas infested the place and everybody had agues and colds from the damp. Nevertheless, Lewis and Clark spent the whole winter organising and writing up the notes they had made on the way out. They longed for some trading ship to call in at the mouth of the Columbia but none did. Their only contact was with the Flatheads and the Clatsops. I found it a moving place, this tiny button of the Westering Nation surrounded by such a wilderness. I bought this medal there for you, a replica of the Peace Medal, with Jefferson on one side and a pair of clasped hands on the other, which Lewis and Clark gave to Indian chiefs along the way to show their good intentions. The originals had holes drilled in them through which each chief could put a ribbon to hang the medal around his neck. What about that as an idea? Or perhaps you could hang it around the Thunderbird's rear-view mirror?

Philadelphia–New York

Sunday 13 April

NIGEL *to Adam*   My happiest day, because I was alone for most of
                  it with Juliet, James and my granddaughters, will
provoke one of my shortest letters.

We went for drinks with Peter and Barrett Frelinghuysen. They live a few blocks away on top of a seventeen-floor 'scraper', with a roof-terrace at different levels including a glassed-in sitting-room and an ambitious garden in tubs. We watched the city prepare itself for the night under a perfect sickle moon. Most cities like London look ugly when viewed from close above, because all you see is the clutter of roof-top apparatus. In Manhattan there are no true roof-tops, for the high buildings terminate in spikes or concealed patios like the one on which we were standing, and the effect is not so much looking down as through. It is strangely still. One knows that a million people are separately busy in the square mile below, and as the lights came on, I could see dimly into the nearest apartments, 'nesting-boxes' as my father described them on his first visit here, but a great calm pervades the place, as if on Sunday evening they all gather themselves to face the coming week. Barrett is a charming woman, vivacious hands, mobile face, very New York. I felt myself drawn into the heart of the city by their animated family talk.

It was fun, too, seeing Clemmie (4) with her streaming blonde hair dancing across the avenues, a surer means of stopping the traffic than red lights, and James in pursuit, not so much pushing as slaloming Flora (1) in her wheeled chair. We ate in their colourful apartment. All my affection for them welled up. Juliet told us marvellously the story of Princess Michael of Kent's royal protest against the proposed title of her book, *The Wandering Princesses*. She wants it to be *Queens from Another Country*, which Weidenfeld & Nicolson, New York, think might be open to misinterpretation. James, who has now risen to be President of his finance firm, has developed into a delightful and articulate person. Never did I think all those years ago that I would have a son-in-law strong enough to turn down an offer from one of the Rothschilds to open their New York office, but he has, wishing first to consolidate his position with Savory Milln.

New York

Monday 14 April

NIGEL *to Adam*   I'll not bother you with my engagements in the morning, but come directly to the moment when I walked down Fifth Avenue to visit Juliet in her office. Once an American said to me that he thought London the most civilised city in the world because you could stand in Piccadilly Circus with a bun in one hand and a glass of milk in the other, and nobody would give you a second glance. I replied that I thought it proved the opposite – that we are so absorbed in our own affairs that we have no time for anyone else's. In New York people are intensely interested in each other. A crowd gathers sympathetically round a man doing handturns on the sidewalk. Strangers talk, nod, smile in the street. There's something unexpectedly compassionate about this violent, seething city. I've noticed it too when watching joggers in Central Park. All ages, colours, occupations, sexes, bounce along merrily together. I cannot see Peter Quennell and your old nanny jogging through Hyde Park side by side, but their equivalents do here. In Manhattan you'll find a three-storey tenement squeezed between two vast columns of steel and glass, because the tenement-owner is not prepared to sell. A down-and-out shares a park-bench with a prosperous banker. They don't talk, but they accept each other's presence without pity on one side or resentment on the other. It's a most democratic, cosmopolitan, generous and tolerant place to be in. Perhaps those who live here don't think so.

The Weidenfeld & Nicolson office is on the fourteenth floor of the same building which houses our publisher, Harper & Row, and Juliet's has one of the most spectacular views in the world. It was strange and exhilarating to find the shy, can't-do-it girl who left Benenden School elevated to this height, figuratively and actually. Her bosses, Dan Green and John Herman, both took me aside to say how well she's doing and how much she's liked. Everything is completed neatly, efficiently, gracefully. You should have seen her passing the pages of our letters through a copying-machine of the size and complexity of the Iron Maiden of Nuremberg. The copies spewed out, already collated.

Downstairs, in the Harper & Row office, I talked to Mike and Cornelia Bessie about our book. Juliet tells me that you complained that there wasn't enough about people in my letters. I thought they pullulated with people. So let me say that Cornelia fixes her eyes upon me with solicitous attention, while Mike lies back in his chair, more avuncular, and both cosset this part-author with suave, professional encouragement. That do?

While I was dressing in the hotel for dinner, I heard on the TV news of the American raid on Tripoli, *while it was still going on.* That's instant history for you. My reactions? First, excitement. Second, admiration for the audacity of it. Third, doubts, (a) whether this operation of war is not too violent a response to a chain of isolated terrorist incidents; (b) whether it will lead to further Libyan terrorisms, further US military action, till we reach the point where neither Khadafy nor Reagan can afford to leave the other with the last insult, the last shot, and go to war, full-blast; and (c) that this will widen the US–Russian breach, the US–Europe breach and the US–Arab breach. So by the time I knotted my black tie, I was against.

The news gave to my subsequent party something of the character of the Duchess of Richmond's ball before Waterloo. It was the Spring Ball in the Metropolitan Museum. You must understand that this is *the* event of New York's season. About 150 privileged people sit down, eight to each round table, in one of the Museum's largest halls, decorated for the occasion like the Hanging Gardens of Babylon. Our tables (plural) were a gift to sixteen of us from Ann Getty. I sat next to her. Our relationship so far is exploratory. She was the calmest, perhaps the wealthiest, certainly the loveliest person in the ballroom, red hair tumbling on bare shoulders, and for the first time in years I was awed by a woman's presence. Awed people are exceedingly dull people, and I felt in her quiet replies to my agitated questions a wonder that this could be the man who partnered George Weidenfeld in his first ventures.

I had a brief word with George, reminding him that this was the first time we'd ever met in New York (a statement which he considered as carefully as a million-dollar deal – he was always a man to seek for possible but unintended subtleties), and with Marietta Tree, whose voice, even on the telephone, makes me go wobbly at the knees.

We were the last to leave the ballroom. The waiters lined up in two long rows each side of it, expectantly. That was not the end, for while we were dining, a crowd of other people had been pouring into the Metropolitan, also evening-dressed, and younger, prettier, livelier, but denied our dinner because they could afford only $ hundreds for their tickets. All the downstairs rooms were thrown open. Dance-bands played between medieval statuary, around the Egyptian temple, facing the American Wing, drink-tables everywhere, smoking permitted, frivolity encouraged. The gorgeous young women danced between the pictures and the statues, rivalling their prototypes in paint, marble, alabaster and bronze. What a scene it was!

Portland, Oregon

Monday 14 April

ADAM *to Nigel*   Shultz and Weinberger are on the TV, crammed behind the microphones like two naughty school-boys, brazening it out. Shultz is the bully, adopting a kind of robotic indifference, Weinberger, smaller, whiter, the anxious sidekick. What an agonising quandary for this country! How is it that America has come to be so uncertain over the exercise of power? Or perhaps that is the wrong way of putting it. The double memory of the Tehran hostages and of south-east Asia, the one a hopeless impotence, the other a nightmarish over-commitment, hang over this Libyan crisis and divide the American mind. I only hope it doesn't get worse. At least the Russians seem to have been squared in one way or another. Bombing Libyans won't start a world war.

These issues, this scale of things, arrives on the television. Portland is much more friendly. By great good chance Kanthi Barry had a plan to visit her mother in Tacoma, just south of Seattle, which coincided with my timetable. So she arrived here yesterday from LA on the aeroplane and is going to show me around the Pacific North West. She emigrated to California twenty-five years ago when she was 18 and has come back only rarely ever since. I think at heart it is a sort of Californian pity that has brought her up here. 'What on earth are you going to do?' she asked me in Los Angeles. 'I'll look around.' 'Well, there's plenty to look at but there's nothing to do!' she said. That's how converts think. We're going to visit the scenes of her childhood and teenagerdom tomorrow to see exactly what it was that drove her south.

Today we walked around Portland. It's very nice. That's the word. The Mayor, Bud Clark, who at the moment like every other mayor is dealing with a corruption/cocaine-dealing scandal associated with one of his aides, comes to work every day on a bicycle. If the Transamerica Tower is the new symbol of San Francisco, Mayor Clark's bicycle is the new symbol of Portland. It means Returning the City to the People, Ecoawareness and Healthy Living. No American novelist could survive in the new version (widely called Renaissance, but utterly lacking the violence and verve of that epoch) of Downtown Portland. There is not a speck of grit in the place. Parks have sprouted up everywhere. Office-blocks have been demolished to make way for them; a four-lane highway along the banks of the Willamette River has been ripped up and replaced with a long (and frankly rather dull) strip of green. Sidewalks have been widened and trees planted in them. Smoked-glass booths looking like the top half of coffee percolators are intended, I think, to be bus-stops. Portland is actually installing a tram system. Everything, as I said, is becoming very nice. You would love it. Suburban gloss is reinvading the inner city. Victorian warehouses are being refurbished to house sushi bars and bread shops called 'The Very French Bakery'. The place is still in transition and some sights must make the city planners agonise. The nice Oregonians for whom all this is intended are not good at occupying public spaces. They move rather quickly in button-downs from the office (on the twenty-eighth floor of the required all-sheen tower) to the pink-tableclothed $22-entrée Italian restaurant without much pause in between. The public spaces are slightly uncomfortable moments of transition between the dependable structures, mildly frightening chasms separating the McIntosh Apples from the *tartes aux pommes*. One square is entirely paved with bricks on each of which the name of a citizen who has contributed to (preferred words: 'participated in') the Renaissance is carefully incised. But the names underfoot do not belong to the people who spend their time in the square. They are winos. (Old word: 'derelicts'; preferred words: 'street people' or even – but this is very radical – 'mobiles'.) I tried to see someone in the City planning office to ask them about this but everyone was busy with budget hearings. Kanthi and I did talk to someone in a bar. His tie said Giorgio Armani and he saw the problem of the derelicts in Downtown Portland as closely allied to the problem of Libyan terrorism. This was political gymnastics, but he straddled the gap with the help of a rum and coke. His name was Chuck and, as he saw it, the policy options fell into two camps: zap them or talk to them. He was in favour of zapping (both derelicts and Libyans) because they weren't susceptible to persuasion. Bud Clark was adopting, as he saw it, a Jimmy Carter approach;

doing nothing. He was all for the 6th Fleet when it came to the Libyans and bussing when it came to the derelicts. Kanthi was speechless with Californian sophistication.

Chuck had a friend who ran a restaurant. And the friend had a problem. Some derelicts, he said, used to spend their days sitting on the pavement outside the restaurant – not nice for Renaissance men and women. So Chuck's friend – Chuck gave his thigh a little slap at this point – installed a hose pipe all around the outside of the building a foot or two above the pavement. The hose had a small hole made in it once every 6 inches. When the winos sat down, the owner simply turned on the tap and soaked them. Wasn't that something? Nothing like clean sidewalks for a nice town.

It's one of those not very extraordinary coincidences that I should pick up a bunch of letters here today from you that extol all the virtues of prettied-up American suburbs (p. 77). You want a Safeways to look as if the Royal Oak Foundation would invest $2 or 3 million in its preservation, and gas-stations to appear suitable for one of your dinners for 16. Well, I don't. You know I don't. I wrote a long piece once claiming that the National Trust æsthetic – that Brylcreem gentility – was a sort of pollution in itself. You may have been laying it on a bit thick, but there's no doubt about one thing: we're both born propagandists. You manage to dress up the staggering banalities mouthed by your senator (pp. 88–9) as if he was Jefferson himself. I can just imagine the colour-blindness of a Maryland Republican senator's children.

New York–Newport, Rhode Island

Tuesday 15 April

NIGEL *to Adam*   I've been allowed to keep my Wonderbird! As this is the end of our first month, and of the first third of our journeys, I had to rebook with Avis. At first the girl (Cagney eyes, Lacey hair) said that I must suffer a change of car. I pleaded. I said that the Ford was the loveliest car I'd ever driven, that we were virtually married, and that neither of us would tolerate a divorce. I had no need to play my trump card, that if allowed to keep it, I'd write nicely about Avis, if refused, nastily. After consulting Miami by teleprinter (further heart-stop), she agreed, and wished me luck in Green Bay, my next reporting-centre.

Tacoma, Washington

Tuesday 15 April

ADAM *to Nigel*   Forty-foot placards about the apple maggot greet you
                         as you cross the Columbia River into Washington.
'There you are,' Kanthi said. 'What did I tell you? That's Washington for
you – green metal bridges and apple maggots. You must see why I left.' We
were about 20 yards into the state and it was as though we were revisiting
Poland. The Ku Klux Klan has announced a scheme to Balkanise the United
States and turn Washington into a white sanctuary. Bumper stickers on large
Dodge trucks are popular here. The favourite a few years ago said, 'If you
can't shoot a deer, get a hippie.' This sits rather uneasily with all the talk
about the Pacific Rim, the dawn of the Pacific age in which the world will
turn away from the Atlantic and Tacoma will become New York. There's a
terrible fear that California will scoop all the riches and Washington will
remain the eternal top left hand corner.

Mixed in with the envy of California is a fear and a contempt. There is a
process, widely and frequently referred to, known as Californication, which
involves the building of houses called La Hacienda, wearing clothes with
colours in them and forgetting that most of the world's jetliners are built
outside Seattle. The louche low body of the Catalina, with its blue and gold
California plates (Washington plates are straightforward white and green),
felt like a little capsule of corruption. We drove up Interstate 5 at the regulation
speed. (When this freeway was first built the Highway Authority had to
broadcast messages on the radio to the people of Washington to encourage
them to drive as fast as the speed limit. Most of them now have edged up to
about 50.) We passed on the right the Millersylvania State Park where Kanthi,
as a Junior Lifeguard, had taken midnight swims in the freezing lake; and
then on the left the dome of the state capitol in Olympia, at the southern end
of the southernmost arm of Puget Sound. Far away to the east the permanent
snows of Mount Rainier were hidden by a low, grey ceiling of cloud. It rains
a lot here. The old joke is that you never get a tan in Washington; you rust.
The Catalina roof began to leak on to the steering wheel and Kanthi said that
if there was one element in Washington which had made her leave it was the
sky; never torrential and never sunny – just the eternal leaking of a damp
grey fleece.

Tacoma welcomed us, The All America City, and we swung off the freeway
towards Puyallup where Kanthi had been born and where she had lived until
she was 18. 'I know where I am now, I know the roads,' she said, 'but they're
twice as wide as they were.' Mount Rainier suddenly appeared through the
clouds, buttercup yellow in the sunshine. 'That's how I remember it,' Kanthi

said, 'always there, sticking up like that ...' We passed row on row of car-lots. Korum Mitsubishi, Dodge Cars and Trucks, The Car Capital of the Pacific North-West. They went on for a mile and a half. 'Oh my God,' Kanthi said. 'It's so *junky* ... It's worse than I ...' and then held her hand up in front of her mouth. 'It's so different. There were none of these cars. It was fields and farms. There were daffodil fields here and berry fields.' And then, pulling herself up, she said, 'I have fond memories but I don't, I mean I'm not attached,' and then looked out of the window.

She didn't know where she was for a moment, but then recognised a street name and we turned off down it. We passed a miniature Hampton Court. 'That's the Elk's Hall. That's where we had the Junior Prom. It was meant to be an all-night party but it was highly chaperoned. I jumped out of the bathroom window at the back with a boy. I can't remember his name now. He wasn't supposed to be there because he was older. I can't remember who it was now. It'll come back to me.' She found her house, a small brown wooden building on a corner lot, which her father and his father had built in 1948. 'It used to be a light tan, with shrubs all around it. There's just that one thorn tree now. And you see that house there, that's where my uncle's cow pasture was, with the electric fence around it. And that white house there? That's where I used to bicycle over to see the Howdy Doody Show. It was the only TV in town.'

She showed me the fields now covered in houses where she used to walk up and down in a Lauren Bacall raincoat, up and down between the lines of raspberries smoking a cigarette, trying to feel tragic. 'All I thought about was getting out, getting to California.' And then we had a cup of coffee somewhere. The woman behind the bar asked Kanthi where she was from. 'I'm from Los Angeles,' she said without a thought.

Newport–Hyannis–Nantucket Island,
Massachusetts

Wednesday 16 April

NIGEL *to Adam*   Here's an illustration of the amazing telescoping of American history. I know you don't like ancestors, and I promise that this is the last you'll hear of one, but you must know a strange fact about the Sackvilles and the offshore islands on the New England coast. In 1637 Edward Sackville, 4th Earl of Dorset, petitioned Charles I as follows:

Certain islands on the south of New England, viz. Long Island, Cole Island, Sandy Point, Hell Gates, Martha's Vineyard, Elizabeth Island, Nantucket

Island, with other islands near thereunto were lately discovered by some of Your Majesty's subjects, and are not inhabited by any Christians. Prays a grant thereto with the powers of government as have been granted to other plantations in America.

The petition, now among the Calendar of State Papers in London, was annotated, 'Reference to the Attorney General to prepare a grant'. So presumably the Earl acquired Long Island, Martha's Vineyard and Nantucket for less than the cost of a string of beads. I don't know if he ever came here, or when he sold the property. We'd be very rich if he hadn't.

The country through which I drove this morning was described by the Pilgrims as 'a hideous, desolate wilderness, full of wild beasts and wild men'. That was in 1620. The untouched forests away from the coast (there's little farmland) still look pretty grim in their winter brown and black, and one must seek New England towns like Guilford and Newport to discover how quickly the settlers made homes like home. A surprising number of wooden houses have survived fire and restoration since colonial times, neat in the eighteenth century, arrogant in the late-nineteenth, when Newport became the equivalent of Cowes, only grander. I walked the road which Mary Leiter (Curzon) took to church, when she turned all heads to marvel at her loveliness.

I caught a ferry at Hyannis for the 30-mile, two and a half hour, trip to Nantucket Island, wishing to vary our road-bound routes by a nautical diversion. It's not an interesting journey, merely a transit. On arrival you enter a harbour like a Hebridean port with classical touches, a Stornoway with columns. The surprise comes when you walk from the quays into the town. You find houses by the hundred which have either remained untouched for two hundred years, or been beautifully restored. That a remote foggy island, at first mainly inhabited by whaling men, could have achieved this standard of elegance and prosperity is astonishing. This is what Ullapool could have been like, if only the Scots had had the enterprise and the taste. Tomorrow I'll visit more of the island, but my first impression is that I've never seen a small town less flawed. The main street, cobbled, is what Jane Austen might have known in Alton, every shop-front different but fitting the composition of the whole. The side streets, in one of which I'm staying, are flanked by substantial houses, white and grey, clapboarded and shingled, some with porches, outside steps and railed galleries on the roof, Greek Revivalled in many cases, never Gothicised. They form a street which is long, curved and slightly uphill, and but for the power-lines brutally scrawled across the façades from giant post to post, would be a perfect illustration of what Americans, in remote corners, have achieved and kept. I'm lucky to have come here before the rush of the tourists. They ruin its peacefulness, and the locals, who depend on them, hate them.

I was met here by Kate Stout, and we dined together in a sophisticated and very expensive tavern in the town. You'll remember her as one of the American girls who helped Jo and me with the editing of the Virginia Woolf letters. She's an expert on Nantucket, having run and presented the news programme on the local TV station for a year, and is now about to found and edit a newspaper called *The Nantucket Map and Legend*, which will consist of 60 per cent advertisements and be distributed free. That's very typical of Kate. Alert, fearless, enterprising, spruce (she was dressed tonight in a green gabardine jacket, red sweater and pearls), a touch tomboyish, a touch maverick, conscious of her worth and saying so, she charms and exposes herself to snubs with equal brio, resigns from committees when thwarted, founds her own in rivalry, badgers editors and newspaper proprietors to help her career, usually succeeds, makes money, saves it, risks it, a New York girl at heart countrified (she was raised in Kentucky). All this I like and admire. I wish the *Map and Legend* well, but Kate's worth more than that, and one day she'll make it.

Nantucket–Boston, Massachusetts

Thursday 17 April

NIGEL *to Adam*   I'd forgive you anything for sending me the Jefferson/Lewis and Clark medal (p. 108), but then I've nothing to forgive you for, except a sentence or two in your letter of 8 April about our relationship. I'll come to that later.

I got up at 5 to walk through Nantucket's idealised streets, and fell in love with them all over again. The cedar shingles in which most of the walls (not roofs) are clad fade quickly to grey, as soft as a dove's feathers. There's not much brick. It was too expensive to import. The dovecots are varied by porches, dormers, outdoor stairs, gables and gazebos, giving to each of them an individuality within a common theme, like a collection of people recognisably of the same race but with different eyes, noses, mouths, ears. The waterfront is the least interesting part, and a waitress in a café was cross with me when I asked for bananas, working herself up to hate the tourists. I bought a newspaper. The Pentagon spokesperson said that the Libyan mission was 'a near-flawless professional operation. I don't think there's been anything like it in US military history.' Really?

Kate and her friend John came to fetch me for breakfast in her loaned cottage on the edge of a lagoon, 6 miles from the town. It's apparently made of odd pieces of washed-up crates, but inside it's cosy, with a ladder-stair to a bedroom, and she could happily write the great Nantucket novel there if it wasn't for *Map and Legend*. Breakfast was good, and then we toured the island in her borrowed car.

My verdict on Nantucket is that the town is lovely, the beaches excellent, the country hideous. There are only two small farms in the 13 miles of its length. Almost the only crops are new houses. The rest is covered with scratchy oak-scrub, called euphemistically 'moors'. Kate said that they have the beauty of an unkempt wilderness, but in that uncertain tone of voice which the Scots use to assure you that there's nothing more romantic than sheep seen through driving mist. In an attempt to lift our spirits a fraction, the island authorities have planted daffodils along the verges of the three main roads. Yet Nantucket is regarded as a paradise. I'm not quite sure why. Consider its disadvantages. Fickle weather; the harbour can freeze 13 feet deep in solid ice; plane schedules are interrupted by fog; saline air, which smokes a windscreen; flies which bite; water-shortage; few entertainments off beach and boat; very expensive; ugly countryside; hoardes of tourists (usual pop. 5,000, summer pop. 45,000); short season. Kate, hurt by this recital, produced her list of advantages. An island (always a draw); isolation (geographically, I admit, but no longer figuratively); pretty town (yes, yes); beaches; clams.

She must win this argument, because she's in love with the island, and people from as far afield as Florida and California have chosen to build their holiday-homes here. We walked a mile across their lawns (this is literally true, for a right-of-way runs past their picture-windows, which causes them acute annoyance, but there's nothing they can do about it). In mid-April there's not a single holiday-house inhabited. One can see September 1985 issues of the *NY Times* lying on the floors. Wooden staircases lead down the bluff from lawn to beach. I walked toe-deep in the Ocean, saying goodbye to it, for you and I are about to turn irrevocably inland.

I flew back in a plane for eight. From the air Nantucket looks like a sole swimming desperately towards Europe. Thirty miles in 10 minutes, excluding long motor-rides along the runways at Nantucket and Hyannis. I rejoined the Thunderbird by taxi and drove to Plymouth, because I wanted to see The Rock.

You know about The Rock? It's supposed to have been the place where the Pilgrims first set foot ashore. It is a large glacial boulder inscribed 1620, and lies at sea level under a classical porch like the Erechtheum. A booklet describes its provenance with scrupulous honesty. It has been moved several times to give it a nobler setting and the legend greater authenticity, and once broke in half during removal. About the year 1741 a very old man called

Elder Faunce said that when he was a boy his father told him that this is where William Bradford stepped ashore to save his feet from getting wet. Perhaps. But the story was not published till 1832, and was by then a century-old recollection of a century-old recollection of the twenty-year-old recollections of a man who was not even there. However, I gazed at the symbol reverently.

Finding my way to the Howard Johnson Fenway in Boston was hell. The expressways run for miles without an escape-route, and once in the city streets, lost, frightened, hooted at, I was twisted in every direction but the one I wanted, by Right, Lane Must Turn Right, Wrong Way, Do Not Enter, Detour, and so on, till two hours later I found a slit which admitted me to my drink and bed. All my concertinaed annoyance was dispelled by finding your letters, two pictures of you with your Catalina, and TJ's medal. You must have thought, 'He'll like that.' He loved it.

Perhaps it was a peace-offering for your letter of 8 April. I quite agree that the urgency of our daily occupations prevents us from answering each other's letters in detail. I needn't tell you how much I enjoyed your account of motor-racing (p. 101), nor need you comment on Gettysburg (pp. 98–9). We both take it for granted that those things have been digested. More disturbing is that you should have felt as a teenager 'hopelessly powerless in any conversation' with me, and that I destroyed any attempt by you to communicate with me. Allowed your 'sallies' to dry? Engaged in 'absurd formalities'? I don't see our past quite like that, and I'm deeply sorry if I widened a gap which I was trying desperately to close. But I was aware of it. I found it sad that there should have been mutual awkwardness, and it is difficult to explain, for we never had a quarrel and shared many interests. I think it was due to the fact that we both sensed that a father–son relationship was more difficult than a father–daughter's, though it should be the opposite, since you were experiencing exactly what I'd experienced – school, dawning sex, sport, work, the Shiant Islands – and maybe it was the very reflection of my experiences in yours that made me take them too much for granted and nip off your revelations because they were so familiar, while Juliet's and Rebecca's weren't. There was also my belief that you were a very private person who would resent intrusion. A mistake, the same that I made with my mother, who longed for an intimacy which I denied her because I thought she'd hate it. Curiously, you have sometimes aroused in me a certain alarm, because you were developing so fast, had abilities which I didn't, love-affairs of which I knew nothing, political and social attitudes which I didn't share but was afraid to challenge. If I could snub you, you could also snub me. Perhaps I should have gone to a psychoanalist after all. It would be easy and sentimental to conclude that *Dodge* has broken the ice and that henceforward we will enjoy a relationship that approaches the norm. I don't believe it. We will continue to respect, appreciate and love each other, but it will be with the same diffidence. Perhaps this will be the only time when we will even mention it.

Edmonds, Washington

Thursday 17 April

ADAM *to Nigel*   All morning in the Quinault rain forest on the far north-western corner of the United States, where the Olympic Mountains wring 200 inches of rain a year out of the Pacific clouds. Everything is spongy with the wet. Take a cubic mile of these mountains and squeeze it and it would shrink to something the size of your fist, running with water. Kanthi and I climbed up along a rough trail, the other end of the world from my hard, dry Santa Lucia mountains in California. (I know my side of this trip will never recover from having been in California first.) But this was magical in its way too, a dense cold jungle in which the limbs of the cedars and the hemlock are hung with the grey-green clubmoss like orang-utan hair and where the smell of rot, a fungal underlife clogs the nostrils. I could never stay in a place like this. The brain looks too like one of the shrivelled and contorted mushrooms that cling to the fallen trunks. There is the vision of sitting contemplating the damp in a rocking chair while moss slowly encompasses the body, turning it into a strange soft submarine coral. There is part of me which loves this softness, this encroaching and enveloping softness of the moss, like a cat against the shin, but there is a side of me which shudders at it too, which wants to scrabble through the musty green-brown skin, patched in places with its own sort of primitive half-flowers, to find the granite underneath. Moss is the most animal of plants and this rain forest was its kingdom. It's a place where growth, life and death are all accelerated in the wet, like one of those too-fast films, and where stands of Douglas Firs 100 feet high can be seen to have sprouted on the bodies of fallen trees lying supine below them, their forms still discernible in ferns and moss-mounds. (I suddenly remember something I was told in Morton yesterday, under Mount St Helens. In the summer after the eruption, the first plants to flower in the devasted zone were found to be growing in the corpses of the elks which the eruption had killed.) This rush, this rot, this everywhere-detritus, this extraordinary vitality, this instant recycling, this carelessness with past forms, passed over, this survival in tiny corners of fragile beauties, the oxalis and the queencup, this sudden harsh vulgarity – all this reminds me of America.

Now I am staying with the Wambachs in Edmonds outside Seattle. I took the ferry across Puget Sound from Bremerton. This huge inlet of the sea is a simple down-fold between the Olympics on the west and the Cascades on the east. (Isn't there a genius in American place-names?) It's like a northern version of the San Francisco Bay, if far bigger and nowhere crossed by those marvellous bridges. The city towers of Seattle faded in from silhouettes to buildings as we came across the sound, the cloud down low over the islands, and rain in the wind. Kanthi was going back to California and we said goodbye at the pier. She is coming to see us both in the autumn. She has given me a lovely time here, tempering Washington with a bit of California. We move on. Don't you always want to stay longer? Three months seemed such a long time before I got here. Now it's a rush from one place to the next. My scheme – it evolved by itself – is to stay in one place several days and then drive a long way to the next, skipping everything in between. That's the only way I can see it working. Otherwise it turns into a dribble. Nothing's worse than a dribble.

The Wambachs are the ideal Americans. Hal (38) photographer, jazz enthusiast, entrepreneur; Anne (27) gardener, plantswoman, landscape designer; and Sam (5) expert manipulator of Gobots and discoverer of new paths through Puget Sound jungles. Sam had to take his mother aside a few minutes after I got here to explain in secret that he liked me very much but he couldn't understand a word I said. So I'm now exaggerating my Los Angeles accent and things are going fine. We've just had salmon on a barbecue. I have listened to a few of Hal's 12,500 jazz seventy-eights. Hal has explained to me the damage done to the American male ego when beer cans were no longer made of steel. Crushing an empty aluminium can means nothing by comparison. Sam has demonstrated his Gobots five times. Anne is taking the whole day off tomorrow to show me around. This is a great country.

Boston

Friday 18 April

NIGEL *to Adam*   My guide through Boston could not have been more aptly chosen by Valerie Henderson, his friend and previous collaborator on Public Radio. He was Peter Davison, longtime resident, poetry-editor of the *Atlantic Monthly*, consulting-editor to Houghton Mifflin, and now married to Joan Goody, the best-known woman architect in Boston and perhaps in all America. Peter is bearded like a Holbein, alert eyes, friendly, engaging, very knowledgeable. You'll want to know what he wore, but I've forgotten.

His plan was that we would tour literary and publishing Boston, and although we started off like that, we extended a great deal further. Two first impressions. First, the centre of the city is unusually open. A large landscaped garden and the adjoining Common are left completely free of buildings in its very heart, as if you expanded St James's Square in London a hundredfold. Second, there's not much of mid-eighteenth-century, Revolutionary Boston left. The old quarter, Beacon Hill, was rebuilt in what we would call the Regency style, but remember the architectural time-lag – it could be London *c*.1780. Very bricky, ruddy, plain patterns of doors and windows, neat, urban, civic then, Yuppie now, climbing the Hill with conversational ease. Around the open centre are clubs, apartments, official buildings and the smarter offices. We entered two of them – Little, Brown and Houghton Mifflin, the great publishing houses. HM was my father's publisher, and in his honour I was greeted by Robie Macauley, the senior editor. I asked him whether it was considered improper for publishers, like certain ones which I won't mention, to seduce another publisher's authors by offering them higher advances and royalties. He replied that it was not a thing that HM would ever do, but he had heard that it was done sometimes elsewhere. Very proper. Very John Murray-ish. A TV crew were making a film in the rooms next to his own. He had not even asked what the film was about as he stepped over the coiling cables. I was much impressed. HN would have approved of HM.

The commercial district, very dramatically, is occupied by high-rise buildings, still rising, one of them the design of Joan Goody. There are two conflicts at work here. If you are to make your city centre lively and efficient, you must approach it by wide elevated roads that inevitably disrupt the serenity and the plan. And if you tear down antiquated office-buildings to make room for new ones, you have destroyed part of its history. I thoroughly approve of the liveliness – and at street-level, you walk, not drive – but I think they have carried too far their laudable desire to preserve. Victorian façades of pretentious ugliness have been carefully propped up like Hollywod filmsets while modern offices are built behind. There's enough Victoriana elsewhere to pay tribute to the recent past. For instance, on the waterfront the better warehouses of the period have been skilfully adapted for apartments. So has the old market place, a splendid series of galleries round a long open court, which reminded me in appearance and atmosphere of a Moroccan *soukh*, a medley of open-fronted stores and hot-food counters, an enormous peripatetic restaurant.

We lunched at Peter Davison's magnolia-decked club on the mall, the St Botolph's. I asked him how Boston's character had changed. Is it still the country's intellectual capital? It would like to think so, and what with the MIT, Harvard, its Medical School, Law School and Business School, Boston's distinguished publishing houses, modern architecture, its museums, the *Atlantic Monthly* and the *Boston Globe*, it can still make a fair claim to the title. The life of the city is enormously enriched by them. More surprisingly, it has become the centre of a thriving technological industry. Up to 30 miles around Boston factories have multiplied (including the Polaroid, the invention of the Bostonian, Edwin Land), and the men and women who direct these industries are not only rich and pay their employees well, but have a deep interest in cultural matters. The museums, music, theatre and architecture benefit enormously. Perhaps its symbol is the Hancock Tower, very tall in green glass, some ten years old, which rises like a giant spear thrust up from below the ground, simple but changing patterns and colour as you walk around it, and sprouting from its distant roof-top a crew-cut of aerials and antennae to indicate the mass of high tech it contains below.

After lunch we drove over the water into Cambridge to view the Harvard campus from outside. Peter said that the professors do not live in the town any more. Only lawyers and psychiatrists can afford to. It looks very graceful, especially when seen across the Charles River, and is still the Mecca of every aspiring young American intellectual, although since the Kissinger era, Peter said, it has been more concerned with politics 'and power'. I did not meet any professors or students, being more than happy with the company of Peter and his pretty daughter Lesley.

Edmonds, Washington

Friday 18 April

ADAM *to Nigel*   What a day. First to the Snohomish Saw Mill. (I set off on another diary description of my day and feel bad that these letters are not like letters, because we're doing too much, because they're public, because both of us – at least to each other – are bad at private communication. Perhaps it's unavoidable, perhaps it will get better. The word 'you' doesn't appear enough because the idea of 'you' is squeezed out by the idea of 'me'. I wrote to you about this last week but, because of the lag, I have no idea yet what your response is. It's as though we're in different countries, in different time zones. How strange it is to think of our two sets of typed out diary letters travelling these huge distances. Neither of us knows the circumstances in which the other will read what we have to say. It's two books at once, two lives at once, parallel but unconnected, similar but distinct, essentially unshared, the two sides of a mirror which doesn't reflect quite properly. This is saddening, an odd, tentative spreading of feelers out from one side of a continent to the other. That may be the most articulate metaphor of all.) Anyway, I loved my sawmill. Yesterday the only traffic on the road to the rain forest was vast logging trucks, going up to the forest from Aberdeen empty, coming back down, like toys with sticks, loaded with only three or four vast Douglas Fir or Sitka spruce. (I must remember to say that whenever I see the television weather-map in the mornings I always look across to see how you're doing. At the moment it's wetter here and colder with you.)

Logging is a raw, frontier enterprise, a primary culling of a first resource. For all its industrialisation and mechanisation, the timber business connects directly with the pioneers. Cutting, clearing, using the lumber – that's what the first white men did here. The business is in a terrible way. Mills have closed down all over Washington. High interest rates have meant a drop in house building and the lumbermen have suffered. They even ship raw timber straight from the forest across the Pacific, where wages are lower. It can be cut and processed, shipped back here and still be cheaper than finished lumber produced in Washington itself. This may be the real shape of the Pacific future – an exploitation of the American market by the countries on the far rim. But the Snohomish–Seattle Saw Mill has survived because it specialises in high quality Douglas Fir 'clear' – that is wood without any knots in, which is used in houses for its plain, pale beauty.

That sounds straightforward enough, but the process is wonderful. Douglas Fir trunks – 50 feet long and 5 feet wide – are brought in from the forest and dumped in the mud. Everything is on this inflated American scale. An enormous tractor with an enormous pair of crab claws loads them on to an enormous conveyor belt 50 feet wide which feeds them into a 'barker'. This is where the noise begins – a wrenching, harsh stripping of the bark from the trunk which emerges naked and bruised. This skinned corpse is then fed in towards the saw – a steel belt, 1 foot wide and 16 feet long. (Men walk around with replacement saws, two men inside the steel hoop, holding it around their bodies like a jagged corset.) Another man in a glass cage operates a giant cradle, fitted with heavy, blunt arms that manipulate the trunk into place. Inside his cage he has electric buttons. His fingers jump at them like a typist's and the tree is tossed around in its cradle until it's in place. Then the whole cradle, like a small train, slides up a track to the saw. A clean, dropping whine as the blade cuts and a perfect slither falls off from the trunk leaving one side smooth and clear. Back comes the cradle, more tossing, as if the tree weighed a pound or two, and then another perfect slice, and then again and again until the beam is squared, all this against the background of intolerable noise. It's the deftness on such a scale that is so thrilling, no clumsiness in it, an absolute confidence. An old man, Bob Waltz, showed Anne and me around. He had founded the mill in 1941. At the end of the tour, after he had shown us the finished planks destined for Melbourne, Australia, he told Anne, with his arm around her shoulder, that he was dying of cancer.

And then a two hour tour – all laid on by Anne – of the Boeing factory in Everett. What can I tell you? The unpainted aeroplanes are the sort of green you find inside an oyster shell. The wing span of a 747 is longer than the first flight taken by the Wright brothers and the engines of a 767 (an ugly, dumpy thing) are each wider across the middle than the fuselage of a Flying Fortress. Poor Anne was bored out of her mind. A 747 at the beginning of the runway is too heavy with fuel to take off. Only by the time it has burnt some fuel going down the runway can it fly. A 747 belonging to Boy George was having its tail adjusted in a building which, the lady told us five times, is the biggest in the world. 'You could put 10,000 average American homes inside this building,' she said. Anne tried to find the way out but the lady told her not to be creative because Security gets uptight with creative people.

And then on to meet a man in the Fisherman's Terminal. (It was sweet of Anne to fix all this for me, but even she thought we were taking it a bit far after a while.) The man was an Alaskan salmon fisherman. He was about to leave for the Aleutian Islands having spent the winter making nets. I haven't the energy to tell you about him because after that there was a dinner-party in a restaurant, a film in a wraparound cinema about the space shuttle, a tour of Downtown Seattle in Anne's car and a visit to a hip café on the University of Washington campus where students wore berets and read Camus, then some more jazz records back with Hal, whisky and sleep. We'll have to meet up and talk one day.

Boston–Walpole, New Hampshire

Saturday 19 April

NIGEL *to Adam*   I have spent today driving north-west towards Canada, and visiting two scholarly couples who put me to shame by their married love for each other and the excellence of their lives.

First I called, for lunch, on Dr Philip Phillips and his wife, at Bolton, Massachusetts. Their house bears the signs of having been much lived-in and loved-in. On the walls hang portraits of the family by Brad Phillips, who has developed a phenomenal skill for catching a likeness and a character. His portraits are almost photographic. There is one of his father, sitting in a chair looking tired and reflective, which struck me as a summing-up of Phil's whole life. *Perfectum est*, it seems to say.

But his life is by no means finished. He has been, and still is, an archaeologist, specialising in pre-Columbian American history. I wanted to talk to him about that, but it seemed wrong to pester such a scholar with superficial questions at lunch. However, afterwards he took me into his neat study and showed me a few of the books he'd written. He seemed more anxious to impress me with Ian Graham's *Corpus of Maya Hieroglyphic Inscriptions*. 'None of us will ever match him for his care and persistence. What he has done is of inestimable value to scholarship,' he said, turning over Ian's photographs and drawings of these gaunt *stelae*, which nobody has yet been able fully to decipher.

My other couple, Henry and Frances Francis, live at Walpole, up the Connecticut River valley on the Vermont–New Hampshire border, in a large 1812 brick house. Both are in their eighties. They were friends of Berenson, and of Ben and Luisa. He was Curator of Paintings at the famous Museum of Art in Cleveland. She told me that when she was a student at Radcliffe, finding herself one afternoon with nothing special to do, she went to a bookshop and bought a copy of *Jacob's Room*. It totally transformed her life. She feels for Virginia Woolf, whom she never met, a devotion of an intensity that I've never encountered before. All her books, diary-volumes, letter-volumes, are ranged in a special bookcase. Every other part of the house is filled with books of the kind you'd see in any comparable house in England. In my bedroom I have only to turn my pillowed head to find *Pale Fire* (Nabokov), *To the Finland Station* (Wilson) and *The Group* (McCarthy).

What trouble they took for my visit! As she has been very ill, and he is lame, they now rarely leave the house on expeditions, and live for most of the winter in a single room. For me they threw open the whole house, lit log fires, gave me an excellent dinner and bed. This is a remote place, which fills with snow and the very river freezes solid. The snow and ice have gone, but spring has not yet arrived. They have retired here because New England was where both were born. Their feeling for it is akin to a Yorkshireman's for the dales. I could not help thinking that my rapid transit through their country and my brief lodging in their house were in some way impertinent, their cultured lives and gentle hospitality a reproach to my hectic habits.

Walpole–Burlington, Vermont

Sunday 20 April

NIGEL *to Adam*   Vermont, I've decided, is not at all like the Scottish Highlands. It is fluffier (with trees) and less precipitous. Eighty per cent of the State is still forested, and only in the northern part where the valley broadens round Lake Champlain is there continuous farmland, the first I've seen since Virginia, and the barns, silos and white farmhouses spread attractively across it. There was the familiar sight and smell of cow-dung on unmetalled roads. There were pretty villages like Brandon and Orwell, usually with a Georgian-type church, but the houses lose something from not being fenced from each other, 'a shell of boards', as William Cobbett described a typical American house, 'while all around is barren as a sea-beach'. It's smartened up since then, but still no garden.

For an hour I walked part of the Long Trail which extends 260 miles from the Canadian to the Massachusetts border. Within a minute of leaving the road you are in virgin forest, pine-needles and fallen maple leaves underfoot, a river in spate to one side, foot suspension bridges which sway when you walk over them, relics of a camp-fire, solitude, recollected terrors of the wilderness. Then I drove to Ticonderoga.

Its name, like Wandewash, vaguely surfaced in my mind from history lessons at Summer Fields, and I had to be reminded of its significance by the metal memorial plaques. It was the main southern outpost of the Canadian French, played an important part in the Seven Years and Revolutionary Wars, was successfully defended by Montcalm against Abercrombie, captured by the English, recaptured in 1775 by the Americans, and two years later recaptured by General Burgoyne The struggles for this tiny spot twice determined whether Canada would remain independent. Napoleon would simply have bypassed it on his way from the St Lawrence to the Hudson. But as it was one of the few fortified camps in northern America, it became for all three sides a symbol, 'the key to a continent'. The small armies converged on it across almost trackless wildernesses. How did they manage it?

Ticonderoga was closed. So was the ferry that leads to it from the Vermont to the New York State shore. I asked the ferryman why. Foolish question. 'Because until a few weeks ago you could have driven across the lake.' No such convincing answer was given at Ticonderoga itself, for there was no one to give it. Simply a notice saying 'Closed till May'. However, a small postern was open on one side of the barred road-gate and I walked unchallenged to the fort. It has been beautifully reconstructed in stone and brick. Cannon stand ready at the embrasures. The moats are grassed in. Memorials, some in French eulogising Montcalm, one in English referring to 'the unfortunate' Abercrombie, solemnise the approaches. Finally, an angry notice on the main door of the fort says, 'Do not enter. German shepherd police dogs.' It's interesting that the word 'German' should still be regarded as the ultimate deterrent.

The country is beginning to turn Canadian. French house-names, French on the radio, a French TV channel in my Burlington motel. It's strange to feel European again.

Massacre Bay, Orcas Island, Washington

Sunday 20 April

ADAM *to Nigel*   Don't you love this address? It's an island in the
                         Sound, a one-hour ferry ride west of Anacortes. The
cloud is down low again, but here it's beautiful. The Douglas Firs come down
to the water. There are flaky madrone trees in between them, the thin skin
of bark peeling away to reveal an ochre core. Every rock is mossed. Vast logs
are washed up on the shore line and left there. They are too salty to burn. A
small tea-house pimples the end of a sliver-island in the bay. White floppy
dog-violets spangle the moss carpet. A sloop is tacking down the Sound.
Someone saw the spout of a whale from the ferry yesterday. I missed it.

I'm staying with some friends of the Wambachs, Doug and Mary Bayley.
He too is a landscape designer and this afternoon we visited one of his works.
A local man had made a million out of Greeting Cards. An architect built him
a cappuccino-coloured house on the shores of the Sound. Doug surrounded it
with moss and rocks, planted rhododendrons on sections of the roof and
daffodils on a wide slope beyond it. He says he wanted to bed the house in
and that's exactly the effect: a rather chic house sitting in a soft moss duvet.
It looked lovely. But even better than this was a walk this morning up into
the interior of the island, away from the crowded shore. Doug is full of the
history of the place. Massacre Bay is named after a terrible incident in the
1840s when Indians from Vancouver Island descended on another party of
Indians who lived near Seattle but had come here for summer camp. The
Seattle Indians were murdered. This felt close.

Doug's grandfather, or was it great-grandfather, had been Mayor of Seattle
and when he had become frustrated with the way his banker was handling
his money, he simply went down to the bank and shot him. This was
thought to be OK and he remained Mayor. So near! But up in the woods,
above Doug's Japanese house looking out at his misty Okinawa landscape of
sea and islands, it came closer still. He showed me the ruins of the log cabin
that had been built by the original settlers of this part of Orcas. They were
called the James Brothers. The roof had fallen in and the walls were leaning,
slimed with moss. Alder saplings had invaded the one room and fir and alder
had already colonised most of the meadows they had cleared. But fragments
of their memory survived. A row of three small pear trees in blossom were
the remains of their orchard. A lilac tree behind the cabin was on the point
of flowering. The sprays already smelt sweet. The pale single daffodils that
dotted the old, invaded meadows had been planted by the Jameses, brought
from somewhere further east to decorate a frontier life. This was wonderful –
private, on that particular edge of near-oblivion. It's like the moment before

you sleep. What had happened to the James Brothers? Doug didn't know for sure. The records were scanty to say the least. But around this and other cabins he had found a large number of bottles. He suspected the drink had got them in the end.

Burlington–Montreal, Canada

Monday 21 April

NIGEL *to Adam*   The frontier between the United States and Canada is very good-neighbourly. I had expected that before checking into Canada, I must check out of the US. But they totally ignored my departure. Canada received me in the guise of a Camay girl in Mounty uniform. I was passed to a young man who asked me what I intended to do in Canada. I muttered something about Queen's University in Kingston. Why? So then it had all to spill out. It was not impertinent bureaucracy but friendly curiosity.

The first difference that struck me across the border was the wild disregard for scenic amenities. The plain between the frontier and Montreal is a terrible mess. Silos cluster in pairs like the shuttle, ill-fitting garages and wrecked cars litter the too-abundant land. Was it for this that Ticonderoga was fought? I'm being unfair. The immediate approaches to Montreal across the St Lawrence are very fine, and so are the roads. I found my motel more easily than usual, and looked around for something to do.

The trouble is that I have only one friend in Montreal, and he couldn't make our assignation. As the three-million population were all indifferent to me, and with reason, I decided to take a look at them. I took a trip on the Metro. It's as clean and efficient as Washington's. I gathered little about the Canadian character from observing the other passengers, for they are just as isolated in their thoughts, just as well behaved, just as certain of their destinations, just as tired by the day's work or the prospect of a dull evening, as commuters anywhere. You would have started a conversation with a stranger. If I did, my advances would fail to carry conviction. I'm an unpickupable man.

People were hurrying into the Velodrome. I could watch a bicycle race! Another disappointment. The Velodrome was entirely occupied by the *Salon de la Femme*, an event which takes place once a year to show the women of Montreal the latest in fashion, food and beauty-aids. The wooden cycle-track, banked to 80° at the curves, was just visible under a fairground of boutiques. I walked around. At the first stall I was invited to vote for one of five women who appear regularly on TV. Large photographs of the famous five helped one's choice. I voted instantly for Number 3, Marie Tipo, as she had lovely teeth. I talked to the Ford Man about the Thunderbird. I watched a plump woman practising on an exercise couch, and another demonstrating a rotary rubber-pad which would take years off her apparent age. (An intellectual-looking man, standing next to me said to his companion, '*Dieu, que l'humanité est laide!*' but I think he pinched that *mot* from Gide. I've heard my father quote it.) The most popular stall told your horoscope. There was also a parade of mannequins in lovely coloured clothes, and pairs of very young children acted brides-and-bridegrooms. It was all quite enjoyable, but where was it getting me in my misson to discover how Canadians differ from Americans?

And what a way to spend half a day in historic Montreal! I have forgotten to say that it poured with rain unceasingly. For the first time since we started our journey, I'm feeling a little homesick, as if I were abandoned all alone in Limoges. If only Harper & Row had managed to arrange for us to broadcast to each other between Montreal and Vancouver!

New Westminster, Vancouver, British
Columbia, Canada

Monday 21 April

ADAM *to Nigel*   'You're going behind the Tweed Curtain,' Doug
                         Bayley said to me this morning. 'Canada will be
home from home.' And so it is. I told a Canadian about the Tweed Curtain and he said: 'It's envy that makes them say that. The Americans are frightened of their own violence. Canada has never had a revolution and there is no tradition of violence in this country. And there is something in America which is both contemptuous and envious of that ability – you can call it a tweediness if you like – to do things in a less flamboyantly aggressive manner.'

This man, who was on the ferry from Orcas to Vancouver Island this morning, was whistling in the dark. The attitude of the elephant towards the mouse is not envy but indifference, even if the mouse squeals and peeps at the top of its voice. Canadian sense of national identity suffers from that. To be envied is something Canadians can only dream of. And the sensation of being no more than the thin furze of unshaved hair across the top of the vast body of the USA – that is not conducive to a sense of national integrity. I feel like an honorary US citizen for the time being and adopt, by some awful instinct, the same condescending air which, in real Americans, infuriates Canadians so much. I was brought up short when the man on the ferry said 'third-class powers like ours', meaning Britain and Canada.

I wrote to Olivia on the ferry and when stopped between sentences, staring into the fog, a woman said to me, 'May the blood of the Lord pour down over your worried brow and wash you, my son. Yes, may it wash you, the blood, and may you be clean.' I told her I'd had a shower in the Bayleys' only last night. 'You are not there with me in my meaning,' she said. 'I mean the blood of the Lord Jesus Christ which can save you and which is more of an effective cleaning agent than any number of cleaning brands you might like to mention to me by name because none of them, not one of them, will clean you in your heart.' I lit a cigarette and asked her if she thought my heart was dirty. 'Now you're not talking to me quite straightforwardly. My son, Bismarck, he sometimes likes to talk sceptical like you because he hasn't yet allowed the Lord to come down into his heart and make it clean.' 'Is Bismarck here?' I asked, clutching at straws. 'No, he's at home, he's in Tulsa. That's Tulsa, Oklahoma.'

Dodie then explained how God had made her clean. Once upon a time, no date given, Dodie had been an addict of *General Hospital*. She had watched it – religiously was the word she used – every day, maybe even several times a day once she had purchased a video. She confessed it now: at one time in her life Dodie had been a *General Hospital* junkie; she had been mainlining soap. But then something happened, something snapped in her life. She got rid of her husband – he was drinking too much – she got rid of *General Hospital*, and as a replacement for both she got the sweet Lord Jesus Christ Himself Our Saviour and Protector.

'Do you want to be born again now, I mean right now?' Dodie suddenly asked me with a little quiver that ran down her body like a ripple in a test tank. 'No thanks,' I said quickly. 'Do you want to be born again Now?' she shouted. 'No,' I said. 'How did you know you were born again?', I asked her in a hurry. She calmed down. 'Well, that is the most interesting part of this story. I was reading the Bible, Maccabees II, one morning back home in Tulsa, Oklahoma, and a good friend of mine, Gil, – that's not her name, but it's what we call her; her name really is Maria, but that name has a Catholic side to it to my way of hearing and I don't like to think of the idea that my friend Gil has a Catholic name at the back of her because the Lord is a jealous God and *will* not tolerate, no, will *not* tolerate the adulation and adoration of graven images which are said to be of the saints who are no more to be worshipped than you or I or this ferry boat here is to be worshipped. Where was I?' 'Gil had come round to the back door,' I prompted. 'Oh yes. She was quite excited with herself. "Have you heard the news?", she shouted at me, well she more like screamed it if I'm going to tell the truth. "Have you heard the news, Dodie?" she screamed at me. "What news?" I said. And do you know what she said to me? "Elizabeth Taylor is going to be in *General Hospital* in June!!" And it was at that very moment that I realised that the

Lord had touched me in my heart. Because not until that moment when Gil came round had I even heard that Elizabeth Taylor was going to be in *General Hospital* and before, I mean before the Lord touched me and washed me in his blood, I was always the first to hear that kind of thing on the block.' Dodie was shuddering with the emotion of recalling this turning-point in her life and took off her glasses to wipe away the sweat or the tears or both.

'We had an Australian pastor who had a voice like yours,' she said looking at me glassless with the lost-yak look of the acutely myopic. And then, glasses back on, 'Do you like rock music? You look the sort of person who likes that kind of thing.' It turned out that rock music was one of Lucifer's tools for levering people away from God. 'Am I in Lucifer's power?' I asked, suddenly entranced. 'Well you're not in the Lord's and if you're not in the Lord's then Lucifer's got you!' Dodie said triumphantly. 'He's got you all right. I can see it. I could see it when I first saw you sitting here writing this letter here of yours. I thought to myself: "There's one of *his*," and I was right, right on the button. I knew you hadn't been chosen. I said to myself, "That boy there has not washed himself and soaked himself and I like to say *submerged* himself in the blood of the Lord."' This was too much. I said I had to get a cup of coffee and went down to the car deck where I finished my letter to Olivia. These are grim distortions of a moral idea.

I'm here now in George Sackville's house in New Westminster. Dr Sackville, who is not here at the moment but away on holiday in Fiji, has achieved a miracle of re-enactment in his house. The façade on to St Patrick's Street hints at Tudor without being pedantically exact in its mannerisms. There is a charming flavour of 1920s clubhouse to it as well. On the left hand side, between the house and the fence, the Sackvilles have added a sun patio loosely modelled on Tintern. It's very effective, but not until you are inside does the ensemble of 'England across the Seas' reach the peak of its achievement. Vague memories of teas with great aunts in the New Forest are suddenly brought back to life by the brocaded armchairs with wings, the wall-to-wall grey-green carpeting, the brasses on the walls, the prints of hunting and ancestors. 'Home from Home' I've written in the visitor's book, where you, on your visit to the Sackvilles' previous house in 1979, simply wrote your name, with no message of encouragement or affection. This was thought to be deeply wounding. I took up two pages to compensate. The climax of the house, ingeniously tucked away behind the kitchen so that it comes as a surprise, is the pub. In this Dr Sackville has outdone the English. I don't know of anyone who has a private pub built into their house in England, but here in New Westminster, British Columbia, it has happened. Everything is regulation quality: dark-brown wood; tall shiny pumps on the bar (which, unfortunately, are no more than decorative); a pub sign – The White Cockatoo

2 (version 1 had been in the house you visited); pictures of Lord Kitchener and Earl Haig on the walls; ashtrays the size of dinner-plates which say Double Diamond on them; a collection of brass snuff-boxes (I think); a section of Edwardian stained glass – as I say, it's a miracle of re-enactment. The only thing missing is Dr Sackville himself. It is rather difficult to imagine the creator of this performance piece in Fiji.

His house and I are both being looked after by a young woman called Deborah Dunlap. She has a bad back and for a while I hung upside down in the metal contraption she has in her bedroom, intended to relieve the pain. For a brief moment, before she wheeled me back upright, I felt slightly alarmed, as memories of the Bondurant exposure returned. But no crashes this time either.

Montreal–Kingston, Ontario

Tuesday 22 April

NIGEL *to Adam*   To judge the Canadian countryside by what one sees each side of the main Montreal–Kingston road would be as unfair as to take the view from the M1 as a sample of England. It's dismal. This is the very land which was broken in by the evicted Hebridean crofters when they exchanged one sad life for another. It looks as if it had just recovered from a long illness, which indeed it has – the winter.

But turn off the road to the south, and almost immediately you find the shores of the St Lawrence. This has been beautifully landscaped. Parkways lead you by bridges from island to island, each a luxury lawn dotted with birch and maple. I had it all to myself, indeed too much so, for when I reached Upper Canada Village, a reconstruction of an early settlement, I found it closed. Only the village store was open. I protested mildly to the manageresss that the village, which is one of the few three-star tourist attractions in Ontario, is not on show till 15 May. She gave me the official answer, that the weather till then is uncertain and cold (but today was beautifully sunny), that the village has to be undressed from its winter protective garb, and that the off-season staff was minimal. I did not find any of this convincing, and nor, apparently, did she. She has to turn away hundreds like myself. Several miles onwards, I found a lock on the famous Seaway, with a ship passing through. It has been open since 4 April, when the ice melted. I passed this information to the manageress. The lock-keeper was awash with statistics about this engineering triumph, but to me the chief impression was of its simplicity. It is far easier and quicker to slide an oceanic tanker through it than a row-boat through Sonning Lock on the Thames. And so, by the 1,000 Island Parkway, I arrived in Kingston.

Kingston is the city of Queen's University and several military establishments, and was once designated as Canada's capital before it was transferred to Ottawa, further from the menacing Americans. It has a classical cityhall and lawcourt, a harbour with yachts, two large old forts, and the impressive University Campus, but the shopping and residential streets are more town-like than city-like, modest in scale and style, leafy, domesticated, neat, with terraces and crescents, more nineteenth-century Scottish than twentieth-century American – in short and at last, distinctively Canadian.

My guide around all this was Susan Dick, who teaches English at the University, specialising in Joyce and V. Woolf (what a door-opener that woman has been for me!). She took me to her office. I picked from her shelves a bound dissertation on 'The Contemporary Symbolic Novel' by one of her students, and opened it on the following sentence: 'The realistic novel strives, above all, in Gombrich's sense of realism, to render a mimesis of appearance.' What on earth does this mean? Dr Dick explained that 'mimesis' meant imitation. Then why not use the more normal word? Why 'render'? Why 'appearance'? For that matter, why Gombrich? Why do young men and women think it necessary to use unintelligible jargon to state the simplest of propositions? I raised the question again with three other teachers of English who gave me tea out of bone-china cups. They said they did not teach their students to write like this, but the students did so because they thought it was expected of them. Their textbooks are written in the same style, and they must include plenty of Gombrichs to indicate that they have read all the relevant literature. But what would they think if their students wrote clearly, interestingly and wittily, like Francis Parkman's book on La Salle which I had just borrowed from the University Library? They would welcome it with great relief. There seems to be a teacher–student gap in communications somewhere.

I stayed the night with Donald and Frances Holman. She is Kit Walton's aunt. They live in a house on four levels but only one storey, if you get my meaning. It stands on a bluff overlooking the St Lawrence just short of the point where the river widens into Lake Ontario. One of the 1,000 islands lies offshore anchored like a small battleship. It is very beautiful, and my entertainment was superb.

They gave a dinner-party for ten. I talked to General Richard Evraire, Commandant of the National Defence College here, about northern Canada, which he, exceptionally for a Canadian, has visited several times. He said that there is a problem with the Eskimos. They have accepted western ways to the extent of adopting our weapons, food and drink, but in the process they have lost nearly all their ancient skills, like farming, hunting, fishing and igloo-building. When they run out of bullets, they starve, or appeal for state-aid. On his last visit, his companion asked an Eskimo how his situation might be improved. 'By giving me a fix,' the man replied. Did the General think that these enormous wastes could be more thickly inhabited? Would the northern territories look any different fifty years hence? 'In no way,' he replied. Canada will continue to be essentially a band 100 miles wide and 3,000 miles long.

Then there was Ronald Watts, who until a year ago was Principal of Queen's University. I told him how surprised I had been to find Quebec Province so much more French than when I was here ten years ago. Was the independence movement still as strong as ever? No, he said, because Quebec has gained almost everything she wanted without it. Their language is spoken universally in the Province, they have their own schools and a large measure of self-government. Financially they are treated generously. They feel themselves to be French Canadians, and that satisfies them.

It is much the same with the attitude of Canada as a whole to the United States. Canadians would say that they are North Americans, but they feel more attachment to Britain than the French Canadians do to France. The Crown still counts for a lot. Canada is buzzing with self-confidence. They turn increasingly towards the United States for their trade, and away from Europe. And what about the cultural influence of America on Canada, I asked. Television, newspapers, pop music, design of buildings, sport? They accept it because there is no means of avoiding it. But there's still a great difference between the two nations. Canadians are less prone to violence and emotional flurries like the American response to the Libyan raid. The Professor had been shocked to witness at Berkeley, as you had, policemen with guns controlling student demonstrations. That would never happen in Canada. 'We're more American than the British,' he said, 'but more British than Americans.' The other guests sitting with us nodded sagely in agreement.

*New Westminster, Vancouver, British
Columbia, Canada*

Tuesday 22 April

ADAM *to Nigel*   Out late last night with the Sackville children and their wives. A blur of retsina in Taverna Greca or somewhere. The lampposts in New Westminster have crowns attached to them. The Sackville children have no idea how we are related. There's a horrible suspicion that nobody in the world is quite sure how we are related. That induces a sense of vertigo. The Mrs Sackville I sat next to is an air hostess. She went on strike last year to try and raise her salary from its present level of $27,000 a year. I was too drunk to work out the sterling equivalent of $27,000 Canadian. The evening ended with a photograph of me in the White Cockatoo wearing a policeman's hat. This kind of thing is not what I'm here for. Not a mention all evening about the Canadian sense of national identity. TWA hostesses get $35,000 a year US, which isn't fair.

A rather more applied attitude this morning. On the radio a man is talking about the Tinkerbell syndrome. Do you remember *Peter Pan?* Tinkerbell begins to go out at one point. She's fading away. The only thing that can save her is the shouting of the children in the audience. The children have to want Tinkerbell to survive more than anything else in the world if she is to have a chance. The children scream and bellow and slowly, flickeringly, Tinkerbell brightens back to life. The Tinkerbell syndrome, the man claimed, was essential to any understanding of Canada's idea of itself. Canada doesn't really exist; it's an assertion not a country, which is why Canadians have to be so positive in their indifference to the USA. Deborah tells me that for three years she lived within 2 miles of the border and *never* crossed it. There was no conscious rejection; it was simply that she had no desire to go there. It was another country. But there are people in Canada, she said, who are simply unaware of the fact that Canada is different from the USA, who think that Canada has a Congress and a President and who watch the A-team and buy gas across the border because it seems cheaper over there.

I've been walking around Downtown Vancouver. The sun is out. I asked someone the way and she said: 'All you've got to do is look up the street. If there are mountains at the end of it you are looking north, if not, you're looking south.' Where else in the world could that be your guide to a city? I know you're a fan of Vancouver. I am too. I got your latest batch of letters here (10–16 April), describing all the careful, nurtured sweetness of the east. And of course there is none of that. Instead, an architecture to match the mountains and the ocean, gloss and height and glamour. The shiny buildings reflect sunlight on to the older brick blocks across the street, a slightly wobbly wash of light like the reflected patterns off water on to a ceiling. All this sounds static and achieved but Vancouver is in the grip of Expo fever. The whole city is getting ready for a party and is preening itself. New smooth carpets of tarmac are being laid on the Downtown thoroughfares. Mortar is being gouged out and replaced. There is not a piece of rubbish to be seen. It's as if the city were preparing in front of its dressing-table mirror, mascara on the eyelashes, buffing and brushing the more raggedy patches, cupping its hair up at the back to raise the bouffant, practising the smile, glittering the eyes in anticipation. Vancouver is about to perform and it's damn well going to show that the Rockies are not the barriers to civilisation all easterners imagine them to be.

The Expo site is a long crescent along the shores of False Creek on the south side of Downtown. It's fenced off and closed at the moment. All you can see are glimpses of the pavilions and of the fun rides. I've been trying to get in there all day and there might be a chance that tomorrow morning I can get a private preview. Meanwhile, it's exciting enough to float about on this bubble of optimism. I have an inkling that some of the pavilions on the main site are done a little on the cheap, but the Canada pavilion is a marvel. By a majestic propaganda stroke it is not on the Expo site itself, but on the other side of town, on the waterfront, facing the mountains of the Cascade range across the bay. It is a huge white marquee, three blocks long and peaking into five crests like the mountains beyond it. This is a brilliant image – pure, clean, optimistic, adding enough fuel for Tinkerbell to burn like a supernova. So this is all plus. Minus are the various crabby stories which appear in the papers and have a fatal attraction for me. Hoteliers, hoping to make a killing on the crowds (they are expecting 200,000 people to visit the Expo on peak days), have evicted old men who had nowhere to go and couldn't afford the new prices. One of them has died. Others have been shoved out on to islands in the Sound where they are having the time of their lives living it up in the hoteliers' summer houses. There is fear that all the prostitutes of the continent will congregate around the hotels. This story is called Sexpo 86. But the biggest worry is traffic. The Expo organisers have been dilatory in getting this organised. The Vancouver traffic commissioner says that 'gridlock' (i.e. total traffic jam in which the intersections are blocked in one direction, blocking them in the other, producing rage and paralysis) will not happen. Others are convinced it will. There is a new 'urban transit system' called the Skytrain, which runs from the Waterfront to New Westminster. They are very proud of it here because it is somehow driven along by magnets. I've used it today. It's far too small. My knees didn't fit. The man next to me poked me in the cheek when trying to read the paper. It was crowded even half-way through the afternoon. Its inadequacy will be the scandal of Expo, an exhibition which is intended to show all that is best in modern transportation.

It's now late in the evening. I've come back from a long talk with Andy Dellinger. The only message I had from Dr Sackville was that I should visit him. Dellinger lives far out of Vancouver on the banks of the Fraser River. That much I could tell from the map. I had imagined he might be another friendly anglophile like Dr Sackville. Not at all. He was the most fascinating man I have met on this continent, an embodiment of its history. (Ah! History! At last!)

I must say how much I enjoyed your account of the War College in Carlisle (p. 102) and of the party in New York (pp. 110–11). For a short moment I envied you all that. And it's a good symmetry that you're taking ferries almost on the day (16 April) that I am over here. This continent writes itself, doesn't it?

But I have to defend myself over this nonsense (p. 106) that I haven't penetrated yet to the deep seriousness and sense of destiny that makes America a nation. I'll tell you why in my month in California I paid no attention to history, to the 49-ers *et al*. Because California has forgotten its history, because its frothing effervescent surface, which you see as febrile and I see as the chaotic symptom of an unprecedentedly dynamic society (Los Angeles is growing by a *million* people a year!), obscures the past by virtue of the sheer volume of the present. The 49-ers mean as much in California today as Hengist and Horsa do to the people of Cranbrook. They're the sort of thing you name ferries and football teams after. They have passed into Kitsch history which guidebooks describe, tourists read and forget and bores in county planning offices dredge for a few new street names. Silverado Ave equals Aethelfrith Cresc.

But more seriously than that, the reason I have not dwelt on the history as you have is a conviction that the purpose of our being here is to dramatise our experience of America, not to convey some Olympian, distant vision of the whole. We are laying a thin mosaic path across this continent, tessera by tessera, not blocking out some Greek Revival cartoon. We are here – I read this in Steinbeck – to discover and display 'the small diagnostic truths which are the foundations of the larger truth'. That is exactly how I see it. We are here to draw the picture, not write the caption.

I know you disagree with every word of this and that too is symptomatic of the difference between us. Your unwillingness to recognise or acknowledge any unconscious or subconscious part of the mind has always amazed me. (This may seem a sudden jump, but there's a connection. The rational mind will always want to set its knowledge and experience in a recognisable framework, which in its broadest sense will be historical. The more willingly irrational mind (that's me) is ready to ignore history in favour of a more immediate chaos.) Something comes to mind now which I must have read years ago – perhaps it was in Hawthorne – that America is, or was then, an extraordinarily graphic map of the human mind. The thin, civilised strip of the east coast is the zone of conscious rationality, where order and control are the guiding principles. From the west, out of the huge, unknown continent, or at least out of the continent whose outlines are half-guessed at, part explored by the pioneers, part simply dreamt-of, came the great rivers, carrying waters from hidden mountains. I know Jefferson's purpose in sending Lewis and Clark out here was political and commercial, but there has been more to the history of the American West than the simple exploitation of a resource. I'm told there is a science nowadays called Psychogeography. Would you like me to enrol you in an Open University course, a two-year BA with Honours? This is my contribution to the literature: the exploration of the American West was a penetration of the American (or European?) unconscious. And it has been a tragedy because the exploration involved killing something (the natural/unexplored/bison/Indian) which the culture loved. Lewis describes beautifully how herds of elk and deer wander along the banks of the upper Missouri, coming close to their canoes out of curiosity and fearlessness, and goes on to say how he shot a couple. What else was he meant to do, or what else was he meant to think? you will ask. And the answer is *nothing else*. But that's the whole story.

I've ignored Andy Dellinger. He had a friend with him called Wilhelm and their stories have run together in my mind. I will tell them as if they were one. *He* arrived in Canada before the war. (We were in a boat house, shored up on piles, on the banks of the Fraser. A great iron stove in the corner with a chimney going out through the wall made it hot. Half-way through the conversation Wilhelm suddenly jumped up and rushed outside, down the jetty and into a dinghy. He rowed it out into midstream where a Douglas Fir trunk the size of the tower at Sissinghurst was floating out to sea. Wilhelm captured it with a hook and rowed it back in, tying it up to the jetty like a launch. It will be a year's firewood.) This is an interrupted story. I must finish this quickly. Arrived before the war. Logging. Ferocious anti-German prejudice. During the war Ukrainian tried to kill him (Wilhelm) by pulling a log out from under him. Kicked in logging. Became a hairdresser in Vancouver (Wilhelm) or a gold miner in the North West (Andy). Placer deposits not hard rock. Reckoned he averaged $8 a day on the gold for four years, at a time when average labourer's wages were $2 a day. This was the triumph of independence. Wilhelm turned to Indian artefacts. Made packet. The bottom fell out of that. Now trading oil paintings. But I must stop. More caption than picture today.

Kingston–Toronto, Ontario

Wednesday 23 April

NIGEL *to Adam*   I reached Toronto by 1 p.m. My friend here is Honey Thomas, the author and scholar. (You once met her when you were 16. Taking her to the Bull, you enquired innocently, 'Would you like a beer, Honey?', and the locals looked up in astonishment.) She brought with her a novel by Susan Kenney called *Garden of Malice*, which describes, thinly disguised, me, Jo Trautmann, Sissinghurst (transferred for the sake of anonymity to the Fens), Vita and Harold ('Viola and Sir Herbert') and even 'Cory and Stella', the two head-gardeners. I've hardly had time to do more than glance at it, but that glance shows me that we all (except Jo) come out of it very badly indeed. I welcome Jo to my 'Abbey' in these words: 'Let me show you where you'll be staying. Your digs, as we say in Britain.' The whole thing is a monstrous caricature. I'll send Kenney a single line of protest, 'There are no oast-houses in the Fens,' and that will be that. She'll not be re-invited to Sissinghurst.

Honey drove me round Toronto. She kept up a brilliant running commentary about the city, of which she is clearly proud. It's a metropolis. The wealth and culture of Canada have centred here. In the very middle is the tallest edifice ever erected by human hand, the CN tower. In the reception-hall at its base are drawings to scale of other comparable buildings – the Sears Tower in Chicago, the Eiffel Tower, the Great Pyramid – and all are dwarfed by the Toronto needle. Two thirds of the way up is a swelling, or ganglion, which contains a revolving restaurant and a circular belvedere. We went up in the lift. It takes just 58 seconds to reach the ganglion, and the young woman who works it had timed her statistical patter to end exactly as the lift stops. The view is indeed amazing. It's not exactly a building, more a column on which you perch like Simon Stylites. As we were completely enclosed by thick windows, not a sound reached us from far below. The little cars, all looking identical from this height, move along the expressways as if engineless, while the railway tracks, occupying twice the width of the roads, appear deserted. Never have I seen a more graphic illustration of the revolution in transport. For the same reason, acres of ground round the clustered towers of the business centre are sacrificed to parking-lots. Why not put them underground, and build on top?

The best news of the day is that you have won the Somerset Maugham Prize for *Frontiers*. Juliet told me on the telephone from New York. The only person who hasn't heard the news is the author. We don't know where to find you. It's a wonderful success for you. You will receive in addition to the accolade, £1,500 towards your future travels.

*New Westminster, Vancouver, British
Columbia, Canada*

Wednesday 23 April

ADAM *to Nigel*   I know the reason for the difference in our letters: you do it at 5 in the morning and I do it at midnight. Not much passion at 5, not much reason at 12. It's now late after another long day. It began at 5.30 this morning. I had to get into the Expo site by

6.30. Driving through the sunny suburb streets. New Westminster, being avidly royalist, is making a special effort for Charles and Di on 2 May. I'm told seven hundred journalists have been accredited for the tour. Into the Expo site, my name was with the security guard at the gate and up to the International Media Center. That felt more like it. And then a whistle-stop three-hour tour of Expo 86 with Diana Barkley, Publicity Co-ordinator. She was charming. It was freezing. And Expo – this is balloon-popping – looked slightly disappointing. For some technical reason to do with the administration of large international shows, the different countries who are participating (eighty-six, Diana says, but I can't believe it) have not been allowed to design their own pavilions from scratch. As far as I could gather this is because the show is not a general fair but devoted to transport and communication. It is an absurd rule made up by some committee in Paris. Only the Canadian provinces and Canada itself have been allowed to design their own pavilions. The rest have to make do with rather ordinary modular units, which are little more than brightly painted Portacabins. I remember at Summer Fields looking at the pictures of Expo 67 in Montreal – their exciting bubbles, their odd coral growths, their absolute difference from everything I had ever recognised as buildings. But Vancouver doesn't live up to that memory. It is like a slightly glorified industrial estate, with only the Canadian provinces standing out from it – British Columbia has a great greenhouse, Ontario an amphitheatre, Saskatchewan a grain silo in mirror glass, the North West Territories an iceberg. Nice Diana Barkley enthused over the 260 performances a day, the floating McDonald's, the hula-hoop track called the Scream Machine, the incredible artwork called Highway 86, which is an arcing strip of freeway, curving up and down as if laid along the back of a Brontosaurus, on which hundreds of vehicles from a submarine through penny farthings, running shoes, Mercedes limousines and light aeroplanes have been fastened and coated in concrete. The artists come from New York. It cost many millions of dollars. So this was a privileged look, in virtual isolation, at something which in a few days' time will be inundated with exhausted hot people. Like any party, in the moments before it begins, there is the mixed feeling in the air: nervous anticipation, a worry that it will not go right (Diana told me the site was 96.8 per cent ready), and a doubt as to the reasons we all go through with these things, which are noisy, busy, crowded pleasures at best, painful and exhausting or boring at worst, inducing a sudden desire – in me anyway – to sit on top of a mountain looking at the moon. I didn't say any of this to Diana who gave me a delicious breakfast and a lapel pin saying Expo 86, which I've worn all day.

'If you're going to piss money down a hole, I suppose that's as good a hole as any.' That was Paul St Pierre on Expo. 'God knows how many millions they're wasting on that thing.' Mr St Pierre is another candidate for the most extraordinary man in Canada. He is a huge man with a belly like a bison's head and guns, snowshoes and Indian masks up on his wall. He was Liberal MP for the Coastal Chilcotin constituency, a wild and beautiful ranching country north of here, the size of England with 71,000 constituents, not one of whom, as he says, gave a shit about politics. And for a time he was part of the Canadian delegation to the UN in New York, the worst time of his life. The government had issued a set of rules and guide-lines to survival in the city. Wise Canadians were *never* to step into a lift if there was only one other person in it. Alone or with at least two others was acceptable. They were *never* to step out of a cab if it was not directly opposite the door of the building into which they were going. Even 20 feet of pavement was thought to be too dangerous. These weren't rule-of-thumb hints and tips. They were government instructions.

He is now well out of that world, living in a small house half an hour out of Vancouver for part of the year, spending the rest of it in Mexico, almost out of touch. He writes novels and stories about the Chilcotin country, set in the late '40s and early '50s, treading the fine line of nostalgic realism, in which the weather is violent, men say their first word of the day at 7 in the evening and Cattlemen's Associations refuse desperately needed government aid out of a sort of instinct. We hardly talked about his stories (one of them begins 'On a day as cold as a witch's tits . . .') but as we talked he took all the pleasure a sophisticated man can summon in enriching what he said with the brutally coloured language for which the West is famous, while confidently discussing the ethnographic complexities of the British Columbia Indians, their eight languages as deeply separated from each other as Finnish from Basque or German; the metabolic particularities of the Indian gut which for purely physiological reasons is unable to metabolise milk or alcohol; the cramped economics of ranching today, as irrigation makes farming possible in lands that until only a few years ago were able to feed a couple of cows and nothing else. I had whisky at 11 in the morning. He had red wine, saying that he had already drunk enough whisky in his life for his daily intake to remain above average even if he never had another drop.

And we talked about British Columbia. 'It is, it always will be and it always has been a Yahoo place,' he said. 'I don't know why. For completely different reasons Quebec and BC are different, they set themselves apart. Quebec because of language, British Columbia because . . . well, I couldn't say I'm sure I know why. The Rockies, the Rockies, people always say the Rockies, but I can drive to Calgary in a day from where I'm sitting. Whatever the reason, the fact is that British Columbia congratulates itself on its ignorance.

Ministers go to Ottawa requesting aid without even having read the Act under which they hope to get that aid. We had a Prime Minister of British Columbia walking his pet cat around the docks in Vancouver on the end of a lead because he heard there were a few too many rats down there. Is that what prime ministers in civilised parts of the world do with themselves?'

This Yahooness comes to a head, he told me, over the treatment of the Indian problem. When in the middle of the nineteenth century British Columbia became a fully fledged province the land belonging to the Hudson's Bay Company became Crown Land, but the Indians' rights to that land had not been extinguished. The people in London advised the people out here to do something about it but for over a century nothing has been done. 'The Yahoos hope that if they close their eyes then it will all go away. But it will not go away. It is an essential question, the question of who owns BC. The Indians have become very sophisticated now. There will be no more stumbling speeches in broken English. There will be none of the futile dramatic moves of that militant phase in the '60s, the blocking of roads and so on. That has evolved into something more serious, a patient well-based campaign in the courts, orchestrated by clever and articulate lawyers and, as I see it, it will end up as very expensive indeed for this province. Some time in the not too distant future the Government of British Columbia will have to buy those crown lands from the Indians, and that will not happen without a great deal of pain and anguish.' He offered me a slice of frozen elk to take away with me, but I had to refuse it. I was impressed by this man.

And then on to be interviewed by a woman in the *Vancouver Sun*. I said the spiel, that I thought of us (that is you and me) like two TV channels side by side, and people could flick from games shows (me) to culture (you) at will. Or simply, if they preferred, stick with the diet they liked best. I hate being interviewed. I hear myself saying one thing after another of undiluted inanity as the woman's pencil scribbles away. Never mind. And then a long tour with the woman who arranged for me to get into Expo, an English journalist here called Moira Farrow. Our only connection in the world is that we have both written for the *New York Times* but she treated me like a long-lost son – a car tour of Gastown, Japantown, the city beaches, Stanley Park, the Guinness bridge and, best of all, the totem pole museum on the edge of a cliff near the University. A wide concrete ziggurrat, with a glass wall facing the sunset, houses those faded monuments. The sun dropped off into the ocean, my last sight of the Pacific before I too turn inland, and we went back to Moira's house where she gave me pork chops in a sauce.

Now back in the Sackvilles'. Messages everywhere to ring Olivia no matter what time. I call her in her early morning. She has been sleeping with the phone beside her all night. She tells me about the Maugham Prize. I drink a beer with Deborah. She asks me what I think of *Frontiers* now. I tell her it is a pompous, pretentious and lazy book. Then I come and write all this to you. And now I go to bed.

Toronto, Canada–Niagara Falls, USA

Thursday 24 April

NIGEL *to Adam*   When I woke up in Toronto, I knew that something splendid had happened, but it took me a few seconds to remember what. Your prize! Then I got your letters (April 14–20). You were quite unaware of your triumph. I'm pleased that you met the Wambachs (p. 121). It was the least blind date that I'd tried to arrange for you, as I knew you'd like each other. What a day you had with Anne!, but you were too exhausted to describe the night.

Crossing the US border at Niagara was a much more formidable affair than entering Canada from Vermont. The trouble began when the frontier-men discovered a Syrian visa in my passport. What was I doing in Syria? I was on a Mediterranean cruise three years ago, following the Crusader trail, and we landed for a day to visit Krak-des-Chevaliers and Aleppo. Did I make any Syrian acquaintances then, and have I kept in touch with them? This I denied. But I was sufficiently a suspect terrorist for my entire baggage and car ('Stand 10 feet away from it') to be searched. I stood aside with the sweetness of total innocence on my face. The only suspicious thing they found were my binoculars. I explained that they were for looking at Falls, birds, horse-races and distant fortifications. Fortifications! That was a grave error on my part. All my money was counted, my air-tickets and hotel vouchers examined, my sponge-bag, twice, for drugs. Then we came, as I knew we would, to *Dodge*. I produced the sketch-map of our two routes. Instant relaxation. Would I mention my Niagara crossing? Would I mention them? I most certainly would.

The frontier is extraordinarily dramatic. The allied bridge crosses the water half a mile downstream from the Falls, and as the cars stand in line awaiting investigation, you look across to the famous Canadian Horseshoe Falls and the slightly less famous but still spectacular American spillway. Who said that we would not describe tourist sites? I did. I shall break the rule for Niagara, as I spent $36 on a specially conducted tour.

The first surprise is that the Falls should be there at all. One expects cascades in rugged, desolate country where millions of gallons of water suddenly erupt down a sheer mountain side. Ontario and New York State in this region are dead flat, heavily populated and loaded with factories, convention-halls and generating stations. Down the centre of all this flatness is a gorge, and at the top end of the gorge are the Falls. Of course, they haven't been there very long on the geological scale of time, about ten thousand years, and won't be there much longer, since all cascades, as you know, self-destruct. The rate of erosion is 2 feet a year. Eventually Lake Erie will slide uninterestingly into Lake Ontario.

Still, while it lasts, it is a phenomenon well worth seeing, if only because Niagara is America's Stratford – you have to go there at least once in a lifetime, preferably on your honeymoon. We had a honeymoon couple in our group of twelve, who walked about nervously hand-in-hand as if they expected to drown and preferred to drown linked together. Our guide, Tony, an elderly man slightly hard of hearing but never short of speech, reeled off the statistics, for this is a very statistical place, but I'll give you one of my own calculation. The two Sissinghurst lakes containing a million gallons would disappear over Niagara in 0.75 of a second.

Tony took us first to the calm water half a mile above the Falls. It is fun to watch a ripple (someone's bath-water from Chicago) gradually communicating to its neighbour that something terrible was about to happen. They break first into regular white-tops, then criss-cross in agitated alarm, sometimes recoil from the brink, start boiling, gather speed to 30 m.p.h. and plunge. The transition from horizontal to sudden vertical is quite smooth and only 3 feet deep. The water rolls over in the shape of the arm of a comfortable sofa. In falling it changes colour from white and dark-blue to green, a trick of light which Tony skated over rather hurriedly when I asked him to explain. The Falls are not very high, about 200 feet on the Canadian side, and the drop is obscured and shortened by rising clouds of spray which contain a perpetual mist-bow. The American side, separated from the Canadian by an island, is sold short. It would naturally receive only 15 per cent of the Niagara River, but the Canadians, in a charitable gesture to their neighbour, 'lend' to the US (how can it ever be repaid?) sufficient water to make the American Falls more worthy of their stature. Even so, they are comparatively less impressive, for huge fallen rocks litter the base, and all attempts to remove them have failed. The Horseshoe water has excavated a pool 180 feet deep immediately below.

Then we went underground, underwater. This requires special clothing. We were dressed head to foot in yellow sou'westers, and looking like the Ku-Klux-Klan, we descended by elevator to a catacomb of tunnels between the falling water and the rock-face. At intervals unglazed windows open on the inner side of the cascade, about half-way up it. There is no impression of a deluge. It is more like the steam-room of a Turkish bath – clouds of disintegrated water coiling round and round and even upwards, an effect of thick mist seen from an aircraft. The noise is like that of a thousand horses galloping over the hardened plain outside Samarkand.

That was the highlight of the tour, worth every one of my $36. Further down the gorge, Tony showed us the whirlpools, the barrels in which intrepid men and women have taken the plunge (it's now forbidden by law), and three giant power stations which generate electricity for half America. His statistics gathered more and more zeros, and his hyperboles might have been a description of the temples of Rameses on the Nile. But it was getting dark, we cold. When Tony suggested that the group might care to leave the bus to examine more closely the biggest flower-clock in the world, there was not a single volunteer. In the gathering dusk we looked through the end of the gorge to the plain that fades into Lake Ontario, and returned to our hotels, the honeymooners to ecstasy, I to my onion soup.

Kellogg, Idaho

Thursday 24 April

ADAM *to Nigel*   I've driven hundreds of miles today and arrived after dark, a motel pull-in off the freeway. This is the country to drive in! The ever-going emptiness of the roads, the scale of the mountains matching the desire to cross them. I just sat on the accelerator all day, up the valley of the Fraser River to Hope and then into the mountains and the forests, stopping only for petrol or a Snickers, smoking, listening to music. A public service broadcast played half the Trout Quintet and then faded; Aretha Franklin came on a millimetre down the spectrum. At Hedley a board said $47 million of gold had been taken from a brown mountain between 1904 and 1955. Sliding by. On the eastern side of the mountains the forest drops away and I suddenly realised it was the forests on the west coast in Washington that had oppressed me. Here at last was a beautiful dry treelessness, dusty green and purple in the rain shadow. Orchards and vineyards lined the valley of the Similkameen down to the United States border. Sage brush dotted the grass, you could see the heavy shapes of the hills, and here and there, gaping out of them, the toothless mouth of a mine.

I crossed the border on a tiny road near the small town of Nighthawk, Washington. Two neat border posts with their flags stood on either side of the parallel. It was a beautiful valley, that smoky green that fringes into purple in the grass, a weather-honed corral just down in the dip from the road. The border guard wore a miniature pair of handcuffs, gilt, as a tie-pin. 'They're for little people,' he said. 'Have you been here long?' I asked him. 'No time at all. It's just under nine years now and I haven't even got myself a horse.'

He was right. I suddenly recognised where I was. This dry, empty, horizon-rich and scarcely-coloured place was the northern tail, the last tenuous extension of the American West.

More mountains to cross, a forest road up and over the Sherman pass at just under six thousand feet, snow sprinkling the windscreen and dusting the road. All I did was drive, loving every minute of it, sucking up miles like spaghetti, down to the flooded valley of the upper Columbia, and then in the dark to Spokane, America spreading out to the south in front of me, a continent of miles, a coast-to-coast invitation. I am glad to be back in the States. As someone in Wolfie's Saloon, here in Kellogg, said to me just now, 'When I was in Canada it felt as if I was in a foreign country.' That was exactly my sensation.

I picked Kellogg on the map because I liked the name. It's just down the road from Smelterville which was the other option. This is mining country but times are bad. Six years ago (all this from the bartender in Wolfie's – only me and her in the bar) 4,000 men were working in the Kellogg silver and nickel mines. Now that figure is down to 200. Many have 'relocated' as she said (another horrible euphemism like 'let go' for 'got rid of') but there are still 1,300 people unemployed in this town out of an adult working population of 2,000. 'We don't even look at the silver price in the paper any more,' she said. 'It's just gone too far down. There are going to be quite a few pretty big holes made in Bolivia before that mine gets going again.'

Here, starkly, was the flaw in the idea that America is the land of freedom. Other people's power to control the silver market, to drive prices low enough to make Kellogg's Lucky Friday mine uneconomic, to push 3,800 Idahoans out of work – that huge force in the shaping of America is somehow smeared over by the dominant myth of the individual struggling on the frontier. Nothing should be allowed to interfere with his ability to do that, the story goes, as if Nelson Bunker Hunt were some kind of 1830s mountainman, for whom any sort of control would spell disaster. The bartender's husband was off in Alaska. He was getting himself ready to take up the placer claim he had near Nome. 'That's all you can do. It's no use crying your eyes out down here in front of the hockey on the TV.'

Butte, Montana

Friday 25 April

ADAM *to Nigel*   I've arrived in heaven. It's snowing, 28° Fahrenheit
                       and this is the most fascinating place. It too was a
mining town, the greatest and richest in the west. In the 1890s, inconceivably,
Butte had a population of 130,000, only slightly less than Los Angeles. As
cowboys and Indians were fighting each other a few miles to the east of here,
a gut-busting, violent, dynamic mining city was living as hard as it could on
the richest hill in the world. Miners from Ireland, Scotland, China, Cornwall,
South America, Finland, Italy, Serbia poured in at first for the gold, of which
there was little, and then for the silver, of which there was slightly more, and
eventually for the copper, of which there were unimaginable amounts, and
for which, with the beginning of the electrical industry, there was an almost
limitless market. By about 1950 more than 250 underground mines had been
sunk into the hill, some of them a mile deep. There were underground battles
fought with dynamite and pickaxes between rival claimants for the same piece
of ore body. There were violent political battles between the three great
copper kings – William Clark, Marcus Daly and Augustus Heinze (he looked
like Oscar Wilde) – who emerged on top of this pullulating mass of voracious
humanity. Clark built an enormous Elizabethan mansion with Tiffany windows and turrets in 'Uptown' Butte, as they say. Daly had an even larger
apartment building constructed next to it in order to block the view. All this
when your grandmother was flirting with Rodin. But even these monstrous
and ruthless men were eventually bought out by the Anaconda Company.

They didn't bother with underground shafts. After about 1955 they opened
a giant pit, a mile wide, destroying Butte's prettiest park, the Columbia
Gardens, and removing nearly 1.5 billion tons of rock. Even this has shut
down now and poisoned water is filling the hole, now officially called a 'Toxic
Water Repository'. The thousands of miles of tunnels in the hill are flooded
too. It is an extraordinary thought as you walk about in the mostly deserted
streets of Uptown Butte, where department stores modelled on Florentine
palaces and Miners' Halls on Tuscan villas rot above the second storey, that
underneath the entire hill, like three or four blocks of Manhattan stacked on
top of each other, is this flooded, poisoned, excavated world, poking up into
the light in the few iron headframes like gallows that stand around the hill.

Anaconda pulled out of Butte in 1982. All the juice of the town – the banks,
the main post office, the shopping mall – has slid down off the hill and on to
the 'Flats', where it has pooled out as an undiluted slick of average America.
The old Uptown is left like a stage set in which the buildings are real brick,
but many are boarded up. The hotels advertising fireproof frames in red and

yellow letters on their sidewalls have now been turned into the shoddy offices of lawyers and insurance agents. This, as you know, is the sort of place I like more than any in the world, where an extraordinary derelict beauty emerges, neither contrived nor worked for, but thick with a skeletal silence that I could drink for days.

Now very late, it must be 4 in the morning. There's an aerobic class on the TV. I've been in the Silver Dollar Saloon all night. Butte has another side to it. A band called the Players from Paradise Valley near Livingston played straight-down-the-line old-fashioned American rock and I danced with girls I hadn't even talked to and then talked to one called Robin for hours. She's a DJ on the radio station here and last week shaved her hair off. She was wearing a 1920s strapless affair and danced very nicely. And then an even longer talk to a miner called Tom Satterley, who isn't a miner any more but draws geological maps. We talked solid geology through all the variations of Rainier and Bud. Do you remember I had a phase a few years ago when I wanted to be a geologist? Well, it all came pouring out. Tom, a huge man, with an interest in Arthurian legend and neolithic stone circles, has also tapped straight into the mother lode of poetry that's buried inside all the technicalities of rock. Of course, I can't remember a word he said now, but it was a *mélange* of feldspar and opportunity, of colliding continents and subducting plates, of molten granites rising from hidden zones and endless veins of hot liquid metal, spreading like an excitement into the crust. And then there would be more music and we would dance with randomly chosen girls and Robin would talk about rock music and Tom would lecture me on Glastonbury legends. This is a wonderful country. I've never been happier in my life.

Warren–Cleveland, Ohio

Saturday 26 April

NIGEL *to Adam*   The Avalon Hotel is too expensive for me – $85 with dinner – but there seemed to be no choice. It's surprising that small towns have no motels at all, and larger ones like Warren at most two. Yet it is a smart holiday resort. Pretty women drive themselves around it in pretty cars. The car parked next to mine is festooned in pink and yellow rosettes, signifying honeymooners. The Avalon lies between two golf-courses. Early in the morning I borrowed one of the electric golf-carts and rolled over the fairways. I asked the pro why people didn't walk, as the main purpose of golf is exercise. 'Perhaps because they're lazy,' he replied shortly. Later I joined them. There's all the difference between the expert and the amateur golfer. The expert swings his driver like an extension of his arms. The amateur stands hunched, anticipating humiliation in every wobble of his club, and then attacks the ball with the awkwardness of a sickle instead of the smoothness of a scythe. Practice, it seems, never makes the amateur perfect.

The approach to Cleveland follows a pattern that I'd not seen in Canada, and very different from your Portland niceness. First come lovely suburbs for the rich, then 5 shattering miles of shopping-malls and gas-stations, next Victorian and inter-war houses decaying into ugliness, then the city centre shining with high-risers, and finally Lake Erie. The middle section is mostly inhabited by blacks. One sees them driving in decent cars, and there is much laughter in the streets. But I'd hate to be involved in a traffic-hassle with a black. He would probably be more resentful, and I more apologetic, than we would be if of the same race. There's no doubt that there is a form of apartheid here, even though the law forbids it. You rarely see a black and white walking together, or bunched in the same car, and while the affluent whites *behave* courteously towards the blacks, they still *think* segregationally, as we do too in England (at least my generation does). With 40 per cent of the young Cleveland blacks unemployed, many of them illiterate in spite of education, feeling deprived, *being* deprived, living apart, being so immediately identifiable by their colour, it is not surprising.

Central Cleveland on a Saturday afternoon is very empty, all businesses and most shops closed. I found a café in the main street which appeared clean and even palatial from outside, but when I ordered fish fillet and French fries, they were uneatable. Could I have a roll and butter? No roll, no butter. I thought of the twenties song:

> The waiter bawled
> Right down the hall,
> 'We don't serve bread
> With one meat-ball'

which expresses all the melancholy and humiliation of the Depression. It wasn't a waiter but a waitress, not meat but fish, and she didn't bawl, she spoke. But the tawdriness and sloppiness of fast-food counters saddened me in just the same way, and I left my uneaten meal for the sunny walks beside the lake.

Later I went to Cleveland's Museum of Art, which is superb. The collection – Oriental, European, American – contains everything from shining medieval armour to contemporary twists of battered metal. My main purpose was to see one picture, which Ben flew (he hated flying) 4,000 miles to see, Georges De La Tour's *The Repentant St Peter*. From a dark cloak emerge the saint's clasped hands and his uplifted face, bearing the same expression of pleading generosity as I've often seen on Quentin Bell's, our Chairman, when I've argued too hotly at a Charleston committee-meeting. I also found something unexpected – Marie Antoinette's bed, which Sir John Murray-Scott ('Seery') bequeathed to my grandmother, and which she immediately sold to pay for central-heating at Knole. A Terbrugghen, a Savonnerie carpet, nineteenth-century American landscapes, Greek marbles – I spent two happy hours recovering from the fast-food.

My hosts for the night were Harvey and Penny Buchanan, friends of the Francis's of Walpole. He is Professor of Art History at the University, and she organises teachers' courses at the Museum. He looks a bit like Geoffrey Howe, she a younger Frances Partridge. Their house lies twenty minutes east of Cleveland in a countrified setting. From their back porch you could imagine yourself in Sussex. The weather has leapt from winter straight into summer. A dandelion-spangled meadow with a white barn in its centre (all that it lacks is a piebald horse) extends towards a thin spinney. Wild cherry, daffodils and tulips are in flower. The house was originally built in 1834 by the first immigrants from Connecticut, and now it is one of many in the village of Gates Mills, each standing on a minimum of $2\frac{1}{2}$ acres and subject to stringent aesthetic regulations imposed by the village community. No building of modern design is permitted, nothing higher than three, preferably two, storeys, and even the windows on the side away from the road must conform to the general impression of English country gentility.

Having contrasted this idyllic scene with the mess I'd seen on the approaches to Cleveland, Harvey explained with the aid of a biscuit (the city centre) set in the middle of a red napkin (the now decaying inner city) and his hands (the affluent suburbs like the one in which we sat), how waves of immigrants, the railway, the car, and the Second World War, gradually made Cleveland what it is. Over dinner we discussed the social implications of all this, then turned to the Museum and the arts. We three were alone, with wine and salmon. It was infinitely preferable to the large dinner-parties which I've attended, when one gets to know everyone slightly but nobody well.

Outside Livingston, Montana on the
banks of the Yellowstone

Sunday 27 April

ADAM *to Nigel*   I'm staying on a ranch. Jon Foote's name had been given me by David Barry (I will be forever grateful to that man). So I rang him. 'Yeah, sure, come along!' he said down the phone. So I arrived yesterday. It is one of the most spectacularly beautiful places I know. (Are there too many superlatives in this book? I can't help it.)

A timber house and barn stand near each other on either side of some massive cottonwood trees. There are one or two small paddocks going down the Yellowstone and in them horses, wearing quilted blankets, snort and whinny. Cut wood and bales of hay are stacked around the yard and a couple of mud-encrusted pick-ups are parked at one side. All this sounds contained and enclosed but I have left the best until last. Beyond the river to the south – it is shallow and fast running here divided by islands and lined with cottonwoods which are now just coming into yellow, celery-coloured leaf like old men waking – beyond all that, about 7 miles away, are the mountains, the Absarokas. They come in and out of the clouds, sometimes like this morning bright and present, at others hidden in fog, so that all you see are the low tree-covered skirts. People say that you would tire of a view like this. I can't imagine it.

When I arrived yesterday all I knew about Jon was that he's a Yale man, an architect. That was the run of it. As I parked the Catalina in the corner of the yard (it's started to fall apart by the way – various functions that were electrically automatic in Los Angeles are now of necessity manual) there was a cowboy putting grease on a muck-spreader. Everything about him was as it should be: the white hat marked with sweat on the line where the brim joins the crown, dirtied with thumbmarks in the dimple near the top, where a hand lifts it off in greeting; the old Levi jacket, the Levi jeans, the heeled and pointed boots caked in mud; the positive stance and the absolutely un-troubled straight-down-the-barrel look. This was the Yale architect. He is a wonderful man and I am having the time of my life here now, staying with him and his wife Jennifer and son Nathaniel. Jon I suppose is in his 50s, Jennifer in her 30s and Nathaniel (from whose mother Jon is now divorced) 19.

You must know those occasions when shared enthusiasms and equivalent histories spark a feeling of utter friendship with someone whom you have only just met. They are rare enough to be treasured and it is the feeling I have with the Footes. We have done little else but talk since I got here, about my history and their history and our attitudes to fathers (but I took the signal in the Boston letter (17 April) loud and clear – no more naked investigations of the FSR for the time being. I will only say that I liked your response very much and that it's curious how we both know to bury the critical word deep down in the middle of a sentence.) Anyway – throat-clearing – the really fascinating thing about Jon Foote is how the Yale man, who is the scion of an old New England family, whose ancestor arrived in the New World in the 1630s, who was persuaded for a short time to consider banking as his life, who until he was 40 lived a laced up existence as an east coast architect – how this man has ripped straight through all that to become the cowboy I met in the yard. That's not putting it quite right, because it sounds as if his life here is a simple rejection of all that east coast performance. It's subtler than that. On the ranch here he and Jennifer breed, train and ride cutting horses. (I will explain about that later – as usual America is flooding me with stimuli I simply cannot keep pace with.) But Jon also practises as an architect and teaches at the University of Montana Architecture School in Bozeman. He hasn't rejected the east but has adopted the west. It is not a rejection of that conscious, controlling element of American culture, but a fulfilling of it, an extension and deepening of it that has attracted him here. And that is where the cutting horses come in. When a cowboy wants to take a single cow from a herd he isolates or 'cuts' it from the rest of them. Like all the cowboy skills, this is now a sport in which the elegance and exactness with which the cow can be cut and then kept away from the herd is the measure of the skill. This sounds simple enough but the whole point of cutting is that the rider is never allowed to tighten the reins on the bit in the horse's mouth. For the $2\frac{1}{2}$ minutes in the ring the reins must stay slack all the time. The only control the rider has is in training (or 'tuning' as it's called) the horse beforehand and the use of his spurs during the ride itself. It's a sport in which an extraordinary degree of understanding has to be developed between the rider and the animal, as the cow, trying to get back into the herd, flits and dodges around in front of the horse, and the horse, sweating with the intensity of its concentration and effort, springs, twists and throws itself back and forth in front of the cow. It is extraordinary how thrilling this drama is. Jennifer is a star at this but the point I'm getting to is that Jon, in 1984, this Yale architect, was the Montana Cutting Horse Champion. If anything can make this country whole – this is a metaphorical way of talking – it seems to me that one achievement does it. It is that breadth of enterprise and energy and commitment and achievement – *none* of it at the expense of any of the civilised values Europeans congratulate themselves on so widely – which makes me admire this country. There's the serious heart of it for you. But with Jon Foote – and you can see I'm amazed by this man – it goes a step further.

Two weeks after he won the Montana Championship he was riding his favourite mare on the dirt road that goes by the top of his ranch. It was broad daylight. A woman he knew slightly came towards him in her truck and ended up careering straight into Jon and his mare. The mare's leg was broken and so was Jon's back. Average people might have been destroyed by this, or at least embittered by it. Not Foote. His back is agony much of the time but he insists on riding, even doing some cutting again. 'The physical pain', he told me, 'is virtually unbearable but the emotional pleasure makes it worth it. Almost.' This man represents the very best of this country. We are going down to Jackson Hole later this week to see something of the buildings he is putting up there.

By the way, I had a good set of letters from you in Butte. It was interesting that Professor Watts in Kingston (this was 22 April) should have thought that he saw guns at Berkeley. He *may* have seen them. He certainly would have wanted to see them, but the fact is that when I was there, anyway, there wasn't a gun in sight.

Cleveland–Bloomfield Hills
(near Detroit), Michigan

Sunday 27 April

NIGEL *to Adam*   I regret that I shall not see another hill higher than
                                  a few hundred feet while this trip lasts. I've entered
the plains sooner than I expected. The State of Ohio is cut by by-roads into squares just as they were ruled by the original surveyors, and the farms stand like chessman on a vast board. It is difficult to find one's way off the main highways, because there are no signposts, as there are no villages to point to, but it is pleasant to be lost in the lanes. I'm astonished by the fertility of the soil. It looks as if a farmer could make a decent living off 100 acres. Nearer Lake Erie I bypassed huge industrial towns like Toledo and Detroit, for my destination was neither of them. I was visiting Cranbrook–Kingswood School in lower Michigan.

The school is sister, or you might say daughter, to our own Cranbrook School in Kent, but only in so far as they share a name, and that not by chance, because the father of its founder, George Booth, came from our Cranbrook. The father made a fortune in newspaper publishing. I met George's son Henry, now 90, alert, impressive, busy in the office of his father's very English country mansion, and he told me how he had visited Cranbrook to see his grandfather's house, near the windmill. The sudden association was very strange.

In every other respect Cranbrook, Michigan, is very different from the Cranbrook School of which I was Chairman of the Governors for ten years. There is no adjoining town. The setting is park-like and lush. Quiet roads serpentine through glades and meadows, and at intervals stand the large suburban houses of the wealthy of Detroit, the smaller houses of the school faculty, the associated junior and middle schools, an Academy of Art for postgraduates and a Science Museum. It is quite a complex, reeking of education. The school campus is highly enviable. It was planned by George Booth in 1927 and designed by the Finnish architect, Eliel Saarinen, as a large quadrangle surrounded on all four sides by varied buildings in brick and stone and half-timbering, which gives the impression of a Scandinavian version of an English college faintly Americanised. It is calm, muted and edifying. The girls' school,

Kingswood, 15 minutes away on foot (but the children bus – why not bicycle?) has been amalgamated in the past year with the boys' school, and this was also designed by Saarinen, more feminine, less traditional, art-deco. You must imagine the two campuses as something not unlike Welwyn Garden City, but less crowded, much more rural.

Cranbrook–Kingswood is an independent school, fee-paying, with scholarships to help less wealthy parents. At dinner with Margot and Ben Snyder, which was also attended by the Headmaster, Sam Salas, I asked whether the school was considered élitist. No more than Eton, was the reply, and in fact less so, because two-thirds of the children are day-pupils from the neighbourhood. It is true that at first the grander universitites like Harvard looked with some suspicion at an independent school outside Detroit. They thought it couldn't be serious. It is extremely serious. Its moral, educational and athletic aims are the highest. The brochure issued to pupils and parents describes them in terms that might have been derived straight from Arnold's Rugby. The Headmaster defines them thus in his Introduction: 'To instil in you a deep sense of respect for yourself and for every human being' (a tall order), 'and to enable you to take responsibility for the common good.' Kingswood's school song, pure Benenden, leads off with the verse:

> Beside a lake, beneath an oak-clad hill,
> Stands Kingswood School, a mission to fulfil,
> Of leading youth to great nobility.
> Gladly to serve humanity.

How could one sing that with a straight face? I suspect the girls don't, any more than they take literally the rules about 'attire'. There must be no jeans or T-shirts for either sex, but I saw many of both in both. Pearls, bangles and silvered ear-rings cannot have been in George Booth's permitted inventory, but they are worn without exciting protest from the faculty. Tomorrow I'll find out more.

Cranbrook–Columbus, Ohio

Monday 28 April

NIGEL *to Adam*   I am back at school. It's not Puyallup High. Under the guidance of Fred Roth, head of the English Department, I toured the campuses and attended two classes, each of sixteen boys and girls. The first discussed James Joyce's *The Dubliners*, the second a collection of short stories by the American writer Bobbie Ann Mason. The atmosphere is more like a university seminar than a school lesson. The relationship between pupils and teachers is informal. They interrupt. They throw and field questions. Discipline does not figure at all, because the assumption on both sides is that there is no need for it. The children are articulate and deeply attentive – most of the time, for someone had doodled on the table before me the initials of a loved one. The table was round, and the eighteen of us (counting the teacher and me) focused inward with wrapt concentration. I made no contribution beyond explaining at the start who I was.

I was struck by the large number of children of Asian origin. Three of them (and one black) were among my first sixteen. I gazed, without her noticing it, at one girl who may have come from Korea. Goodness knows what her history, or her parents', may have been. But here she was at Cranbrook, beautiful, silent (I longed to hear her voice), listening with a profound desire to understand the doubly alien culture of James Joyce. She ideally represented the new wave of immigrants into this country, and America's eagerness to share its bounty. A few others were European or South American (Sam Salas himself is Chilean). I talked to a very bright youth of 18 from Bolton in Lancashire, a chess Grand Master you might have thought him, who had come here with an English Speaking Union scholarship. When pressed, he said that the educational level was lower than that at home (I saw no sign of that), but he found the school atmosphere freer, less competitive, more congenial. A black girl, a dancer, to whom I talked during the school lunch, was equally at ease; she would not have known the meaning of segregation. Many others came up to me to ask what I was doing here. There's an explicit friendliness about the place, to which the fine architecture and gardens make a subliminal contribution.

Afterwards, Fred Roth took me round the main buildings and sports grounds. By British standards they are lavish, except that by an inexplicable decree of George Booth there must be no swimming-pool, a rule which they hope to bend. The indoor and outdoor tennis-courts, the gymnasium, the battery of weaving looms, the Gothic church, the science laboratories, the associated museum, all amount to an educational opportunity that can have few equals in the world. The only course missing from the syllabus is what we would call Home Economics, specially cooking. I asked why. Because the girls would regard it as fixing them for life in the kitchen, and the boys will develop into Yuppies who take their wives to a restaurant every evening. What very contemporary reasons! It is a matter of pride that all Cranbrook–Kingswood pupils move on to higher education, but then so do 50 per cent of all American children. It's an incredible proportion compared with ours.

I left Cranbrook with reluctance to drive south. My visit there had been a spur off my planned itinerary, and I was back on the wide fields of Ohio to find a night's lodging in Columbus. The trees here are all in fresh leaf. It's summer again. The clocks have been advanced an hour. I too look across the TV weather-map to see how you're doing.

T-Square Ranch, Livingston, Montana

Tuesday 29 April

ADAM *to Nigel*   I'm still here, looking at the Absarokas across the valley. Jennifer says it's one of the problems they have: people stay far too long. She said it, waited and then gave me a great hug to show she didn't mean it. The clouds have gone, the willows and the cottonwoods are greening up. I'm typing outside in the mountain sunshine (the ranch is 400 feet higher than Ben Nevis, but it's only the light that would make you guess it, thin and hard, concealing nothing) and the ticking of the typewriter sounds trivial in the outside air. A hawk with khaki wings and white primaries at the tips is hunting, circling and then flapping in a mundane, businesslike way, over the far bank of the Yellowstone. The Absarokas are bunched and folded, cut by one deep valley, opening a gap that's filled at the far end with a blunt white summit called the Elephant's Head. The horses nibble in the paddock. Nathaniel is writing songs on the guitar which he plays down the telphone to friends in New York. Jennifer is preparing her horses for a cutting in St Ignatius at the weekend. I'm going to Bozeman with her later to watch her tune the star, a rather misshapen animal called Tiny, who is, apparently, a world class cutter. Jonathan is designing an extension to a hotel. It's strange how his physical appearance changes, the shape of his face alters, as he plays his different roles. As the architect he tightens and sharpens; as the cowboy he opens and expands. We've talked about this. He sees it as a dialogue, not a division, between the adult and the child in him, each one at ease with and enriching the other.

I've been killing dandelions all morning and fertilising the grass. Doug Bayley on Orcas told me that dandelions came over with the Pilgrim Fathers and they are now the commonest weed in America. 'Just like the guilt,' he said and I've been merciless, zapping each bright vulgar head with some vicious capsuled poison.

I went for a long walk yesterday afternoon up on to the hills, with my hands in my pockets and one or two breaks in the cloud. 'He had run up and down America,' I had read in a novel by Tom McGuane the night before, 'unable to find that apocryphal country in any of its details.' So hands in pockets, with the Footes' dog called Jake to kill the rattle-snakes and to keep me company. Sweet Jake, who likes playing football with stones, didn't seem to mind the prickly pears, the nasty little cacti that cover the grass and gave Lewis and Clark such a frightful time on their portage around the Great Falls, spiking their already spiked feet through the useless moccasins. Jake danced all over them, chasing the gophers, cocking his head sideways like an interviewer over the entrances to their little holes. I caught up with him at one point, standing stiff and still except for a slow wag of the tail, staring into the middle of a low and bushy juniper tree. 'Go on,' I said without thinking and he leapt in with a scrabble between the branches. All I could see for a moment was his orange wagging tail sticking out from the juniper. Then a reverse and he emerged with a gopher – a grey, squirrel-like thing with a measly bit of string for a tail – in his mouth and a smile in his eyes. He flipped it around so that the head was between his jaws and then he crunched it. There was no screaming, just the noise of Thomas digging around inside a bag of crisps as Jake destroyed the gopher's skull. A gout of dark blood came out between the gopher's lips and Jake looked at me for a moment before walking over to a corral where he dropped the dead animal in a piece of melting snow. It looked as if it had been dead for days, its fur separated and wet, its pathetic anatomy displayed on the snow. Jake licked its face and then walked off, swaying and wagging as before.

I followed him, over and under the barbed wire fences, which are invisible from a distance but divide the open range every few hundred yards or so. The country, patterned with snow like a skin-disease, a blotching, rolls on for ever to the north, rising on one side to the blunt and rusted bluff of Sheep Mountain, like the side of a tanker that has somehow beached here, and climbing beyond it to the snowy massif of the Crazy Mountains. This is not really the country for walking. Nobody has ever walked here. It's too big. It goes on for ever. The nearest I have ever come to it is in the Auvergne, where France rolls out for hundreds of uninterrupted miles every way you look. I reached the small rise I had been aiming at for a couple of hours – a non-destination, a little wrinkle in the crust – and smoked a cigarette looking back over the valley of the Yellowstone. Jake lay full length on the snow as if we had arrived. Cloud pulled away at the peaks of the Absarokas. Clark had come back this way in 1806, his half of the expedition (Lewis was returning on the more northerly route) in two canoes tied together, tearing down the current 90 or 100 miles a day, reaching for home through country that was rich with game. This must have been the happiest of times. Clark was wildly optimistic about everything he passed: rivers, which in fact are shallow, gravelly streams, he reckoned suitable for all sorts of heavy trading vessels. Their confluences, where there is no more than a small ranch today, crucified on the agonising economics of raising beef that sells for only 50c a pound *on the hoof*, Clark thought would be the prime sites for the great western cities of the future. You can see why. This country is too beautiful for any realistic assessment. Jake and I followed our tracks down through the snow back to the ranch here on the river, where the mayflies are hatching. Jon says that I must not forget to mention how brutal the winters are here.

Columbus–Cincinnati, Ohio

Tuesday-Wednesday 29-30 April

NIGEL *to Adam*   Cincinnati ought to have a beautiful riverfront, but hasn't. The Ohio is historically more important than the Mississippi, for it was downstream from Pittsburgh to Cincinnati and Louisville that the great tide of pioneers flowed until the railways were built, and it is lovelier. Jefferson described the Ohio as 'the most beautiful river on earth' (that he never set eyes on it did not diminish his enthusiasm). 'Its current gentle, its water clear, and its bosom smooth and unbroken by rocks and rapids,' except one, at Louisville. But Cincinnati turns its back on the river, and its five bridges are in different ways ugly. Its beauty lies within it. This was the place where Frances Trollope spent many unhappy months and wrote of it insultingly. But today no other American city is so civic nor so civil. There is no great pressure of traffic in the centre, for the expressways divert it; there are open spaces like Fountain Square where you can stroll and sit; and, best of all, pedestrian ways on several levels from building to building and by bridges across intervening streets. I've never seen anything like it. It's as if you could walk the length of Bond Street without ever emerging into the open air, passing through office lobbies, department stores and restaurants in an unbroken chain. The shops are luxurious, the cafés set out like those in the great piazza of Venice, but indoors. I had to come away with something from this elongated, glittering bazaar, so bought a pair of socks.

A baseball game was scheduled for 12.30, a Business Man's Special to attract the lunchtime crowd, and I followed them into the stadium, thinking that between us we must cover at least one sporting event. (I'll leave Rodeo to you.) The enormous stadium lies on the river, but pays no tribute to it, being, like all stadia, wholly self-centred. It holds in its bowl 55,000 people when full. Today there were barely 15,000, because the home team, the Cincinnati Reds, are in disgrace with their supporters for having lost nearly all this season's games. Their opponents today were the Montreal Expos, easy meat for the Reds anyone would have said six months ago, but again the Reds went down, 0–8.

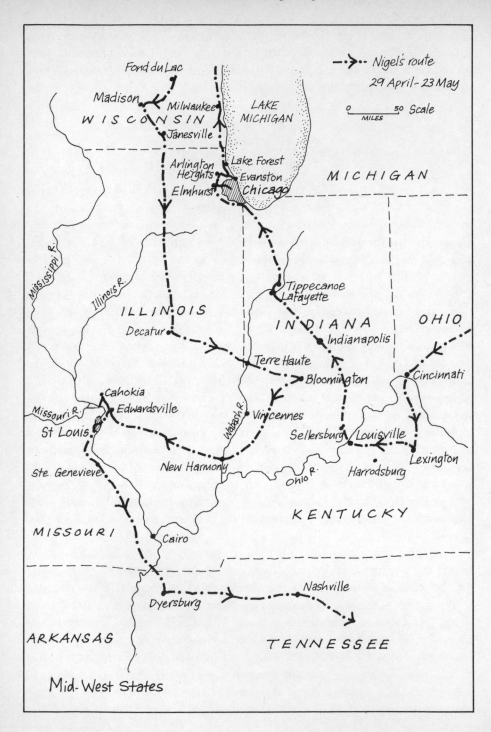

Fond du Lac
Madison
Milwaukee
W I S C O N S I N
Janesville
LAKE
MICHIGAN

Nigel's route
29 April - 23 May
0   50 Scale
    MILES

Arlington
Heights   Lake Forest
                 Evanston
Elmhurst   Chicago

M I C H I G A N

MISSISSIPPI R.

Illinois R.

I L L I N O I S

Decatur

Tippecanoe
Lafayette

I N D I A N A

Indianapolis

O H I O

Cincinnati

Terre Haute
Bloomington

Cahokia
Missouri R.   Edwardsville
St Louis

Wabach R.

Vincennes

Sellersburg Louisville

Lexington

New Harmony

Ohio R.

Harrodsburg

Ste. Genevieve

K E N T U C K Y

M I S S O U R I   Cairo

Nashville

Dyersburg

A R K A N S A S   T E N N E S S E E

Mid-West States

I was disappointed by the first live baseball game I've ever watched, for a simple reason – I could not grasp the method, the scoring or the rules, and being ignorant of what was supposed to happen, I found what did happen unintelligible. It would be the same for an American watching his first game of cricket. I must have been the only one of the 15,000 unable to follow the play, and the electric scoreboard was little help, for it assumed familiarity not only with the system, but with the entire life-stories of the stars, whose portraits appeared from time to time in lights. My neighbours on the bench were two elderly women who cheered and jeered with total comprehension and partisanship. To ask them for explanations would have spoiled their enjoyment. But at half-time the board signalled a message which even I could half decipher:

	R	H	E
Expos	4	5	0
Reds	0	0	0

Clearly the Reds were in trouble.

I'll give you a short résumé. The pitcher winds himself up like a piece of mechanism and hurls the ball at the batter who strikes at it with a bat little broader than a broomstick. Sometimes the pitcher's aim is out-of-true, and the batter disdainfully ignores it. Sometimes he flays and misses. Then he throws away his bat in disgust. More often he smites it hard, and the ball sails into the outfield or the spectators' stands (when this happens, the finder of the ball is allowed to keep it). Then everyone runs from base to base. I'll not go on with this. It gets too complicated, and you've often seen it on television. I bought a book of rules a hundred pages long, but the only one I understood was the first: 'Baseball is a game played between two teams of nine players each. The objective of each team is to win by scoring more points than the opponent.' That, after all, is the objective of most games.

Afterwards I talked to a man in a bar who was ready to enlighten me. I asked him why the pitcher almost always seemed to be the hero, not the batter. The pitcher has only to throw; the batter has to hit a missile coming at him at 90 m.p.h. from 60 feet away, an amazing feat of eye and timing. He explained that in fact pitching demanded even greater skill, as he has only a narrow 'window' at which to aim, between lines right and left and the batter's knees and head. Compared to American Football, he found it a dull game, and the Reds, his home team, lamentable. After a series of defeats, they go into each new game with a load of humiliation and self-reproach, augmented by the vocal contempt of their fans, who do not hesitate to boo an incompetent player, not just once, but whenever the ball floats in his direction. It is the sound of accumulating derision which must often have echoed through the

Roman Colosseum. So the team loses again, as they did today to Montreal. I asked if the manager would be fired. Perhaps, but it's rare.

We have now completed half our journey, and in celebration I had my hair cut and my clothes laundered, and took the Thunderbird to have its face washed and innards examined by Avis at Kentucky Airport. It has taken me four thousand miles, most of which was getting in and out of Boston, without a fault or a drop of added oil. Like you, I have found rushing from place to place unrewarding, and I plan generally to stay two days in a single place and drive the third. I've been two nights in Cincinnati, and will be three in Louisville, with Lexington in between, just to put me in an equine mood for Saturday's Derby.

T-Square Ranch, Livingston, Montana

Wednesday 30 April

ADAM *to Nigel*   After watching Jennifer tune Tiny yesterday in a covered school near Bozeman, we had dinner in a smart restaurant. The tuning was a little uneventful at first. A lot of loosening up and riding round and round in circles. Then a few cows were brought in for Tiny to do his stuff. He wasn't paying attention and the essence of cutting is attention. The horse has to be thinking of the cow and nothing but the cow. When the cow even hints at moving to the left, the horse must follow. If there is even the slightest lag or reluctance or laziness in its reaction, the judges will strip points away with disastrous effects. World Championships have been lost in the last few seconds as a horse starts to think of something other than a cow. You've got to pity the poor animals in a way. And that's Jennifer's trouble. She's far too nice. She loves Tiny and doesn't want to make it hurt. Tiny – it's just like raising children – knows this and makes full use of all Jennifer's sweetness and generosity. But Jennifer knows he knows it and today was the day that Jennifer was going to let him know she knew that he knew. This involved spurs. She strapped on a pair of spiky asterisks **. Tiny began reluctant. He was OK turning to the left. It was turning to the right that was the problem. But Jennifer really dug in and, for the first time in her life, drew blood from his flank. She felt terrible about it but she knew it had to happen. A horrible woman from White Sulphur Springs with a voice like over-ripe Gorgonzola twitted and reproached Jennifer and Jennifer paid no attention. Then there was a pause and Gorgonzola creamed on about her knowledge of animals, human and equine. Then Jennifer climbed back on Tiny and five more cows were brought into the ring. For the first time I saw what this sport was about. It was thrilling. As the cow jigged here and there trying to get back to its fellows clustered up in the back corner of the ring, Tiny, dancing on the springs in his legs and his muscles, headed it off, half dancing, half wrestling with the intentions of the other animal, his whole body taut and elastic, a desperate sweat-soaked intensity in meeting the cow's every move. When I think of horses I think of them moving steadily and easily in the one same fluid direction, but here was a creature in the sort of dense crisis I associate only with hawks or jaguars. Every resource Tiny had was being poured into that moment, each of his legs was moving independently, his head was down low, his eyes wide and open, his flanks and shoulders dark with sweat, while Jennifer, a mask for a face, held on to the saddle horn, apparently above it all. This moment can't have lasted more than twenty seconds, but it was worth all that waiting and all that horrible Gorgonzola. As soon as he had done it, Jennifer stopped. She had tuned him. He was now ready for the cutting at the end of the week, when he would remember how she had hurt him.

And then on to dinner in a scarcely lit restaurant, where we met yet another remarkable man. Never in my life have I met such a string of extraordinary people as on this trip, articulate, courageous, open-hearted people. Saul Benjamin is in his 30s. He had been born in a poor, raw district of East Los Angeles, and after a rough childhood, somehow got himself to Yale, won a Rhodes scholarship to Oxford, had written poetry there which had won the National Poetry Prize and is going to be published by Faber in a book called *Stradivarius at 92* (age, not temperature), worked for two years as Mondale's chief issues analyst in the White House, was offered a job at Yale but didn't want to return to the sort of set up he knew too well and instead has spent the last year or two creating an Honors Programme in the University of Montana in Bozeman while writing a book on Dostoevsky and Hegel and fighting a losing battle against those forces in the state which are cutting away at funding for education. An amazing man, passionate in his opposition to all those forces of inequality and privilege which perpetuate the establishment, which prevent anyone less remarkable than himself from emerging and doing what he has done. I just sat back and listened after a while. I thought of all those people you have been meeting on the East coast, all the people I know in England, so cosy in our structures, playing the one game we have always been taught how to play. Here was a man who had fought his way into that world and could now be reaping all its easy rewards, but had chosen not to. I kept asking why in different ways, but he always slid past the question. Jonathan made an argument for the burden of privilege. Saul filleted it and Jennifer, who had a complicated and even confused childhood, half east, half west, half nurtured, half ignored, said that she envied us three the same one thing: the certainty of a strong background, whether Connecticut, East LA or Sissinghurst, which we could either hold on to or reject, or perhaps even both at the same time. At least we had something there, something which either in the negative or the positive could make us what we were. Nothing, in effect, is more comfortable than swinging between poles. It's the absence of poles that is difficult.

Cincinnati–Lexington, Kentucky

Thursday 1 May

NIGEL *to Adam* Lexington has always been a familiar name to me as the centre of the Bluegrass country where the horses live. It is one of the cities in the US which the Queen has often visited, brought here, to witness the ceremonial mating of stallion with mare. But for me Lexington has another, less conjugal, association. With Harrodsburg, not far away, it was the terminus of the Wilderness Trail which Daniel Boone pioneered in the 1770s from the passes I saw weeks ago on the Blue Ridge Parkway in Virginia, the first toe-hold, you might say, which Americans established in the Indian country beyond the Appalachians.

There's not a great deal here to remind you of that historic fact. I found a plaque which mentioned that a party of hunters had camped here in 1775 and gave it the name Lexington. Another which stated that 'On this site stood the first blockhouse'. On this site today stands a multi-storey car park in which I stabled the Thunderbird. A statue or two, equestrian of course. And a strange aberration, a stone plinth marking the navel of the city, on which is perched the model of – a camel! Otherwise Lexington is a normal American city, striving to assert itself, and succeeding, by high-rise office blocks, the tallest and newest sheeted in blue glass, hotels and shopping malls. No place rebuilds itself so rapidly. A church proclaims proudly that it is the fourth church to have occupied the site in little more than a century. The Victorian buildings, apart from two private houses, one of them Henry Clay's, the greatest of all American senators, are undistinguished. Perhaps I was expecting too much. A town famous for its origins as a wilderness settlement of log cabins, and which has since prided itself on its 'development', was not until recently interested in preserving relics of its past.

The surrounding country is lovely. The grass is not blue but Irish-green. As I drove here from Cincinnati, the dull plains of Ohio were replaced by little hills garrisoned by soldier-cypresses and horsefarms coralled by slab fences painted white. I visited the most famous of them, the Kentucky Horse Park, which is the equestrian equivalent of the most luxurious Holiday Inn.

The white and grey stables, separated by lawns and show-rings, are as neat as rows of bedrooms. The horses trot, prance and jump with a gliding, stealthy, catlike suppleness, and are bedded, fed, shod and harnessed in public. Each stall is labelled with the horse's name, its breed, its parentage, weight, height in hands, and sometimes its performance. It is a living, working museum. One stable, built in knotted pine and encrusted by shining brass fittings, is reserved for champions. It is the Presidential Suite of the Inn. Only four horses are deemed worthy to occupy it, and each stable opens at the back onto a private paddock. I looked into Forego's eye (fifty-seven starts, thirty-four wins), and Forego looked back at me. There was nothing very special in that look. Nearly all horses have benevolent faces when at rest, and they seemed quite unconcerned to be partitioned from each other, and from the public, in a zoo. They are very beautiful in figure and movement, just like Stubbs's Whistlejacket. They convey no sense of anxiety, apprehension or envy.

Jackson, Wyoming

Thursday 1 May

ADAM *to Nigel*   You won't believe this, but I have just had another meeting with an extraordinary person. ('Extraordinary' is the most over-used word in all these letters. But there's nothing to be done about it.) I came down here with Jonathan. The Catalina is dying. It won't go round corners at less than 25 m.p.h. without a great deal of prodding and hauling. The steering wheel gets hot after 100 miles and so we have long pauses looking at the mountains. It was a lovely drive, even so, skirting round the edge of Yellowstone, where the roads are still blocked by snow, up the valley of the Gallatin where elks in the distance chewed at the low willow bushes by the river; where we were arrested and fined for speeding (more about that later), before coming down into Idaho, Mormon potato country, with potato barns like aircraft hangers and churches like brick garages with spires, with the constant, changing presence of the jagged Teton horizon to the east. At last, after about five hours, we crossed a high pass and dropped down into Jackson Hole, a wide and beautiful basin, rimmed by the mountains. But all this was overshadowed by the Meeting with the Remarkable Man.

This trip is changing under me. Instead of watching the people I meet, watching them more like puppets than people, I'm becoming involved with them, affected by them. It's like the lady in Santa Cruz said, I'm losing some of that English reserve. I feel like a set of false teeth (this is a strange comparison but it's one of the dominant images on TV commercials) suspended in some chemical solution that is lifting away years and layers of un-revised consumption ten times faster than all the brushing I have ever done.

This evening's dunking was the most severe of all. After Jonathan had a meeting with a lawyer, we went to a bar a few hundred feet up the side of the valley. Instead of mirrors and bottles of Johnny Walker behind the barmaid, there was a huge uninterrupted window, 30 feet long and 10 feet high, framing the Tetons, a battered saw-blade of a ridge, stretching away to the north. After a minute or two there, a tall loose-looking man came in. 'Ah here's Gerry,' Jonathan said. He sat down next to me.

This was Gerry Spence, America's greatest trial lawyer. Jonathan had talked to me about him before. He comes from the poorest of frontier families, his mother intensely religious, wanting him to be a preacher, his father bicyling to work at the railroad tie-plant in Sheridan, Wyoming, to save the few cents it cost for a gallon of petrol. But the job at the tie-plant was only incidental. Everything important that Gerry Spence's father did happened out in the mountains, where he was an expert hunter and killer of animals, as much of a mountainman as there has ever been. He fed his family with his gun, bringing home the carcasses of antelope, deer and elk for them to eat. Gerry never ate a piece of beefsteak until he left home at 16, only the gamey, wild meat of the animals his father had killed. That virtually undiluted idea of life in the American West has survived in his son. He began his career – it was the natural momentum of it – representing the interests of the estab-lishment, above all the insurance companies, saving them vast amounts of money by his brilliant persuasiveness in court, effortlessly destroying the cheap lawyers whom the victims were able to hire. He was surviving as his father had taught him, looking out for his own, hunting and killing, the only difference being that Gerry Spence's forests and victims were in the courtroom. He ran for Congress as a Republican but wasn't elected. And then, I think about fifteen or sixteen years ago, he had a change of heart. He met one of his victims, a poor old man who had been run into by a woman in a car, but who had received no compensation because Gerry Spence had persuaded the court that he didn't deserve any. He met him hobbling around in a Safeway supermarket, crippled and pathetic. The same evening Spence decided never to represent insurance companies again. He saw that they were the embodiment of everything that is mean, brutalising, dehumanising and exploitative in American culture and from that moment he has represented the individual against them, winning a string of outstanding victories and multi-million dollar awards for his clients.

He fought and won the Silkwood case, in which a young woman had been contaminated with plutonium from a nuclear fuels plant – they made a film about it – and got $10.5 million damages for her three children. (But this was overturned at appeal.) He saved a lawman called Ed Cantrell from the death sentence. Cantrell had shot another policeman in a car straight between the eyes. Cantrell said that he shot him in self-defence but the dead man's pistol was still strapped in its holster. Spence argued – and this is where the history of the west breaks straight up through the surface of the present – that Cantrell, as an old, experienced and brilliant gunman, could tell from the look in a man's eyes, well before he moved to his gun, that he wanted to kill him. There was a great deal of evidence surrounding this – the unbalanced state of the dead man's mind, Cantrell's own character and record – but that was the core of it: unless Cantrell had acted on that recognition he would have been dead himself. As it was he was saved by the quickness of his draw, a little more than a quarter of a second between the thought and the death. That was Spence's case anyway. There are many who are still sceptical about it.

Jonathan had told me all this before Gerry Spence arrived, by chance, in that bar. But for some reason I forgot it. This large man, with both his hair and the skin on his face hanging down from the bones in his head, with heeled and shiny snakeskin boots and a vulture's beak for a nose, ordered a beer. He was large and loose; I didn't recognise the power in the man. We started talking about *Dodge*. I explained about the two sides, about the attempt to explore the FSR. He looked coldly at me. Not a hostile look but one of penetrating honesty, not withering but desiccating. 'I'd like to do that,' he said. 'But none of my kids is smart enough.' And then I said, forgetting this man shelters many, many vulnerabilities behind his strengths, 'That's exactly the sort of brutal and inconsiderate parental attitude that makes it necessary.' I just flipped it out, like throwing a $1,000 chip on a roulette table as if it were a penny. He hardly reacted at first. This is a cliché for a gunfighter, isn't it, but it's true. He stayed slow and calm and I realised that I had raised the stakes without thinking about it. I had the sensation of standing at the end of a long strip of iced highway, watching this juggernaut sliding towards me. I blushed and held my hands up to my mouth and chin. I hunched my shoulders together and leant forward. He stayed sitting back in his chair. I don't know why I felt this panic. It wasn't as if he was going to kill me, but it felt as if he could. 'How's it going?' he asked, with his blue eyes unframed in their sockets, the little diagnostic muscles around them staying quite still. 'Oh fine, fine,' I said. 'We must have written 50,000 words each by now.' 'And have you made any progress?' 'Yuh, we've talked about some of the things we haven't talked about for years.' 'And have you talked about your mother?' I had to think. 'No. That's strange isn't it? I don't think either of us has even mentioned her.' 'Are your parents still married?' 'No, they were divorced about fifteen years ago.' 'How old were you then?' 'I was 12.' 'Do you resent that, their divorce?' I had to think again. This was a steep dive in. 'No, I don't think I resent it. No, no resentment, but a feeling of hurt which I don't quite understand.' 'Have you said that to your father?' 'No.' 'Don't you think you ought to say that to your father?' 'It's sometimes difficult to say these things.' 'What's difficult about it?' 'I don't want to hurt him.' 'What are you telling me? Are you telling me your father can't take the truth?' 'In some ways, yes.' 'Are you telling me your father is a coward?' 'In that sense, I suppose he is.' 'But now wait here. You've put that label "coward" on your father. Are you a coward too?' 'If it's cowardly not to want to hurt someone like that, yes I am a coward.' You can imagine by now that the whole bar was listening. A girl on the other side of the room threw me a smile like a lifebelt. Jon discreetly ordered me another glass of whisky. I stared out of that beautiful window at the Tetons in the grey evening. 'Do you know what I'm hearing from you?' Gerry went on. 'I'm hearing that you are intimidated by your father, that you are not telling him what you need to tell him because you are afraid.' 'It's more complicated than that. I guess I am or certainly have been intimidated by him in the past. I have already said that in a letter. But I am also afraid of hurting him. The two are mixed up with each other.' 'And what did he say when you told him that he frightened you?' 'He replied in a nice way, but said in effect he didn't want too much more of this.' 'He was shutting you down.' 'Yes, I suppose so, in quite a civilised way, he was shutting me down.'

We then had a long wrangling argument about that word 'civilised'. 'Here you are,' Gerry said, 'clinging to this idea of being "civilised" as if your life depended on it. A young man like you shouldn't be holding on to that. You need to dare to say to him what you need to say. And if you don't dare do that, if you don't get down into those barren places with that man, if you reach the end and you haven't done that, then this book that you are writing will be a failure. And do you know what it should be called? *Two Cowards to Dodge City*.' 'That may be the truest title of all,' I said. 'You have to dare to say the things you need to say,' he went on. 'Those are difficult, though, aren't they?' 'Tell me something that it's difficult to say.' 'That you want to hurt someone and not hurt them at the same time.' 'You can say that and I can say that.' 'If you can say that, you're an exceptional man.' 'Yes, I am,' he said, and Jonathan slid another whisky across at me. Without my noticing it, all the tension in my body had gone and I thanked Spence for what he'd said and for the first time his eyes smiled.

He then left in his snakeskin boots and of course I talked about it all with Jonathan. He said he had been struck by two things I have said to him in the last twenty-four hours. When we left his architect's office in Livingston, I had told him how refreshing it was to hear the junior architects in the office telling him what was wrong with his ideas. No intimidation. And then, when we were arrested for speeding outside West Yellowstone, how I had shook and gone white over a $5 fine and then said to him: 'I have yet to reach that critical moment in my life when I am arrested by someone who is younger than me. Then I will relax.'

I know at times that you have been frightened of me and I have used that knowledge. I think the biggest step we'll take is recognising our mutual fear and envy. That seems to me a long way down the track and we can stick with our original title.

Lexington–Louisville, Kentucky

Friday 2 May

NIGEL *to Adam*   When I complained a few days ago that I would never see another hill, I erred. Kentucky is made of hills. The Interstate winds through their cleavages with sweeping elegance (I am attributing to the road itself the imagination and skill of its designer), and although this is written at 6 am next day, which you say is an hour bereft of all emotion (p. 140), I can still feel the pleasure of fingertip steering through this beautiful countryside. The garden which the Boone-followers imagined but didn't find, they created unconsciously by their crippling labour, leaving just enough of the forest to vary the pattern and suggest the past. At intervals, where the ground is flat enough there's another horsefarm. The grazing horses are silhouetted against the green. What is there in that familiar shape which makes it so evocative? A barrel supported by four poles and terminating in a bent club-head would be a child's drawing of it, but the reality is perfect and serene.

I am staying at Louisville with Cy and Wig MacKinnon. Cy (Cyrus) is the husband, formerly President and Manager of the Louisville *Courier-Journal*, and Wig (*née* Helen Wigglesworth) is his wife. This is the fourth time I've stayed here. The last time, Thanksgiving Day 1980, was the only occasion since school when I've sung solo in public. Their house stands in one of those parklike suburbs with which I've made you all too familiar, and I have a large bedroom overlooking a maple in full leaf bisected by the tall white Federal columns of the porch.

We lunched in a more isolated country house belonging to Jim and Jane Welch, a party of about fifty sitting at round tables on the lawn. But before joining them, Wig and I were invited to mount a nineteenth-century dray pulled by four horses the colour of conkers. I expected to drive only to the car-horse-park. We drove 5 miles. The owner–driver was Dinwiddle Lampton, a squire straight out of Fielding, and he had with him a little step-granddaughter who ought to have been called Heidi. He wore a grey tophat, and his groom, mounted behind, a black one. Why do I have to come to Kentucky to experience exactly the sensation of travelling through rural Hampshire in 1810? The lane of course was smoother, but so narrow that the wheels canted now on one verge, now on the other, as we swayed from side to side, ducking to avoid the trailing flowers of the locust trees. We were followed at the gallop by six retriever dogs. We trotted, the horses not quite in unison, for they find awkward the juxtaposition of rumps bouncing off each other, and the heads of the two leaders turned from side to side as if in argument. They sweated whitely under the harness. Soon we emerged from the wooded hills into the flatlands beside the Ohio, and this was the spankiest moment of our spanking drive. On the left was a reach of the river like Cliveden's Thames, only much broader, on the right the grazing-meadows, and finally the stables where with a shout and a shudder we stopped. Heidi helped the older passengers dismount, and we returned to the lunch-party by pickup truck.

I sat with Roberta Henderson, the Marietta Tree of Louisville. A few years ago I said to her, 'Whenever I think of Louisville I think of you,' and then seeing on the face of her husband, Ian, an expression of slight surprise, I quickly added, 'But then I think of Louisville only once every six months,' to which Roberta replied that I'd spoiled the nicest compliment she'd ever received.

We all went to the races after lunch. The Kentucky Derby, tomorrow, is the culmination of an entire week's racing, and today was the day of the Oaks, with eight less prestigious races preceding it. The course, the Churchill Downs, is not beautiful. For one thing, flat racing in America has to be dead flat, and the track is not of grass but sandy brown earth. The surroundings are small houses tightly packed, and their front yards are turned into parking-lots for innumerable cars. It would be a great improvement to build a new racecourse on the flat meadows beside the river, but when I suggested it, the reaction was as if an American proposed that our Derby or the Grand National should be run in Windsor Great Park. Churchill Downs is the most hallowed arena in the United States.

The lack of any scenic attraction is compensated by the people and the convenience of the stands. The MacKinnons have a box almost opposite the winning-post. Do not imagine a floral Royal Enclosure. It is like a pen in a sheep-market, furnished with six chairs, railed off from its many neighbours by metal tubing, and raised some 20 feet above a wide group of less desirable boxes on a level with the course. It is a mark of distinction to have an upper box, rented year after year. When a couple divorce, the most acute controversy is to decide who is to keep it. Behind the stands is the many-windowed Tote.

There is much less rowdiness than you would find at an English race-meeting. The atmosphere is one of animated decorum. Dress, you might say, is optional. Some women sport cart-wheel hats, but no man a topper. Others come in whatever they happened to have cooked lunch in at home. It is undeniably a social occasion, but there's much more interest in the racing than you'd find at Ascot. I was making notes of all this when a man in the next box leant across to ask me if I was a sportswriter. 'Sort of,' I replied.

Louisville, Kentucky

Saturday 3 May

NIGEL *to Adam*   Derby Day. As this is the event of the day for all America, it must be the event of the year for the place where it happens – Loo-uh-vull. Consequently the weekend is given over to a chain of parties, of which I've already attended six, and there are at least two more to come. All my parties were in the houses of the upper-upper income group, which will raise the short hairs on the back of your neck, so let me not excuse, but explain, stung by some comments in your latest batch of letters which I received here (22 April). I'm concerned that as we draw geographically closer, we seem to be drifting temperamentally further apart.

Why do I care so much for the history of this country, and its influence on today's society, and you hardly at all? You, who poured so much history into *Frontiers* and *Wetland*. Why have you never mentioned the Spanish culture of the Pacific coast, and why do you say that the 49-ers mean nothing to northern California, Oregon or Washington, when the character of these States was shaped by the Gold Rush? When you come to the western plains, Pike's Peak and Santa Fe, I don't expect you will be indifferent to the story of the waggon trails, but only once so far have you given me the feel of history, when you visited the Lewis and Clark camp at the mouth of the Columbia and sent me the Jefferson medal. I feel the influence of history all the time, even when I'm in a lovely house sipping mint julep and a band is playing waltzes in the background. I stood today on the terrace of such a house (Owsley Brown's) overlooking an Italian garden, a meadow with horses, a great sweep of the Ohio, and beyond, on the Indiana shore, an ocean of trees stretching to the horizon. I know that the forest is intersected by great roads, and buried among the trees are innumerable farms and houses, but they are invisible. It is the same scene, apart from the garden, which General George Rogers Clark, the Washington of the West, saw from this hill when he founded Louisville during the Revolutionary War later named after Louis XVI. And why did he site the future city here? Because the Falls of the Ohio were the only interruption on its course to join the Mississippi, and cargoes had to be portaged round them. But come closer. The house behind me was built in 1920 by a Justice of the Supreme Court. Not history? It is. It represents the best merging of English domestic architecture with the American, and contains in its beautiful rooms works of art of several centuries and cultures, including the most modern. It is, in its way, a summing-up of the American achievement, a consummation of the Dream, the best use that can be made of great wealth accumulated by great effort.

This brings me to another point in your recent letters. Why do I meet only the rich, and you only the relatively poor? It is not simply a matter of generation, or my opportunities compared to yours. I would like to, and will, see more of people like your Andy and Wilhelm, and Jon Foote. You find derelict Butte 'the sort of place I like more than any in the world' (p. 149). This I think paradoxical or perverse. It makes me suspect that you would enter the Owsley Brown house with reluctance or a sneer. Is it that you consider great affluence in some way improper when there are still so many poor in this land? But consider, Adam, that these people, or their grandfathers, were once poor too. America was created by the poor. Log-cabin to this white house. And it is not as if the present generation are idle and impotent. Another of my hostesses, Polly Brown (no relation to Owsley), co-ordinates the activities of the world-famous Audubon (Humana) heart hospital in Louisville. Among her guests were doctors, lawyers, businessmen, the people who run Louisville's opera, theatre, orchestra, ballet, museums – all achievers, crowning their careers or thrusting upwards. In conversation it takes but a sentence, a question, to discover beneath the dinner-jacket or the gown a man or woman who has striven, still strives. It is quite different from London's aristocratic society, where real accomplishment often ended with an ancestor. These people have no ancestors beyond perhaps a grandfather who emigrated, destitute, from Poland, and they bring up their children not to rely on their parentage. I think that at heart you must approve of this motivation, and of their enjoyment of earned wealth. If not, you must explain your values clearly. And you are wrong to say that I refuse to recognise any subconscious part of the mind. That's my whole point, that Americans draw subconsciously on their past to stimulate their present. I see evidence of it everywhere. History *is* the subconscious.

But the Kentucky Derby. There were seven preliminary races, warmers-up, which aroused only mild attention until their orgastic climaxes. The eighth was the Derby, delayed more than an hour after the preceding race to heighten tension and swell the Tote-take. There were parades of girls in southern crinolines, of buglers in scarlet tailcoats, of soldiers and police. We stood for

'The Star-Spangled Banner'. We stood again for 'My Old Kentucky Home', which brought cheers and tears at its conclusion – this was a genuine emotion. The race on which experts have speculated since it took place last year, and everyone else for a fortnight, was about to be decided in two minutes. This narrow span, not a window but a single pane of time, is what makes the event so dramatic. The susurration of talk from 150,000 people rose slightly in pitch, and there were cheers for impromptu events like a dog running loose across the track or a hat blown askew by the wind. No hysteria, no drunks, no breaking of bounds. Controlled enthusiasm was the keynote, an evident pleasure at being here.

There were sixteen horses in the Derby. It was the most open for years. At least eight of the sixteen were possible winners. I backed two to win, at $5 each, Bold Arrangement because it was the only British entrant, and Rampage, a tip I'd been given at lunch-time. I watched my horses parade directly in front of our box. They looked good, tiptoe trotting, chestnut-gleaming, and then they returned, led by acolytes, to the starting-gate. Possibly you watched the race on television and saw more than I did. The streaming cavalry charge veered round the first corner and into the back-straight almost out of sight. Then the pack re-emerged bunched, seen from our perspective almost motionless for some seconds, to straighten out into a short line of multi-coloured jockeys. I lost my two horses in the chromatic flurry. The cry went up, 'Shoe! Shoe!', which I knew meant Willie Shoemaker, America's veteran jockey, their Lester Piggott, as he streaked past the post on Ferdinand, a 16-to-1 winner, two lengths clear. Bold Arrangement was second, Rampage fourth. I had not done badly, but lost the $10 I'd won on Oaks day.

There could never be a better example of the American love for a winner. Bold Arrangement slunk into the background, his feat totally ignored. Ferdinand was ridden slowly around for the photographers, genuflected to the Governor, was garlanded, led to a lawn which no hoof other than a Derby winner's is allowed to mark, and looked quite unconcerned – no expression of triumph or dismay has ever crossed the face of a thoroughbred. Shoemaker smiled. He is 54, thrice previously a Derby winner. His warm and gentle personality was evident through my binoculars. The crowd shared his pleasure, *post coitum felix*. I have never sensed such a mood of mutual congratulation.

We dispersed to the parties. All house-guests are automatically included in their host's invitation. I went to two. At the first, mint julep sprayed from the three orifices of a fountain, and you held your silver cup beneath. The second, Polly Brown's, was like something out of *Gone with the Wind* (Louisville is essentially Southern). We drove up to a portico hung with fairy lights in the shape of trees, and all the upper bedroom windows were lit to give the whole house an expression of welcome. From within came the sound of a dance-band. In the garden was a vast marquee. I enjoyed it far more than last night's party in the Club. There was more room, and sufficient quiet away from the band to talk. I met a former British Wimbledon star, Kay Stammers, a man who knew all about the navigation of the Ohio, a couple who invited me to stay with them in Wisconsin, a doctor, an attorney. It was an occasion which I would have wanted you to enjoy, and I think you would have.

Kemmerer, Wyoming

Saturday 3 May

ADAM *to Nigel*   Days ripping past. Just driving in the West, through the grasslands and past deserted farms and 20 acre lots for sale, no takers, migrating deer pausing on the roadside, raw rough broken dirt roads and the roof down and my one Van Morrison tape in the Catalina, now restored to life by a visit to a garage, all its various juices sucked out and replaced with new, and the sunglasses on and a cigarette in my mouth, thinking of that lawyer who wears a cowboy hat and a fringed buckskin jacket in court and the strange morality of getting these huge damages for his clients and taking 50 per cent himself, retreating after a trial to his 35,000 acre ranch in the mountains. 'God must have been a cowboy at heart . . .', a terrible band in the Liquor Locker here in Kemmerer played over and over like a litany and women with Loretta Lynn hair-dos circled and gyrated in contained arabesques and high-waisted jeans while the men in belt buckles the size of television sets stood solid with their beers by the bar.

Jonathan took me to see a beautiful house he had designed for a surgeon outside Jackson, where you cross a wooden bridge over a stream into the front door and inside, as you move from room to room, the height of the ceiling changes above you, like moving through different tents, and through each of the windows the mountains appear in a different frame. I telephone Olivia from roadside telephones where the Snake River pours through its gorges on the long way to the sea and for the first time I don't want this trip to end, I don't want to recognise that America runs beyond the limits of this book, that it's too much for the time. And it is strange how, driving through as I have been doing, noticing only the biggest elk horn arch in the world across the road in Afton, the empty site of the city of Fossil, which the railway business created and the withdrawal of railway business destroyed, noticing only these bubbles in the great stream of this continuous country, it is strange how, in this rubber-cushioned automobility I feel closer to America than in

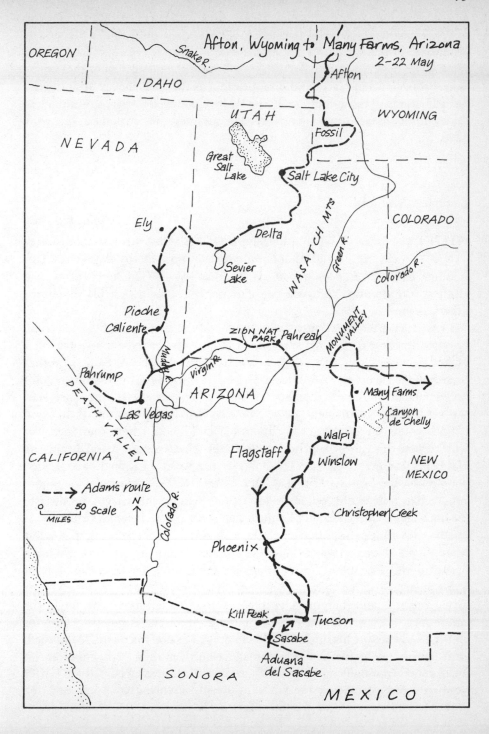

Afton, Wyoming to Many Farms, Arizona
2-22 May

Adam's route
Scale
0 — 50 MILES
N

any amount of digging around for the fact and the detail. The West is soaked in the idea of movement and transience, of not staying but going, where towns are hinged to the roads and not, as they are in Europe, vice versa. I like the sense of dryness coming on from the south, of the tenuousness of that grass-skin, breaking up in places and disappearing, as the rock shoves up into grit-hulled buttes and those endless Charlie Waite clouds roll on past a meaningless horizon. People talk to me about Freedom and here, for a moment or two, I have it.

Louisville, Kentucky

Sunday 4 May

NIGEL *to Adam*   You'll be relieved to hear that there was an easing-off of entertainment on post-Derby day. The Mac-Kinnons had a dozen people to lunch, but that was all. The lunch-party, like all those I've attended here, was out of doors, and some people played tennis, others swam.

I met after a ten-year lapse Sallie Bingham, the liberal, slightly maverick, novelist daughter of Louisville's leading family who have been involved in a widely publicised row about their newspaper interests. First, Sallie's brother turfed off the Board all his women-relations on the grounds that women don't understand business, and then her father, who held the controlling share, sold the newspapers to outsiders. Sallie has been hugely involved in all this, and is now writing an autobiography about her childhood, which sounds as if it will be something like Angelica Bell's about Charleston. I asked her if she was being discreet. 'Discreet? I couldn't write a word if I thought about what people will think of my writing.' She is a strong, adventurous person whom I much like, refuses nine out of ten invitations because she shares your distaste for high-life, is now married to a third husband, and writes like a dream.

It's interesting, this reaction of the rich-born. There was another guest there, Smith Bagby, who was raised in a house with forty servants. He has a beautiful wife, Elizabeth. I'm developing a senile tendency to say aloud what I'm thinking. Talking to her, I suddenly heard myself say, 'Goodness, how lovely you are!' and then quickly, to cover up, 'Please forgive and forget the compliment'. 'Forgiven', she replied, 'but not forgotten.' Anyhow, Smith, for all the advantages of his birth, decided to branch out on his own. He founded, with partners, a textile firm which made a lot of money ('It's important to make your own money, not inherit it'), retired at 41, greatly helped the Carter campaign and presidency, and is now deeply involved in promoting the economic interests of third-world countries. He's one of the few Americans in his circle who deplored the Libyan raid, and says he finds himself in 'a gray area', as I did when I was a Conservative MP, associating with the Republican rich, but rejecting many of their attitudes. But then America as a whole is in a grey mood, especially in deciding its world role. There's uncertainty about how it should use its power, and we will continue for some time to see displays of that power which have no firm aim and no clear conclusion.

I spent an hour in the afternoon with Roberta and Ian Henderson in their garden, and supped alone with the MacKinnons and their son Peter. They are a happy family. Cy has a manner which causes everyone to unfold. You can watch them weakening, or uplifting, to his charm. He was exactly the right person to introduce the new technology to his newspapers, ten years ago, without creating a Union riot. He would have made an excellent congressman, for, while he is a principled man and deeply experienced, cheerfulness keeps breaking through. Wig is much more than a good hostess. She is considerate, active, immensely companionable, and has a genius for stimulating the shy. What a happy time I had with them! I hope you may call on their daughter Anne, who longs to meet you. I spoke to her on the telephone. I made a mistake in telling you that she was an ex-acrobat. That was her sister. Anne helps edit Wyoming's newspaper.

Salt Lake City, Utah

Sunday 4 May

ADAM *to Nigel*   This is an arrival. 'This is the right place,' we all say as the freeway drops down the canyon. Brigham Young didn't need a vision to recognise it. The ring of mountains and the plain in the bowl is a picture we all have ready-made. But I have a new indifference to arrivals, and the first thing I did was simply not appropriate. There's a phrase floating around in my head – I think it's Henry Miller's – about love always leaving him confused, but one thing he *could* understand was 'bought sex in the afternoon'. Olivia says I should give you a long description of it, but I'm not going to. All I can say is that she was charming and so was I.

Louisville–Sellersburg, Indiana

Monday 5 May

NIGEL *to Adam*   Cy MacKinnon drove me to the Humana heart hospital (Audubon) in Louisville, and left me there, not
as a patient but as a reporter. I had said that I wanted to visit an American
hospital and compare their health service with ours. I had meant something
much more modest in scale and reputation than the Audubon, and hoped
merely to talk to a young Dr Kildare for a few moments, buy Cy and Polly
Brown insisted that I see the best and be treated like a VIP, when God knows
I didn't feel like one.

Polly, who is its Clinical Director and runs the staff and administrative side,
received me in her office. Here was my hostess of Derby night transformed into
a busy executive, the link between the two characters, her smile. She walked
me along the corridor, reeling out information. The hospital deals only with
heart cases. It has nearly five hundred beds. It is almost brand-new, founded
in 1983. Every patient has a private room. We looked into some of them as
we passed, occupied mainly by elderly people recovering from one of the
most serious of operations. The windows look over a carpet of tree-tops
towards the river, to give the patients the comfort of outside normalcy, Polly
explained, and for the same reason windows on the opposite side of the room,
which can be closed by Venetian blinds, show them what is going on in the
service-room (that's not the right term, I'm sure) where nurses are busy with
dressings and medications, to involve them in the life of the hospital and
reassure them that nothing sinister is going on behind their backs. As much
thought is given here to psychological recovery as to physical. It is no empty
boast of the Audubon that the patient's needs must always come first. There
is one-to-one nursing during the most critical post-operational period, and
constant monitoring of the patient's condition by electronic machine. At least
one surgeon is always on call. So tender is the care that I felt the place to be
faintly numinous.

Polly opened a door, suddenly, into the Open Heart Recovery Room. I was
taken aback by the sight of two men lying unconscious on padded stretchers,
their faces half-hidden by tubes to help breathing. Electrodes and intravenous
lines were attached to different parts of their bodies. But what to me was so
pathetic, indeed shocking, was the colour of the exposed flesh, face and feet,
alabaster white, and seemingly cold. I have never seen a human being
apparently so close to extinction, but the monitors with their jumping lines
showed that their hearts were beating regularly. The nurses moved around
quietly, like acolytes attending an embalming (the religious parallels were
never far from my mind). They are accustomed to the sight, but what must

it mean to a patient's family, who are admitted to this room an hour or two after the operation, while he is still unconscious and reduced by it to a ghost? I was thankful not to be taken into the theatre where another operation was in progress.

Polly took me to meet Dr Allan Lansing, the founder and Chairman of the hospital. I ask you to imagine my sense of total inadequacy at being confronted by one of the foremost heart-surgeons in the world and expected to question him about his work. And what must he have thought of my ignorant intrusion? I found the contrast between his white coat and my Brigade tie actually debilitating, but he was very patient. This briefly is what he told me, and what I learnt later from publications.

The Audubon (its full title is The Humana Heart Institute International, Audubon) carries out three types of surgery – open heart, heart transplants and the insertion of an artificial heart. Its advanced work is still experimental and educational, pushing the very frontiers of medicine ('We are learning all the time'), and it is the leading hospital of its kind in the world. Even I had read of its reputation in English newspapers. It admits patients from many countries, and prides itself on never turning down a heart-case which qualifies for its special skills, irrespective of the patient's ability to pay (for those who can, it is very expensive). I do not trust myself to quote statistics, and it might be a betrayal of confidence to do so, but the proportion of recoveries to deaths is high, depending on the patient's age and the complexity of his heart-lesions. Dr Lansing personally performs about two operations a day, and he has six surgeon colleagues. Each operation takes about two hours. Some are emergency cases, the majority scheduled months in advance. Heart transplants take longer, and are rarer. The implanting of an artificial heart is still more rare, 'purely experimental' still, and this is the only place in the United States where it can be performed.

I asked Dr Lansing if I could see an artificial heart, and he gave me in charge to a young technician, a true Kildare, with a bleeper, who took me to his laboratory and put into my hands a white plastic heart, with small pieces of metal inside, about the size of two closed fists held together, with orifices, valves and two tubes dangling from it. It seemed to me an enormous object to implant in the human body, but it is no larger than a normal heart. If the patient recovers from the operation (and here again I must tread delicately, without quoting figures), he is attached to a large electrical apparatus to keep the pump working and the valves opening and shutting in a timed sequence, to maintain for a few years, or perhaps only months, the 40 million heartbeats we annually experience without noticing them. 'Life sustained by and tethered to a machine' is the published description. Unable to work and only with difficulty to travel, I wondered whether I would wish to endure it, but

'Kildare', like all his colleagues, regards life as a sacred trust. The perfection and simplification of the strange artefact is their constant aim.

I was taken to lunch in the new Humana building which houses the staff who manage their eighty-six hospitals, some abroad, including London, which has two. Only Polly Brown and Bruce Macleod, the Executive Director of the heart hospital, were with me. We talked briefly about the American health service, as I did again later with George Atkins, Vice President. They defended it eloquently. Medicare and Medicaid, and private and industrial insurance, take care of all but 30–40 million Americans. These are the ones who may suffer severe economic hardship if one of the family falls seriously or permanently sick. It was proposed a few years ago, chiefly by Ted Kennedy, that 'catastrophic coverage' should be given by the Government to families in those circumstances, meaning that the medical fees would be partly paid by the State. The medical profession was divided on it. Some suspected that it might be a step towards total State medicine. It is no longer a live political issue, but it may be revived. They admire aspects of our National Health, but were guarded, as I was in advocating it.

Afterwards I was taken round the Humana skyscraper of twenty-seven storeys by Kathy Knotts. It was designed by Michael Graves as the most efficient of offices, but also as an architectural feature which would enhance the appearance of the whole city. It was completed in May 1985 and cost $60 million. It's magnificent. The granites and marbles were brought from as far apart as Finland and Italy to create on the floors and columns coloured patterns as splendid as in a Roman imperial villa. The offices are cool and pastel. The women employees dress and move to match. Its elegance is of the kind to induce elegance. The view over the river from the gazebo on the top floor is superb. But ask me whether it is a beautiful building and I would be as lost to explain it as the intricacies of a Bach fugue. I believe whatever I'm told – that it 'makes a gesture towards the city and the river', the first by its street-level loggia, the second by flying buttresses. It may be so, but externally it looked to me like a vast piece of sculpture.

Stunned by all this, I crept away from Louisville to a small town just north of the river, Sellersburg, and found there an excellent Day's Inn where I could write and sleep.

Monday 5 May

ADAM *to Nigel*　　The keel's coming back upright. I spent all day
yesterday with the McCoys. I had to stop myself
from making the appropriate joke and it only slipped out once in an unguarded
moment. Mr and Mrs McCoy quite rightly disregarded it and went on with
their conversation as if I hadn't said anything. Mr McCoy – I never managed
to catch his first name, even though I craned to hear it (there was a brief
period when I thought it was Byron, but that turned out to be somebody
else) – is a lawyer and thinks of Spence as a magician, little more, a weaver
of spells. Mrs McCoy – without any doubt at all called Lauri – dislikes all
Republicans no matter what and doesn't like Spence's arguing in favour of
uncontrolled gun ownership. I suddenly realised that I didn't either, but the
answer to that is simple: people do not consist of the banners they hold up
for public inspection.

The McCoys and I had breakfast together in a restaurant in Downtown
Salt Lake – it was the second breakfast I had had, but I didn't say that – and
then they took me up into the mountains, where it was snowing (having been
92° the day before) to a party in a completely triangular house (not plan but
section). Byron and Joan were the hosts. We watched the snow, 6 inches in
three hours, building up on the trees, drank wine cooler and ate marzipan
cake because it was Joan's birthday. I talked to a man who built Minuteman
missiles and had taken the best photograph of Halley's Comet I have seen, a
little wisp of straggled out cat hair above the Wasatch Mountains, their sides
lit by the rising sun. He didn't want to talk about missiles, so we stuck with
azimuths and the Square of Pegasus. Then I talked about plural marriage to
Joan. She told me a terrible story. Before making the long trek out to Utah
her grandfather had got engaged to a woman in England. He was too poor to
marry her and the purpose of his coming here was to make himself enough
money so that he could. He came and while building up his fortune, which
was a slow and grim process, married a Utahn girl. (Doesn't Utahn sound
like the name of a tribe in the Pamirs?) She bore and raised seven children
by him in the time it took him to accumulate the money. Finally there was
enough and he sent it off. They waited for news of the Englishwoman's
arrival, but she never came. And she never returned the money. Which is the
worst part of the story? The behaviour of the Englishwoman or the institution
of polygamy.

Sellersburg–Indianapolis, Indiana

Tuesday–Wednesday 6–7 May

NIGEL *to Adam*   I've been lazy after Louisville, leaving myself three days to trickle slowly towards Chicago, and I've gained an hour by switching to the Central Time Zone. I had meant to devote these three days to studying the history of Indiana, and how it slowly emerged from the wilderness, but I've been discouraged by your implied criticism that there's too much history in these letters already. It will recur later. I next considered taking local politics as my theme, as a Senate Primary is taking place in Indiana, but I could find no excitement, no public meetings, and in fact only 16 per cent of Marion County's registered voters bothered to go to the polls. The candidate supporting the awful Lyndon LaRouche (see Leesburg, 9 April) lost to a Valparaiso professor, I was glad to read. So I read my books, wrote letters home, and watched the President's televised press conference from the Tokyo Summit. I cannot help admiring Reagan's dexterity on occasions like this. He deflects questions brilliantly, knows nearly all the reporters by their first names, charms the cynics and defuses the impertinent. It was a virtuoso performance in his best style.

I also watched, this time live, American couples at breakfast. It's a phenomenon. They eat gargantuously, as if this was the only meal of the day. The newspaper might furnish matter for conversation but they do not read it. They scarcely speak. This does not greatly surprise me, because they have just emerged from a common bed and have nothing left to say. I know that I'm strange about this, perhaps mentally twisted, but I crave the privacy of a single bedroom, where I can read or write as late or early as I wish; and remain selfishly free from having to consider another person's nightly needs and habits. I like travelling alone, sleeping alone, often eating alone, and returning to an empty house or room. I think that Americans must be unusually uxurious. What I was observing at breakfast was not over-familiarity with a partner, but *love*, the pleasure of a lifetime's companionship, however stout or dull the husband or wife has become. It's something I envy. I think of Olivia, stout only because of her pregnancy and never dull, joining you in a few days' time, and wonder what both of you will think of this confession.

I went to the Indianapolis car-race track or Motor Speedway, not to drive, nor even to watch a race, but to see the world champions in practice. The Indianapolis 500 takes place on 25 May. You should watch it. It is being televised live for the first time in its seventy-year history. It is the most famous car-race in the world, and the Speedway is used only on this single occasion, not even for preliminary races. But the competitors practise on it for a month beforehand, and are required to undergo lap-trials to reduce the number of entrants from a hundred to the thirty-three who will actually line up on the starting grid. The fastest wins the pole position.

It was very hot, 82° (I thought of you in the snow!), and the open stands were bakeries. I wondered how the drivers in their fireproof suits could endure it. Occasionally a car would stop at the pits below us, and mechanics gathered round, nursing it, keeping it alive, attaching plastic tubes and metal leads, as in the Recovery Room at Audubon, and in half a minute it was off again, with a cough. Attendant girls of startling beauty kept the scores. They wear dark glasses, to repel not the sun, but ogling stares.

Hemingway is quoted in the Official Program as saying, 'There are only three sports – mountain-climbing, bull-fighting and motor-sports. The rest are merely games.' If you measure sport by danger, I suppose this is true, but I would hardly call heavyweight boxing a game.

On leaving the Speedway, I did not exceed 125 m.p.h. on the Interstate.

Salt Lake City, Utah

Tuesday 6 May

ADAM *to Nigel*   First I recorded a song to send Olivia on her birthday, which is this coming Friday. 'Blue Moon,' I sang standing in a shopping mall, 'you saw me standing alone . . .' and so on for a few verses while strangers peered in through the window of the booth. I lost track of the tune rather early on, having to gobble up the most important part (something something something *there for*, something something something *care for*) before the music ran out. I sent her that, a Mormon book about wives (similar to 'Blue Moon' in its way, telling wives that what they were *there for* was to *care for* their 'weary warrior'), $20 of flowers to be delivered in Cambridge on the day and a thundering Brigham-Young-style warning that 'Blue Moon' was not to be played to the eighty guests she is having to her birthday party. The man who owned the recording booth was called Sharman W. Smoot, but unfortunately he was not there to be interviewed about his name. Instead Tinna Powell dealt with everything. She said I sounded cute. That was the last adjective I would have chosen. The express postage cost twice as much as what was being posted.

After a great deal of searching in the suburbs I managed to find the main post office and your letters waiting there. A wonderful description of Niagara! (pp. 144–6) And some truer remarks about the blacks in Cleveland (p. 150) than all that creamed-off nonsense the Senator gave you in Washington. After reading them in the car, I went on through the pouring rain to visit the

Temple Square. I had a tour all to myself of a building devoted to explaining the Book of Mormon. A rosy cheeked and rather plump young woman called Deanne was my hostess. She looked me straight in the eye as I asked her about Moroni and Co. (I was dying to ask if she thought Proph. J. Smith, Jun. might have been making a small *joke* in giving the heavenly revealer of the golden plates a name that was so open to puns. But I didn't.) At first we stuck to fairly open country. Why did the Mormons consider other Christian churches so inadequate? We were not going to have the rational historical answer – that exclusivity is the only food on which seedling sects can survive. No. The reason was that other Christian churches like mine for example, did not have divine – or at least angelic – authority. She was as nice as she could be about this, but the fact was that Henry VIII simply didn't measure up to Moroni when it came to real authority. We both thought this was a shame. It would be so much nicer if some sort of Moroni equivalent had appeared at Hampton Court in 1528. Then Deanne and I could be friends. But we were friends anyway, weren't we? Oh yes, no question: distinct in terms of enlightenment but friends for sure.

Then we waded through a series of dioramas explaining the wads of undiluted drivel that go to make up the Book of Mormon. Here was Proph. J. Smith, Jun. being visited three times in one night by Moroni. Moroni, living up to his name, said exactly the same thing on all three visitations. It reminded me of the Harmetz's car in Los Angeles. Whenever you climbed in and shut the door, the dashboard asked, 'Are you ready? Sure? All right then, why not put your seatbelt on now?' And it occurred to me that a Mormon businessman might make a killing by customising a limousine – the Cadillac Moroni – so that the exact words Moroni used to Proph. J. S. Jun. would emerge from behind the steering-wheel whenever you exceeded the speed limit, a reminder of the spiritual dimension. But no mention of that to Deanne either. On through the digging up of the golden plates, the three witnesses and the eight witnesses, Proph. J.'s amazing ability to translate from Egyptian, Arabic, Aramaic etc., despite ignorance of those languages. Not a glimmer of doubt in Deanne's eyes. Not of doubt anyway, but a certain defensiveness that was all but perfectly camouflaged. I suddenly recognised this look from somewhere else. A woman a little older than Deanne had shown me a Nazi concentration camp outside Riga in Latvia. She worked for Intourist and I had asked her about the Soviet liberation of the Baltic Republics. She had the same look, of the divided mind, knowing on one side that what the other was saying was a fraud and a lie, and at the same time holding the two halves tightly together to prevent them falling apart, like a man afraid of some terrible dissolution wrapping his arms as far around his own body as they will go. Then we had a film showing how the Mayans and the Incas were in fact tribes of Israel that had crossed the Atlantic at various times. Thor Heyerdhal was rolled in to show that it could be done, even though he had come on a reed boat and the Book of Mormon talks about nothing but large timbers.

Someone said to me yesterday that there was a single difference between LSD and LDS: you take one with a grain of sugar and the other with a grain of salt. This of course is quite ridiculous. What is amazing about the Mormons is the brilliance with which they have made themselves rich, the courage with which they came here in the first place, the strength of purpose with which they have held to their aims. It is this combination of all that is best in the American mind with all that is worst in its sludgy and self-deceiving heart that is so difficult to understand.

Delta, Utah

Wednesday 7 May

ADAM *to Nigel*   I've just come back from supper in the cheese factory here with a man who is trying to keep his ranch going. He was alone, I was too, and so we sat down together. He was called Dail Christensen and looked like a Viking. He's a Mormon, a good man and over his head in debt. Beef prices have dropped out of sight, half what they were four years ago, because people in the big industrial markets in the north are turning away from steak to fish and chickens; because the great steak-eating sector of the economy – this is how he put it – the heavy-duty industrial workforce in the rust belt, has itself taken such a hammering in the last decade and now can't afford to buy steak; because the federal government, trying to do something about the milk glut, has instituted a Diary Herd Slaughter Program, which is flooding his market with cow meat; because the beef lobby in Washington is not as organised or powerful as either the milk or grain lobbies; because the prospect of an American equivalent to the Common Agricultural Policy is anathema both to this administration and to the spirit of America as a whole. Land prices in Utah, for agricultural land anyway, have come down 50 or 60 per cent in the last few years. 'If you had $100,000 dollars in your pocket,' he said to me, 'you could go from here to the Canadian border, putting ten thousand down here, another ten there, and you could buy yourself a strip of land that went the whole way up the Rocky Mountains. It's that bad.' This was an alluring prospect. I said I would talk to Olivia about it next week. 'But don't think you're going to borrow any money out of these banks!' he said. 'You've seen some of those rates on the television for cars? What are they saying now? 5.9, 6 per cent? You're not going to get that for ranching. We're talking more like 12, 15.' What was he going to do about it? 'I don't know. I just can't tell you for sure. I'm working twelve hours a day, twelve days a week,' he laughed, 'and last year, I reckoned it up, I was getting paid $1.25 an hour. I don't know about you, but I don't suppose there are many people in the *world* who are working for $1.25 an hour, not with the cost of what you have to buy here. But there's not much that can be done about it. All I can do is wait and hope for some kind of a change, something that'll pick up that beef price.'

We ate our steaks in the cheese factory restaurant. He told me about his brother who is trying to make a living out of grain just outside Tetonia, Idaho. 'I was talking to him on the phone yesterday. He liked the sound of that nuclear explosion in the Soviet Union. "If we can get that fall-out coming down over that Ukraine grain crop," he said to me, "then we might get some kind of money for the wheat we're growing here." But, I'm telling you, he's worse than what I am. There's a hundred million tons of surplus grain in the world today. That is not good news for the American farmer. *Saudi Arabia* has a farm surplus! Can you believe it? That desert?' Wouldn't he leave? 'There's no job for a ranch hand in the city. I can fix cars. But most everyone in the world can fix cars. And you're not going to get me behind a bar. And besides, I don't even have anything to sell. I'd be leaving here with nothing. The bank would be getting everything I had. I guess you could say it was some sort of trap. Stay and you get nothing. Leave and you get nothing. You could say it *was* a very sad state of affairs, the sort of state of affairs, if that's the words you want to use, that made my grandfather Christensen leave Denmark in whatever year it was. But he had the United States to come over to didn't he? And where have I got to go to? Where have I and my brother and our families got, where can we go now? There isn't anywhere in the world. All we can do is hope and pray and trust in the Lord.'

Indianapolis–Chicago, Illinois

Thursday 8 May

NIGEL *to Adam*   As I drove through northern Indiana, flat hedgeless fields and scattered farms, I remembered that this country was first discovered by the French from Canada. The passage from the Lakes to the Mississippi was easier than west across the Appalachians, and the light Indian canoes, which the *coureurs de bois* soon adopted, made the short portages simple. It's fascinating to explore these portages today. At certain points the rivers which flow north into Lake Michigan rise only a few hundred yards from the springs which feed the Illinois, the Wabash and the Ohio, so that there was a virtually uninterrupted waterway from Quebec to

New Orleans. I found one of them, and walked the narrow gap, marvelling at the geographical chance that almost decided the fate of a continent.

But the French were not settlers. They built a few forts like Vincennes and Lafayette, and allowed the Indians to hunt right up to their stockades, enticing a very few of them inside to become Christians. In 1763 the whole territory between the Lakes, the Ohio and the Mississippi became English for less than twenty years, and then American. The settlers poured in. Land could be had for as little as a dollar an acre, and the soil and climate were the best in the United States. I have been reading de Tocqueville, who visited this area when it was crystallising:

> This migration never halts. It starts from the depths of Europe, continues across the great ocean, and then goes on through the solitudes of the New World. Millions of men are all marching together towards the same point on the horizon; their languages, religions and mores are different, but they have one common aim. They have been told that fortune is to be found somewhere towards the west, and they hasten to seek it.

They found it here. De Tocqueville goes on:

> It is hard to give an impression of the avidity with which the American throws himself on the vast prey offered him by fortune. To pursue it he fearlessly braves the arrows of the Indian and the diseases of the wilderness, he goes prepared to face the silence of the forest and is not afraid of the presence of wild beasts. A passion stronger than the love of life goads him on. An almost limitless continent stretches before him.

I went to Tippecanoe near Lafayette. This was the scene of one of the best-known battles with the Indian tribes, in 1811. There is little to mark it, but I found the grove of oaks beside the Wabash where a handful of men on each side engaged in ghastly atrocities. The Americans (I'm not forgetting that many of them were also Europeans) felt no shame in what they were doing. It was a war of extermination. They wanted the land, and the Indians, their equals in dignity and courage, must go. The conflict was justified because it was inevitable, 'manifest destiny', and their descendants think so too, just as we instinctively take the side of Vespasian when, as a young general, he massacred the Britons in Maiden Castle. It was the strangest form of empire-building, without national leaders, plan or strategy, but it worked.

For the pioneers life must have been atrocious. A child could not wander to fetch water from a stream without risking capture and a tortured death. And when they traded with the Indians, what did the Americans give them in exchange for beaver-pelts and buckskins (hence 'buck', a dollar)? Horses, firearms and whisky, which turned them into what Theodore Roosevelt described as 'the most formidable savage force ever encountered by colonists of European stock', or so befuddled them with drink that they signed away lands they didn't own. Down the rivers floated the family raft, with cow, grandmother, bed and the piano balanced on it, till they found an unoccupied site, felled the trees and planted the first seeds among the stumps. It was in these circumstances that Indiana was first populated. Churches, schools, courts and a form of government soon followed. There was the satisfaction of constant victory over constant odds. This is where Lincoln was raised.

Is it not more rewarding to travel this country with such memories and reflections in one's mind than to have it wholly occupied with current business and one's ears dazed by pop music? What an accomplishment the two last centuries have seen! When Indiana became a State in 1816, there was still not a mile of metalled road. Now I approached Chicago steadily at 60 miles in each hour. I circled its vast industrial suburbs to the Ramada Inn at Elmhurst. At dinner the waitress gave me chicken which overlapped the plate at each end with four times as much as any human should want to eat at a sitting. 'Please', I said, 'take it back to the kitchen, and leave me this one piece.' 'Shall I wrap up the rest of it for you to take away?' she asked, astonished at my frugality. This is the contrast.

Las Vegas, Nevada

Thursday 8 May

ADAM *to Nigel*   For the first time on this journey – and the Catalina and I have now covered 5,000 miles (we're running at the rate of 10 words a mile) – I have travelled west today. Until now I have been cutting across the historical grain of the country, clipping through people's arrivals like the layers in a club sandwich. But today, on my drive west from Delta to a junction of three roads in the middle of a Nevadan nowhere which took me south again towards Las Vegas, I was going with the current, with the historical current, that is, and across the geographical grain of the country. It was a succession of basins and ranges, the road cutting clean and straight across the flatlands and then curling and twisting up to a pass, where the next wide mountain-rimmed bowl appears. All this so easy and fluent in the Catalina on the empty road, a callous non-repetition of the agonies people must have gone through crossing this dry country for the first time, threatened by Indians, drought and each other. The only signposts to left and right pointed to distant wells and hidden valleys. The map showed a dotted blue amoeba to the south called Sevier Lake (Dry). I expected a white mirror of a salt flat, but the spring rains had changed it into a wide blue lagoon, the colour of the sea in Eleuthera, with the snow-capped mountains bright and present behind it. I drove down across the crusty grit of the desert to its shores, the sage brushing up under the belly of the car and swallows flitting in front of me. The water was dense and salty, lifeless, a liquid desert, and I flicked stones across its flat, flat surface playing ducks and drakes. I love this sort of desert for the reason that I don't like forests. Everything is clear and essential here, nothing muddled. There is too little happening for confusion. The mountains display their structures as if a geologist had sliced through them, their layers, their hardnesses and softnesses are all revealed. Granite bulges in elephantine globules; limestone chips and cracks; sandstone crumbles and disintegrates in striped, spreading fans; and the strips of quartzite, where the mineral liquids have squeezed in between the other rocks, stand out like the veins of fat in paté.

I had meant to stay the night in Caliente, just south of Pioche, but for the first time in my life I rejected a motel room. Its smell had more layers to it than the mountains I had been passing all day. I said No to the woman who then wrapped her arms across her chest. 'It's too much money, isn't it?' she said. 'No,' I said, 'it smells horrible.' 'I can make it $17, if you like.' 'I wouldn't take it at any price.' 'I don't know why people travel round the place if they don't take enough money with them.' 'Yuh, stupid isn't it?' I said, and drove off to the Caliente Laundromat where I put the entire contents of my suitcase in a washing machine as preparation for meeting Juliet tomorrow. The poor thing (the washing machine) groaned and creaked with the unprecedented task. A woman in a cowboy hat, watching her clothes revolving behind the front-loader window next to mine, said Caliente was a crazy town. It didn't look too crazy to me. 'Oh it's crazy all right,' she said.

Caliente was not for me. I've driven here to Las Vegas, 160 miles through the desert night. It was after 11 when I crested the last rise in the dark and saw this oasis pooled out in front of me. Not the green and the dun of Palmyra in the Great Syrian Desert, but a wide slick of sodium and neon in the darkness of the Nevadan night. It sucks you in, takes you in. At first one or two utilitarian gas stops and other undemonstrative buildings, but then the tempo quickens – it's like your ripples approaching Niagara – the lights begin to move, to trace out every lineament of the strip, to bathe the entire façades of hotels, to coat surfaces the size of football fields, but curved and folded, with infinite electric sequins. The night disappears or at least becomes no more than the thin slivers of a black flesh contained and clothed in this rustling, riffling electricity. Wedding chapels, hotels, casinos, fun parks, more casinos, words – desert, oasis, Sahara, Aladdin, saloon, girls – lurch at you, clamour for you in a barrage of noise, a tunnel of electric demand like an invented jungle, with the people and the cars crammed down the strip between them. I knew where I was heading. Juliet had booked us in to this hotel, the Flamingo Hilton, and at last after miles of exposure to lesser displays, there it was, flaunting its fluorescent pinkness for twenty-eight storeys into the night. I'm now here, on the twenty-eighth floor, looking out at the cool green waterfall of Caesar's Palace – nothing moving in the lights there, just a radioactive glow – in a sweet smelling room. It's one o'clock in the morning and I'm going out to see what it is that people do here.

Chicago

Friday 9 May

NIGEL *to Adam*   I wrote about Chicago's past in my biography of Mary Curzon (Leiter) who was born here. Now I want to write about its present. I didn't dare face the traffic, as it is a frightening city, so went to the centre by train from Elmhurst with a mob of commuters.

It does justify in a way its reputation for toughness, but this applies to any great city where the stresses build up. As soon as the lights turn green, cars streak off the stop-line with the fury of Indy 500 cars off the grid, indifferent to pedestrians who are frantically trying to escape. Receptionists, who are there, after all, to receive, look up angrily from their personal telephone calls, which they have no right to be making, as you approach the desk. Barmen pretend total lack of comprehension of English spoke as she should be spoke. Postal clerks declare that no express mail exists between Chicago and Las Vegas, when it does. All these examples are taken from life, my life, today. But put against that the assistant in the Public Library who told me that they held not one, but three copies of *Mary Curzon*; the dancing of a Bulgarian troupe on a temporary stage in the central plaza, where I shared my popcorn with the pigeons; and the taxi-driver who told me that there was no longer any violence in the city centre, and 'If people object to my colour, that's their problem'. I liked that.

But the point is that Chicago is beautiful, *beautiful*. It must be the only city in the US to rival New York in the number of high buildings and its atmosphere of metropolitan urgency. Yet it is less hectic, the streets freer of traffic outside the rush-hours and better paved. The glass skyscrapers reflect each other with a shimmer that extends all the way down a long avenue. Walking towards Lake Shore Drive I found the Art Institute, where I lunched, a yachting harbour and a broad expanse of grassy parkland between the lake and the serrated row of tall buildings which confront it, an approach by water which must be one of the loveliest in the world. Alas, this approach is now denied us. The airlines, and people's impatience, have killed passenger traffic on the Lakes.

I wandered happily around in the sunshine, entering one or two of the great office buildings unchallenged, which you could never do in London. The most beautiful of all is the Amoco building, designed by Perkins & Will in 1974. It stands isolated at one end of the lakeside park so that you can see it to full advantage from a distance. It is eighty storeys high, a rectangular shaft of grey marble undecorated except for bevelled corners and, at the foot, fountains and terraces in a Lutyens manner, and two rows of flags of all the States in the Union. It is the proportion of height to breadth that I found so satisfying, the same pleasure which a Wren or Palladian house gives me, here translated into a slim pillar of infinite grace. How much preferable it is to the architectural tricks I saw in the more recent buildings, which are sliced into glacis at the top or mount in a rolling series of staggered hoops. I went inside the Amoco. The main hall is split into different levels, broad stairways and escalators connecting them, a marbled ice-rink of a floor. I enjoyed the surprise of it all. To those who work here its splendour must soon seem ordinary.

On returning to Elmhurst by train, I was welcomed by you telephoning from Las Vegas. We discussed this correspondence, and agreed that the occasional note of father–son controversy is all to the good, for being unalike, we must be seen to be unalike.

Las Vegas, Nevada

Friday 9 May

ADAM *to Nigel*   It's Olivia's birthday. I've spoken to her three times on the phone today. Poor Thomas has chicken-pox from head to toe, but 'Blue Moon' and the flowers arrived from Utah. Olivia didn't like the book about wives. One of its sections was devoted to 'Introducing Your Wife At Parties'. Acceptable was: 'This is the light of my life ...' Unacceptable was: 'Here's the ball and chain ...' I'm keener on love than you are because without it I feel lonely. But loneliness, and I don't like loneliness because it's more like a bellyache than a real heartache, is now going to disappear from my life for a few weeks because Juliet is coming now (I'm at the airport, typing this in the back seat of the car, my head sticking out of one window, my feet out of the other) and *Olivia* next Thursday. What more could anyone ask for? There is nothing better than meeting people you love in remote places.

I have half an hour before her plane gets here to tell you about last night in this strangest of strange places. I had never been to a casino before my 1 a.m. introduction this morning and I had made two assumptions about them: that gambling would have an air of risk and excitement about it (which was fed by the neon light show down the Strip – this had to be a place of extremes); and that the heightened air would be surrounded by some sort of exclusivity, some hedge that would make you feel you had entered a special zone where special things happened, where spectacular rewards became somehow available. Neither of these assumptions were right. This is a town based on the marriage between the supermarket and the casino. There are no uniformed porters at the gates, checking your ID or ushering you in. There are scarcely any gates. The casinos have vast mouths opening out on to the strip, more like garage doors, or those great holes in limestone country through which rivers disappear into the ground, than the entrance to a building. There is no lobby or foyer – you flop straight into the gambling cavern, packed with machines and tables, frantic with the rattlesnake noise of a thousand machines – 'slots' as they are called after the mean little mouths at finger height. Just one of those machines tells the whole story of Las Vegas. That little slot looks a meek and ungreedy thing, only taking one coin at a time. The bright little whirling face is as full of smiles as the Strip itself, fecund with all those fruits and lucky 7s that are going to bring you happiness. On the right hand side is the lever for the moneypump, a nice chunky, reliable version of the lever you pull down at a petrol pump to start the juice flowing. The machine makes no noise as you put the money in the slot. That is the silent little offering, an unimportant part of the ritual, but pull that lever and the machine starts to sing, little bubbly messages of happiness and hope ringing out as the fruit-laden cylinders roll in front of you. And then, if they land up right, ecstasy! In joy and delight the machine pays you its money to the sound of bells and a deep heartfelt vomiting into its great tray-shaped mouth at the bottom, a deep full-bodied belly of a treasure chest designed for riches. But if the cherries don't line up right there is nothing but silence. You have failed. The machine doesn't like you. It's not giving you 'unconditional positive regard' and you had better try again. No instrument has ever been designed that so accurately disguises and distorts every one of its functions. For rapacity it substitutes generosity, for mechanical greed affection, for taking giving, for using helping, for hopelessness hope. It's as if a knife were disguised as a sofa.

There are pictures all round the machines, on the walls, even on top of the machines themselves, of big winners, of dazed people from Illinois and Hawaii with a casino executive and a large number of dollar bills. There are limousines standing around some of the casinos just waiting, *begging* to be won. That's what I wanted – a cool, black Trans-Am with black windows in which to meet Olivia at Phoenix. So I spent $20 discovering that I wasn't going to. That was in the Frontier. Then I moved on – God knows what time it was – to the MGM where I watched a woman, with a substantial bosom that rested on the table, destroying eight men at poker. Her chips piled up in front of her like a model of Downtown Seattle. The men maintained their appropriate faces. She scooped in each new load as if they were scones at a WI fête. 'Poker for you tonight, sir?' some sort of floor manager asked me. 'Not tonight, thanks,' I said and mooned off towards the Black Jack. Not a happy face in the room. The little short-skirted waitresses exhausted, the dealers deadpan, knowing, the players dead in the face, dead in the head. The chandeliers were Barbara Cartland hair-dos. Surely I should go to bed. 'Lost a lot have you?' a man suddenly said to me. 'Yes,' I said at random. '$100.' 'What were you playing?' 'Black Jack.' 'Well, there you go. It's a bad game. What are the odds? 23 per cent? Something like that. You'll never win at that game. Craps. That's the game.' 'What are the odds on that?' 'If you play it right, if you play the numbers, you're well up there in the 80s.' I had no idea what he was talking about. 'Craps is your game.' 'OK,' I said.

The man and I had a drink together before heading off for the Craps table. He was Mike Netti, an ancient Italian from New York with a carbuncled face and an entire caucus of frogs in his throat. I think he was about 68 and had been gambling and dealing in Vegas for 40 years. 'May the Lord be my witness,' he said, 'Craps is the game.' He told me I should write his biography and it should be called 'I have gambled, I have won and I am in rags.' I said I'd think about it. Before the Craps we had a quick go on Keno. This is very like Bingo – a $3 stake for a $40 win. Mike insisted on using his steady numbers. He always used them and he was still here today, he said. So I said OK. The lucky numbers were: 14 and 6 (because his younger sister, who was slightly simple, had been born on June 14), 8 and 10 because his father had died at ten past eight in the morning) and 57 and 63 (because his father was 63 at the time, which was in 1957). So we wrote the numbers on a piece of paper, waited for the game to come up, while Mike told me that a gambler (a) didn't mind if he lost, as long as he could play the next day, and (b) didn't mind if he was playing with a quarter or $10,000. I didn't understand this. 'Well, there you are,' he said, 'you're not a gambler.' Then the Keno numbers appeared on the board. June the fourteenth and eight o'clock were all among them and so we won – $40. Mike kept twenty and I kept twenty – my stake, his numbers. Then off to the Craps table.

I think that it was about 3 in the morning at this stage. I was ready to drop. Mike had a strange look in his eye. He held my biceps with a crabby hand as we left MGM and walked down the Strip to an altogether less salubrious place called Little Ceasar's. This was Mike's regular. I cashed $100 and gave them to Mike. I know this was crazy but it seemed an interesting thing to do at the time. We leant up against the edge of the Craps table and Mike began to perform. It's the most complicated game I have ever seen. The table is about 12 feet long with deep sides, so that the dice which are thrown from one end to the other don't bounce off on to the floor. People bet on the throw of the dice. Further than that I couldn't trust myself to explain. There were four other old men playing at the table, a man with a stick who collected the dice and returned them to the thrower, a man who paid and collected the bets, another man doing the same thing at the far end of the table, and a general supervisor who smoked all the time, talked to the other officials in a tone of patient contempt and wore a Gucci tie pin – and me in my jeans and Caliente-laundromated pink shirt.

Mike started playing with my money. I watched in a fuddle. Mike was in a glaze, talking code to the stick man, occasionally telling me 'You watch, Adams' – an early misapprehension – 'you watch where I put them Adams. Stick with the numbers – remember what I told you about those numbers,' while I thought 'What numbers?' 'Press that ten,' Mike said.'Ah,' I thought, '*ten* past eight.' 'Give me a hard six,' Mike shouted again across the table as I remembered June. Come to think of it, *my* sister had been born in June as well. Things couldn't be that bad. And to my amazement Mike started to win. Gradually we evolved from red ones meaning $10, to green ones meaning $25. '*Never* go on the *big* 6, Adams, ' Mike said, his eyes gleaming with a sort of passion, 'always go on the numbers.' 'Right,' I said. All I could think of was the little stash of plastic money gradually accumulating in front of Mike. 'You're going to go home happy,' Mike told me. I started thinking about the Trans-Am again. And then suddenly, Mike was dishing out tips to the stick man, Gucci and Co. Was everything OK? 'I know what I'm doing,' Mike said, invoking the Lord again. Then it was all over. Mike cashed in the chips. I got my $100 back with another $200 on top of it. Mike got $250. That seemed fair enough. 'Remember Adams,' another claw on my biceps, 'never gamble, don't waste your money.' 'OK,' I said and went off back to the Flamingo where the mindless hordes were stuffing their money into machines. I felt infinitely superior. 'Craps is the game, you know,' I said to one of them. 'Oh ya,' he said, 'tell me about it.' Of course I couldn't.

Chicago

NIGEL *to Adam*   The metropolitan area is enormous. It's as though
                        Sevenoaks and Windsor were incorporated in
London. It takes an hour to drive on the fastest roads from its extremities to
the centre. I was anxious to discover the social symbolism of all this, and was
lucky to sample it at three levels – to lunch with people in the middle range,
to lunch on the second day with upper-middle, and, in between, to dine and
sleep with the upper-upper, respectively in Arlington Heights, Evanston and
Lake Forest. My hosts, in the same sequence, were the Paul Fullers, the
George Rapps and the Charles Meyers. None of them when asked, say that
they come from Chicago. They say that they live in Arlington Heights,
Evanston or Lake Forest, and if this does not make a sufficient impact, they
add, 'North of Chicago'. Nobody worth knowing lives south. But Chicago is
the magnet. They visit it periodically for its arts and restaurants. They are
proud of it. They faintly resent the term 'America's second city', believing
it, in all but finanical clout, to be the first, and I have come to agree, for the
most paradoxical of reasons, its sobriety and its brilliance.

At each of my parties I asked them to define from their different angles
why outer-Chicago is such a pleasant place to live. This is the sort of question
which they never ask themselves, and consequently delight to answer. First,
there is Lake Michigan, a private ocean, where you can sail (but rather dully,
I thought, for you can only circle and return to your starting-point), and
where, in August and September, when it has hotted up, you can swim. The
trouble is that all the Great Lakes have risen recently by a couple of feet,
obliterating some of the best beaches. Secondly, the city's cultural attractions.
Thirdly, the congeniality of their closed societies. Arlington Heights does not
meet Lake Forest, nor Lake Forest, Evanston. But they seem to lead, at
different economic levels, much the same sort of life. The tennis-club, bridge-
afternoons (never for high stakes), shopping, hair-dos, distant holiday homes
(Evanston's in Maine, Lake Forest's in Colorado), private schools and universities for the kids, charity committees, and for the men commutable offices
in the city. The women seldom work for pay. At my Evanston party I asked
what effect the feminist movement has had on their lives and attitudes. There
was uncertainty in their replies, slight embarrassment (their husbands were
listening intently), but it appeared to be negative or fading fast. They admitted
that the problem of the blacks is unresolved. In these residential white suburbs
they seldom meet them, but they spoke sadly of the poorest schools where
many black children simply give up hope, seeing no future for themselves in
a society biased against them, stay away from school, and drift into indolence

and sometimes crime. There's a feeling of communal guilt about this. For instance, when a lawyer said that black teenage girls usually keep their illegitimate babies because they can claim child-welfare for them, there were cries of protest round the table, as if he had said something highly improper.

My three rendezvous were subtly different. The Fuller house in Arlington Heights is neat and clean (what importance Americans of the middle class attach to cleanliness, like the Swiss and the Dutch!), linked to its neighbours by a common lawn running beside a leafy surburban street. In Evanston the Rapp house is much larger, facing the Lake across a strip of park, but here again the houses are contiguous, not screened from each other, and of different styles, colonial on one side, modern (windows rounding the corners) on the other, as in an Expo. Lake Forest houses are secluded by trees and large gardens, and the area so security-conscious that when I had difficulty in finding the Meyer house, I was nonplussed by neighbours clearly unwilling to tell me where it was, and there are no signposts. You are expected either to know your way around Lake Forest, or not go there.

The Meyer house is lovely, rooms opening into each other with spacious discretion. I had a bedroom with two canopied beds. Their dinner-party, of ten, was of silvered excellence, served by two maids. I like this sort of thing. You don't. Susan Meyer is a beautiful woman with an amused enquiring mind, ever ready to analyse her privileged life. Her husband is more serious, contemplative, quick to agree or disagree, stimulating. Their guests were all, like me, elderly. I wonder why they do not mix the generations more. But it was a highly convivial party. Having lived so long and travelled so much, we all had friends and experiences in common. Nobody grew tired sooner than I did, and I was allowed, before any of the others, to go to bed. I explained that I always get up at 6.

How can I summarise all this? That Chicago is a happy, stratified society. That money counts. That they have fashioned for themselves a surburban life more vigorous than our own. That women are equals to men in all but work. That the segregation of the classes gives no offence to anyone. There is no snobbishness, simply a legitimate ambition to rise from Arlington Heights to Evanston, from Evanston to Lake Forest. There's no mutual antagonism, no pretence, no looking disdainfully down or enviously up. The assumption is that after a certain age you will settle for the social status you have reached, make your friends in that category, share the benefits which the whole vast city offers, and be grateful not to live in New York or Los Angeles.

Las Vegas, Nevada

Sunday 11 May

ADAM *to Nigel*   Juliet has come and gone since I wrote to you at the airport. It was so nice having her here. I only wish she had come to visit me in a place that was a little more humane than this hell-hole. I'm leaving tomorrow morning as soon as I get your latest letters from the PO. But first of all I must thank you for sending the dollars with Juliet. It's incredibly kind of you and it means that Olivia and I will have a lovely luxurious time. I now feel extraordinarily flush. Juliet handed them over with a great flourish almost as soon as I met her at the airport. We gave each other a good look up and down. I said she looked lovely. She said my hair was too long and that I should wash it more often. This is the role of older sisters. Then an inspection of the Catalina – wrong colour but OK otherwise. Then I said about five times in a row how lovely it was to have her here – some sweetness and gentleness in a place that doesn't even know the meaning of those words. Then we swam off together like Hansel and Gretel into this sucking black whirlpool of iniquity. No that's the wrong word. It's not positively bad enough to be called iniquitous, but it is somehow both bland and deceitful at the same time. We went together to a show at the MGM Grand starring Engelbert Humperdinck. Juliet was deeply reluctant but I insisted it was the sort of thing one had to do on a trip like this. There was no chance of finding anything more civilised than Engelbert in Vegas. He in fact was the acme of Vegas high culture. She, as ever, was game, even after 6 hours on the plane from New York. Engelbert is in the line that descends directly from Stewart Granger and Errol Flynn. Massively handsome in a hidalgo way, with more hair than a horse, and a semi-self-deprecating English sexiness. Or at least so the lady from Denver, Colorado said, who shared our table. She had seen him at a show in Dallas in 1972 and he had *touched* her. The other man on our table enjoyed Engelbert's few jokes with a vengeance. He used to open his mouth to its full width while Engel was still mid-joke and then at the punch-line make four loud and separate barks. The formula never varied. Juliet had never seen human beings like this. I told her the West was full of them. Engelbert gradually divested himself of his clothes as the evening wore on until at the sweat-soaked finale – Denver held three fingers up to her mouth in awe – a young woman was summoned on to the stage to *kiss* him. Complete fascinated silence accompanied this act, while the conductor of the band, who was the spitting image of Edward Macmillan-Scott, maintained a surreptitious rhythm with his right toe. As the girl, her life transformed, stepped off the stage, Denver was at last able to let out the breath she had been holding for $2\frac{1}{2}$ minutes. For the whole of yesterday Juliet kept seeing Englebert in restaurants, in traffic jams, while buying a sun hat, but I never caught sight of him myself.

Most of yesterday was taken up with a long trip out into the desert to the west of here to a place called Pahrump, which is known for one thing only: it is the site of the most famous brothel in America, called the Chicken Ranch. We didn't find it, but I'm told it consists of about six caravans on the very border of Clark County Nevada, smack in the middle of the desert. Las Vegas is in Clark County and prostitution is illegal there. In bordering Nye County it is legal but only if the brothel can be moved at a moment's notice. Hence the caravans, decorated inside, so I'm told, with plush velvet and plastic, antiqued models of the Venus de Milo.

But as I say we didn't find it and the real point of the trip was to show Juliet the desert. Anything to get out of Vegas and its strangely puritan sterility. There is no joy in it. The only real happiness was a small ceremony in one of the instant wedding chapels. A man called Gregory and a pretty woman called Holly, both from Chicago, went through the 3 minute service and a 4 minute photo session together, with no one in the congregation except Juliet and me. I asked them afterwards why they had come here. Gregory said they had been planning it for 2 years. They wanted it to be 'special' and they didn't want any of their friends and family to come because they wanted it to be secret. I didn't ask why. They were going on honeymoon to Florida. They both looked very happy.

Last night, in a rather manic way, we went to another show. This was the Lido de Paris. Women in diamond-encrusted G-strings and no bras were wheeled around in gondolas against a Venetian background. The same ladies in leopard skin G-strings and no bras then appeared on elephants in front of a jungle background, and then ostrich feathers, etc. I can't think who likes this sort of thing. We left, looking for some kind of something that had some worth in it. And where did we end up? A restaurant belonging to Liberace where we drank the most expensive wine I have ever drunk and ate something called 'surf 'n' turf', which is steak and lobsters mixed up together. That is the only solace in a town completely bereft of every value, of every form of true happiness, of any human worth. Why do people come back here?

Juliet has now returned to her children – another 6 hour slog across the continent. I'm amazingly grateful to her for coming all this way. I would have been a small black puddle under a roulette table by now if it hadn't been for her. This evening I have been sitting smoking in my room, refusing to encounter any more of this city and instead reading the Book of Mormon. Hear this: 1 Nephi, Chapter 12, Verse 16: 'And the Angel spake unto me, saying: Behold the fountain of filthy water, which thy father saw; yea, even

the river of which he spake; and the depths thereof are the depths of hell.'
That's Las Vegas: the Devil's jacuzzi.

Milwaukee, Wisconsin

Monday 12 May

NIGEL *to Adam*   I drove to Milwaukee last night, and explored it this morning. There's a good waterfront and some decent modern high-risers behind. As in Boston, they have decided to save some of their older buildings, but the trouble is that the city's visible history is so short that their 'historic buildings' often mean the ugliest (apart from the Germanic City Hall, which is marvellous, and must be kept), and they are now stuck with them until some brave mayor dares to say that an American city centre should be constantly renewed, like Chicago's, and history banished to the districts where there are some good Victorian houses. The people are pleasant and many of the women very elegant. An article in the official guidebook says that Milwaukee has a reputation for being stolid and stodgy, 'but Milwaukeeans don't mind'. If I were a Milwaukeean, I would mind very much indeed, and it isn't true.

I found your letters here. I envy you your mountains and torrents after all my flatness and coastal development, and you may envy me the Great Lakes, in reality placid seas which give these mid-West cities an unexpected Mediterranean flavour.

The most important part of your letters was your conversation with Gerry Spence (pp. 167–8). I would not have admired him as much as you did. I find his pleading for injured people (for 50 per cent of the take) almost as distasteful as his championship of the insurance companies, and was glad that you eventually came to consider his morality strange. I wish you had challenged him on that, but you were too shattered by his bullying of you and, at one remove, of me.

If I were reviewing our book, I would pick out one phrase in your letter of 1 May – 'our mutual fear and envy'. What a bold move that was, like suddenly jumping out a knight to harass the pawns, and it's true. In what, on my side, does this fear and envy consist? I think it is fear of your criticism, envy of your talent. There are so many things in my character of which I'm ashamed – indolence, lack of warmth in my personal relationships, uncertainty of judgement (politics, the arts, business, people) – and you have an unerring gift for spotting them. Then I fear your occasional anger, as when I told a journalist that some of your written sentences were not immediately intelligible, and you reacted with extraordinary hurt and violence, saying that I have too logical a mind and ignore subtleties of expression. Or when you respond to some moderately élitist opinion of mine not with argument but with contempt. Then envy. I envy you your youth, your future compared to my past, your gift for fluent and irradiated writing, your firm judgements, your emotional depth, and in a way (though I may often deplore it) your capacity to disregard the feelings of others, a take-me-or-leave-me-alone attitude, while I retain a schoolboy's fear of being rejected, and act unnaturally when confronted by someone I greatly admire, like Harold Macmillan or the Audubon surgeon. If you, at 28, can take such people in your stride, what will you be like at 48? A most formidable personality. As I have never been formidable, I envy it, as well as fear it, in you.

Then you touched on something else with Gerry Spence, the breakup of my marriage. You were hurt by our divorce, and though you were too kind to tell me so before, you told a complete stranger, but only when forced to. Of course, I knew that there was a risk of hurting you, but I think the hurt was a temporary shock and disappointment such as any child would feel if the parental link is broken, more than any permanent psychological damage. You may also be subconsciously comparing my marriage to your own, Olivia's longing for you during this separation, and yours for her. Why could Nigel and Philippa not have created an equivalent bond? I will not go into the reasons (some things are too painful and private), but it was as much my fault as hers. The effect upon our three children was not in any way disastrous, and curiously enough it is one of the things in my past that I reflect on with least sense of guilt towards you. So while I don't want to pursue this subject, I feel that your hurt cannot be very deep, and that you should have mentioned it to Spence may have been because he expected that reaction, and you were anxious to assert your normality and sensitiveness after your slashing remark in reply to his mild criticism of his children, which I thought as cruel as some of his probing questions to you. Why should it be so dreadful for him to say that none of them is smart enough to sustain such a correspondence as this, when you knew nothing of their other qualities?

It might, in fact, be quite a good idea if some American father and son (or daughter) wrote *Two Roads to Wolverhampton*, but then our island is too small. They would always be bumping into each other. The 'you' would have to start in the Outer Hebrides, the 'I' at Sissinghurst.

Springdale, Utah

Monday 12 May

ADAM *to Nigel*   I collected your letter this morning from the Las
                         Vegas post-office and read the promised screed about
history and the rich (pp. 171–2) while a man scrabbled in the dustbin beside
me saying to no one in particular that he wasn't looking for people's letters,
just for their magazines. His mind must have gone. And I'm sorry if you were
upset by what I said about history and the implied criticism of your spending
your time with the rich. The question of the rich is easier than the question
of history. I haven't exactly slummed it myself. I haven't been to the sort of
parties you have been to because there aren't so many parties of that kind on
the West Coast anyway, because I don't have the friends you have here, and
because people of my age don't, on the whole, do that kind of thing. I haven't
been avoiding rich people. I've even stayed with some. Nor do I approach
people who have money with a sneer. It's much simpler than that. As I see
it, the whole purpose and pleasure of going on a trip like this one, that we
are now on together, is to expose oneself to the unfamiliar, to find excitement
and even revelation in that. I have a great appetite and longing to immerse
myself in lives that don't remind me of my own, in experiences which can
show me more of what I am like. The obverse of that is a sense of frustra-
tion and discomfort when I find myself contained and restrained inside a
polite and comfortable situation with which I am already familiar. I know
I would have gone crazy with that string of parties you had up the East Coast.
I would have become rude and riotous, not because the people were rich
(I have no trouble in accepting that people should enjoy the rewards they
have earned), but because the situation would have been polite. Nowhere, I
imagine – and this probably is a prejudice – in those parties would I have
met, and talked to, as I have, a Gerry Spence or a Jonathan Foote. Now
I like the sound of Sallie Bingham (p. 176). There's just my type. And I
know, for God's sake, that she's just your type too. You don't like stuffies.
You've been polite about the stuffies you've met on your side. But the people
I admire, and the people who I am single-minded enough to think are ob-
jectively the most admirable, are those who have breadth and strength and
staying power enough to achieve something, and who, having achieved it,
then have the courage and wisdom not to settle themselves into the padded
niche those qualities could so easily have bought them. There is a famous
Gide division between the *subtils* and the *crustacés* in human beings. It's
not the rich I don't like, it's those crusty, rigidified lobsters who are not my
favourite people. I like honesty and change and frankness and freshness.
I wouldn't sneer at the Owsley Brown house but I would hate with a

passion the snobbery of the set-up at the Derby. I just don't like that kind of thing.

What is honest and strange – or perhaps sadder than strange – is what you have just written from Indianapolis on May 7 (p. 182), that you like being alone but that being alone makes you lonely. I've heard you say it for years and its something in you not wholly worked out. You *love* being taken up by people, you love Americans because Americans socialise you (if that can ever be a transitive verb) and you hate the dead, cold reticence of the English. I think you want to have the best of both worlds in this – to be able to push people away and say 'Now is my privacy,' and then to appear later and for them to say 'How wonderful! There you are again'. What this doesn't take into account is any reciprocal right they might have to say 'No. You must not go away now. You must stay here and listen.' That is something I have never known you submit to.

But history's more complicated. I have to rush to the post. I will write about it next.

Springdale, Utah

Monday 12 May

ADAM to Nigel   Of course you are right about history (pp. 171–2), and to say that history is the subconscious of a nation is a good way of putting it. But there is a crucial American paradox over this: the history of America, or at least of the American West, consists of an indifference to history. The men and women, the trappers and traders, later the farmers and settlers, who came up the rivers, who pushed their handcarts, who came in the waggon trains, who eventually journeyed on the railroad, were doing what hadn't been done before. They were rejecting the restrained and enclosed life of Europe or the East Coast. It was a radical thing to do, based on a refusal to accept everything their ancestors had accepted in a world dominated by the inhumanities of repressive, seigniorial systems. That radical urge for individual freedom lies deep in the heart of America. The Lewis and Clark expedition is, in a way, a great exception in the history of the discovery of the West. It was organised, sponsored and financed by the President, a great reaching out by the federal government to the far Pacific coast. But from my perspective, from this side of the country, it is not the expedition itself which is representative of America but a small incident that occurred on the way *back*. Three of its members, who – I would have thought with my European mind – would want nothing more than to return in triumph to St Louis and to the settled East, decided to leave the Corps of Discovery and remain in the wilderness, living the life of mountain men, indifferent to their role in history as the great pioneers. To my mind those three are the essential Americans, the Americans I admire and envy. Of course their lives and decision were the product of history, no more than bubbles on the great stew of Romanticism that had been cooking in Europe since the Renaissance, but they didn't know it. Seeing themselves as individuals, they were doing their individual thing.

Our difference over this is simply the result of a difference in temperament. You see, and like, the Jeffersonian control, the building of a great and ordered civilisation. I see those three 'lighting out for the territory', as the saying goes. You have been making your way through the colonnades and structures of that civilisation. I have been bumping around in the froth of bits of individualism. This is an old and famous polarity, one which, I am sure, is more obvious in theory than in fact.

I have been ten times happier here than I was in Eastern Europe or I would have been on the East Coast. I haven't wanted to abstract my experience of the West into a recounting of its history because that would be to remove myself from it. Instead, I have tried to live it day to day. I hope you understand that. It would be wrong for either of us to expect or hope that we would resemble each other too closely in this. One of the agonies of America is that the two parts of its soul are so unlike each other. I see us swimming on opposite sides of a reef. You are digging into the coral structure, the building of polyps over hundreds of years. I'm looking at the barnacles, the anemones and the sharks.

Milwaukee – Green Bay, Wisconsin

Tuesday 13 May

NIGEL *to Adam*   Today I enjoyed the privilege (I mean it) of talking to Professor Francis Prucha of Marquette University, Milwaukee, one of the leading authorities on the frontier period of America's history and the Indian tribes. I was surprised to find him wearing a dog-collar. He is a Jesuit priest, like several of his colleagues, and Marquette is named after Jacques Marquette, the Jesuit who rediscovered the Mississippi in the seventeenth century. I was uncertain whether to call him Professor or Father. We settled for Professor. He is a man of about 55, quiet, firm, friendly, indicating with a shy gesture, when I asked, the row of books he has written. For an hour we talked across his desk, a tape-recorder between us but no ashtray, and at lunch in the grim seminary where he lives, no wine.

I asked him the question that has puzzled me since I drove through the empty lands of Virginia and the Carolinas. Why had the colonists left them for the ghastly life of the wilderness? 'Ghastly life!' he replied. 'Your words, not theirs. There was the country, the game, the opportunity, and they were free. Their letters are full of wonder at the beauty of the forest, even those written during the painful 2,000-mile trek to Oregon. They found it heaven on earth.' Their farms in the old colonies were exhausted by the cropping of tobacco and cotton, and in Ohio, Indiana and Illinois they found a fertility unimaginable in Connecticut, where to this day you can see the stone fences of their abandoned farms. Economic progress advanced with astonishing rapidity. There was enthusiasm, and much hard work. 'If life is tough today', they said, 'next year we will have a frame-house, and the year after we will sell corn on the market.' Their success buoyed them up. There was so much land to spare that if a neighbour's pressure proved too much, you simply moved further west and sold your land to speculators. Prucha does not take a romantic view of all this. The pioneers were speculators too. Of course to us their lives would seem brutal ('I couldn't stand to live in a place without air-conditioning'), but to them they were generally happy, exciting and self-sufficient – his own grandmother had raised a large family in western Wisconsin, needing to buy from outside scarcely anything but kerosene.

As we strolled through the campus towards lunch, we were deafened by a student pop group playing to maximum volume, amplified, and wondered why it was that for the only time in history the popular music of the day appeals only to the young people of the day, and how long this craze for noise can possibly last. But when I left the Professor to drive north, my mind was full of what he had told me. The farmlands of Wisconsin are beautiful, and I was seeing them at their gentlest and in their youngest green, for here summer has taken a step back into the freshest spring. This country was virgin territory only 150 years ago. The descendants of the Irish, the Germans, the Dutch who first tilled these farms are now fledged Americans, and the attachment which they still feel for their countries of origin will surely fade in a couple more generations. Green Bay is an example. It is neither green nor bay, but industrialised and wholly American, with a famous football team, the Packers, which has twice won the national championship. A ship from Piraeus was docking in the harbour. That was one thing that pleased me. Another was that Avis, in the Green Bay airport, allowed me to keep the Thunderbird for a third month, and we will remain linked till Dodge City. The mileage-counter, by a strange coincidence, recorded exactly 10,000 miles since we were married in Atlanta.

Tuesday 13 May

ADAM *to Nigel*   A small signpost in the desert this afternoon pointed
left off the highway to 'Pahreah Old Town'. A dirt
road trailed off between the rabbitbrush and the cheatgrass and I took it, a
twin wake of grey dust filling the view in the mirror behind me. A thin layer
of dust covered everything in the car. In front of me the tomato red rock
peaked into stubby towers like a ruined Herstmonceux and below them
pleated skirts of a softer sandstone spread out in their exact stripes of purple,
grey and brown. It looked good and someone in Hollywood had chosen this
place to build a set for a western – three or four wooden buildings, looking
like western bars and stores should do, with hitching posts, falsefronts and
other places for cowboys to lean and drawl. This was not the place. The track
ended by the movie set (and it's interesting that in the Hollywood imagination
the West should look like a sightly antique shopping mall with a photograph
from *Arizona Highways* in the background) and beyond it a more realistic
version survived.

I parked the Catalina and walked. Flies crawled on my face and hands. I
crossed the floor of a washed out gulch, the crust of mud there flaking up in
polygons like chocolate flake on the top of a mousse, down into the valley
where the old town had been. The first thing I came to was the cemetery,
made distinct from the desert only by the barbed wire fence and the stubs
of old gravestones made of the hopeless, crumbling sandstone that had
disintegrated like teeth. But there was also a bronze plaque detailing the
deaths in Pahreah. 13 people, 8 of them women, had died here between 1877
and 1892, 6 Smiths, 4 Smithsons, 2 Twitchells and 1 Mangum. The catalogue
of Smithsons was the most articulate of these inarticulate memorials. Allen
Smithson, aged 61, had died in September 1877. (They were all Mormons
here.) Two years later Dennis A. Smithson died. He was 18 months old.
Then two years after that the two girls died, Susan in January when she was
just 17, and her younger sister Margaret three months later.

The cemetery was up on the bad land above the flat floor of the valley. I
walked on down towards the settlement itself over the scrubby red earth –
what can have induced them to think that anyone could live here! – through
the scattered, barley-like grasses and the odd Indian paintbrush. Mud slides
spread out in places across the track and scarab beetles crawled an inch an
hour over them. A dribble of a river came out of the canyon to the north,
occupying no more than a tenth of its bed. The rest of it was crusted with
salt over the grit grey dust. The whole valley was a dried up, dead version of
somewhere that could have been a beautiful farm – if it had been in Virginia

or Wales. Everything was as it should be – the high land for the rough grazing, the flat bench between the hills next to the river, where some corn or even fruit could be grown. With some irrigation, those Smithsons must have thought on arriving here, some sort of good life would be possible. It was the classic American landscape: wilderness with potential. But it had been too much. On the far side of the river were the ruins of the settlement. Almost nothing was there – a single collapsed range of log houses, the adze marks still on the timbers, a few nails sticking out of them. A cottonwood hedge on the northern, windward side had died in parts and grown into mature trees in others. Some way away, hidden in the scrub, was an underground hovel for animals. It is a place where the threat of extinction, the strangling drought, can never have been absent from men's minds.

When I was there, I thought it must have been drought that had driven men away. Not at all. The first attempt to settle Pahreah in 1865 was made impossible by raiding Indians. The white men left after a couple of years. In 1870 the town was resettled on the site of its paltry wooden ruins today, under the director of a Presiding Elder of the LDS church called William Meeks. A church and school were built. There was a post-office here by 1893. They tilled the land, raised their crops, fostered a few animals and survived until the turn of the century. And then the disaster. It took the most ironic of forms – a flash flood, ripping down from the canyon, carrying away people and houses, animals and the fragile fields. That's why there is so little left here now – most of the place was literally removed by that innocent-looking river. I walked back to the car thinking of Sissinghurst and all its permanencies.

Green Bay–Brillion–Janesville,
Wisconsin

Wednesday 14 May

NIGEL *to Adam*   One of the unexpected features of mid-Wisconsin, which at first appears almost wholly rural, is that it is full of small towns which support thriving manufacturing industries. I went to lunch in one of them, Brillion, with new friends, Michael Ariens and his wife. Michael recommended a route, off the main roads, through Fond du Lac and Madison, to Janesville, to stay the night in a Ramada Inn. The country is lovely – rounded hills, small woods of oak and maple, farmhouses as neat as Swiss chalets, Hereford cattle, mounds of Indian corn. At one moment I was so enchanted by it all that I heard myself muttering aloud that earth has not anything to show more fair, as Wordsworth once wrote of a very different scene.

Phoenix, Arizona

Thursday 15 May

ADAM *to Nigel*   By the time I got to Phoenix, dazed with pop music, as you would say, I could think of nothing but the present – 7.40 this evening, to be precise, when TWA flight 133 would lock into Gate 6 at the Phoenix Sky Harbor, and the first class passengers would emerge and then the exhausted, brightened crowd of the tourist class, with Olivia in among them and William in among her. I spent all day making preparations – buying a small silver brooch of a roadrunner with a turquoise eye from a small roadside stall in the Navajo reservation north of Flagstaff; picking up some dollars from a bank in the suburbs of Phoenix; booking into the smartest hotel I could find – the Hyatt Regency, where the lady who turns down the bed covers leaves a small chocolate on the pillow to make you feel happy and where the glass-walled lift emerges from the atrium at the eighth floor to a sudden view of the spreading city; reserving a table for two in a restaurant at the top of a skyscraper; finding out where Gate 6 was; changing into the cleanest, most uncrumpled clothes in my suitcase as if it were a stranger I was preparing to meet. Then to the airport an hour and a half early, where I read 150 pages of a book about the Canyon de Chelly, went to the loo three times (mostly to check my appearance in the mirror) and paced up and down as if I were an old-fashioned father waiting for news outside the delivery room. Two months is a long time. I tried to concentrate on the Anasazi. 'The year 1492 was a bad one for the first Americans,' my book said. 'This was the time when Columbus blundered into the New World on his way to India, and, through his lifelong refusal to admit he hadn't hit his goal on the first try, the Navajo and the Pueblo and all the other native Americans became known as Indians.' The plane was late – first 10 minutes, then 20, then half an hour. Headwinds. A lady warned me about the desert (scorpions and rattlesnakes), Mexico (corruption and an exaggerated masculinity), and Europe (Libyans and fall-out). 'It's not a good time for Americans to be out of their own country,' she said. I asked her if she thought the motive behind the Libyan raid was to keep American tourists at home and give a boost to the domestic economy. No, she said, it was to stamp out the cancer of terrorism. I said I didn't know cancer was susceptible to stamping. She said I didn't understand.

And then the plane arrived and Olivia came out of the little doorway and everything was fine. This was the only meeting I had come to America for. She was sleepy and excited. I was plain excited and, like thirty-two other people around us, we had a long hug next to the baggage collection roundabout. Now she's sleeping. A man on the next table in the restaurant sent her a bottle of champagne because she looked so lovely. Neither of us ate any of the vastly expensive food that we ordered. Olivia said she knew she had arrived in America when the TWA pilot, bidding farewell to his passengers, had said: 'Have a nice day and, *please*, be nice to each other.' I thought that was a lovely thing to say and she couldn't understand why I had lost all my sense of irony about America. I said I'd tell her slowly in the next few days. 'Can't you see how fat these people are?' she said. I honestly hadn't noticed. The first thing she's going to do with me tomorrow is take me to a hairdresser and remove the hippy look I've been cultivating over the past nine weeks.

Terre Haute–Bloomington, Indiana

Friday 16 May

NIGEL *to Adam*　　　　Bloomington is the seat of Indiana University, and one of its most famous institutions is the Lilly Library. It has special associations for me. Three years ago they acquired from me (that's a euphemism for bought) over ten thousand letters written by Vita and Harold to each other, from their first meeting in 1911 to her death in 1962, probably the fullest correspondence between husband and wife to have survived entire. The Lilly also bought Vita's early diaries and the diaries of Lady Sackville. Now why did I sell them our family archive? Because I was being pestered by students to read them, and Sissinghurst is no university; because they were at risk there from fire, theft, flood and beetle; because Bloomington is placed fairly centrally in the United States where students could have access to them from either coast; because the Lilly has a reputation, among much else, for its collection of twentieth-century literary manuscripts; and because (don't let me balk the ugly fact) I needed the money. I saw the archive there today, neatly packaged by date in boxes and folders, arranged in long catacombs, low-lit, humidified or de-humidified, purring with contentment. I was shown round by Saundra Taylor, the curator of manuscripts, who has a nurse's tenderness with them. My host was the librarian, William Cagle.

Among other Nicolson documents which he showed me were my father's letters to Bruce Lockhart, and I was able to read them for the first time. I came across the following sentence: 'Americans always either condemn on ethical grounds, or try to dismiss by ridicule, those symptoms of civilisation which they can never share themselves.' He also wrote that in the US he felt far more of a foreigner than he ever did in western Europe. I don't believe that either of us share these prejudices. It is simply not true (and I don't think it was true in 1933) that Americans are any more philistine than the generality of the British. Harold came to his conclusion because he was lecturing to women's clubs and enduring a surfeit of hospitality which he would have disliked just as much in Harrogate or Cheltenham. He was tired and bored. But, in spite of these excuses on his behalf, his superior attitude riles me. I feel less of a stranger here than I do in Paris or Rome. The intellectual level at its best (Father–Professor Prucha) is as high as our best, and the mush of television and bar-talk is no more trivial than ours.

I suspect that you consider me over-indebted to my father, and it's quite true that he influenced me far more than I have you. But Ben and I reacted strongly against his élitism, his contempt for all values that were not his own, his covert anti-Semitism, and his innate belief, derived from his own father, that true civilisation can exist nowhere outside a few European capitals. The Americans are not the sneery, diminishing people he pretended. If anything, they care too much, and are swept away by emotional gusts like the hostages, the shuttle, and now the fear that a trip to Europe is a one-way ticket to almost certain death.

I loved your story of Las Vegas and Juliet's visit. Your account (p. 189) of your descent on the city at midnight is the best thing you have written in these letters. I had warned Juliet that the last person a young man wishes to accompany him to Las Vegas is his sister, but her presence, and Olivia's imminent arrival at Phoenix, in no way inhibited you, and in any case, you hated the place.

I thought you replied excellently (p. 201) to my letter about the rich. Yes, that's it – you don't disapprove of riches, you simply seek in this country the unfamiliar and the impolite – and it makes me feel guilty of my acceptance and enjoyment of situations, raised to the power of three, which I've known in England. Where we differ is in your wanting people who have made money to reject its material rewards. That's a very puritanical streak in you. How would my heart-surgeon fit into your scheme of things, or Cy and Wig MacKinnon?

In the desert, just west of Gate's Pass,
outside Tucson, Arizona   *Friday 16 May*

ADAM *to Nigel*   We're sleeping in the car, with the roof down, looking at the muddy stripe of the Milky Way and listening to the coyotes howling and yapping away in the desert. The Catalina has really come into its own. I crumple up in the back seat, Olivia lies full stretch in the front. She notices the shooting stars, I see the satellites moving through the constellations like blips on an oscilloscope. We both think it's incredibly romantic. I feel I'm no longer on a trip but a holiday. It's obvious enough that if you are not alone in a foreign place you are much less exposed to it. Steinbeck says that travelling with someone else 'interferes with the ecology of a journey'. That's true, but it's negatively put, as if a friend were some kind of pollution. I have a suspicion that may have been exactly what Steinbeck meant, but the terrible secret is that, even if I'm noticing a tenth of what I was before, it is a much, much *happier* way of seeing a country. Joint gloom is far more difficult to sustain than the singular variety. There's the benefit of that cosy, uncommunicative state of breakfast-time love you find it so difficult to understand (p. 182). If it sometimes trims the peaks, it certainly fills the troughs.

So what can I tell you about today? We went to a Phoenix hairdresser, where Olivia gave instructions to the *artiste*, Lorie, and she clipped and sliced for half an hour until I emerged partially yuppified. 'A neat head of hair is much easier to manage,' she assured me. Olivia was banished from the cutting booth while the work of art was created because Lorie said she needed to have some 'space' if she was to feel comfortable in what she was doing. In this way faint whiffs of the Californian ethos have drifted across the desert to Arizona. But it has been transformed on the way. Lorie herself had lived several years in Palm Springs but 'couldn't handle all that money'. There's no sense here of the Californian edge of things, of experimenting to the hilt with whatever is new simply because it is new, but the hedonism has survived the desert crossing unchanged. Again and again people answer my question 'Why are you here?' with the one-word answer: Sun. That is not a stimulating motive in life but it does at least have the virtue of simplicity. There are vast colonies of retired people who are here for the one reason that it's sunny in the winter time, preparing for heaven by tanning their wrinkled bodies. I heard the most fascinating statistic on the TV this morning: 90 per cent of Americans think they are going to heaven. Sun City West, the retirement spot, where you are not even allowed in if you are under 50 and where old people can escape the monstrous presence of the children they have brought up on the basis of undiluted individual freedom, is simply the foyer to the Pearly Gates. Arizona, I mean the society in Arizona, is like a California that has been turned off, a jacuzzi without the jets.

After the haircut and a quick swing round the Art Museum (a *wonderful* collection of cowboy pictures, many of them very early, the '70s and '80s, but already made romantic, with an instant and mutual feeding of art into life and back again), and then off down here with the sunset at our backs and the Catalina creaming through the purpled desert.

Bloomington–New Harmony, Indiana

Saturday 17 May

NIGEL *to Adam*   New Harmony is a doubly pleasant surprise to find in southern Indiana. It is a small and very pretty town, with an inn well away from hustling traffic. And it is absorbingly interesting. In the early part of the last century, two communities were founded here, both famous then and famous still, the first by Germans, the second by the Scottish philanthropist Robert Owen. Although Owen's venture failed, the Germans under George Rapp succeeded to an extent that is almost unbelievable. On the very edge of the wilderness they built a town, much of which survives, of lovely little houses, great dormitories in brick, two churches and much else, and farmed 20,000 acres around it. They also established industries which were known throughout the West for the quality of their products. They were communist, celibate and deeply virtuous, and in spite of it (perhaps because of it) the community made a huge fortune. Astonishingly they abandoned New Harmony after ten years, sold it to Robert Owen, and built another town, called Economy, in Pennsylvania. The sect died out in the early twentieth century for the pathetic reason that being celibate they had no children to succeed them.

I won't write more about New Harmony because I've described it in a long article for the *New York Times*. All I need add is that I stayed comfortably at the inn, went riding in a cart drawn by two slow horses, talked to several elderly ladies, and read the town's history far into the night.

New Harmony – Edwardsville, Illinois

Sunday 18 May

NIGEL *to Adam*   What a lot of letters we will get saying, 'You passed my door, and you didn't call in!' and others beginning, 'Sir, Our client, Mr Clinton B. Dykstra, has had his attention drawn to a passage on page 165 of your book ...' We will ignore the latter tremulously, but the former we will regret. How right you were to say that our small contacts in this country are like isolated tesserae from a vast mosaic.

Today was typical. I crossed the entire State of Illinois from east to west without stopping. I was making for Edwardsville, just north of St Louis, where I was to stay the night with Joe and Genevieve (Gen) Hill. They are the parents of Kathy Hill-Miller, who helped me with the Woolf letters, taught English at William and Mary College, then at C. W. Post University in Long Island, from which she is temporarily detached to teach at Cologne

University with a Fulbright scholarship. She lives in Bonn with her husband
Fred and their small son. What chances disperse the American people across
the world! Kathy was born in a farmhouse not far from here, showed promise
at the local school, was encouraged to become an academic when there was
no tradition of scholarship in her family, and has since made for herself a
promising career. Her father is a chemical engineer, just retired, her mother
a registered nurse. They told me that they had been a bit scared to meet
Kathy's 'intellectual friend'. They need not have worried. I am not intellectual,
and I do not scare.

They took touching pains to welcome me. A Union Jack, borrowed from
a neighbour, was hoisted on the outside deck where we ate our barbecued
dinner overlooking the valley. A Sissinghurst banner hung in their living-
room. Two of my books lay open for signature. I was given a bedroom
furnished in antique style, with a multi-coloured quilt and looped lace curtains.
Gen Hill is a generous, lively, kindly woman to whose care I would readily
entrust myself in the severest illness. She has her peculiarities. She piles
bundles of unread magazines into large baskets, hoping to get around to
reading them some day. She planted a green-ash tree immediately outside her
kitchen window, to shade it in hot weather, she explained, but it blocks the
lovely view, and when she points out some distant item of interest, one has
to go on all-fours to see it. She can be critical of her country, saying things
like, 'Everything here has to be new, otherwise it isn't any good.' She maintains
that Kathy can twist her father round her little finger. All this Joe accepts
with affectionate indulgence. He is a man evidently accustomed to taking
responsibilities, but gentle, domesticated, and has a winsome smile. He is
unaffectedly modest. There is nothing in the house to indicate his past
profession, the chemical plants which he has helped to build in many parts
of the United States. Instead, there are photographs of Kathy in every corner,
and holy oleographs and symbols, for they are devout Catholics. Everything
is neat. Dishes are washed immediately the meal is over. Bananas lie in
regulated clusters. Clothes are racked. Pens in vases. But the effect is far from
sanitised. The house contains the magpie collection of a joint lifetime, as if
Mrs Hill could not bear to throw anything away, like the magazines.

You get the picture? It is a very happy one.

Tucson, Arizona

Sunday 18 May

ADAM *to Nigel*   We've been living the life of tourists, my wife and I.
First a visit in the early morning, before the heat
blankets the country, to a fascinating desert museum. Bloat-bellied lizards
and rattlesnakes in sandy glass boxes; a gopher-snake whose skin you were
allowed to touch ('Just like your poly-vinyl handbag, isn't it?' the ranger said
to Olivia; she doesn't have a poly-vinyl handbag); a leopard padding back and
forth in a cage like me in the airport; ocelots in a miniature canyon; and
everywhere the wonderful, odd plants of the desert in flower. The king of
them is the saguaro, the symbol of Arizona. It is the nearest a living thing
comes to a telegraph pole, or at least a telegraph pole with a couple of telegraph
pole branches sticking out of it halfway up. Some of them are nearly twenty
feet high, perfectly vertical, ribbed and fluted like a cylindrical accordion, so
that when it rains the body of the plant can expand to store the water,
gradually drinking from its own reservoir during the dry season, shrinking as
it drinks, the pleats in its skin slowly folding in towards each other. This is a
miracle, isn't it? At the top, which is slightly rounded, there is a crown of
plain white flowers. Humming-birds drink the nectar from them, pushing
their heads and needle beaks deep inside the petal cups. The only ugly objects
in the museum were the human beings. If any of us had been on show in a
zoo somewhere there would have been an outcry. How could the zoo keepers,
a beautiful reporter on *60 Minutes* would have asked, let these animals
degenerate into such a mis-shapen, bored and useless state? How baggy and
unfit we have become! But we were not the only fallen creatures there. The
lizards looked as nasty as we did.

And then on in the growing heat – it reached 103° in the shade in Tucson
this afternoon – to the Kitt Peak National Observatory. This restored all faith
in human beings. Almost the only interest Olivia and I share (apart from
Thomas Nicolson) is astronomy, and Kitt Peak, as I'm sure you know, is the
Delphi, Mecca and Bali of world astronomy rolled into one. 7,000 feet
above sea level and 3,000 feet above the Arizona plateau, on top of a small range
called the Quinlan Mountains, is a collection of sixteen telescopes through
which people look at the universe. The telescopes are all housed in white sun-
proof domes and are dotted around the crest of the mountain like a high tech
mushroom farm. All the astronomers were fast asleep in their dormitories and
of course, in the sunshine, most of the telescopes weren't working. But we
talked to lay guides – it was oddly like visiting a monastery where the priest-
monks were resting – about background radiation and the age of the universe
(this was really an opportunity to swank superficial knowledge) and to hear

about strange things. Did you know there were alcohol molecules floating about between the galaxies? Or that all the light ever collected by all the telescopes in the world would only be the equivalent of the light from a pocket torch for 4 or 5 minutes? These things are difficult to believe. It would have been lovely to come here at night, but that isn't allowed. Only real astronomers can look through the telescopes and they have to apply months in advance for their one or two nights of observing. But we did see something neither of us had ever seen before. At one corner of the mountain top there is a huge *solar* telescope. It is about 300 feet long, most of it underground. A mirror at the top reflects an image of the sun down a long cooled tunnel, where it is then reflected back up into an observing room, where the scientists examine the great circle of light, as big as a table-top, for its blemishes and contortions. We weren't allowed in there either, but the image is reflected into another little room where non-professionals could look at it too. We rushed over in great excitement and there it was, the complete white disc, wobbling slightly in the heat shimmer, and towards one edge of it, tiny but quite distinct, a pair of *sun-spots*. This was marvellous. They would have been nothing on a photograph. You would have thought them blemishes in the printing process. But here on Kitt Peak they were for real, blemishes on the sun itself. Olivia gave me a long, detailed and patient explanation of solar magnetism, the 11 year cycle, the contorting effects of a rotating, heated sphere of hydrogen and helium, the solar flux and the solar wind. I followed in part but with great enthusiasm. She was over the moon, so to speak.

And then – but I'm running days together; there was a night in here somewhere, in which a Lebanese in a restaurant said Olivia's emerald was as beautiful as she was – we went to Mexico. A tyre exploded at one point as we were bowling along at 75 aiming for the border crossing at Sasabe. The Catalina swerved here and there like Gareth Edwards playing for the Barbarians but we came to a stop all right and I put on the spare. The desert is much hotter when you're not going along. Olivia says it reminds her of Chobham Common.

We came to the border. A US immigration woman, with a revolver hanging from her belt, came out to the car and peered in. 'I thought we might just pop into Mexico,' I said. 'What exactly do you mean?' she asked. 'I thought we might just go over the border and get a drink in a bar. It's hot isn't it?' I repeated. She looked at us as if we were some strange form of marine plant life. 'I wouldn't do that if I was you.' 'Oh?' 'I wouldn't go into any of those bars they have there if I was you. *I* wouldn't go in there myself. My husband wouldn't take me in there.' 'What, not even with that thing on your hip?' I have to admit she smiled. 'I wouldn't go in there with an M16 with the safety catch off.' 'Oh good,' Olivia said. The poor customs woman looked a little nonplussed; she can't seriously have thought that we would turn round and go all the way back again.

We said we'd see her again and moved off towards the border fence. It's a scraggly thing, eight or ten strands of untautened barbed wire. It would have been useless as a boundary between fields, let alone countries. The American tarmac comes up to the fence, meets a cattle grid and spreads out in a little pock-marked apron, a yard and a half wide, into Mexico. From there the dirt road trailed south into Mexico. The wreck of a couple of light aeroplanes lay to one side between the prickly pears and the flowering mescal. Some unadorned brick houses, with the mortar slapped in between the courses, sat low down in the dust. Four or five children without shoes played with a softball next to them. Dust, dust and dust, dust and poverty. We bumped and rumbled down the rutted street to the infamous bar. Women in turquoise nylon shifts sat on the concrete steps of their houses smoking vacantly. Nothing picturesque about this poverty, only a suffocating grimness. A minute here explains the scale of illegal immigration into the US. The figures aren't known for certain, but it's thought that about 5,000,000 illegal crossings are made across the southern border of the USA every year. In the Tucson district alone, the Border Patrol catches about 50 a day, and the number caught may represent no more than a fifth of the number who enter the country undetected. That adds up to 90,000 successful illegal immigrants a year. Against this flood, a border patrol is about as effective as a picket fence across the Mississippi. We found our bar, a concrete garage with a man and a box of beer at the far end. No one spoke a word of English. Olivia spoke in Spanish to a sheriff in a straw cowboy hat. He'd had a few beers and was a little too relaxed for any information. There were pages out of *Penthouse* on the wall and the sheriff started to talk to her about the various figures displayed, so we left.

'Glad to have you back here,' the customs woman said. And so, although part of me was loath to admit it, was I.

Edwardsville–St Louis, Missouri

Monday 19 May

NIGEL *to Adam*   Joe and Gen Hill drove me across the plain to the Mississippi. I insisted, first, on seeing the place where Kathy was born, in Granite City, which may sound grim, but was then open farmland, and they lived in the farmhouse, since demolished, only a grassy patch and two trees surviving to mark the spot. Americans can do terrible as well as fine things to their landscape, and Granite City today is one of the most terrible. One can accept two huge oil-refineries, but was it really necessary when the town was expanding to let it grow without plan or theme, allowing each owner to build what he liked where he liked, and fill in the gaps with tawdry malls and gas-stations? Or to destroy the old farmhouse and the church?

We left all this urban desolation for the river, at the actual place where Lewis and Clark started their journey in May 1804. I was seeing its beginning; you saw its end. For me it was a stirring moment. Lying athwart the natural drift of the pioneers from east to west, the Mississippi marks much more than the boundary between States. It was once the frontier between Americans, French and Spanish, and today is still the Great Divide in people's minds, more than the Rockies watershed. It is noble, determined in quite a sedate way, slithering along with a burden of flotsam timber carried down the central stream, now unrapacious, tamed, eternal, and useful still. A long tow of barges slowly beat north against the current. So much history and literature too – de Soto, Marquette, La Salle, Mark Twain, Paul Robeson, Jonathan Raban – and Lewis and Clark. A circular monument with inscribed tablets marks the otherwise deserted beach. We looked across to the confluence of the Missouri on the opposite bank, a slight break in the distant tree-line, no more, and no apparent interruption or addition to the main stream, no change of colour, no drama. Simply two great rivers uniting without fuss. If one regards each as a tributary to the other, the Missouri, which is the longer, should have given its name to the whole river basin as far as the Gulf, but the Mississippi visibly takes command, 'receives' the Missouri in unmistakable pre-eminence, martriarchal for all its masculine attributes, Ol' Man River, Old Glory, and slides more than rolls along, investing the whole centre of the US with beneficent power.

When I left the Hills, I drove into St Louis to see the famous arch from close quarters. It rises on the banks of the Mississippi in an heroic sweep of stainless steel, 630 feet high at its apex, and 630 wide at its base. It was designed by the Finnish architect Saarinen (whose father built Cranbrook School), and was finished in 1965 after his death. It has great symbolism. The shape is a reminder of Jefferson's domes, and is a gateway to the wide plains. It is a single dynamic thrust, like the flight of Glenn's space rocket. In section it is triangular, tapering towards the top, and a car travels inside the legs to an observation platform, but it is so popular that I failed to get a ticket.

It seems to me that the intention was sublime, the engineering fabulous, the assertion intensely dramatic. What worries me is the curve. A parabola is not a shape in nature, but a geometrician's. It is awkward, inconclusive. One instinctively wants a rainbow, and is given a splayed hairpin. I longed to push the legs together, or link them. I wonder what you think. I enclose a postcard.

Christopher Creek, Arizona

Monday 19 May

ADAM *to Nigel*   This morning, in unbelievable heat, relieved only by
                       two 5lb bags of ice cubes which Olivia bought at a
gas station and which sat on our knees as a substitute for an effective air
conditioning system, we drove to Phoenix, collected your letters from the
General Delivery and then came on up into the mountains here, where it's
cooler and where the head of an elk is attached to the wall of our log cabin.
In the desert Olivia's hair gets so dry that it sticks out sideways like uncooked
vermicelli. We both enjoyed your description of my terrifying contempt
(p. 200). But you're wrong about the most important part of it. I am short
and contemptuous when I feel weak or threatened. When I feel confident,
then I can be more generous. It's just like the desert plants: they're spiny
because in that environment they have to avoid being eaten. In lusher places,
where life is not so marginal, plants can afford to offer themselves as food,
can turn themselves into blackberries or even peaches, because they are sure,
in the end to benefit from it.

But I must answer what you say about your divorce (p. 200). It's not right –
and it's not your part – to say 'Your hurt cannot be very deep'. You have to
take it from me that it was deep at the time and that I was unable to talk to
a single person about it for 9 years. And the moment when I did, in the end –
it was at Cambridge – I remember almost more clearly than anything else.
And I have to tell you that for you to say 'the hurt was a temporary shock
and disappointment such as any child would feel' shows an ignorance of the
strength and depth of children's feelings that is nothing short of staggering.
It was dreadful at the time. Not that I don't believe it was the best thing you
could have done, given the circumstances. It was certainly the better choice
between two pretty bad alternatives.

Winslow, Arizona

Tuesday 20 May

ADAM *to Nigel*   A dreadful day, a disaster of a day, a complete waste
                       of a day, one of Olivia's precious few days here was
spent in a *garage*. I knew the day would come when the Catalina would simply
refuse to do what it has to do. Today was that day. The engine started off all
right, the reassuring roar, that slight shuddering of the bodywork which
shows it wants to go. Then the click of the gears into Drive and – nothing.
It wouldn't go anywhere. I walked to a garage half a mile away and explained

the problem. Larry was all ears as I described the symptoms. Or at least I thought he was but when I'd finished he said, very slowly, 'Now wait here. Could you please explain that to me in English without quite so much of your gabbling. You're just not talking the language I talk.' As he said it, I knew this was true because Larry, like the Ancient Egyptians, made do without vowels. His was a discourse consisting entirely of consonants. 'Yr tlkn fstr thn a Mxcn, n I cnt kp p wth y thr,' he said. So I went through it again, describing the Ctlna's dffrntls and trnsmssn, as well as its prfrmnce on the rd so far. A great beam of recognition spread out from under Larry's mstch. That was the first success in a barren day. He had understood, but the news was bad. 'My eardrums were sweating with all that talking back there,' he said (expanded version), 'bt I hv to tll y, the nws s bd. Wr talkn bt a nw trnsmssn n thts 4 r 5 hndrd dllrs.' Oh God. So the Catalina was dragged in on the back of the rcvry vhcl and Larry slid underneath. 'Thts gt a smll ndr thr tht I dnt lk th smll of,' he said. We had to telephone around the state for a new transmission and at last one was identified down the road at Payson. 'What smell is it?' I asked Larry. 'I wldnt vn lk to dscrb t t ya.' Gaining confidence in my ability to understand anything he said, Larry launched off into a cnsnntl dscrptn of the history of Christopher Creek. One word – pch – featured regularly in the generalised mass of letters. Only late this evening have I realised what it was. The Apaches were an important ingredient in the early history of the place. More than that I could not say. After hours of hanging around waiting for the new transmission to arrive, poor Olivia flaking out in the roadside bar trying every combination of 7 Up, Mountain Dew and Sprite the barman could mix, Larry suddenly had a brainwave. 'Hv y chckd th trnsmssn floooid?' he asked, those vowels suddenly ballooning out of nowhere, like an idea bubble in a cartoon. No, I hadn't. Larry checked it. It was wy dwn lw, so we poured in a couple of quarts, started up the old Cat, and there we were, ready to go, raring to go, and we've been going ever since. 'Bye bye and thank you,' we said to Larry. 'Bye bye,' he said, with a huge round-mouthed effort and a wave. We're now in Winslow, a zero nowhere rail-town, where some Indians (from India, I mean) are running the Best Western motel, hating every minute of it and pining for the sweetness of Chepstow, Monmouthshire that they have left behind.

Ste Genevieve, Missouri

Tuesday–Wednesday 20–21 May

NIGEL *to Adam* What a pleasure to discover this place by accident! It lies on the Mississippi some 60 miles south of St Louis, and is the oldest town on the west of the river, founded by French-Canadians in 1735 from the north and Creoles from the south. Later, Germans poured in to work the local lead-mines. Its character bears traces of all this. Loggia-ed houses from the French period, peaked buildings from the German, a steepled Catholic church, and modern additions in decent brick and timber. It's utterly delightful. I am staying two nights in the Inn St Gemme Beauvais. Beside the Stars and Stripes it flies the fleur-de-lys, and there's a notice outside, *Logement à louer*, but all this, like their annual Jour de Fête, is due, I think, to recent romanticism, for the town is wholly American. There is one inhabitant, I was told a little dubiously, who can speak adequate French, and a shop where they make German sausages.

The people, as in all small towns, are friendly. When it became clear after a word or two that I was English, I was questioned closely about Princess Di and the fogs that permanently envelop London. In a baker's shop I saw a notice advertising the human chain which next Sunday is to stretch from New York to Los Angeles, passing through Ste Genevieve itself. I set a girl of 10, Susie, a problem. 'If six million people stand hand-in-hand across the 4,000 miles from coast to coast, how many people will be needed to cover the 1 mile through Ste Genevieve?' Susie knit her sweet face with the effort of calculation. Eventually she came up with, 'Two hundred'. 'Go down two grades,' said her grandmother, who I suspect was finding the sum equally stubborn, and I had to supply the answer.

In the office of the local newspaper, I talked to the editor, Ralph Morris; in the finest Creole house, the lady-guides; in the church, the priest; on the river, the ferryman; and on its far bank a man who transplants trees. So I had no lack of willing informants. The most interesting was the ferryman. I crossed the Mississippi four times with him, for he makes the trip with cars, tractors and small trucks dozens of times a day. How wide is the river at this point, how deep in the centre, how fast the current? The treeman had answered respectively, a mile, 60 feet, 7 m.p.h., but the true (ferryman's) figures are 600 yards, 40 feet, 3–4 m.p.h. Treemen, he implied, are all liars. Did the floating debris worry him? They seemed to me like spears aimed at his hull. No, only if they were more than 20 feet long, and then he diverts them by turning his articulated ferryboat aslant. Do dead horses, cows, dogs, people float down the river? Treeman, 'The whole time'. Ferryman, 'Animals rarely, humans never' (but in the local newspaper I read that a St Louis corpse was fished out last week). How does he avoid crossing the path of the vast barge-tows which pass in each direction about twice an hour? By radio, searchlight signals at night, and long-established custom. By what name does he refer to the river? Never the Mississippi, never Ol' Man River, and the term Old Glory must have been invented by Raban. It is always 'the upper river' and 'the lower', the dividing line coming at Cairo where the Ohio enters from the east. Had he read Mark Twain? At school they had studied *Life on the Mississippi*, but he'd never got around to Tom or Huck. (He had a perfect Huck lookalike as his assistant.)

He reduced the whole romance to the level of a monotonous job. I had to return to my books to rediscover it, and read once more the stories of Marquette and La Salle, the first white men to travel the river between hundreds of miles of uninhabited forest, La Salle to its mouth, where he raised the flag of France and named the whole vast river-basin Louisiana after his King. The river has changed its course many times since then, but its appearance is almost exactly the same today, stretches 10 miles long bordered by cottonwood trees, and bluffs on each bank which, had it been a European river, would have been crowned by castles and mansions, but here are left to a few grazing cows.

Then came the steamers which could force their way upstream to St Louis and Pittsburgh in a couple of weeks, and the whole hierarchy and drama of the river-pilots, to whom the young Samuel Clemens was apprenticed. He describes in *Life on the Mississippi* how his master, Horace Bixby, 'silent, intent as a cat', navigated by night the shoals of Hat Island, which could have torn the bottom out of his boat.

> The watchman's voice followed from the hurricane deck – 'Labbord lead, there! Stabboard lead!'
> The cries of the leadsmen begin to rise out of the distance, and were gruffly repeated by the word-passers on the hurricane deck.
> 'M-a-r-k three! . . . M-a-r-k three! . . . Quarter-less-three! . . . Half twain! . . . Quarter twain! . . . M-a-r-k twain!'

I love the terminology, the excitement, the tradition. Those were the great days of the river. Now you have all the aids of signals, radar, radio, to make the passage unadventurous for the giant tows, and no pleasure boats except the famous tourist paddle-boats venture on the stream. 'A few years ago, there was an Englishman . . .' I had to remind him of Raban's name.

But the Mississippi can still be treacherous. Almost every year it floods into the outskirts of Ste Genevieve, and twice recently, in 1973 and 1982, the town was inundated, doing enormous damage. It was declared by Reagan a national disaster area. Why did they not build a levée, I asked Ralph Morris, like the ones I'd seen on the Illinois shore? They did, to protect farmlands north and south, but there's a gap opposite Ste Genevieve because two creeks enter here, and it would cost $35 million to siphon them over a levée. 'So this historic place could be washed away?' 'It could. And that's why we've been agitating in Washington to have the levée built. There's support from the Army engineers, but opposition from the politicians. It's thought to be too expensive for such a small town. It's likely to be refused.'

I think it unforgivable. Ste Genevieve is a lovely place. I felt the first touch of the West here, although the plains were unexplored by the French before the Louisiana Purchase. A 1804 map in the museum marks them as *Grand espace de pays qui n'est pas connu.* But in the inns (such a relief after the motels) there are man-sized bar-counters, divided doors that swing, gas-globe chandeliers, and armchairs covered in red plush velvet. One expects to see a Stetson, barmaids in low-cut brocade, a gambler or two, but not yet. It is all unfaked, jolly and very hospitable.

Canyon de Chelly, Arizona

Wednesday 21 May

ADAM *to Nigel*   I had never met a man who had killed a man before today. K.J. Mackenzie – that's how he introduced himself – laughed at the end of nearly every sentence. 'Yuhu,' he said in the Winslow Tire Company this morning, looking at me through his one eye, 'Ah killed him'. He laughed while looking at us all around the edges of the room. Mackenzie is a tall man and big across the chest. He wore a sort of khaki safari suit, hanging loosely about his body. He stood out from the rest of us in our blue jeans as a vaguely military man who was so used to the idea of uniform that even when in ordinary clothes he appeared to be wearing one. I suppose he was about your age. 'Ah was Special Agent to the Atchison, Topeka and Santa Fe Railway at the time,' he said. 'Tell them about it KJ,' Mr Matlow, the owner of the garage and hunter of bison, said, before sitting back with folded arms to hear the story once again. KJ pulled up his safari shirt. Tucked inside the waistband of his trousers, between the trousers and his pants, was the gun that had done it, just stuck in there, without any kind of elaborate holster, but with its muzzle nestled into a leather pouch. He gave me the gun. It was a 44 revolver, a big, black bit of metal. He flipped open the fluted cylinder, took out three of the bullets and gave them to me. They were fat and short, really like stunted slugs, with brass caps at the tips. 'Don't drop them' KJ said, 'those are explosive caps on there.' It took me a moment or two to realise what this meant. These bullets were not intended to wound or to catch someone a glancing blow. If KJ hit his man the bullet would explode. Mackenzie told the story. It was simple enough. He began at the crisis, the climax. A Mexican was coming at him in the stock yard in Winslow. He had a knife in each hand, one 8 inches long, the other 6. 'He was coming at me, and he was saying that if I didn't kill him he would kill me, so I killed him. I shot him here', KJ spread his hands in a double web across his stomach, 'and that killed him, always does,' and then a long bout of rolling laughter. 'He's a real character, KJ,' Matlow said. 'What did it feel like?' I asked. 'Oh it didn't feel like nothing,' KJ said.

We drove north through the incredible country of the Navajo Reservation. This must be one of the most beautiful places on earth. The mesas stand out on the horizon, sharp-edged or whale-backed like islands on the Minch. The colours are all smoked, the grassy plateau lifts and drops in billows. Now and then there is an Indian hogan, usually surrounded by the wreck of a couple of cars, one of them helplessly upside down like a beetle. I tried to persuade Olivia that this sort of undividedness with all its invitations to the horizon, was the best landscape there was. She didn't agree. She liked fields, organisation, interruptedness, detail. Here the place you chose to set up home was too arbitrary. It was all yours but there was nothing telling you what to do with it. She saw it as a huge and mildly frightening *tabula rasa*.

We were heading for a place which, I guessed, would be more to her liking. Right in the middle of the Navajo Reservation, which is enormous, over sixteen million acres, is the reservation of another people, the Hopi. They have a small (640,000 acre) pie-slice of territory called, with all of Washington's sense of poetry, District 6. The Navajo and Hopi are deep in a bitter and complicated argument over an area which is neither strictly part of the Navajo Reservation nor part of District 6, but was designated in 1962 as a Joint Use Area. Extremely valuable coal deposits have been found in part of it. A white mineral company wants to strip-mine it, but whom should they pay? The Hopi claim the land as undividedly theirs (although, concentrated in their villages in District 6, they have never used it) while the Navajo families that have been settled there (illegally, according to Hopi lawyers) refuse to move unless massively compensated. About 10,000 Navajos and 20,000 acres of land are involved. This is what the public meeting at Berkeley was about (p. 97), although the issues, I now realise, were utterly distorted there. It is not simply a case of white capitalist greed destroying the fabric of Indian life. It is not even Indian greed destroying the fabric of Indian life. It is the classic border problem of interpenetrated rights to which, historically, there has only ever been one answer: the overwhelming use of force by one side or the other to establish its claim. That's impossible here, as it is in Ireland, and the dispute will dribble on, as it has done since 1882 when the Hopi reservation was first set up to protect them from encroachment by the far more numerous and active Navajo, with minor acts of violence between the two sides. The other option – large amounts of federal dollars – is not appropriate because of the Indian beliefs about land. It is seen not as a simple resource, but as the reservoir of everything that makes the people what it is. In this sense the land is sacred, the embodiment of everything that matters. How this conception can survive the activities of a strip-mining company, I don't know.

The story of the Navajo-Hopi dispute goes on for ever, but there is one line to be traced through it. The Hopi are almost certainly the descendants of the Pueblo Indians who built the great pre-Columbian civilisation in these canyon lands. They are farmers not pastoralists. The Navajo are part of a later wave of people who came down from the North in the twelfth or thirteenth century, as hunters and gatherers. (It's strange to read these terms again, repeated slightly out of order from the prehistoric history of England.) There has never, for any length of time, been a community of interest between these peoples. Olivia said it was like the difference between her and me. She was a Hopi, settled in her mesa-top stone village, unshifting, permanent and agricultural. (All this was a symptom of missing Thomas, for whom she is now pining.) And I, in this scheme of things, was the Navajo, shiftless, careless about domestic arrangements, marauding and disloyal.

We drove up on to the first mesa in the Hopi Reservation. After the Pueblo Revolt in 1680, the Hopi took their villages up on to the defensible mesas and there they are today. Notices warned visitors not to behave badly. Our guidebook told us not to go into people's houses without knocking and not to pick at the jewellery that the Hopi might be wearing nor to ask how much they would sell it for, as this would be rude. God knows what white people must have done here in the past. The village of Walpi is built on the end of a finger of rock, cliffed on either side and with long, protective views to north and south across the grasslands. It has a stronger sense of place and permanence than any white settlement in America. It is the only village I have seen where the houses touch each other. They are packed together like boxes in a warehouse, with a dusty lane leading in and out between them. The twin tree-poles of ladders stuck out through the roofs of the hidden kivas. Olivia said she hated doing this to a place, hated looking in on somewhere that had its arms tightly bound around its chest in a sense of privacy and difference that is almost absent in white America. We bought a rattle for William from the man who made them. It was a painted gourd with a cottonwood handle decorated with tadpoles and the rising sun for the beginning of life. We had a rudimentary talk, the fault not of his English but of my reticence. His name was Del Fritz. He had been given it at school, he said, so that he would feel more part of the system. His real name was Suma and in Hopi that meant something like 'the knot as it is being tied'. He was trying to persuade his wife, who had been labelled Del Ramirez at school, to return to their Hopi names. It is a sign of the times that this seemed a more obvious move to Olivia and me than it did to the Hopis themselves. There is a sentimentality in our culture now which imagines that before the coming of the Spanish or the Anglos, the Indians were living a wholesome, integrated, happy life which our arrival disrupted. Blaming the Hopi-Navajo dispute on the intervention of white capitalist forces is a symptom of this, but if there is one virtue in that dispute it will be to stop the pendulum swinging from Indian as Hopeless Savage (still prevalent in Winslow Tire Company) to Indian as Primitive Perfection (increasingly prevalent in parts of urban California, for example). Olivia and I came away with one idea: tourism gives no access to other people's lives. There is no knowing in a half-hour talk, particularly with people who have as strong a tradition of self-protection as the Hopi.

Ste Genevieve–Nashville, Tennessee

Thursday 22 May

NIGEL *to Adam*   A driving day, nearly 400 miles, as I'd given myself a treat by staying two nights at Ste Genevieve instead of making half-distance to Nashville. To my disappointment the road does not follow the Mississippi but heads south with Roman straightness towards Memphis, and I missed the confluence of the Ohio in Cairo. I crossed the river by a bridge near Dyersburg, and went into the Welcome Center because it looked welcoming and I wanted a break from the unstoppable rain.

Six huge men sat round a table. The hostess, whose helpfulness was advertised outside, was nowhere to be seen. The men looked up as I entered. I was the sole visitor that afternoon. One of them, a giant in anorak and sea-boots, approached me beaming. Clearly the official greeter. 'Cun a' be ain as't to ye?' he said. The Tennessee accent, the ugliest in America, hit me like a steam-hammer. 'I come from England', I said, 'and you must speak nice and slow for me to understand you.' So the tortured syllables were expectorated one by one (but I can't reproduce the new version phonetically), 'Can I be of any assistance to you?' (too pretty an enquiry for so burly a man). I asked if the other men were truck-drivers. No, they all worked here. I saw no evidence of it.

Then the boss appeared, Tom Turner, Manager of the Dyersburg Welcome Center in the Department of Tourist Development, State of Tennessee, his card said. He was all affability. He took me to the wall-map to give me directions, and gave me a copy of it. He pressed on me a Tennessee cookbook, a plastic bag with more welcomes printed on it, and several brochures about canoe trips and pioneer villages. Would I care to enter the lottery for a free night's lodging in Nashville? I would. The necessary form could not be found. Would I like a cup of coffee? Please. The machine needed fixing. All this time the jolly sextet round the table cross-questioned me. Princess Di? How many children did I have? Where are they? It was the friendliest frontier welcome of all time. Another tessera.

The road onward is beautiful. It deserves an engineer's Oscar. Half Tennessee is still forest, part evergreen, furry, firry, but most is cottonwood and oak. The road winds through them, smooth as cream, in great amorous curves for 120 miles, crossing at intervals stupendous rivers. The difference between this and the Black Forest is that in Germany every hill would have a building perched on top. Here there is little habitation, a few isolated cabins. How strange it is to pass in a few seconds for the only time in one's life a place where someone lives for ever.

Olivia telephoned to Nashville from the Arizona–New Mexico border, and I spoke to both of you. You had been sleeping in the open desert among the rattlers. She said she preferred it that way.

Farmington, New Mexico

Thursday 22 May

ADAM *to Nigel* It is so easy to be seduced by the myth of paradise among the Anasazi ruins. Olivia and I walked down into the Canyon de Chelly this morning at 6, when it was still cool and there was no one else about. The canyon is a cut about 500 foot deep down into the plateau of north-east Arizona. Above it everything is dried out and marginal, but in the cut of the canyon itself there is a lushness and a dampness that turns the world green. There are twelfth century ruins pushed into little cracks in the cliff and everywhere the glorious colour of the rock. It's red, but to say it's red is not good enough. It's raw red and cooked red and vermillion and magenta and the green of the cottonwoods is giant new lettuce. Can you imagine this? Olivia is going to repaint our house entirely in these colours. By the time we left the ruins, which are like a small Hopi village, unroofed, and built in finer masonry – and it's a shock to remember that these houses are older than any domestic building in England – other Americans were coming down the path from the top of the canyon. We loathed the sight of them. They loathed the sight of us. Olivia made us hide behind a tree while

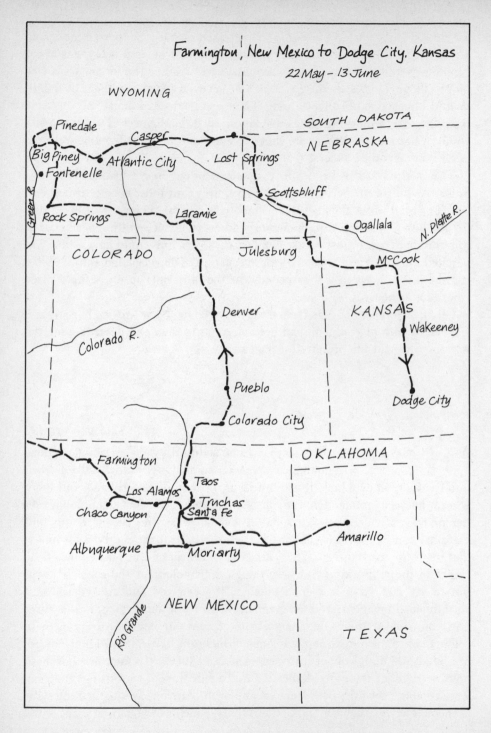

Farmington, New Mexico to Dodge City, Kansas
22 May – 13 June

a romantic couple in their mid-thirties wandered past, so that their happiness wouldn't be alloyed by our presence in paradise.

On the way here today we gave a lift to two Navajos. The first was a fundamentalist pastor who despised everything to do with the traditional Navajo religion, saying it consisted in nothing but sun and moon worship (completely untrue) and banging on about Olivia's soul. 'What's your technique for getting to heaven?' he asked her four or five times. He was very right wing. I drove fast through the spectacular country so that conversation would be impossible and we could all look at the view in its silent wisdom. We dropped him outside Monument Valley. (Olivia's verdict: in need of bridge-work.) Next passenger a 25 year old Navajo drug dealer called Jimmy who tried to sell us some dope *en route*. No deal. Apart from commercial transactions, Jimmy was as silent as the pastor had been loud. He averaged about two words every 3 miles and spent most of the time polishing the lenses of his green and gold shades. In both Navajos there was a terrible deprivation, narrowed into intolerance in the pastor, spread out and whacked into nothingness in Jimmy.

Nashville–Chattanooga, Tennessee

Friday 23 May

NIGEL *to Adam*   At Nashville Airport I checked with Eastern our tickets to Kansas City–New York on 14 June, and booked our flights Dodge City–Wichita, Wichita–Kansas City on the same day. The only plane leaves Dodge at 6.30 am., I suppose because it was at that hour that they started moving the cattle.

Nashville calls itself the Music Capital of the World – well, of a certain type of music. I could not leave without sampling it. Near the city centre lie all the recording studios and the homes of the stars, round which you can be conducted just like Beverly Hills, but the action takes place some miles out, at Opryland USA, or at least the action I wanted to see.

It is a vast fairground. Neither of us have previously seen the Americans at play *en masse*, and here they played as if in heaven. It costs an amazing $15 even to get inside the pearly gates, and extra for the performances (one has to give one's name. 'Nixon?', suspicious. I spelled it out), but this did not deter thousands from entering, boys and girls and large numbers of retired people, the older men wearing comic hats to simulate the return of youth. I tried to buy a T-shirt for the roasting plains ahead of me, but could not find one that was not overwritten by an embarrassing slogan or printed with the picture of a star of whom I'd never heard. There are shooting and ball-tossing galleries at which I dreaded to win a polar bear three times my size, overhead railways, swings, zoos, cafés, linked by broad alleys kept spick and paintwork span, and by piped rock and country music, some performed in open-air orchestras. Let me explain the difference between rock and country. In rock the team stands sideways, craning and crooning into a single mike. In country, they stand apart, each with his own mike, and wobble a little with the syncopation. I prefer country, for the rock always seems to be anguished, the country harmonious.

To discover more, I went to *Music, Music, Music*, an hour-long song-and-dance show in a theatre. Most of the audience were middle-aged and tired, the performers all young and bouncy. The object was to transfuse a little *Elixir vitae*. One of the dancers looked exactly like Olivia, so I focused my attention on her. She sang 'Singing in the Rain' and 'My Heart Belongs to Daddy', and danced a waltz, a tango, and many medleys with the others, as in *Chorus Line*. I admired her greatly. The histrionic smile never left her face on stage, but as I was seated to one side, I saw with amusement how quickly it shrank when she skipped into the wings. The show was entirely sexless. For while the girls were pretty and the young men handsome, they were clothed head to foot (not a navel visible) in cowboy costume, idealised, and their amorous gestures and glances were totally anodyne. There was not a single blue joke. How different it would have been in Blackpool! It was *Oklahoma* plus, *Cats* minus, drawing deeply on the romance of harvesting in the prairies, with bits of Broadway added. At the finale there was a brilliant piece of stagecraft. A sort of elongated crane descended and in a single movement whipped up the gorgeous cloaks and southern ballgowns they were wearing, leaving them in chequered shirts and lederhosen. I would like to see it repeated. I cannot make out how it was done. The audience clapped. Olivia clapped back. Then the figure of Liberty rolled forward, the symbol of America's marvellous past and present. The audience rose to its feet. The whole performance was unashamedly jingoistic, strangely moving as the only part of their history they chose to remember, but remember through the distorting lens of sentiment. The golden boys and girls of the plains is the image they most treasure here.

I drove south-east to Chattanooga through glorious country (Tennessee is now my favourite State), approaching perilously close to Atlanta – perilously because this detour will create a jagged line on our map when all should have been predestined curves. Chattanooga? Chattanooga? Why was the name so familiar? Not for its Civil War battle, but, of course, for the movie *Chattanooga Choo Choo* and its song. The Choo Choo was a railway station, and is now a Hilton complex. The young man behind the Ramada bar had not seen the movie, and could not sing the song, but I could, and hummed it to him.

Chattanooga–Birmingham, Alabama

Saturday 24 May

NIGEL *to Adam*   Your account (pp. 202–3) of America's history contains a flaw. It is not the only example of Europeans flooding into an unknown continent. The colonising of Africa and parts of Asia was almost contemporary. Both experiences illustrate the extraordinary vitality of the West, not just of the USA, and what we see in the frontier story is a more brutal form of colonisation. They murdered their Indians; we educated ours. So when you praise the pioneers for rejecting the tamer life of Bohemia or the east coast of America (I agree with that), one must also admit that their motives were self-seeking and their methods unscrupulous, which puts 'freedom' in a rather different light. For the 'inhumanities of the seigniorial system' they substituted another just as cruel – massacre, misappropriation and slavery – as you subconsciously acknowledged when you retreated in shame from the Indian reservation.

You return to your thesis that the liberated American who rejects the rewards of his ordeals represents the noblest of his kind, and you hold up as types worthy of your admiration and envy the three followers of Lewis and Clark who remained in the wilderness. I don't have the books to remind me of what sort of men they were. They may just as easily have been vagabonds, criminally inclined, as true adventurers, but given that they were mountainmen of the hardiest calibre, I see nothing more admirable in their renunciation of civilised life than in Lewis's acceptance of the Governorship of the very territory through which I'm now passing, and where he soon died. Your preference for the maverick comes close to admiring the outcast just because he is an outcast, Patty Hearst because she joined her kidnappers in a bank-raid, and your analogy of the barnacles, the anemones and the sharks is a romanticising of an aspect of America which to me is far less important than the political, economic, scientific and cultural achievements of men and women who did not remain in the wilderness.

Why do you respect non-conformity so much? Here's an example. Today I entered a sleazy motel, economising for once. The youth at the reception-desk was engaged in a long telephone conversation with his girl-friend. After ten minutes (I'm not exaggerating) he looked up at me, still telephoning, with a 'Huh?', expressive of his contempt for an elderly gent with a fancy accent who drives up in a swishy Thunderbird. I walked out, throwing over my shoulder, 'And I won't be coming back'. Now, he was non-conformist worthy of your approval, but you'd have been equally (well, perhaps not equally) outraged, and pleased by the girl at my next motel who greeted me with a conformist, but not deferential, smile. Where do you draw the line?

Perhaps when we meet in Dodge City we will discover together an American who represents an ideal on which we can both agree. He will be a Marlboro man, a rancher with 10,000 acres, stubborn, proud, successful, slightly bar-nacled, who has made money in the hardest way, lives in decent comfort, is indifferent to books and Englishmen, and still rides the ranges with his sons.

I enjoyed your account of meeting Olivia in Phoenix (p. 207), how you arrived at the airport 90 minutes early, met, hugged, and in your shared excitement left the Hyatt dinner uneaten. This is something I really envy, reciprocated love. Olivia wrote to me that this is the best holiday she has had in her 26 years. 'There is everything to live for – do you know what I mean?' Of course I know. I am glad you brought in a single ink-spot of Mexico (p. 214) to set, geographically and culturally, against our Canadian experiences. And how much I agree with you about the general ugliness of mankind (p. 213). When so much money, so many magazines, are devoted to pruning, preening and paring the flesh, the effect is negligible. There is no substitute for youth. But as you observed in your observatory, even the sun has spots.

Having visited the Chattanooga Choo Choo, where the Hilton guests sleep in old-time stationary wagon-lits, I drove south to Birmingham. I was astonished by the extent of the forests. The cities are carved out of them at intervals of 100 miles, like the space stations of the next century, and, wanting to see what lay behind the endless screen of trees, I turned off the Interstate and found beautiful houses scattered among the glades. Worship of nature, comfort in a pseudo-wilderness, pride in good design, the consolation of privacy, love in a hot climate – all this I read into the secluded mega-cabins of Alabama.

Santa Fe, New Mexico

Saturday 24 May

ADAM *to Nigel*   On the way here a couple of days ago, we came across the mountains on a dirt road and then dropped down to Los Alamos. Olivia was feeling deprived of intelligent company, so we scanned the map for a concentration of brain cells. Los Alamos had no rival. She didn't particularly want to talk to anyone clever. She just wanted to be surrounded by clever faces. In some rather oblique way she finds this flattering. So we drove through the thick smell of the pine woods and through a few high flowery meadows before coming to the nuclear capital of the world. There they were, leaning against the corners of the coffee-coloured buildings, ambling pensively on sidewalks, holding their chins: brains. The mild dis-illusion/disappointment Olivia had been suffering for a couple of days in her husband/America vanished on the spot. It was like ordinary people's reaction to a fairground – a brightening of the eyes, a lifting of the pulse. I was slightly anxious about taking an uninvited swing around one of the most sensitive installations on the continent, but Olivia experienced none of that. She set off like a neutrino, straight through a couple of swing doors, out of which the scientists were emerging, every one of them with an identity/security label attached to their shirts. The only I D I had was a passport in which 70 per cent of the visas were from communist or Arab countries. Visions of an F B I arrest and interrogation never entered Olivia's head. But I had to follow her. So I too went through the swing doors, putting on a brainy face to show that I was so deeply engrossed in the problems of nuclear super-symmetry in the first fractions of a second after the Big Bang that I had forgotten my plastic identity card that day. Olivia had disappeared. I peered into cool, whitely lit rooms where banks of white computers were making invisible calculations, but Olivia was nowhere. Had she already been arrested? I saw a sign to a cafeteria. You probably had to have a PhD to buy a cup of coffee there but I reckoned it had to be a low risk option, so I bought a cinnamon bun, calculated the sales tax before the cashier rang it up so as to demonstrate my qualifications, and sat down to plan a strategy. (The Los Alamos café is the only one in the world where salad is sold at 18c an ounce. You select your beetroot and spring onions and a scientist then weighs them on a set of electronic scales.) What to do? I looked around the room. Shop was being talked everywhere. Nothing remains of the frontier spirit at the time when Oppenheimer and Groves took over a boys' school on this remote moun-tainside in 1941, gathered the best minds of the generation to develop the bomb and spread the rumour in Santa Fe that they were building submarines up here. All that has gone: now comfort, carpets and discreet lighting with a waterfall outside, many miles away from the lino and chipped enamel of the coffee room in the Cavendish at Cambridge. Then I saw her. Over on the other side of the room, Olivia was discussing Chernobyl with a group of four nuclear scientists gathered around her. 'They had it coming, didn't they,' she was saying. 'Their maintenance programme is notoriously sloppy.' The scientists were nodding in amazement and agreement. They were discovering astrophysicist friends in common. If only she had got in touch with them before we had gone to Kitt Peak. Back on to the sun-spot cycle. My wife will never cease to amaze me. She then saw me with my solitary bun and waved me over like a hostess. Quick introductions to her lifelong friends and then we had to go. 'You're rather tense, aren't you?' she asked me as we swung out again through the swing doors. 'A pity, such interesting people.'

And then we drove down here. My friends from Los Angeles, David and Kanthi Barry, have flown in for the weekend. And they have a friend here, a wonderful woman called Sallie Wagner, in whose guest house we are all now staying. It's up on a red gravelly hill covered in piñon pine and juniper, her drive lined with silver sage, the whole place alive with innumerable fluffy dogs she has saved from various appalling fates on roadsides. She is in her 70s, full of extraordinary life and enthusiasm, with a laugh that's the most infectious I have ever known. Before the war she ran a trading post in the Navajo reservation, miles from anywhere down dirt roads at a place called Wide Ruins and has had a long and deep friendship with the Navajo, about whom she knows everything, and for whom, long before the splurge of emotional enthusiasm for the Indian in the '60s and '70s, she has held a proper and unsentimental respect. Her house, a cool, thick adobe building, is filled with Indian things, masks and drums and paintings and rugs. She has given Olivia a small drum for Thomas to play. It is made of hollowed out cottonwood covered with rawhide. He'll love it.

I picked up your letters and you will want me, I know, to respond to the question about the St Louis Arch (p. 216). (I loved your description of the great Miss-Miss confluence!) I'm looking at the postcard even now. The snow's nice, but the arch . . .? Do you know I really don't care about things like this. I get the point, but I knew the point anyway and to my mind that sort of point is far, far better left unmade. I'm sure it had to be a parabola to get the required look of *thrust* and *future* in it – and that's why it does *not* have the look of Jefferson's settled domes – but how much better it would have been if it wasn't there at all, or, like one of Christo's sculptures, there for a week and then remembered as more beautiful than it was, a half-non-shadow on the mind's sky.

We've had a fine time wandering around Santa Fe. You know the complexities of this place – its three inter-connecting layers of Indian, Spanish and Anglo, each making its contribution and all flowing together in the wonderfully plastic material of the adobe. No line is sharp in the town. All the corners are rounded, all verticals are no more than near verticals, sloping inwards towards the roofs. It is strange that a place of such cultural complications should have a coherence that is only outdone by the Hopi villages. In the great central square, the Plaza, bad artists sell bad art – one creative character, offering to paint Olivia's portrait, showed her a picture he had done of Barbra Streisand as a model. She refused the offer. Under the long wooden arcade of the Palace of the Governors – which has been reshaped but was originally built in *1609* – Indians display jewellery, silver and turquoise, on sheets. I bought two presents: one, for Kanthi, a bunch of multi-coloured Indian corn, plaited together in a purple pony tail at the back. (Do you remember the corn that used to hang under the tower at Sissinghurst? Vita must have brought them from New Mexico.) And for Olivia, a Zuni necklace made of coral, with small stone animals, hunting talismans, strung along it. The Zuni who made it was called Bob Davis. I said to Sallie how terrible it was that Indians should now have these everyday American names. Not at all, she said. It's of the utmost arrogance to think that people should not have the names they want to have. Besides, the real name of an Indian is secret and almost never used. A name has power in it and an Indian will use his proper name only in an emergency, when he needs it. That's like Odysseus in the Cyclops' cave, isn't it?

There are few things Sallie dislikes more than what she calls the 'bleeding heart' attitude to the Indians, the self-gratifying display of guilt, not only for its sogginess, but because it allows the Indian to say 'You owe me this, you owe me that,' eroding his self-reliance, his need to do something for himself. She told me a very funny story. She was in a trading post on a reservation a few years ago and an over-sympathetic white woman was there, cooing and clucking. She tried to talk to one of the Navajo women but was getting no answer. (It is an Indian response to react to gush with silence.) So the white woman turned to the Indian's baby. 'What lovely red hair! Does his father have red hair?' 'I don't know,' the Navajo woman said, 'he didn't take his hat off.'

Birmingham – Anniston, Alabama

Sunday–Monday 25–6 May

NIGEL *to Adam*   Anniston is one and a half hours east of Birmingham, a prong off my planned route, and I went there for two reasons, to see a smaller southern town and talk to some of the people who run it, and to stay with Brandt and Josie Ayers, friends of the MacKinnons. He owns and edits the local newspaper, *The Anniston Star*. Josie is a beautiful woman who in certain lights could be mistaken for a college girl though she must be nearing forty, and she's clever, effervescent and affectionate, all the best qualities one associates with the South.

Next morning I was driven by Brandt to the office of *The Anniston Star* to interview, in succession, a Baptist pastor and the Mayor of Anniston.

The pastor, Dr Nelson Kuykendall, came dressed in a business suit. When I said that I had expected him in robes, he replied that he wore them only for funerals and baptisms. As this was Memorial Day, a holiday set aside to commemorate the dead of America's many wars, we talked first about war, of which his church cannot disapprove without antagonising its congregations, but he had had considerable difficulty with Vietnam. It is not the business of the church, he said, to comment on public affairs, but on private morals it is adamant. Morality is lax and getting laxer. Pre-marital sex, which was pre-viously practised knowing it to be sinful, is now practised with the excuse that it is natural. Once children would feel ashamed of putting their aged parents in an Old Folks Home, now they don't. Family ties are loosening. There's increasing disharmony at home. Abortion is widespread. If this continues, said the pastor, 'we risk the downfall of our country', but he said it with sadness more than reproach.

He is disturbed by the continuing separation of black from white. I put it to him that his church does not set a very good example by keeping its congregations apart. In his Golden Springs parish he has not a single black communicant. Only once has he baptised a black person, and that was eight years ago. He explained that Golden Springs is a predominantly white community, and while he would never refuse a black man entrance to his church, they just didn't want to come. Both races prefer to worship separately, since the black tradition is more colourful, their music throbbier, gayer, their responses emotional and loud – 'they hold the notes longer'.

The Mayor, Bill Robison, who took the pastor's seat opposite me, agreed. He is an enlightened man. He does everything a Mayor can do to give the blacks more confidence, in major ways like upgrading their housing and schools, in minor ones like holding seminars to teach them how to apply for jobs. 'It is important that they should understand what opportunities are open to them, and cease blaming the whites for their status in society, which may have been justified once, but isn't now.' Anniston is an expanding city. New industries are replacing the old. It has a tradition, from Sam Noble's day, of a multi-racial town, and what's needed is confidence among blacks in their worth.

At dinner we had Molly and Tom Bartlett, she with a profile as beautiful as Nefertiti's and a wit to match, and he is Chancellor of the University of Alabama. He is a brilliant man. His flow of talk is as different from mine as wine poured from a perfect claret jug is from tea out of a pot with a chipped spout. He spoke of the resurgence of the South, the new quality of life in a place like Birmingham (one of his campuses), and the changing attitude of the two coasts to the Sun Belt. We talked about race, about the coming influence of biochemistry, about the arts and politics, the mystique of the Deep South and its history. It was the liveliest and most prolonged conversation I've had since coming to this country – but what's the use of trying to reproduce it? Such talk is evanescent, but the impression endures.

Sunday 25 May

A D A M *to Nigel*   Today was Hands Across America Day. We left Sallie with much kissing and hugging and drove south to Moriarty to meet the line. It's been a beautiful day, cool and one or two clouds, the Catalina purring with the pleasure of it. We were late and had to tear down the road to Moriarty to get there by one o'clock. At one point it looked as if we wouldn't make it. But just on time we arrived at the T-junction and there it was, just like the logo on the T-shirts, a string of people holding hands across America, a bumpy rhythm in the line going body hands hands body hands hands body hands hands from New York to Los Angeles. Through Moriarty the line was continuous, so we turned west to find a gap, along Route 66, everyone getting their kicks (Note: that is a reference to a pop song with which America was doped and dazed a few years ago), to the point where it trailed down on to the Interstate. A horse held reins across America at one point. There was a man in a gorilla suit, a woman painted and dressed as a clown. I popped out to ask the man why he was in the gorilla suit. 'I've got to get myself some attention, haven't I?' he said. And then within a mile or so we found a gap, a huge gap, quarter of a mile long, with a man and his wife standing in the middle of it holding hands. This was the most touching sight all day. So we parked and held hands with them. The telephone engineer from Albuquerque, his wife, David, Kanthi, Olivia and I in the middle of the big gap. We would have filled one T-shirt. People on the radio sang the song from somewhere else. We chatted and looked out at New Mexico. In the distance there was an abandoned homestead gone grey with age and the sun. Then, at 1.15, it was all over and people climbed back into their cars for the traffic jam into Albuquerque.

This whole exercise, as you no doubt know, was intended to remind America that there are poor people in the country. I don't think it did anything of the kind. A man on the television, when told that 50 per cent of the money he had helped raise would go on administrative costs, said that he was more interested in raising consciousness than money. But how on earth does holding hands raise one's awareness of poverty? It is extraordinarily symptomatic of an American optimism, of always looking on the good side, that the holding hands — such a wonderful image — came to seem more important than what the hands were being held for. Outside Albuquerque, on one of those boards on which supermarkets and motels display their latest deals to passers-by, the owner had put up HOORAY FOR AMERICA! in two feet high letters. The intention behind Hands Across America was to say OH DEAR FOR AMERICA! Instead it was a great party. This is not the result of an indifference to need – 89 per cent of Americans give money to charity every year – but a complete disconnection between the coast to coast demonstration, even with its gaps, and the cause that had prompted it. It came to be a wonderful achievement in itself, a national picnic on which, of course, one held hands not with the poor but with one's own friends and family. It was a sort of national reassurance that everything was all right, exactly the opposite effect of the one that was intended. This was why Reagan's joining in was such an astute move. If he had held to his original position (Poverty is Ignorance) then the joining of hands might have become a really powerful national protest. As it was, the whole event was intensely forgettable.

Olivia and I said goodbye to the Barrys at the airport here. We are now in a motel next to the runway. Olivia's plane leaves tomorrow morning, which makes me sad.

Anniston–Birmingham–Montgomery,
Alabama

Tuesday 27 May

NIGEL *to Adam*   I returned to Birmingham for lunch, but my date, Cynthia Lewis, who imports and sells British antiques, didn't show up. She had chosen for our rendezvous the swankiest and newest hotel in Alabama, the Wynfrey, and I ate there alone. It lies in open country 8 miles from the city. While that is understandable for a modern hotel which needs space to create its maximum effect, it is more surprising that annexed to it, indeed opening out of it, is the Galleria, a fabulous shopping complex on several floors, as if you took Selfridges and Harrods, piled one on top of the other, and dumped them in Lamberhurst. Would the ladies of Tunbridge Wells travel so far to buy their clothes and luxuries? The ladies of Birmingham do. It was packed. Perhaps it is the attractiveness of this vast bazaar as much as its contents which brings them there. Really, what riches pour into the corners of America! The racks of clothes seem endless, the children's departments the most lavish, all of superb quality and design. But why is it that such clothes almost always look more terrific on hangers than on people?

Birmingham itself is smaller than I'd expected. Its Downtown fades after a few criss-cross streets of high offices into the meaner districts from where Martin Luther King led his famous march on the City Hall in 1963. At first I thought that the smallness of the business quarter indicated the newness of the resurgence of which Professor Bartlett spoke last night. But it's not entirely that. It's the modern city planner's use of space outside, the dispersal of institutional buildings, like the University, made possible by the universal ownership of cars, fast roads, and the availability of so much empty ground. The result is that Birmingham, while not impressive, is a very convenient city. There are no traffic jams in the centre. People are conditioned to travel considerable distances to work, shop, live and play. It's the pattern of the future.

Montgomery, 100 miles south, is different. Here the buildings are more tightly knit together, and the famous Capitol, where Jefferson Davis took the oath as President of the Confederacy, dominates the higher part of the city. By comparison with Birmingham, Montgomery is old. A plaque gives the early date of 1703 for the discovery of the site by Frenchmen prospecting from the Gulf.

I can imagine it bustling at midday, but I reached it at 7 p.m., in rain, when it was dead, dead, dead. Driving round the empty streets, I could see not a single place of entertainment open, and found only one restaurant, in the old railway station. I asked the receptionist how many passenger trains passed through each day. None. The last choo-chooed away thirty years ago. Now there are only freight trains. What else was there to see? The 'old' quarter. A tram standing immobile on the lawn, to remind us that Montgomery was the first city on earth to experiment with electric trolley-cars. On the river, which I visited, the paddle-boat was unmanned. And, of course, the Shakespeare theatre, Montgomery's pride and joy, which I'll see tomorrow.

I rang Juliet at Mulberry, Charlie Atkins's house near Charleston where I stayed two happy nights. She and James have it to themselves.

Amarillo, Texas

Tuesday 27 May

ADAM *to Nigel*   I came hundreds of miles down Interstate 40 yesterday and I will go back almost exactly the same way tomorrow for one reason: the Non-Pro. It is one of the biggest cutting horse contests of the year – not the biggest, which happens in Houston in the winter – but pretty big.

One of the reasons I had come here was to meet Thomas McGuane, who is a friend of the Footes in Livingston, a champion cutting horse rider, a novelist and a hero of mine. I knew he was going to be at the cutting, so I asked where he was and introduced myself. He had all the right clothes on – the crisp white hat, the straight blue jeans – and was as friendly and welcoming as could be. He pointed out the various characters, indistinguishable in their uniforms. That man was heir to part of the King Ranch, the biggest ranch in Texas, which is to say the world. That man owns the Taco Bell fast food chain. That man used to be World Champion Cowboy several times in a row, riding the baddest horses that have ever been born but got so nervous riding cutting horses that he could never raise his score above 210, 212. McGuane himself had scored 218.5 the day before. He was lying fifth. And then there was a disturbance. Milo Martin on Cee Nu Bar had finished and Wes Shahan on Miss Silver Pistol was about to take the ring. Miss Silver Pistol is the current starlet of the cutting scene. Since December last year she has won half a million dollars. 'Just you wait,' Sam Shepherd, the McGuanes' trainer from Alabama had said, 'just wait till you have a look at that little grey mare. Then you'll see what art there is in it.' And I did. She walked into the herd of cows, neither tentative nor headlong, with her neck held low and relaxed, her steps easy, steadily one after the other. The cows didn't panic. They eased apart like a viscous liquid and Miss Silver nosed a small globule of them away from the rest and down the ring. Then, by the subtlest of movements, she managed to start that globule pouring slowly back towards the main body of the herd, monitoring it as it went, so that all she had to do was make a slight movement forward when there was one cow left and it was cut, in her control. This was beautifully done, the arrangement and choosing of the dancers but it was all preliminary to the dance itself. There wasn't an ounce of heaviness or anxiety in the mare's performance – I can't tell you how enthralling a thing this is to watch – no hauling of the horse's body around after the horse's intention. That gap did not exist. There was a constant feather-taut agility, like a clever man arguing, in every one of that mare's movements, the uninterrupted ease of something done right. This is the quality those judges have recognised. Those $2\frac{1}{2}$ minutes alone made it worth coming to Amarillo.

I've just come back from dinner with Thomas and Laurie and Annie McGuane, given to us all by Sam Shepherd. Annie is a genius. She's 6. The Japanese waiter, slicing beef strips in mid-air over a four-foot flame, asked her if she was Japanese. 'No, Spanish,' she said. 'Can I have some more water?' We had fortune cookies. McGuane's said: 'The show off is shown up at the showdown.' He was very pleased with that.

Montgomery–Mobile, Alabama

Wednesday 28 May

NIGEL *to Adam*   One of the advantages of this trip is that we do things we would never do in England, and bother people for favours which we would never dream of asking at home, all for the sake of widening our American experience and strengthening our audacity.

The example I have in mind is my visit this morning to the Alabama

Shakespeare Festival Theatre outside Montgomery. It was closed. Instead of retreating, I looked pathetically at the clerk inside the glass door, and he opened it a chink. Could I, against all the rules, come in? How could I write about Montgomery without describing its greatest achievement? He not only allowed me in. He fetched Donna Sicuranza to take me round.

The theatre is a magnificent brick Palladian building, with a central dome like Ickworth's, rising above two low flanking wings, forming a theatre complex which can have few equals in the world. It was finished only last year, and its cost, $21.5 million, was a gift to his city by a single individual Winton M. Blount, a building contractor and formerly Nixon's Postmaster General. It was an extraordinarily bold move to site it in Montgomery, the heart of Dixieland, where people are traditionally open air, social and sports-loving. How would they take to the classical theatre and ultra-modern plays? They did. They packed every performance and asked for more, perhaps because it was so great a novelty, perhaps because it became almost a social and civic obligation, but mainly because the standard of production is so high and the plays world-famous. The current repertoire illustrates their ambition. *Richard III*, *The Merry Wives*, Pinter's *Betrayal*, Tennessee Williams' *The Glass Menagerie*, Thomas Middleton's *The Changeling*, *The Beaux' Stratagem* by George Farquhar, and *The Imaginary Heir* by Jean-François Regnard. People come from as far away as California, and stay over three nights to attend three performances. It is this sort of enterprise which is changing the whole reputation of the South outside it.

Donna took me first to the costume room. At one large table they were making chain-mail for Richard's soldiers out of the steel aprons which butchers wear to avoid cutting their clothes, at another his crown, at a third a yellow Elizabethan dress. I was struck by the high quality of the materials. They looked real, and apart from the jewels, they are real, 'made to last', they explained, for *Richard III* is bound to return to the repertoire. The same with the wigs. Real hair, which must have left the women from whose heads it was cut quite bald. In the vast hangar where the scenery is made, carpenters and painters were at work, and they were rehearsing on the stages of the two auditoria. The lobbies, dressing-rooms, cafeteria all bear the stamp of Mr Blount's generosity. I was amused to see, in the entrance hall, an exact reproduction of Sissinghurst's Lutyens bench. 'No expense must be spared to make it superb,' he had said, and none was. The whole complex is sited in the park of his considerable mansion.

I came away high-spirited, and drove 180 miles to Mobile. Suddenly the trees broke loose, and there before me was the famous Bay, and beyond it the Gulf, my first sight of the sea since Nantucket. At an isolated dock was moored one

of America's greatest battleships of the Second World War, USS *Alabama*,
and alongside her, a submarine, USS *Drum*. If a theatre, why not the Navy?
I went aboard each in turn. You are allowed to wander everywhere alone.
The sub is a steel tube of electronic tricks, divided by mousehole doorways,
the battleship a vast complex of stages, austere for all its spaciousness (Nelson
was more comfortably quartered in *Victory* than the captain of this floating
machine), but the lines of the hull are beautiful, and the 16-inch guns gave
me an impression of power and anger which will never be equalled by modern
missiles.

But the point is Mobile itself. I had expected a manufacturing town with
a port. What I had not realised is that Mobile is a southern city as lovely as
Charleston or Savannah, lovelier than New Orleans. There is something
unmistakably French about it, with a touch of Spain. Great live-oaks rise
from perfect lawns, and around them are gathered large houses with double
porches, one above the other. Low lights glow from within. Squirrels dance
across the lawns. The heat, even after dark, is that of a tropical glasshouse.

I am staying the night in one of these houses, with George and Vidmer
Downing. She has furnished it with the best of English eighteenth-century
furniture (the rosewood and mahogany silky to the touch), and I have a
bedroom at garden level with windows on three sides. They took me to see
the modernised house of her son, Stanley Ellis, quite lovely, and we dined at
Bernard's, a restaurant in an old mansion, the sort of thing I had sought in
vain at Montgomery. Afterwards we drove round the dark streets. I could
scarcely believe that such profusion of taste could exist in a place of which
few Europeans have even heard.

Mobile—Biloxi, Mississippi

Thursday 29 May

NIGEL *to Adam*   I am staying the night at Biloxi, half-way to New
                    Orleans, mainly because I wanted to swim in the
Gulf. The water is the warmest I've ever encountered outside a bath. No
shock on submerging, no shivering on emerging. The water and the air seem
to be of the same temperature. I cannot equally praise the town. Biloxi is a
holiday resort, and the advertisements along the beachfront compete clam-
orously. One of them says, MAMIE'S RESTAURANT AND Lounge.
'Lounge' is written small because Mamie's lounge is not very big, but why is
the AND in upper case? The guidebook adopts the imperative tense, 'Sun
yourself . . . Savor the sea-food . . . Play golf . . . Vacation in outstanding hotels
. . .', as a variant on the French *Ses plages, ses marinas, son château*, but I hope

Juliet won't adopt the manner for her blurbs, 'Read how ... browse through ...'. I admit the style is catching.

Can you explain the contrast between the American Press and their TV and radio? Local newspapers like the *Anniston Star* and, here, the *Sun Herald*, are aimed at an educated readership. The articles are full and interesting, dealing with important issues at home and abroad, and reprinting the best from New York and Washington newspapers. But on radio and television all you get are snippets, rarely any in-depth discussion of the news, an insult, I think, to people's intelligence. Yet both are intended for the same audience, both depend on advertisers, and both are ephemeral. I find the difference puzzling.

Santa Fe, New Mexico

Thursday 29 May

ADAM *to Nigel*   I'm back here after my yo-yo into Texas. The sesquicentennial is making little impact up in the panhandle. I walked out of the cutting arena for a while yesterday afternoon and went over to the Amarillo Auction Rooms. It's one of the great market places for cattle just across the railroad tracks from the showgrounds, and is sunk in the deepest gloom you could imagine. The buyers and sellers are arranged in a small theatre, steeply banked, surrounding a little *orchestra* (there must be a less pretentious word) where cows are led in, inspected for a moment, and then hurried out. At the back there is a raised box in which the auctioneers sit and babble away the prices. Have you ever heard an American auctioneer? A young man, younger than me, with the required straw cowboy hat and his sideboards shaved away under its brim, sits in utter silence looking at the crowd. They too wear the Stetsons and chew on the end of matches. Three dirty men with electric prods hustle the cattle into the space, kicking them and prodding them with their electric sticks. Then the auctioneer gives a little burble, with his lips kissing the bulb of the microphone and his eyes cruising the room. 'Blmdibbleblmdiddlebm,' he says to get us in the mood, as the cow-handlers bang shut the metal gates and the steers open their eyes wider than they should, revealing the whites. And then the auctioneer begins singing 'Old Macdonald Had A Farm' very very fast, taking a breath once every 25 seconds and interjecting a dollar and cent figure once every verse. Not a single whole word is intelligible. The cow buyers hang their wrists over their knees and occasionally jerk their hands upwards to show they want to buy. (I think. This may have been the signal to show that they were no longer interested.) Lot after lot was hustled into the arena, the cowboy auctioneer sang his song and the cows went out again, owned by someone else, destined for a feed lot in Nebraska or Oklahoma, where they would lose all the toughness of grass-fed beef and, as they gradually plumped up, would tenderise. For beef to be palatable, for the knife to slip through the meat as though it were cream cheese, the cow must have been fattening at the moment it was slaughtered. No one cared less about the cows as animals. They were beef that happened to be auto-mobile for the time being. How stupid, unattractive and boring an animal the cow is! Shoved in here, jerked at there, prodded upward, hurried sideways, made to feel horrible. Here was evidence of one western truth: the cowboy hates the cow.

At no moment is his hatred more intense than when the price is low. And the prices in Amarillo were way down. Some of the scrawnier lots were going for under 40c a lb. Long long faces all around the little theatre. The auctioneer held his chin, drew a breath and ran down the long hill of his burbling while buyers on the telephone gesticulated to bosses far absent in Muskogee and Tulsa. A great gloom, but this wasn't poverty. The men had diamond cufflinks and beautiful new trucks, crisp clean shirts and a certain polish. The only prospect was of a slight diminishment in riches. Men who have ridden high for a long time on the approval, through various subsidies, of state and nation, who have nevertheless proclaimed the unending virtues of Texan self-reliance and the irreproachable market, are now the victims of a glut. I didn't feel sorry for them. They felt immensely sorry for themselves.

Outside the saleroom a man was trying to shoe a horse. The horse tried to kick him so the farrier kicked it back – in the balls. That's Texas. The horse looked contrite and stood still, but the farrier then hit it over the nose with his metal file. The horse blinked and put its ears back. The man then turned around and saw me watching. He joked his way out of the situation: a horseshoer, he said, has to have a size six hat and size forty-four jacket. Do you understand that? It means *stupid* and *strong*. 'And what does the horse have to be?' I asked him. 'Jes stoopid,' he said.

But now I'm back in Santa Fe. I've spent all day with Sallie Wagner going to Chaco Canyon, aways away (Have you heard that phrase?) across the desert to the west of here. It's a remarkable place. You would love it. It is a fairly shallow canyon, with a wash running down the centre and a series of side canyons branching off it at intervals. It's not half as beautiful as Canyon de Chelly. The rock is a dun, sandy yellow which doesn't have much to rec-ommend it, and the shape of the canyon is not as dramatic, but the buildings – and that's what it's famous for – are wonderful. They are Indian towns, built in the eleventh and twelfth centuries, up against the walls of the canyon and spreading out in semi-circles on to the desert floor. All are built in stone, some of the masonry very fine, some a little coarser, and rising in places three or four storeys. There is room for 10 to 12 thousand people in these towns and no one is sure quite why the Anasazi (a Navajo word meaning 'the old ones') chose this dry and distant canyon for their stupendous capital. Why not put it in the far more lush and verdant valley of the Rio Grande not so very far to the east? You might say that the Rio Grande was already occupied by peoples whom the Chaco Indians could not displace. But that is not true and what is fascinating about the Canyon is its role as the centre of a wide network of outlying settlements all connected to the core by straight, level roads, engineered for tens of miles across the desert. This was an urban and organised civilisation which irrigated its fields in the valley, demanded or at least received economic tribute from its outliers (there is a vast midden in Chaco of broken pots, almost certainly brought in by their makers in the outliers and ritually used or destroyed here). Chaco brought Indian culture to a peak it had never achieved before and has never achieved since. It lasted a little more than a century and then for reasons unknown fell apart. There is a theory that Chaco wasn't lived in all the time, but was only the ritual centre of a people who spent most of the year in the outliers, processing along their ritual roads with their ritual pots to the great annual celebrations in the giant kivas of Chaco. That sounds reasonable doesn't it, at least as reasonable as Las Vegas.

Sallie and I wandered around the ruins in our various hats and had a picnic in the car. Sallie had come here in the '30s, dragging her truck down the side of the canyon on a wreck of a road, filling in the gullies by hand with a shovel as they came to them and then sleeping the night in one of the Anasazi rooms, with the sky for a ceiling in a room full of stars. I envied her that. I don't really like visitor centres. I know they are among your most favourite institutions, but I prefer ignorance to nannying, especially when the only information one gets is a declaration of *professional* ignorance. This will infuriate you, as does my preference for the maverick over the conformist. The idea that rudeness is the same as non-conformity is only the prejudice of an innate Tory (p. 229). (That sounds like an essay question for an A-Level General Paper. It occurred to me this morning at 75 m.p.h. on the road through the Jicarillo Apache reservation.) And the idea that romance is incompatible with either difficulty or violence is simply ignorant. (More phrases from a silent period on the road this morning.) But to be serious, I'm not legislating for America and the world. I'm sure it's worthy and necessary that people should take up Governorships for the good of the people (although that idea too is more than tinged with wishful thinking) and I'm sure it's right that the suburb is the most perfect arrangement for a large number of human beings ever devised, but I am not particularly interested in the general salvation. *As far as I'm concerned* – that's the crucial phrase – I like mavericks,

I feel encouraged and cheered by mavericks, not because they ignore fancy strangers at check-in desks, but because I like the air of courage, of having made definite and brave choices, which hangs about them. I know this is romantic. I don't mind that word. I actually like it, and what is fascinating about the West is that everybody knows that the image of both the cowboy and the mountain man is wildly romanticised. The grim and brutal loneliness of both those periods cannot be over-estimated, but that doesn't affect the reality of the romantic idea.

You think of yourself – I think you do, anyway – as a sort of Platonist, and if Plato made one contribution to the world it was to suggest that ideas are real, perhaps even more real than the material world shaped in their image. That is a good idea, the idea of real ideas, and what I like both about the West and the people who identify with the West is their willingness to accept the reality of a romantic idea in the face of all the actual difficulties and uglinesses that life here has always involved. There are armies of paradoxes involved with this, not least the fact that more of the West is owned by the Federal government than is not, and that this zone of 'individual freedom' is more closely monitored and controlled by state and water agencies than any other. Nevertheless the idea of the West (ask Barry Goldwater) is strong and lively enough to survive all that.

It is one of the great paradoxes of American history that the incoming culture, proclaiming tolerance and freedom, obliterated – all but – the culture it found in place. European diseases did most of the damage, but my noble wild men weren't far behind. I'm not advocating a return to the sort of brutality that life as a mountain man involved. It's really no more than a sort of boy scout dream that I have of a good time without responsibilities, a Huck Finn floating on the stream. It is purely and literally escapist. It is no good as a principle on which human society should be founded. It's an abandoning of all the regulated and civilised hierarchies at which your eighteenth century was so good, but I don't pretend otherwise. It ends up with gun-toting maniacs living out violent fantasies in Kentucky backwoods and with ranchers riding the range, thinking nothing on earth could be better than this. That's fine by me. The rewards are worth the risks.

Biloxi–New Orleans, Louisiana

Friday 30 May

NIGEL *to Adam*   I bathed again in the lentil soup of the Gulf, and took the beach road which extends for miles beside the off-white sand through a string of resorts like Biloxi. Man has made nature available, but not improved it, until you cross the Lake Pontchartrain Causeway, which is not a causeway, but a bridge 24 miles long, of which 8 are out of sight of land, fun to drive.

Things went wrong in New Orleans. My Best Western is in an unsalubrious district and the only food available is in a nasty café next door. Your Express letter, for the first time, has failed to arrive. There was a call from the *New York Times* requesting changes to my article on New Harmony. Worse still, the $2,000 on which I'd counted was not awaiting me. The transferring of money in the greatest capitalist state of the world is an extraordinarily rudimentary and over-cautious process. Then I made the mistake of booking a tour of the city with Acadia, hoping to see more of it under a professional guide than by wandering around by myself.

It was a mistake because we wasted the first hour gathering customers from other hotels, and because I'd misjudged the nature and quality of the tour. To me New Orleans is the city of the French and Creoles, of Sieur de Bienville and Andrew Jackson, the weight at the bottom of a long pendulum, the cork in Mississippi's mouth, historically the key to the whole centre of the continent. I had hoped to see the inside of the best of the Vieux Carré's houses, the cathedral, and especially the Cabildo, the finest building erected by the Spanish in North America. I wanted to be told more than I already knew about the river, the life of the port, the character of the people. Then I would spill all of it into this letter.

Instead, our black bus-driver and guide, Fred, had from long experience gauged accurately the appetite of tourists for architecture and history. It is minimal. What they want are anecdotes, jokes, records (widest avenue, biggest Superdome, longest bridge), municipal achievements, the houses of the very rich and, surprisingly, cemeteries, of which we were shown four. Fred explained that in this climate bodies decay completely after a year, and the dust is then shovelled aside to make room for more. The group chuckled with macabre pleasure. He showed us the Garden District with its splendid mid-nineteenth-century houses (I liked that), relating everything to size and cost – 14 bathrooms, 1.8 million dollars – and we had a glimpse of the river, but when we came to Jackson Square and the French quarter, we were driven slowly through without stopping. Fred merely indicated with a wave of the hand these exquisite buildings, and told more jokes. Samples of Fred's jokes:

'Once I was made to sit at the back of the bus, and look at me now!' 'The horses all wear diapers. How would you like the job of changing them?' 'I took a group of forty-four Senior Citizens from New York round the night-clubs. Did they enjoy it!' (imagine that scene). Then there was audience participation. We were not being sufficiently responsive. 'Come on, folks, say something.' I was terrified that he would turn his wit on me, 'our Australian', but I escaped ridicule, remaining totally silent in my distress and disappointment.

After dark I went to a German restaurant in the old city and dined alone, then walked through part of the Vieux Carré. What is there about it so un-American? A mixture of Italy (not France) and Africa, hyped to spasms of extreme luxury and descending to the sleaziest aspects of Soho. Through an open door I saw a black girl dancing topless on the bar-counter. Never, never has a temptation been less tempting, a performance more unappetising. I returned to my motel and awaited James's call, which never came. It has not been a good day, when it should have been one of my best.

New Orleans–Baton Rouge–Lake Charles,
Louisiana

Saturday 31 May

NIGEL *to Adam*　　　　Baton Rouge is a great river-port eighty miles upstream from New Orleans. I saw little of the port, because my destination was a house in the oak-shaded suburb where live many of the Faculty of Louisiana State University, and my host for lunch was one of the most eminent of them, Dr John Loos, Chairman of the History Department and acting-Dean of the University. He is also an expert on Lewis and Clark. 'Amazingly', he said, 'they never had a quarrel.'

He had gathered half a dozen of his colleagues, and we sat around his living-room eating a delicious buffet-lunch. We had Grits. I had asked a fast-food man what it was made of, and he replied, 'It's not made of anything; it comes from a packet,' but Helen Loos explained that it was crushed corn. This led indirectly to a discussion of the southern temperament. It became a sort of professorial seminar, with me asking the questions. In general there was agreement that the southern distinctiveness survives. When I suggested that the division of the country is now more East–West than North–South, they said that this is not really so, because in the south there is less harshness, a willingness among all classes to work together ('Don't mistake me – I'm not against Yankees'), and in southern Louisiana there's a 'French' tradition still, xenophobic, one professor said, jingoist, with a strong Catholic influence. But

I must not overlook how much inventiveness there is in the South. Many important technological developments originated here. They are by no means the poor relations of the north. We talked about the second wave of emigrants, how they leapfrogged across the plains after 1804, the gold-rush and the land-rush, and how it still affects the American character, for instance in their self-reliance, their eagerness to get ahead individually, combined with a readiness to co-operate for the common good. Each professor deferred to another when his speciality came up. I could see the pleasure they took in each other's company under their merry Chairman, the interpenetration of disciplines, the academic freedom of debate, in which I sometimes regret that I've never had a part.

I told them about our book. Someone asked who would buy it – and then hastily added, 'in Britain'. I answered that the American way of life is perpetually fascinating to the British. Besides, our secondary theme, the development of our own relationship, is to me its most interesting part. Then why not simply exchange letters between Sissinghurst and Cambridge? That would not do at all. We needed the stimulus of travel, of discovering a foreign culture together and yet apart, to provoke us to write what we could never have written at home.

After lunch, Dr Loos took me round the L S U campus. It is vacation-time and few people were about. But I saw the astonishing wealth and complexity of buildings which the State and a few private donors have erected for the 29,000 students. There are temples of learning for each of the humanity and science subjects, huge stadia, an Augean stable but very clean, a library with over two million books, halls of residence, a garden for the study of horti-culture. He took me to his own office. I have never seen such a mess of tangled papers, on tables, desks, chairs, the floor. He asked me what I thought. 'It's a disgrace,' I said. 'How can you leave your office so untidy when your house is spick and span?' He laughed. 'At home there's someone else to look after that.'

I liked him enormously. He's an elderly Puck among professors. He told me two things of special interest. The University has decided that it's all wrong to admit any student, whatever their High School qualifications. There must be, and from 1988 will be, a raising of standards, which will eventually result in the reduction of the student body by about four thousand. At the moment there are students at the L S U who simply cannot benefit from higher education, and finding themselves left behind, sink into apathy or drop out. Then, as we passed the fraternity and sorority buildings, splendid colonial-type houses with Greek symbols sculpted above the front doors (Chi Omega is the grandest), I suggested that it was an outdated, snobbish and even cruel system, to select a few boys and girls in the first weeks of their first term as worthy to join these élitist groups, leaving the rejected to brood on their unworthiness. Dr Loos thought there was something in this, but so old a tradition is hard to break. Many students, some of the best, like his own daughter, refuse to be considered for a fraternity or sorority, and it is in this way that the system will eventually change.

The road west across the Mississippi – I headed straight into the setting sun – crosses swamps by mile-long bridges and causeways. In Europe such obstacles would be bypassed. In America they leap them. I noticed rice-fields, the first I've seen, and crossed great rivers, till I came to Lake Charles and am staying at the Hilton. If you and Juliet can, I argued, why not me? A man sat throughout dinner wearing a Stetson. Does this mean that I've reached the West at last?

Taos, New Mexico

Saturday 31 May

ADAM *to Nigel*   America turns through 90° here. This isn't the American West. It's the Mexican North. Or at least that's the image that Taos tries to sell you. It's no longer true – the place is invaded with and dominated by Anglos masquerading as locals. The key material is fake adobe. J.C. Penney's in Taos is modelled on the Governor's Palace in Santa Fe. The girl in the McDonald's drive-thru window, distributing her McNuggets, peers out at her customers through an adobified, sliding, aluminium opening with just a hint (some cultural confusion here) of purdah in the wooden-latticed framework-with-baubles that surrounds her bored and spotty face. Nice New England Girls sell jewellery ('The design is pueblo, but it was actually manufactured in China') under the stars and stripes flying over the Plaza.

Taos congratulates itself endlessly on being 'the meeting of three cultures' and a unique 'intercultural blend of humanity and happiness'. This is self-delusion-cum-boosterism. There are great lumps of unleavened flour and resentment floating around in the melting pot. Inter-racial violence – especially Spanish/Anglo – was commonplace until recently. Now Taos is ridden with a peculiarly horrible sort of Californication. You can take your pick from Tubs of Taos, Massage: A Healing Energy, and Taos Herb Company – any one of which will provide you with a customised combination of Frozen Yoghourt, Acupressure, Lymphatic Goings Over, etc. Then you can decide between the Sun God Motel, the Hacienda Inn, the Kachina Lodge, the El Monte Lodge or the American Artist Gallery House for somewhere to combine a restful night's stay with soaking up the unique Taos

Atmosphere. Then there are bookshops (Moby Dickens) and art shops (Evalena's Gallery of the Setting Sun) where you can indulge your dollars on up-priced rubbish. I said to the owner of one nonsense store on the plaza that Taos had been wrecked by its fame as a tourist destination. He's heard that one before and had an answer. 'This has been a tourist area since 1600 when the Spaniards came.' Convenient date. He was from Oklahoma.

Lake Charles–Houston, Texas

Sunday 1 June

NIGEL *to Adam*   I wanted to see more of southern Louisiana than its great cities, so drove to the Gulf through miles of blowing grass and canalised inlets of the sea or outlets of the rivers (it was difficult to tell which was which), and came eventually to the shore at Holly Beach. It's the most repulsive place I've yet come across in America. Mobile homes, shacks, nasty stores and lodgings, litter the low strand. Angry notices, KEEP OUT, CRIMINAL PROSECUTION FOR TRESPASS, destroy whatever pleasure one could have gained from the beach, which is strewn with caravans and recumbent bodies. I took advantage of the only privilege, to drive into the sea itself. Salt water licked my front tyres.

So west into Texas. The country is so uninteresting, and where developed in towns like Port Arthur so unpleasing, that Texans have made up for it by creating cities like Houston, Dallas and Austin which do justice to their vigour and inventiveness. The towers of Houston are first seen from twenty miles away, rising serrated from the plain like some great medieval castle.

Taos, New Mexico

Sunday 1 June

ADAM *to Nigel*   This afternoon – it's now late and I'm back in the Hacienda Motel outside Taos – I went to a place, a marvellous place up in the hills between Taos and Espanola, where all the Taos bogusness was simply absent. It was a small village, high in the foothills of the mountains, more than 8000 feet up and settled across the broad back of green ridge between the valleys of two rivers. I had read in my guide book that Anglos were not welcome there, so of course I headed straight for it. The all-American welcome of Taos, that awful bright cynical have-a-nice-day-using welcome of American commerce, wears out after a while. I was actually hungry for a bit of hostility. And my village up in the hills, called Truchas, which as you know is the Spanish for trouts, provided nothing of the kind. I found the church, in the middle of a farmyard thick with mud, and tried to get in. But it was locked. A lady, without any doubt a Spanish lady with a Spanish accent to her English – this was extraordinary, a real unleavened lump in the melting pot – told me that I could find the key at Susy Romero's house. No hostility there. So I walked up the village street, with the snowy mountains in front of me and Los Alamos a long way across the valley behind me, past the dotted houses. They have the exposed and inconsequential arrangement of houses in the Falklands or the Hebrides, and although they are all made of adobe, there is none of the false nurturing of the material you find in Taos or Santa Fe. It is covered in plastic siding or cement that is painted green and then scored to look like bricks. There is an aluminium trailer or two parked on the grass and the ruin of a log cabin, roofed with mud, leaning sideways between them. I can't properly convey to you the frontier sensation of this Spanish village. It was a mixture of coherence and exposure, a wholesome reality which Taos has simply abandoned. I wonder if you would find my liking for this sort of place 'paradoxical and perverse', as you did my enthusiasm for Butte, Montana (p. 172). Who knows?

I found Susy Romero's house. She is a school teacher and about 45, looking utterly Spanish. Spanish is her first language and she teaches her 3rd grade pupils in both Spanish and English. That has been a state requirement since 1976. She knew everything about Truchas. Her ancestor, a man whose name appears in the documents as Romero, applied, along with 11 others (there is a biblical air hanging over the whole place) for a land grant, a *merced real*, of 17,000 acres to the Viceroy of New Mexico. The crown granted the land to the twelve men in 1754. It stretches from the grassy meadows down by the river, the Rio Quemado, right up into the mountains on a broad, deep-boned haunch of land between the Rio Quemado and the Rio de las Truchas.

The twelve men and their families arrived here on this virgin territory, an outpost of New Mexico threatened by raids from the Apaches across the mountains, on 1 June 1754. By chance I had arrived precisely on the 232nd anniversary of the founding of Truchas. Susy brought me her English bible and showed me the lesson for today. It was the miracle of the loaves and the fishes. The twelve families heard this lesson read to them on the small patch of clear ground now occupied by the church. When mass was over they named the village after the fishes, the trout, in the story they had just heard.

Susy showed me everything: the rough religious icons called *santos* in the church, which the devout scrubbing of the village ladies over many years has almost destroyed; the wonderful system of channels and conduits by which water is brought down into the village from the source up in the mountains. Water is the life blood of this country more than any other. They could not depend on rainfall to feed the crops, the corn, the vegetables, the hay and the alfalfa. The only reliable source is the slow melting and percolation of the snow pack on the mountains.

Susy took me up there on a rough track into the thickening trees. We reached the point where the one stream coming down from the mountains, the Acequia de la Sierra, met its first watergate, called a *compuerta* in Spanish. There it divided into the Acequia Madre and the Acequia de Llano, the Mother aqueduct and the aqueduct of the valley. Work on these channels was begun immediately after that first mass in June 1754. The twelve men cut them with stone axes. So an old lady told me, although that is difficult to believe. These plain channels, fringed with red willow and irises, you can imagine how beautiful they are, almost literally the branching veins of the place, spreading out from the single source at the wrist into all the fingers of the hand, are each looked after by its own bailiff, a *mayordomo*. This extraordinarily unchanged air in Truchas – isn't *mayordomo* the most eight-eenth-century word you can think of? – reinforced all my loathing of the fakeness sold to an unwitting public by the pasticheurs of Taos.

But it's poverty and conservatism that has kept Truchas as it is. Can you believe that almost all of the Catholic priests who serve these New Mexican villages still come from Spain? I find that incredible, as though Devon and Somerset were still providing ministers for the churches in Maine. It was a beautiful evening today and Truchas looked bewitching, but Susy was insistent that I shouldn't think it a wonderful place. 'It's poor,' she said. 'You cannot know how poor the life is here.' With it being so high, the crops were never reliable. A sudden frost could kill anything in mid-summer. There were regular plagues of grass-hoppers which mowed down whatever had survived the cold and the altitude. It is too high for chilis to ripen and traditionally the people of Truchas have exchanged the peas they can grow here for the chilis grown in Chimayo down the valley, where a sort of worm (that was Susy's description) eats any peas that are planted. I said to her that Truchas appears unchanged. That wasn't true. The most significant event in the history of the village since its founding was the building of Los Alamos across the valley. You could see its lights now against the mountain behind. The young people had gone over there to work, emptying Truchas, Las Trampas, Cordova and Chimayo. Where there used to be three bars and three small shops in the village, now there is one of each.

I asked Susy why my guide book had told me not to come here. She said she didn't want to talk about that. I pressed her and she drove me down a bumpy road, the Nissan truck lurching in and out of the ruts and the puddles, to a smooth bit of sloping meadow, dropping sharply to the Rio Quemado. On the grass was the rusted remains of an old school bus, painted psychedelic. Next to it was the charred skeleton of a burnt house. In the late '60s and early

'70s white hippies had tried to live here, either taking over cabins that had been abandoned by the Spanish or building their own shacks on the common land of the eighteenth century land grant. In neither case were they welcome and the people of Truchas literally stoned them and burnt them out of their houses. A couple of Anglo people do now live in the village, but discreetly, without fuss. That's fine, Susy said. It was the hippies polluting the crucial acequias, making public displays of themselves (I think this meant nude dancing) which the people of Truchas, the Romeros, the Martinez, the Sandovals, the Lopez, the Cordovas, the Trujillos, the Fernandez, used to go and watch 'like watching animals in the zoo,' Susy said.

So it is violence, poverty and conservatism that has kept Truchas whole, an island curiously unaffected by the fast and blurring current of American life, like a reservation which has been self-imposed. That's a crucial difference, an emphasis not on the fence but on a linguistic and cultural heartland. I had dinner with Susy and her mother – mutton and chilis – with a long grace in Spanish before and after. I asked them what the people in Cordova, just down the hill, founded on the same land grant, what the people down there were like. 'Loud, rude and violent,' Susy's mother said. The Romeros were wonderful people.

Houston, Texas

Monday 2 June

NIGEL *to Adam*   I went to NASA, the Lyndon B. Johnson Space Center, 20 miles south of Houston. It was a sad day to choose, because the report of the President's Commission on the shuttle disaster of last January was leaked at about the time I arrived, and it is highly critical. For seven years, it apparently says, high executives ignored warnings that the famous seals on the booster joints were unsafe, and recommends that there should be no further manned flights until late in 1987. There was no sign of distress or protest from the many Bronowski figures I saw strolling to work, and in the Visitor Center, which explains the whole space programme beautifully, there is no mention of the disaster. When a bold woman asked a guide about it, he replied, tight-lipped, that NASA is not yet ready to disclose its own findings. I saw the place where Reagan delivered his memorial address on the shuttle victims, a speech which did more than anything to explain to the British his hold on the emotions of his people.

The layout of the Space Center resembles the most beautiful of campuses. On a simple Texan pasture they erected about fifty grey and white buildings, widely separated by lawns and parking-lots because at the start they feared 'explosions', a friendly scientist informed me. I asked him if he found the crowds distracting, the same silly question that people often ask me at Sissinghurst, and received the same reply, that the public don't enter the private sections, and worry him no more than crowds in a city street disturb the office-workers. But we are allowed to visit some of the buildings where the most dramatic work is done – the complex where they train the astronauts, another where they examine moon rocks, and Mission Control itself.

The last is the most exciting. You climb to a gallery-auditorium separated by a glass screen from another auditorium where the twenty-five top executives sit during a launch. Facing them is a huge map of the world scored by flight paths. Of course, today Mission Control had no mission to control. Instead, it was turned into a television studio to interview Eugene Krantz, head of NASA's operations division. We couldn't hear a word he said, owing to the sound-proof screen, but we could observe him (and he presumably us, though he showed no sign of it), crew-cut, sharp nose, no Einstein in appearance, but a noble head packed with secrets, problems and possibly remorse.

In a huge hangar there was a mock-up of the shuttle, but we were not allowed inside it. A fresh crew of astronauts was undergoing training. We did not see them either. Finally, I went to the Lunar Sample Building and through another screen watched a scientist dressed like a nurse doing something scientific with bits of the moon. Several rocks lay like Crown jewels in a display case for our inspection. They looked just like something picked up in the Painted Desert or on Bodmin Moor. Yet these were the only *tangible* products of the whole multi-billion project.

I'm not scoffing. I thoroughly applaud the space programme, admire the brilliant techniques and the courage of the astronauts. They are not scientists. They are jockeys mounted on unbroken horses. What I would fear most is claustrophobia. The re-entry capsule of the Apollo series (an actual one is on show) had only room for three men lying side by side on stretchers. What must their fear have been, their prayers! This tiny pellet was all that remained of the vast rocket that launched them, and it was dependant upon a parachute and hitting an exact spot in the ocean. We have seen this repeated many times on television, but the sight of the actual craft, its heat-shield scorched and tattered, is very moving. There's a reproduction of the lunar module from which Neil Armstrong uttered his famous phrase. The descent ladder is short of its final two rungs. It was not a 'small step for a man' but a 3-foot jump.

There is an excellent restaurant, shared between the public and the scientists. Eavesdropping hard, I heard one of them say, 'I don't suppose that there's anyone on the face of this earth ...', but lost the rest of the sentence. They speak low, but it's astonishing that one of the most secret places in the US should be so accessible. My only criticism is that the literature on sale is so trivial. 'But there's no demand ...' If there was a supply, the demand would follow.

I've dented my Thunderbird against a concrete pillar when backing out of a garage. I can't tell you how much I mind. One beautiful flank blemished! I rubbed the sore place with ointments, but I fear that the damage is irremediable except by minor surgery.

Colorado City, Colorado

Monday 2 June

ADAM *to Nigel*   We got on to the Rio Grande soon after 8 this morning. I'm such a hypocrite. I don't like Taos because of all its tourist facilities and then I buy myself a white water raft trip from the Sierra Sports office for a day's playing. There were only two customers in my boat, a fat yellow sausage boat like one of those curled up salamis you see hanging from hooks in Italian delis. There was me and Wayne, a man from Pacific Palisades, Los Angeles who did the voices of animals in cartoon commercials. He was thinking of changing profession, but as we pulled on our wetsuits he did his dinosaur-advertising-milk voice for me: 'I like it at breakfast and I like it at night,' he said in a voice that was a slightly maled up version of Shirley Temple's. 'Very good,' I said. Brett, our 22-year old pilot, told us to climb into the boat. 'Have fun,' he said. We said we would. The river was brown and thick, running, Brett thought, at about 3,500 cubic feet a second. That's a meaningless fact. It is deeply cut into a thick basalt layer, at the bottom of a canyon known as the Taos Box. Dinosaur Wayne and I sit on the front of the boat holding strings, while Brett, a handsome, tanned young man who frankly admits that one of the best things about overnight trips is the girls (this, of course, is the ski instructor syndrome) sits in the middle of the boat with a pair of oars facing downstream. We float along. There are a couple of Canada geese breeding in the grasses on the bank and some furry goslings. A night hawk flits on the river, a golden eagle swings on the thermals high above us, and it's the sweetest sensation you could imagine. We're bowling along as easily as on the Beult in April. All this water is going to Texas to feed those innumerable unwanted cows. Brett tries to keep up our enthusiasm for white water by describing the various deaths on the river, how people get swilled around on the backside of rocks as if they were in a washing machine, how lunatic some old woman on the Colorado is, taking eighty at a time on three boats strapped together. Dinosaur and I listen, rather disappointed that our trip doesn't come up to these epic tales. 'You wait,' Brett says. We did. We piddled down a couple of rapidettes, no more ravenous than the riffles on the Hammer Brook and then pulled into a beach for lunch. Cheese sandwiches. I have now conceived an ambition to go all the way from source to sea in the Colorado Basin, starting at the melting glacier in the Wind River Mountains in northern Wyoming and finishing in the saline, used up mud flats at the head of the Gulf of California. Brett says that's over-ambitious but that doesn't matter. Do you want to come? Anyway, lunch over and the fun began. Those few miles, about the last ten of the Taos Box, are *incredibly* exciting. The first is a minor affair called Dead Car Rapid (on the steep slopes of the canyon above it is the wreck of a car in which some one drove over the edge) but a little beyond it is Powerline Falls. The Rio Grande drops about 16 feet here in a single step. It announces its arrival by roaring a little at you when you are still a few hundred yards upstream. Dinosaur thought he might use the noise in his next voice-over. We slid towards it unruffled. Brett told us to hold on tight. We were a little sideways and then suddenly into it, slipping down the smooth tongue of water that licks half-way down the fall, riding on its tight curved ridge and then into the 'rooster's tail', a flicking froth of afterflow, chucking up the blunt nose of the boat and soaking us. 'Oooh,' Dinosaur said in his best bunny-rabbit-skin-milk tones as a 6 foot wave surrounded and soaked him. I was ecstatic, bailing hard, waiting for the next brainless drop into chaos. It's *so* exciting, and it didn't last long enough, but I'm confirmed now in the idea of a long river trip, the first part in kayaks, the rest in these rubber boats. Brett says that it would take at least a year to learn how to do it. I can't believe it. I put my faith in learning on the job.

After getting back to Taos, wet and battered, I drove up here, heading for Wyoming, crossing the Divide again on a 9,500 foot pass, and moving across the language frontier: what were mesas only a few miles ago have now become buttes.

Austin, Texas

Tuesday–Wednesday 3–4 June

NIGEL *to Adam*   On my way here I crossed the country where La Salle, seeking the Mississippi on his return to the Gulf coast in 1667, was murdered by his companions and his body left unburied by the Trinity river. Ever since Montreal the ghost of that great Frenchman has accompanied me. What did he achieve? He founded Kingston, he explored the Mississippi to its mouth, he claimed Louisiana for France, but his colony at Matagorda Bay, where on a previous journey through Texas I saw his statue, collapsed after his death. He was the pioneer of pioneers, and his ultimate success lay in the example of fortitude he left behind.

Of course the country is very different now. The forests and the swamps have all but disappeared, and the plains which once were shaken by the heavy gallop of huge herds of buffalo are now ranches for placid cattle and horses. The small towns are dreadful. What must it be like to spend a lifetime in a place like Giddings, where nature has done nothing sweet and every building is an offence to the eye! I went to the supermarket there, and watched the people pushing giant prams with stores to sustain a family for a week. Even the poor of Giddings, it seems, live well. Their poverty is in the spirit. It shows in their faces.

Austin, on the other hand, is beautiful. The Capitol building, higher by 7 feet than the Capitol in Washington, is one of the great achievements of late-nineteenth-century architecture in America. Its centre is a slender dome topped by a statue of the Goddess of Liberty – or it should be topped, but after removing the statute for repairs, the helicopter dangled the lady for hours in a vain attempt to reseat her. The local newspaper is full of suggestions from readers, of which the best is to magnetise her feet and the tip of the steel pole which is to run vertically through her body. The interior of the dome rises in three galleried tiers, a highly original and effective device, and off the first opens the Senate Chamber on one side and the House Chamber on the other, magnificent debating halls for the rough and tumble of Texan politics. It makes Westminster look tawdry.

Texas is celebrating its Sesquicentennial, 150 years since it won independence from Mexico. I went to see the organisers of this year-long jamboree. 'The name', I said, 'is barely pronounceable.' They replied that it was not chosen by them but by a committee which first sat six years ago. Imagine the committee-members solemnly trying out the word, and deciding it was perfect! Anyhow, the Sesquicentennial has caught on like wildfire. A thousand local committees have been formed in cities and towns throughout the State, and each organises one or more events, from rodeos to candle-lit parades. It is a little uncertain whether the Sesqui is intended to be joky or serious. The official brochure suggests joky, by comic drawings of Indians, fiddlers and covered-waggoners, and by urging Texas to enjoy 'fun-filled festivities', but the Director told me that there's a serious side to it too, to make people aware of the State's heritage. 'What is their heritage?' 'Size and quality,' he replied. 'Texas is big, thinks big, but it also has style.' I said that Giddings didn't have style. 'Ah, but they're a conservative people, happy to live where they live. They cling to the past. The Sesqui will celebrate it.' The Alamo, San Jacinto, Sam Houston. (La Salle? He doesn't figure in the heritage.) The flaw in this picture of proud independence is that Texas, having gained it from Mexico, immediately applied for entry into the United States, and after ten years succeeded.

I went to an Austin night-club. It was more like a large Australian bar, but more decorous. No drunkenness, no ribaldry, not the faintest suggestion of a brothel, simply men chatting up girls who would occasionally dance for them on the bar-top. One of the girls gave me the line, 'What's a nice man like you doing in a place like this?' I said I was studying the American way of life. 'Well,' she replied, 'it's not much of a life for us.' One reason must be that the management don't charge enough. The whole evening cost me only $10.

Austin, Texas

Thursday 5 June

NIGEL *to Adam*   I have quite lost my heart to Austin. It is the only city except Louisville where I have spent more than two successive nights. For one reason, the surrounding country – lakes, hills, parks, the Colorado River – is infinitely more attractive than most other parts of Texas. Then its buildings are excellent, its streets so clean that one would hesitate to drop a piece of confetti in the gutter, its hotels and shops good and cheap, and its people wonderful.

I went to the Humanities Research Center, which is known for its collection of literary manuscripts all over the world, except in Austin. My taxi-driver had never heard of it, nor had the back-up lady at the other end of his radio, but I insisted that it was somewhere on the University campus, and so it was. Wanting an excuse to go inside this treasure-house, I filled in a form requesting the letters of V. Sackville-West, and under the heading 'Qualifications' I put 'Son'. I thought there might be one or two of Vita's letters there. There are hundreds, written to more than a score of people who sold their archives to the H R C, and I picked out those to Richard Church, Hugh Walpole, L. A. G. Strong, Ottoline Morrell and Denton Welch. I sat making notes on yellow paper, in pencil, both provided by the Library. One is not allowed to use one's own notebook. Security is very tight.

How much time people spent writing to each other fifty years ago, how careful they were to keep even trivial notes, how courteous they were – and Vita was the most courteous of all, disparaging her own work, praising her correspondent's. 'I have nearly completed my poem called *The Garden* and simply don't know what to think of it. I never thought much of *The Land*, and this one seems even worse.' That was to Richard Church in September 1945. It was not put on. She genuinely felt herself to be a failure as a writer, and her admiration for Richard's poetry was unforced and unjealous, as it was for Hugh Walpole's fecund novels.

It was strange to read these letters in Texas, especially as I, aged 9 and 10, figure occasionally in those written to Leonard Strong, who was then a master at Summer Fields. Vita's sweetness and modesty scented the air of this famous reading-room. I met one of the librarians, John Kirkpatrick, and his assistant Cathy Henderson, and was asked to sign the door in the cataloguing room. I wrote my name very small near Tennessee Williams's, and then ate my lunch in the campus, sharing my cookies with the squirrels.

LBJ's library is also in Austin. It is not only his presidential archive, but an eulogy-museum devoted to his character and career. He emerges from it as a powerful and saintly figure. Thinking this portrait too good to be true, I went to yet another library where I borrowed Robert Caro's biography, Vol. I, and read it for a couple of hours till closing time. He makes out that Lyndon Johnson had no philosophy, no ideology, just 'a hunger for power in its most naked form, for power not to improve the lives of others, but to manipulate and dominate them. . . . a hunger so fierce and consuming that no consideration of morality or ethics, no cost to himself – or to anyone else – could stand before it'. He had 'a seemingly bottomless capacity for deceit, deception and betrayal'. Seldom can such a hatchet job have been done on a famous man so recently dead. Mrs Johnson is said to be much displeased. However, I wonder if any major politician's reputation could stand such careful scrutiny as Caro's, for to succeed in politics one must be formidable, and formidability is a highly unattractive quality to its victims, and often to read about.

Pinedale, Wyoming

Thursday 5 June

ADAM *to Nigel*   I am now back in my favourite state, a slightly random choice, based on my completely unfounded and commonplace love of cowboys and cowboy country, the emptiest state in the union, with fewer inhabitants than the city of Louisville, Kentucky, and 70 per cent owned by the federal government. I've been jigging around, disrupting the predestined curves you like so much (but you wouldn't expect me to believe in them anyway). I picked up your letters in Denver, looked around for a few Carringtons, found none and left. I enjoyed your description of rock and country (p. 228). The difference is this: both country and rock are based on the idea that it's awful to be alive, but country singers like the pain and rock singers don't. I'm amazed at your stamina. You keep rolling along at the rate you started three months ago. I've been getting slower and slower ever since those first hectic days in California. A week today I will get to Dodge and roll into a second hand car lot. 'I'll give you ten bucks for it,' the man will say. I'll refuse such an insult, drive out on to Wyatt Earp Boulevard, find someone I like the look of and hand over the Catalina like an indulgent godfather. That'll be the culmination, something given back to this incredible country. (Although, judging by the amount of dollars I have spent so far – I can't believe the thousands that have disappeared – I have already been a major stimulus to the tourist economy of the West.)

Since I last wrote, I have spent a night with Peter and Kaaren Iverson in Laramie. He's professor of history at the University of Wyoming there and an expert, probably the expert, on *the* Indians of the South-West. He put me right on various misconceptions. The reservation system, which certainly began as a form of containment and control, a space within which – it was thought – the Indians could be brought into the undifferentiated mainstream of American life, has turned out to be the opposite of that. The reservations, particularly something as vast as the Navajo country, have become secure bases, platforms on which an Indian resurgence can be founded. He spent three years living near the Canyon de Chelly, at Many Farms and is now about to leave Wyoming and return to Arizona, where he is to set up the history department in a new university outside Phoenix.

Here is another in the long list of admirable people we have both met here. I can't believe it is by chance that in these few months I have met more people to admire than in years at home. Why is it that so little of this quality in America, this integrity of purpose, crosses the Atlantic to dilute the anti-Americanism, which in my generation at least is so widespread? It may be that it is less noticeable or perhaps believable at such a distance and is submerged and obliterated by the more raucous and initially exciting fanfare razzmatazz from New York and California. And because events like the Libyan raid do nothing to advertise the real virtues of this country. But then I think I was born with a pair of rose-coloured spectacles bolted on to my eyeballs.

I can't tell you, whacked out as I am, and longing as I am to get to Dodge, New York and home, how glad I am to have made this trip. For any number of reasons – the people I have met (Jonathan Foote and David Barry are both going to be in New York when we are there, and I hope you'll meet them); for the places I've seen; for having talked to you, not a very great deal despite all these words but certainly more than before; for having escaped so much of the deadness of my life in London and all its dull constraints; for having spent some time – if I am honest – in places and doing things where I simply like myself more; for being able to meet people without the weight of a class identity dominating every aspect of the meeting – although I said that to someone not long ago and they said: 'Sure, I'd mistake you for a Liverpool docker's son any day of the week'. So that's another self-delusion; for acquiring an even more confused view of the world than before, the result of one or two prejudices modified and one or two acquired; for having a good time. I can't remember in which book it was that Robert Byron said the purpose of travel was to realise that he came from a pair of little brown islands somewhere off the coast of Holland. That's my feeling now and I long to get back to them. There's a confusion worth having.

Austin–Gatesville, Texas

Friday 6 June

NIGEL *to Adam*   Having read for another two hours Robert Caro's biography of LBJ, I went to see the cottage where he was born, the ranch to which he retreated during his years of power, and the family cemetery where he is buried, all within walking distance of each other, about 60 miles west of Austin. It was not my first visit there. Three years ago I was taken to lunch with Lady Bird Johnson at the ranch, and remember with pleasure how attractive it was, how lively she was, and how excellent the lunch. If I had spent most of my life being a gracious First Lady for the sake of Lyndon's career, I would have given myself a break when Lyndon died, but Mrs Johnson is indefatigable in her hospitality to strangers like me. She showed me his two-roomed birthplace and his grave. Both are of decent simplicity, the cottage restored and slightly smartened up, the tombstone modest for a president. The impression is very different from that which Caro leaves, but not necessarily contradictory.

I made a great loop-drive through central Texas, away from the main roads, stirred by Caro's description of the hardships which the settlers, including Lyndon's forebears, endured. I find it astonishing that men should have exposed their wives and children to such toil and danger. The Hill Country, as it is known, was dominated as late as 1870 by the Comanche, 'the Cossacks of the Plain', who had a reputation for unbelievable cruelty – women impaled on their fence-posts and burned, men staked out to die under a blazing sun after their eyelids had been cut off and burning embers heaped on their genitals. The pioneers lived in constant fear – for what purpose? For the hope of gain. It is true that fortunes were sometimes temporarily made by cattle-drives and by planting cotton, but the soil was soon exhausted, and they lived in poverty among derelict farms or in shabby settlements like Johnson City, 'a tiny cluster of houses huddled together in the midst of immense space'.

This was LBJ's boyhood inheritance. No wonder he grew up tough and ruthless.

Today the country still appears desolate. Trees, too starved of water to grow more than 20 feet high, speckle the rolling hills. They provided shade for the buffalo and cover for the lurking Indians, and one can recreate in imagination something of the fear and loneliness of the mid-nineteenth century. There are occasional cemeteries, very pathetic. I saw one gravestone recording the death of a complete family, 'killed by Indians'. Further north-west towards Llano and San Saba the plain flattens, and I saw herds, never very numerous, of Herefords and Friesians, but seldom much cultivation. The compensations are the great horizons, the profusion of wild flowers, the pink granite, and the Colorado River, which has been dammed at intervals to form beautiful lakes.

The small towns are without charm. I am staying the night in one of them, Gatesville, before continuing to Dallas. Why have the wealth and splendour of such a city not spread beyond its borders to give Gatesville at least a small taste of luxury and style? Why does nobody ever employ a decent architect or landscapist in a place like this?

Miner's Delight, outside
Atlantic City, Wyoming *Friday 6 June*

ADAM *to Nigel*   It's been Cowboy's Delight all day. (I'm now sleep-
ing in the car next to an abandoned mining village just east of the Divide, high in the grassy mountains, my face raw from the sun and no hat.) I've been at a rodeo all day! By now, you shouldn't need to be told that it was undiluted ecstasy. It didn't matter in the slightest that this was a high school rodeo. It was a day in Olympus as far as I was concerned. I talked to the All-Wyoming High School Rodeo Queen. She was pretty and rather bland, telling me, while looking me straight in the eye, that nothing was more important when being subjected to the personal interview section of the Rodeo Queen Competition, than to look them straight in the eye. And smile. So she smiled. I can imagine her without any difficulty in ten years' time being the most terrifyingly authoritarian of mothers. (There is this strange contradiction, which I have yet to understand properly: the people who most loudly proclaim the values of individualism are the most rigidly conservative, frowning on any deviation from that strict gospel. Why is it that when Individualism has a capital I it becomes the most anti-individualist of creeds?)

That complication didn't arise at the rodeo. It was scarcely a theoretical event. The setting was a large dusty arena outside Big Piney, surrounded by a white metal fence about six feet high. Half-way along one side of the arena, with the Wind River Mountains white and distant behind them, were the pens, the tight, gated boxes where the broncs and the bulls were prepared for their rides. And over at one end were the stock pens, where the steers were herded together, and from which they were released one by one for the roping events. All around the outside, horses and the young cowboys milled about, the boys attending to their horses and the elaborate, laden saddles, while the pretty girls, in prettied-up versions of cowboy gear – boots, jeans, hats and shirts all like the boys' but in a perfect one-shade pink or primrose yellow – attended to the boys with a little flutter of mascara. I was the only person there not in the required uniform and the only person secretly frightened of horses, steering wide veering courses around their enormous, dangerous bottoms and those horribly poised hooves. They tell me horses can sense someone's fear at 100 yards.

First there was roping. A steer is let out of the gate; a cowboy chases after it, lassoes it (although no one ever said lasso; it was 'roping') around the neck or the horns. (The boys that were watching unconsciously practised the action again and again, rotating their forearms around the elbows like Glen Miller on an easy beat and then flicking invisible loops way out over the unconscious heads of non-existent cows.) The steer would be brought to a sharp stop, spinning its little shocked body around the end of the rope, now taut on to the saddle horn, and would moo a little. The cowboy jumps off and runs towards his capture, suddenly ungainly and a little clodhopping in boots after the speed and ease of the roping, would struggle for a while to pick the calf up off its feet and then dump it flank-down in the dust, tying its feet together with a double wrap and a clove hitch, finally lifting his hands above his head to show the act was over. He would then walk over to pick up his hat, which had flown off in the first flurry out from the gate. To wear a string holding it on is not thought to be cool, except in a stampede. With the best of them the whole process took less than ten seconds. Now and then the rope would miss and fall disconsolately into the dust. The commentator would say, 'Tough break there, cowboy', and the audience would chat.

It went on all day and I won't describe it to you blow by blow. We had bull-dogging, a terrifying, courageous thing to do, in which a cowboy gallops alongside a galloping steer, then throws himself off his horse and on to the neck of the steer, grabbing and twisting the horns as he does so, pulling the animal over on to the ground. Ideally this is all one movement, but usually it breaks in two – the jump and then a rather graceless struggle to topple the steer. And team-roping, in which one rope loops the head and another is flicked up under the rear legs so that the cow ends up strung out between the two ropes, held tight like a butcher's diagram. And various, very boring girls' sports.

Of course, what I was waiting for was the bronc and the bull-riding. I watched the saddle bronc from the far side of the arena, across from the pens. A clot of hats gathered above and in front of the pen. Detailed fiddling and fixing – you couldn't see exactly what was happening – then suddenly the men drew back, the tall, metal gate was pulled open and the staggering, electric animal emerged, curved down in that single, wonderful arc from its nostrils to the heels of its hooves, jerking and quivering as though some laboratory experiment was sending massive voltages through its body, while the strange appendix of a man, with one hand held high in a flopping, loose and inconsiderate wave, rode the enormous energy, loose from the waist upwards but kicking away manically from his knees down, as though that part of his body shared the energy of the horse, something desperate about it. In the rules you are scored on how well you kick and how well the horse bucks, how near the vertical its neck and back becomes. But as you watch, the division is not between horse and rider, but at that point where the rider's body emerges into free air. Everything above it is supple, thrown around, victim; everything below frantic, active, passionately deliberate. To score at all you have to stay on for 8 seconds, but it's not the length of time you stay on that matters. It's the quality of that conflict for the eight seconds that gets you the points.

I could have watched this all day, just for the courage and skill of it. But it came to an end. There were more mundane sports to follow, but traditionally the last in any rodeo is bull-riding. I went round to the pens to watch this and made friends with a bull-rider called Brad. He had broken two ribs and bruised his kidneys last week when a bull stepped on him, so he wasn't competing today. I asked him why he did it. In return he asked me if I had ever known the satisfaction of daring to do something that frightened me more than anything in the world. The moment of daring in a lifetime's surrender. I told him that, very occasionally, I had known that feeling. I was thinking of that Gerry Spence interview (pp. 167–8). 'Well,' he said, 'that's why I do it.' This boy was sixteen and I felt his junior by about ten years. He took me round to the back of the pens to show me the equipment: the chaps, purple, green and gold, with his initials cut out of one colour leather on to another; the one soft leather glove, its palm sticky with rosin where it gripped the rope; the rope itself, which is wound around the chest of the beast and from which two big cow bells are suspended, both to make a noise and to provide a weight to pull the rope off the bull once the ride is over; the one pair of never-washed jeans, smelling of bull; and the spurs, the rowels fixed and the hank turned in so that the rider can dig them into the side of the bull to get some good purchase.

The bulls were now being fed into the chutes. They were obviously frightened and so were the boys. Each boy was allotted his bull and they all climbed on to the backs of the animals in the pens to tie on the ropes. This was preparatory. The bulls didn't seem to object much, one or two of them shuffling back and forth a little in the pen, but nothing more than that. Then the boys walked up and down getting nervous, building up the adrenalin for the ride. Brad says that those who make most of a show of this are the worst riders. They spend all their nerves beforehand and when it comes to the 8-second crisis they are already used up. Nevertheless, the air of tension behind the pens is extraordinary. Everyone is nervous and their nerves feed off each other. The bulls stink and everyone is sweating, walking up and down past each other in the thin, dusty alley littered with saddles and ropes and kit-bags. All the boys look 35. From outside this pit of tension, the girls look in, leaning up on the fence. Old cowboys joke and smoke out in the arena, while a couple of clowns in red braces and shorts and running shoes prepare to distract the bull if it turns nasty. And then the time comes.

The first boy, his face pitted and ragged with experience and tension, climbs up the outside of the white metal cage in which his bull is standing, a creamy Guernsey-looking thing. 'This one's just a cow,' the commentator says. 'And I bet you didn't know it, but this is how you get whipped cream.' The crowd laughs and no one in the pens pays attention. All consciousness has drained out of the boy's robot face. He carefully settles his legs down over the back of the bull, which shifts suddenly and violently, folding its head back against the bars of the cage and almost trapping the boy's leg against them. He jumps up off its back just in time. People outside ask 'What's the delay, cowboy?', and he lowers himself on to the bull's shit-encrusted back again. Another of the young cowboys takes the long loose end of the rope around the bull's chest and draws it upwards, tightening the girth. The bull shifts and bangs against the sliding door in front of it while the boy rubs his one-gloved hand up and down on the rosined rope, getting it hot and sticky. When that's done, he pushes his hand into a loop in the rope on the bull's withers and has the long rosined tail wound through his fist for a good grip. He holds it right down next to his crutch and brings his body up so that he's resting on the inside of his thighs against the bull's flanks. And then he nods. No words. That's the only signal, the slight movement up and down of the brim of his hat. The gate is pulled open, the bull's rump is given a shove with an electric prod and suddenly the monstrous anger of this huge, creamy animal explodes. None of the quivering electricity of the bronc, just great lumpen rage, with this poor boy, testing his masculinity in front of those pretty girls, jagged round on top of it. No grace in it, just a thumping rejection of man by animal, which lasted four brutal crashing seconds before he was thrown off to the left, the animal turning as it threw him and, ignoring the clowns in their red tights and shorts, looked to see what it was that had been ruining his afternoon. The boy jumped up from the dust holding his left arm just below the elbow and ran limping to the fence.

This was a horrible and brutal show, as different from the bronc as you could imagine, with a stupid grossness in it. I didn't want to see any more, so I thanked Brad and left. Now it's getting dark on my mountain top, so I must sleep.

Dallas, Texas

Saturday–Sunday 7–8 June

NIGEL *to Adam*   I was in Dallas less than two years ago, but could hardly recognise it. It is not only the number of new buildings but their juxtaposition with older ones that plays havoc with a familiar pattern, and that's partly the purpose, to generate fresh excitement, to create new reflections building against building, and to alter the street-lines by placing skyscrapers at new angles. The rigid grid pattern has been abandoned for island sites, forming odd triangles and rectangles which are often filled with small gardens or terraces, or sacrificed, temporarily one hopes, to huge parking-lots.

Then the buildings themselves are changing shape. It's sculptural architecture, a constant experiment with different ways of confining a large number of people under glass without squashing or roasting them. Every geometrical trick is played in three dimensions. They slide, they roll, they break into pinnacles. One appears to be an exact reproduction of Paxton's Crystal Palace, another has a spire, a third is windowless, lit from above, another is sliced into sloping sheets. Two very tall factory chimneys are painted dead-white, crowned with gold. Never has architecture been more hygienic, the cleanliness of inside transferred outside. The city centre scintillates and owing to the frequent open spaces between the buildings, the streets and squares are slashed by shadows, repeating in the horizontal the patterns of the vertical.

I was lucky to have it almost entirely to myself on a Sunday morning. Not a coffee-bar was open. The few people were mostly black, sitting, sleeping on benches, standing at corners, as if staking their claim to a share in a city which on working days is as white-dominated as central Johannesburg.

I walked with dragging footsteps, as if approaching Calvary, to the place where Kennedy was shot. It's a broad highway dipping to the triple underpass, and overlooking it at the higher level still stands (for how much longer?) the mutton-red Book Depository from which, on the sixth floor, Oswald took his aim. Dallas does not hide its face in shame. No spot is marked on the roadway itself, but several memorial tablets describe the scene, one of them on the Book Depository saying that from here Oswald 'allegedly' shot the President, a concession to the theory, still active after twenty-three years, that he had accomplices. The main JFK memorial is on a piazza a little distance away, a polished slab with his full name engraved on it, and set apart is a tablet with the words, 'It is not a memorial to the pain and sorrow of death, but stands as a permanent tribute to the joy and excitement of one man's life.' Much thought must have gone into the composition of that epitaph. I think it wholly appropriate, neither grandiloquent or over-remorseful. After all, why should Dallas carry for ever the whole guilt of the assassination when it was the work of a megalomaniac who could have done it anywhere?

Partly because it was the only public building open on Sundays, and because I wanted to compare Dallas people to their image, I went to the new Museum of Art, and lunched there. Again I was asked if I was an Australian. It's my height, they said. All Australians are giants, therefore all giants must be Australian. The Museum building is more splendid than its contents, for there has not been time, even for Dallas, to fill it with treasures comparable to those I saw at Cleveland or at the Frick in New York, and a big section of it is devoted to contemporary art which appeals to me so little that I feel ashamed. The people look and behave no differently than they do elsewhere. They are not more beautiful, more arrogant, nor more obviously wealthy. Why should I have expected otherwise? Perhaps you can guess. They may be more openly demonstrative. I watched in the auditorium a song-and-dance show, and at its conclusion the audience applauded, and some attempted a standing ovation, with an enthusiasm which seemed to me far greater than the performance deserved. Undoubtedly, there's a certain vigour about Dallas. One notices it in the alarming audacity and impatience of drivers on the freeways. The monsters in my rear mirror seem about to devour me. I'll be glad to get out of the place alive. But can this be truly called a Texan attitude?

Dining at their home with Michael Holahan and his wife Jane (he teaches in the Southern Methodist University here) and three of their friends, I asked them what they considered distinctively Texan. 'Expansiveness' seems to be the answer, a love of drama, of which Dallas's probing skyline is one example, the Sesquicentennial another, and the hectic growth of the oilfields a third. Of course, they have taken a severe knock in the drop in oil prices. Charitable donations have sunk by two-thirds. A Texan who had publicly promised his old university $25 million for a new building to be named after him was obliged to confess that he could no longer afford it; he was finding it difficult to save his own house. So temporarily there is a loss of confidence.

We talked about the cowboys, a myth which still colours the State's personality, how it was sparked off by Owen Wister's novel *The Virginian* (pub. 1902), then by Frederic Remington's idealised paintings of prairie life, and perpetuated by the rodeos and the Westerns. How strange it is that these loutish, rowdy, illiterate men with their monotonous jobs should have become the national folk-heroes instead of the pioneers further east or the mountainmen further west. After all, the whole cowboy period lasted only twenty years, 1866–86. I asked them to explain why it was that these immense cattle-drives to railheads at Abilene, Wichita and Dodge City were necessary, when the railroads could have been brought to the cattle country in mid-Texas instead of the cattle to the railroads. The answer is that the whole movement westwards was along the northern latitudes, leaving Texas wild and isolated – which to some extent it still is. Yet, as Michael Holahan drove me back to my motel at midnight through sparkling Dallas, I felt that there was a contradiction here. The city symbolises the material accomplishment to which the whole country aspires.

Casper, Wyoming

Sunday 8 June

ADAM *to Nigel*   Three miles out of town yesterday morning, as the first scurf of Taco Bell and trailer home suburbs gathered around the road, the Catalina clocked up 10,000 miles since Los Angeles. I gave a little hoot on the hooter and a baby in a stroller outside Safeways started crying. I had a fine drive across empty, desiccated Wyoming, where there are so few children that four hundred High Schools are all that is needed, where one cow needs 70 acres of dry grass to live, and where hundreds of thousands of emigrants trailed across to the boosted dream goal of California and Oregon, their path lined in the drier stretches with the corpses and skeletons of oxen that had died *en route*. I stopped at a couple of the crucial landmarks on the way – Split Rock which could be seen for a whole day before you reached from the east and remained on the horizon for two days after you moved on westwards. And at Independence Rock where everyone painted or carved their name next to the mosquito-thick meadows bordering the Sweetwater River. You can still read many of the names chipped into the granite. A flock of lovely white pelicans wheeled above the river and then sat on its surface dipping their heads underneath as they floated along.

I'm now staying with Anne MacKinnon and her fiancé Jon Huss – they are going to be married in July – up in the Big Horn mountains. She is Assistant Managing Editor on the *Casper Star-Tribune*, Wyoming's main newspaper, and he is now in law school in Laramie, having spent many years fighting environmentalist battles for an organisation called the Powder River Basin Resource Council against a variety of coal, oil and gas companies. They've been giving me a lovely time. We went for a long walk last night on a hill called Muddy Mountain covered, and I really mean covered, so that the hillside was blue, with lupins and sage.

We're just back now, in the most crashing thunderstorm I have ever known, from a canoe trip with some friends of Jon's on the North Platte. No rapids, but a gentle downstream float, past an owl sitting in a red rock niche and swallows diving on the surface of the stream. Then antelope for dinner and homemade beer. I've settled into America now and lost all sense of destination. Only one unfortunate incident: demonstrating the tremendous style and power of the Catalina on the Interstate, I was stopped by a policeman and fined for speeding. I didn't mind too much, but as Jon said, thinking of the policeman, what job can be more horrible than being confronted all day either by hostility or by fake contrition.

Dallas–Wichita Falls, Texas

Monday 9 June

NIGEL *to Adam*   Perhaps we timed this journey a week too long. I find myself dawdling towards its end, and unless you have been making unplanned forays, as you did to Amarillo (trespassing, I protest, on my State), I expect you feel the same. However, the easing of pressure has its advantages. I can wander more, read more, sleep more, and steep myself in the legends of this wide-open country.

After crossing the 98th parallel of longitude (I got that from a book), I left behind the scattered woodland for scrub, and scrub for bare plain. A poster in a Rest Area informed me that trees are still found in part of it, but (this is typical of the Texan love for startling statistics) although they rarely grow more than 3 feet high, their roots can extend as much as *ninety feet deep* to find sufficient moisture to nourish the miniature plant above ground. The plain is divided into great cattle ranches, and about every 20 miles you come to a small town like Saint Jo, which has a large central square taken straight from a Western, with a brick bank-house which seems to be awaiting Billy the Kid. It is the place where a main east–west trail to California was crossed by the south–north Chisholm trail of the cattle-drives. I turned to follow it on a farm road as far as the Red River which divides Texas from Oklahoma, and came across two mounted men coaxing a bunch of cows into a corral. This was the right stuff. With more self-confidence, I would have spoken to them. They looked up with surprise at a strange car, since their road ends abruptly before reaching the river, and it was too far, too rutted, too hot and obviously too private for me to cover on foot the distance to the point where the great herds jostled towards the fords.

When I reached Wichita Falls I spent two hours in the public library reading Walter Prescott Webb's classic book *The Great Plains* and Sam Ridings' *The Chisholm Trail*, and was allowed to borrow for the night *The Virginian*. Webb makes the point that the prairies required techniques and developed a life-style quite different from the eastern wilderness, and it took many years for the settlers to adapt to a country where there was no timber and little water. For the axe, the canoe, the plough and the wooden fence were substituted the horse, the rope, the Colt six-shooter, wells, the windmill, and eventually barbed wire, the railroad and farm machinery. The long waggon-trains had passed over this country towards the Pacific, thinking it useless. It is marked on maps as late as 1850 as The Great American Desert, when it was in fact the most fertile soil on earth. The ranchers were the first to grasp its suitability for raising the fierce longhorns, and then came the farmers with their barbed wire. The two groups competed for land which had been free and undivided.

Well, you know the outlines of this famous story. I simply want to indicate the pleasure it gives me to read a scholar's and a novelist's treatment of it, and then to drive over the byways to see for myself where it all happened, enriched by my new knowledge of how and why it happened, and return in the evening to the balm of a Holiday Inn and a swim in its refreshing pool.

I loved your description of Olivia among the boffins of Los Alamos (p. 231) – just like the child-Christ in the Temple.

Casper, Wyoming

Monday 9 June

ADAM *to Nigel*   I've been in Anne's newspaper office all day, writing on their computers, which they have had, in various different versions, for *fifteen* years. It's scarcely the new technology any more.

I picked up the last batch of letters I'll get through the post from you – before the final bundles we'll exchange in Dodge, like that one occasion – do you remember it? – when we spent Christmas alone together in Sissinghurst, eating an entire side of smoked salmon that someone had given you and nothing else except sausages throughout the day, and exchanging, in a grim little bit of ballet at 3 o'clock in the afternoon, my present to you and your present to me. That was not a very festive occasion.

The newspaper has a grand neo-railway station palace for an office, all air conditioning and white light inside, with the journalists scattered across its floor peering into their screens.

I sat in on the morning's editorial meeting. The editor, Dick High, is a powerful man, very sharp, in his early 40s and full of ideas for hot stories. There is a dam on the Green River north of Rock Springs at a place called Fontenelle. It's been something of a disaster ever since it was built, crumbling and leaking at the same time. With the enormous amount of water coming off the mountains at the moment there is a fear that it might break and a tidal wave will sweep down the valley, destroying everything in its path. The *Star-Tribune* has been running front page stories for days on the danger, with diagrams of rising water levels and close up photographs of worried Bureau of Reclamation officials. But this morning's bulletin, to Dick High's dismay, followed a 'There's nothing really to worry about' line. He was not pleased. The person who deals with statewide news, a nice man called Dan with red hair, got a grilling. 'I don't call this good reporting,' Dick said. Dan said his man on the spot had a right and responsibility to report what the Burec officials had told him, and they had told him that the scare stories on Salt Lake City TV, among others, were way over the mark. 'I am not having this paper simply trying to balance out the bad reporting in other places,' Dick said. 'One piece of bad reporting is not balanced by another piece of bad reporting on the other side of the issue. We've been told for days now that the Fontenelle Dam is a bad dam and now suddenly this morning we wake up and everything's all right. What kind of a story is that?' Dan repeated his point. 'We are not here to save the faces of Burec men,' Dick went on. The rest of us sat around the table saying nothing. Anne hadn't read the piece. I had, and although I didn't say so, I thought the editor was right. Dan looked a little taken aback by the fury of the attack and eventually, ceding rank, climbed down. Of course the story was one in which the accumulated evidence could, quite justifiably, be interpreted either way. Nevertheless this evening Dan was writing the intro to tomorrow's Fontenelle piece. In a heavily adjectival first paragraph we had 'alarming', 'dangerous', 'eroding', 'threatening' and 'rising'. The editor was satisfied.

Anne took me to lunch with an oil man called Harry. By training he's a geologist and by instinct an adventurer, coming out here to prospect for oil, when Casper was still the wild, drunk, whoring town tourists like in retrospect and avoid in reality. He is now about your age and has of course mellowed quite a bit. We had lunch – steaks, out of loyalty to the ranchers – in the dim dining room of the Casper Hilton. Yes, there is such a thing. It's the sort of padded interior where the most ruthless betrayals in *Dallas* are always set. We talked about the business, the rise and fall, the chronic pattern of boom and bust which has afflicted Wyoming in various forms since that first brief period of cattle-based fortunes and cattle-based ruin in the 1870s. At the height of the boom, oil was selling at $38 a barrel. The price has now sunk to between $10 and $12. I expected him to talk about the period of instant oil wealth with a regret for its passing. Not at all. It had been an ugly and a bad time. All sorts of people had rushed into oil who had no training, no understanding, no *care* (that was his word) for the business. The suppliers of drilling rigs, bits, piping and transport had all grown sloppy in the over-demand for their services. He had had to wait months for a rig when he most urgently needed to drill a test hole. I asked him if he had seen the end of the good times coming. And then, with unexpected poetry, he told me that he had felt uneasy at the time. 'If you go down into the Cretaceous,' he said, 'and look at the fossil sequence, you can tell when some change is approaching. The fossils start developing strange and unlikely forms. Shells double in on themselves. They sprout stalks and spikes. They lose their naturalness. That's what was happening to the oil industry. It was becoming unlike itself, over-developed, dangerously extended and vulnerable in all sorts of ways. The wrong sort of people were in it and something had to go.' He was optimistic about the future. The current price is below the cost of replacing reserves. There are only seven hundred drilling rigs now operating in the whole of the US. (Harry himself has seven of them.) As soon as countries like Nigeria, Indonesia, Venezuela and England – a significant look across the table here – learn that it is simply not worth their while to produce and sell oil at this price, the price will begin to rise. A glut is a stupidity. Never again will the $80 barrel seem likely, as it did to thousands of people, now bankrupt, only a few years ago, but a reasonable price, something around $20 a barrel, is a necessity.

Wichita Falls–Watonga, Oklahoma

Tuesday–Wednesday 10 11 June

NIGEL *to Adam*   I wanted to avoid Oklahoma City. I've had enough of cities. After a whole morning spent in the Falls library, I headed north across the Red River, which was so low in water, so sliced by sandbanks, that I could have forded it anywhere. On the plain there are humps and hunks and baby mesas from time to time, but for miles the horizon is closed by the curvature of the earth, like the ocean, people often say, but the simile is wrong. No ocean bears traces that any human being has passed that way before, and here the land is a palimpsest of past and present endeavour – the Indians, the cowboys, the farmers and the oilmen.

I am beginning to like the cowboys more. There are few activities which put a man's courage, skill and endurance to a greater test, more even than war, because battles are short and intermittent, and cow-punching was continuous, sixteen hours a day in the saddle under a cruel sun, and then often a night-patrol to end it. It produced a character – never betray a friend, never forgive an injury, never forget a face, never shirk a challenge – which is worthy of its heightened legend, and if on arriving at Wichita or Dodge City they spend their two months' pay in a single night of debauchery, who can blame them? And did you know that the first thing every cowboy did on reaching Dodge City was to buy himself a new set of clothes? You might follow his example. We have New York ahead of us.

By chance I met an Indian and one of Oklahoma's original settlers. Talking to each of them separately, I felt for the first time the full implications of the long adventure which created this country, and in a sense of my whole journey, finding in these two people symbols of everything that has happened since San Salvador and Jamestown, the slow, arduous replacement of one culture by another.

Both were women. My Indian was an assistant in the information-center just north of the Texan border. I asked her what tribe she came from. 'Comanche,' she replied without a blink. She is not pure Indian. Her father was a German. How did she think of herself – German, Comanche or American? 'Comanche.' She speaks their language, attends their powwows, but she is not wholly accepted by them, owing to her mixed blood. Is she accepted as an American? No, she is a neutral – or did she say neuter? – but her children are Americans, and she has brought them up to harbour no resentment for the Indian fate. Did she feel any herself? Her thin face wrinkled as if analysing for the first time what must have been a deep hurt. Yes, she did. It had been a profound injustice, but who was she to complain? She had a good job doling out information to tourists like me. She gave me a large poster of an Indian brave advertising the attractions of Oklahoma. The brave was her own cousin.

She gave me the address of a ranch-like motel in the country near Watonga, north-west of Oklahoma City, and it is here, where I am spending two nights, that I met my immigrant. She is 83. When she was 6 months old, her parents brought her in a covered waggon from Missouri to settle in the new Territory of Oklahoma. They left their Missouri farm because it was 'awkward', full of slopes and knobbly mounds, and here the ground was at least flat, and it was free. They were given a quarter-section, 160 acres of virgin land, just north of the Red River. She showed me the original title-deed describing the position of the farm in terms of pure geometry, for there were no place-names to define it. The surveyors placed a stone at each of the four corners of the plot. There were no fences, as there were no herds. They grew wheat. A cow had been towed along from Missouri, but it died, and she and her four siblings were raised on Grits ('That's why I'm so short'). Their house, at first a single room, was expanded to three as the family grew.

My reading about the Oklahoma settlement had suggested that it was a terrible life. They were poor, frightened and desperately lonely. They had few neighbours, no visitors, no joy, and lived in constant terror of the Indians. The dreariness of the endless plain induced profound melancholy, particularly among the women. 'There was not a thing to hide behind,' said one of them, longing for some privacy in all this solitude. But my lady's recollection was quite different, which shows the value of oral over written testimony. They did have neighbours. They even had a school. A small town, Grandfield, grew very rapidly. There was a store for groceries there. Though there was no church, an itinerant preacher held a service once a month in different houses. Her mother kept a gun for protection against Indians, but never had to use it. Was it a happy childhood? Very happy. She went to college, married a Methodist minister, and now in their retirement they can spend a holiday week in a place like this.

It is a lovely resort in the middle of a State Park called Roman Nose after a Cheyenne chief who was settled here in 1868, and was then evicted by the awful Custer. Roman Nose spent three years in the prison at St Augustine, Florida. Just think of it! It's a shallow canyon forming two lakes, and amenities like swimming-pools, a tennis-court, a golf course and a nature trail have been added to the many-bedroomed lodge. I wonder why America does not provide more places like it for the traveller, instead of the ubiquitous motels on the outskirts of cities crucified between great motor-roads.

McCook, Nebraska

Wednesday 11 June

ADAM *to Nigel*   This is the last leg, if not quite the ankle of the last leg, of my particular Road to Dodge City. Tomorrow morning I'll leave this motel – it could be anywhere in any one of the thousands of square miles I've crossed – and head straight down to Kansas. This is the country for heading straight. There's no deviation on these roads. Occasionally you kink east or west a section and then resume the longitudinal course across the surface of the planet, heading for the stupendous grain elevators which, like great white cathedral beacons, mark the towns in the general flatness.

It's not entirely flat. I think most people are under the impression that the plains are flatter than they are because they travel across them on the Interstates, which, of course, are intended to smooth them out. If you take the small roads, as I've been doing, you roll up and down in a lovely way, dropping down into the valleys of small streams filled with cottonwoods, climbing back up on the wide brown of a ridge where you see again for miles. Occasionally, on a modern bridge or viaduct, the road is carried straight across, and there, down to the left or the right, is the old way-to-market bridge, rotten and rickety, with one or two planks gone. In England this would have been restored and preserved by the local footpath society, but that's unthinkable here, isn't it. (For the first time we are sharing a landscape! And I have a theory – I'm not sure if it's true – that this farmland, with its wonderful spread, and oasis villages, its combination, in a word, of what you like and what I like, might, at last, provide some sort of agreement between us. That would be a marvel wouldn't it? But I have a suspicion that you might not even come towards me on this one, hanging on to the Massachusetts-cum-Wealden idea of cosy countryside.)

I might be tempted to say that there isn't even a sense of the local in this place. All of it has simply been sliced out like square pieces of an oven-wide pizza. The map looks like that, scarcely a road interfering with the north-south/east-west grid, so that every car travels, every combine harvester harvests, every shopper moves from shop to shop on one or other set of the parallel lines that grid the enormous prairie. That's a wonderful thought. And what I find strange is that this doesn't destroy the sense of place. In a funny way, it enhances it.

On the radio, in between the endless lists of corn and beef prices, and a wonderful announcement that a Los Angeles film company was looking for 'real farm types, heartland types' to act as extras in a Miller beer commercial they are planning to make in Ogallala, Nebraska, I heard that the great Peace March was passing through Julesburg today. So I headed for it.

The march left Los Angeles three and a half months ago, just two weeks before I arrived, and ever since, apart from a hiatus in the near-desert outside Barstow, California, where for almost two weeks the organisation collapsed and the money ran out, they have been footslogging it across the continent, aiming in the end for New York and then down to Washington. I arrived in Julesburg in the topmost right-hand corner of Colorado, which I clipped off on my way here, at the same time as they did, passing the long column of tanned refugees, with a few flags at its head, on the last mile into town. A beautiful day, the monument towers of the grain elevators by the railroad tracks, the one or two streets spread out from them on one side in the necessary grid. The shopkeepers peered out through their shop windows, craning over the window displays with their heads twisted around the corner to see the weird new arrivals, the girls in the one café laying every setting they could.

This was a coming together, not of the two sides of America, but of the two sides and the middle. This was solid corn and beef country, Reagan's rural constituency. The marchers were nearly all from the coasts, lovely Californian girls wearing T-shirts saying 'I can make a difference' in quotes like that, the Mayor of the march, Diane Clark, all in white, telling me that their principle on the way had been *to yield*. That's how they had got so far. And standing around them, chewing matches, the good old boys of Julesburg. I talked to them. What did they think of this crew, now lying around on the grass after their 16-mile march of the morning. I had expected reticence at least, maybe even outright contempt. Not at all. These are the clichés one carts around. They thought it was a fine thing to be doing. And the girls were lovely – 'hanging loose' one of the Julesburg citizens called them – and quite obviously very rich if they could contribute, as they all had done, $3,000 to something like this.

The Sheriff made a speech describing the history of the four Julesburgs – a story of quite outstanding violence, at which the peace marchers smiled, 'yielding' I suppose. And then there was an exchange of tokens – wooden keys, trees, model cars, all that sort of thing – before the marchers set off for the state line and Nebraska. There was no problem of communication here. Each side made jokes the other laughed at. The only real suspicion, if this was not paranoid, was of me, a *reporter* with a notebook and pencil. I was part of the media circus that distorts everything it touches, fuels anxiety and suspicion both inside and outside the United States, relishing discord where the natural state is harmony and so on and so forth. These farmers had far less of a problem in talking to the peace marchers than they did in talking to me. I am, obviously enough, still the outsider in this country.

And that's the point of this story: for everything you hear to the contrary, this is one country, extraordinarily in touch with itself given its size, its climatic, cultural and historical diversity. It does make sense to talk of 'the American way'. I would never have thought, on arriving here three months ago, that that idea would survive a trip like this. But it has and I'm glad it has. The only difference is that I didn't like the idea of America too much at the beginning. Now I can find nothing wrong. Or at least I'm prepared to think that anything that is wrong is necessarily wrong and that virtues are unavailable without compensating – or do I mean complementary? – vices. The only real human failing in this particular vision of the world is a failure to indulge or exhibit either virtue or vice, but to muddle along in some boring muddy basement of existence that doesn't even know the meaning of 'contour'. Perhaps this comes from having spent so long in the mountains: I like ups and if you're going to get ups you've got to have downs. Classically binary, unutterably American! I don't know if I'll ever recover!

Watonga–Wichita, Kansas

Thursday 12 June

NIGEL *to Adam*   I paid my last historical call, to the Chisholm Trail Museum in Kingfisher (excellent it is), and then drove towards Kansas, our last State, our only shared State, apart from your aberration into the Texan panhandle, eager to find your letter at Wichita. As we will be meeting in Dodge City tomorrow, I'll be my own postman for this one.

In Oklahoma there was a rich golden haze on the meadows, and the grain silos stood up from them like the churches from Romney Marsh. I took the wrong road away from Kingfisher, and in trying to recover the right one cross-country, found myself enmeshed in the vast grid of red-dirt roads which are still exactly as ruled by the first surveyors. It is squares within bigger squares within the county square, and that square is precisely aligned to the neighbouring county's. What a neat and horrible method of subdividing 100,000 people! You would have thought that this simple chess-board would make it impossible to lose one's way, but some roads were blocked off, others too rough for the car, and I was forced to make detours, navigating by the sun, for there are no signposts, until eventually I hit a numbered road and could identify it on the map.

So I came to Wichita to find your letter. Do not let us end by quarrelling about romanticism (p. 244). We share it. But mine takes the form of loving the past and yours the present, mine the struggle to create orderliness out of chaos, yours the relics of disorderliness. I like explanations (visitor centers), you ignorance; I the achiever, you the non-conformist. I contend that the 'definite and brave choices' made by your mavericks are far more definite and brave when made by men and women with responsibilities and ambition. I believe that you consider this to be a sign of age and Toryism (good God!) in me. Robin Lane Fox once said much the same, that only a young man can understand Alexander the Great, who was both a maverick and an achiever, but that's nonsense. The elderly were once young, but the young have never been elderly, so I maintain that it's the elderly, not you, who can best appreciate the two strands in this country. We can resolve this only in conversation, for our reunion tomorrow will put an end to this correspondence, but not to the argument.

I have been very happy here. An American visiting Britain would notice differences more than similarities, just as I have done. That is the habit of travellers everywhere. But how much the same we are! The frictions, needs and pleasures of mature countries are 95 per cent identical, and produce the same divisions, characteristics and joys. So I felt at home in America. If, on my return to England in a few days' time, someone asks me if I had a nice time, I shall want to slap them. It is a term totally inadequate to describe an experience so diverse and rewarding.

Dodge City, Kansas

Thursday 12 June

ADAM *to Nigel*   Well, here I am, a day early so that I can sell the car tomorrow. What on earth is there to say? I'm in the Silver Spur Lodge (Best Western, what else?) on Wyatt Earp Boulevard, Dodge City, Kansas. I mean DODGE CITY, KANSAS!!! But it's not quite like that. The exclamation marks came earlier. More like a glass of whisky after a day in the office than scoring a try in the final. That's as it should be: nothing is more off-putting than a screaming climax, if you know what I mean. It's 6 in the evening. I think I'll have a few more McNuggets and go to sleep.

Dodge City, Kansas

Friday 13 June

ADAM *to Juliet*   Dear Juliet,
It was just as planned. I was waiting in the office of the Silver Spur Lodge, drinking my can of 'Squirt'. I had got back there 15 minutes early, at quarter to three, thinking that after half a continent Nigel might be a *little* approximate in his timing, but he didn't turn up until 30 seconds before the hour we had appointed three and a half months ago. 'Aren't I punctual?', were his first words, stepping out of the incredibly beautiful Thunderbird. (Ingeniously, he had parked it so that the dent in the right hand door was hidden. It looks like the sort of machine in which 1950s space admirals drive around the earth station.) Only at supper tonight did he reveal that he had actually arrived in Dodge over an hour before and had hung around waiting for the dramatic moment. As you will realise, I had to

drag this information out of him. Never, *never*, has a man loved schedules so much.

And then, of course, the great question: To touch or not to touch? Well … we didn't. We came close – I'd say about 14 inches – but Nicolson flesh never came together with Nicolson flesh. Very friendly, a lot of eye contact, but no actual touching. The entire staff of the Silver Spur was lined up behind the desk watching (I – and you! the champagne and the telegram! – had told them all about this critical moment), and if anything is less conducive to trans-generational intimacy, it's an audience with an appetite. Besides, neither he nor I regard the physical as the acid test of a relationship, and so it was as good a meeting as anyone could have hoped for. He looks marvellously well – brown and fit and full of energy. (I feel rather ashamed and puzzled that I should be so exhausted while he's still brimming along as though he's just gone for a short walk in the Cotswolds. And what makes it even stranger is that he has driven almost twice as far as I have. My total is 10,798 miles, his only a few short of 20,000. I have a secret suspicion that he's been fiddling the clock. He denies it with vehemence.)

'So what do you think of it, then?', was my first question. 'Fine,' he said. 'Except for one thing. You know your paragraphs are far too long.' Nothing has changed.

But we had a fine time this afternoon. There was an interview with the local paper, in which I said my favourite place was Jonathan Foote's ranch on the Yellowstone in Montana, and Nigel Washington DC. That says it all, doesn't it? And then the photograph, taken by a nice man from the local weekly cow magazine, the *High Plains Journal*, of the two cars nose to nose and their two pilots leant up against the fenders – the Catalina unwashed since Los Angeles, the Thunderbird, except for the carefully hidden dent, immaculate from a shower in Wichita this morning. God knows what we look like.

After the photos we had to get rid of our cars. First thing this morning, I had driven down 2nd Street, cruising past the car lots. I selected as the most promising a slightly run-down place, not too awful, called Hi Plains Auto Sales. It was full of large, louche limousines of various ages, and looked the right sort of retirement home for the Catalina. Rick was inside the office behind a formica desk, smoking Marlboro Lights and wearing a pair of blue shorts. There were red hairs on his legs. 'What do you want for it?' he asked. (That 'it' hurt.) Jon Huss in Wyoming had said I'd be lucky to get $250. '$800,' I said. Rick lit up another Light and consulted a dog-eared dealer's manual. 'I couldn't dance with you at a dollar more than half that.' 'I'd be looking for 6 at the very least,' I said, unable to believe my luck. Rick said he couldn't even stretch to $425. '$400, then?' 'Yup, that's the top.' 'Done,'

I said, and five minutes later was walking out with a cheque in my pocket and a spring in my step. All I had to do this afternoon was leave the car there with the key in it and drive away with Nigel to the Avis drop-off. He thought it was callousness, the ease with which I left the Catalina behind. In fact, it was nothing but relief.

Nigel has taken rather a shine to a girl called Mary in the Avis office, but I'll let him tell you all about her. Tomorrow morning we are coming to see you. I'm longing – and I mean that – longing to get there.

Lots and lots of love from Adam

Dodge City, Kansas

Friday 13 June

NIGEL *to Juliet*   Darling Juliet,
            Adam has shown me his letter to you, and I must admit that it's a fairly accurate description of our meeting in Dodge City. After all the blows we've traded in these letters it was a relief to find our mutual affection unimpaired. 'It doesn't matter how much we insult each other in public,' I said, 'so long as we are nice in private,' and we were.

I'd lunched in a roadside café on my way from Wichita, and got into conversation with a Marlboro man who owned 25,000 head of cattle. He took me to see them in their railed enclosures, and I was so saddened by the sight that I arrived in Dodge City unexpectedly gloomy. It's a pleasant town with a bronze statue of a longhorn bull in the middle and shops where I bought a cowboy jerkin for Tom, and then I timed my arrival at Silver Spur Lodge to the exact half minute we'd agreed. I don't resent Adam's comment about my passion for keeping schedules. It's a neatness of habit, like turning in to a publisher an impeccable typescript.

Adam looked not three months, but six months, older, the extra three betrayed by a new intensity of expression in his face. His experiences have left some permanent mark. Happy, healthy, not, as he says, tired, but full of beans, he organised the despatch by slow boat to Cambridge and Sissinghurst of our two boxes of books. Then came the interviews, the posing for photographs, the farewells to our cars. It is quite true that I thought his parting from the Catalina perfunctory. He should have patted it at least once, like a cowboy his dying horse.

He wants me to tell you about Mary of Avis. 'Hail to thee, blithe Spirit, bird thou never wert!' and if you can explain the allusion in that Shelley quote, it'll be worth the thousands of pounds I spent on your education. Mary was not, as you suspect, a golden girl of the plains. The point about her is that she was totally different from what one expects in Avis staff, rather scruffy, dressed in a singlet, and pestered by her two kids whom I bribed with dimes to stay away. She didn't look like the Mary to whom I'd spoken by telephone last night. She looked like someone waiting for Mary, but was Mary. She was infinitely casual and attractive. I told her about the dent in my Thunderbird, showed it to her, confessed my sorrow and my shame. 'That's nothing,' she replied, 'you should see the state of some of the cars that are handed back to us.' She filled in an accident form to my dictation – date (made-up, as I'd forgotten), Houston, witnesses?, 2 m.p.h. ('Oh, come on!'), the whole interview conducted by me in mildly flirtatious–apologetic tones, by her in mock-officialese, while Adam listened in astonishment to this new (but it isn't new) manner of his lonely, Tory, buttoned-up father.

Enough of this. We'll see you tomorrow in New York. I'm longing to get there, – and feel no shame in repeating Adam's identical last words.

Much love, Dadda

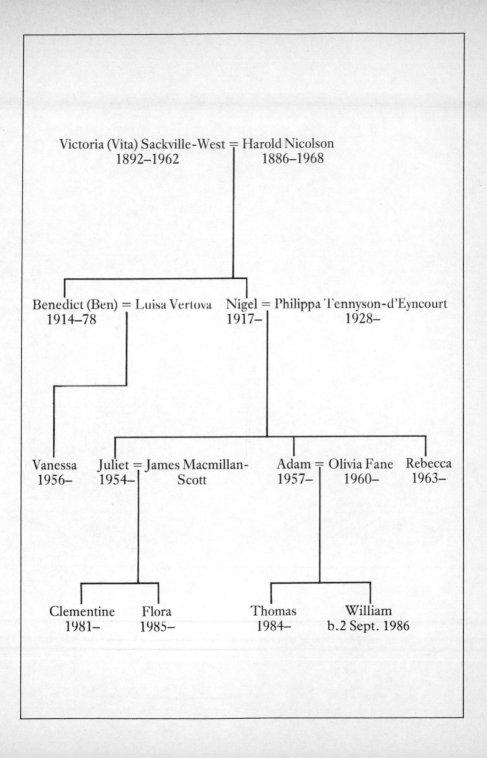

Victoria (Vita) Sackville-West = Harold Nicolson
1892–1962   1886–1968

Benedict (Ben) = Luisa Vertova   Nigel = Philippa Tennyson-d'Eyncourt
1914–78   1917–   1928–

Vanessa   Juliet = James Macmillan-   Adam = Olivia Fane   Rebecca
1956–   1954–   Scott   1957–   1960–   1963–

Clementine   Flora   Thomas   William
1981–   1985–   1984–   b.2 Sept. 1986

Index